Arts and Cultural Programming

A Leisure Perspective

Gaylene Carpenter

Doug Blandy

EDITORS

Human Kinetics

Library of Congress Cataloging-in-Publication Data

Arts and cultural programming : a leisure perspective / Gaylene Carpenter, Douglas Blandy, editors.
  p. cm.
 Includes bibliographical references and index.
 ISBN-13: 978-0-7360-6564-1 (soft cover)
 ISBN-10: 0-7360-6564-4 (soft cover)
 1. Arts--Management. 2. Nonprofit organizations--Management. I. Carpenter, Gay. II. Blandy, Douglas Emerson, 1951-
 NX760.A78 2008
 700.68--dc22

2007042357

ISBN-10: 0-7360-6564-4
ISBN-13: 978-0-7360-6564-1

The Web addresses cited in this text were current as of October 19, 2007 unless otherwise noted.

Photo page 65: Nancy Morgan demonstrating traditional quilting at the Stephen Foster Folk Culture Center, White Springs, Florida.

Acquisitions Editor: Gayle Kassing, PhD; **Developmental Editor:** Ragen E. Sanner; **Assistant Editor:** Anne Rumery; **Copyeditor:** Jocelyn Engman; **Proofreader:** Jim Burns; **Indexer:** Sharon Duffy; **Permission Manager:** Carly Breeding; **Graphic Designer:** Nancy Rasmus; **Graphic Artist:** Kathleen Boudreau-Fuoss; **Cover Designer:** Keith Blomberg; **Photographer (cover):** Background photo by Steve Smith, PhotOregon, courtesy of Raychel Kolen, Eugene Symphony Association; top photo courtesy of Derek Campbell; bottom left photo courtesy of VSA Arts, © 2006 Scott Suchman; bottom center photo courtesy of Joe Wieronski, AIA; bottom right photo courtesy of Hult Center for the Performing Arts/Eugene; **Photographer (interior):** © Human Kinetics, unless otherwise noted; **Photo Asset Manager:** Laura Fitch; **Photo Office Assistant:** Jason Allen; **Art Manager:** Kelly Hendren; **Associate Art Manager:** Alan L. Wilborn; **Illustrator:** Accurate Art; **Printer:** Sheridan Books

Printed in the United States of America   10   9   8   7   6   5   4   3   2   1

Human Kinetics
Web site: www.HumanKinetics.com

United States: Human Kinetics
P.O. Box 5076, Champaign, IL 61825-5076
800-747-4457
e-mail: humank@hkusa.com

Canada: Human Kinetics
475 Devonshire Road Unit 100, Windsor, ON N8Y 2L5
800-465-7301 (in Canada only)
e-mail: info@hkcanada.com

Europe: Human Kinetics
107 Bradford Road, Stanningley, Leeds LS28 6AT, United Kingdom
+44 (0) 113 255 5665
e-mail: hk@hkeurope.com

Australia: Human Kinetics
57A Price Avenue, Lower Mitcham, South Australia 5062
08 8372 0999
e-mail: info@hkaustralia.com

New Zealand: Human Kinetics
Division of Sports Distributors NZ Ltd.
P.O. Box 300 226 Albany, North Shore City, Auckland
0064 9 448 1207
e-mail: info@humankinetics.co.nz

*Dedicated to those students
who are preparing for careers
in arts and cultural programming
and in recreation and leisure management
and to the professors
who are encouraging
their professional development.*

contents

PART III Arts and Cultural Programs in Context 127

preface

This book, the first of its kind, on arts and cultural programming combines concepts associated with delivery of arts and cultural programs and leisure programs in contemporary society. As such, it will be a useful reference guide for leisure professionals and managers working in public or private arts and cultural organizations. This book will also serve as an orientation to the field for advanced undergraduate and graduate students. Conventional and innovative programming approaches are provided along with examples of best practices.

This book is directed toward a broad audience associated with the fields of Tourism, Arts Management, Leisure Studies, Public Relations, Public History, Hospitality, Folklore, Museum Studies, Event Management, Education, and other fields associated with the arts and culture sectors. This book will be of interest to students and professionals who are arts managers, public relations specialists, recreation specialists, public historians, public sector folklorists, arts educators, event planners, festival organizers, cultural policy analysts, community educators, and college and university program managers. College and university students in academic programs who are preparing to work in professional fields related to those venues mentioned above will also benefit from the content in this book.

Why This Book, Now?

The desire to highlight arts and cultural programming for leisure professionals, and to highlight leisure program theory for arts administrators, was a primary purpose for all of those who contributed to this book. Successful arts and cultural programs for children, youth, and adults are markedly influenced by both the context in which these programs occur, as well as the theory that underlies program development. We noted the wide variety of arts and cultural programs that are now available was outpacing any documentation or recognition of the same. We were encouraged by the editors at Human Kinetics to fill this void by bringing together experts in their fields to publish on arts and cultural programming.

Textbooks currently available to arts and cultural managers that address programming typically do so within the context of administering arts organizations. In doing so, they ignore or merely scratch the surface of leisure program theory and concepts. Leisure and recreation textbooks that focus on program theory and concepts tend to reduce discussions related to arts and cultural programming to one chapter or less and fail to recognize the breadth, depth, and numbers of such programs. The resultant effect of minimizing content in these important areas inhibits the potential that arts and cultural programs have to contribute to individuals and organizations.

Arts organizations are competing for the public's free time and attention without all of the tools they need to be successful. Successful organizations are those that plan and implement arts and cultural experiences with the expertise that will enable them to position themselves in competition with commercial, public, private, and corporate enterprises already programming experiences for individuals seeking educational and recreational opportunities during their free time. Leisure professionals often rely on traditional arts and cultural activities that result in producing programs that may lack appeal to the general public.

Organization

Arts and Cultural Programming: A Leisure Perspective is divided into three parts. Part I, Orientation to Arts and Cultural Programming, discusses the contemporary popularity of arts and cultural programs and suggests that the basis for such popularity is embedded in public interest in the arts and in the organizational initiative demonstrated by arts and recreation agencies. Concepts related to program theory and to leisure behavior are presented. Tasks and functions inherent to successful programming are discussed around phases related to program needs assessment, program development, program implementation, program evaluation, and program modification.

Part II, Applying Program Theory to Practice, offers several theoretical perspectives related to the management of programs, audience development, assessment, documentation, budgeting, and marketing of arts and cultural programs. This portion of the book depicts the breadth and depth of approaches used in small, medium-sized, and large organizations and venues.

Part III, Arts and Cultural Programs in Context, explores best practices associated with programming in chapters on festivals, special events, community arts, cultural programs, museums, and performing arts. Each of these chapters includes case studies that readers will find of interest. This part of the book concludes with a chapter on the future for arts and cultural programming. Here, the co-editors take a look at forecasting the future for arts and cultural programming.

An Invitation to Engage

All of us associated with this publishing project invite readers to engage with us in connecting with the multiple opportunities that now exist to plan arts and cultural programs. Significant work in this regard has been accomplished, some of which is described and discussed on the pages of this book. However, numerous opportunities and challenges continue to be evident and the need for people to assist in the facilitation of responses to these challenges and opportunities is crucial. Our hope is that readers of this book will join with us in continuing to create innovative approaches, identify best practices, speculate about the future, and ultimately advocate for the enhancement of quality of life for all that is in part achieved through a variety of leisure-time options associated with the arts and culture.

a note from the editors

This book is a result of our work together over the past several years preparing graduate students in the Arts and Administration Program at University of Oregon to work in a variety of settings associated with the arts and culture. Each of us approached our students from our unique disciplines of leisure studies and recreation management (Carpenter) and arts education (Blandy). As the curriculum for our graduate students was conceptualized, implemented, and revised we came to realize two things. First, there are important associations and intersections between our two disciplines, and second, there was a lack of literature connecting the bodies of knowledge specifically related to our two disciplines.

An initial step in identifying connections between conventional wisdom and best practices in arts education and recreation management began in two courses, Arts Programming (Carpenter) and Community Cultural Development (Blandy). These courses, in part, are predicated on our belief that graduate students preparing for careers as arts administrators benefit both from knowledge about leisure programming and that students preparing for careers in recreation benefit by having a deeper understanding of arts and cultural programming. Students participating in these courses understand the significance of comprehensive programming and learn how to design programs that are more competitive in the vast marketplace of leisure arts and cultural options available to children, youth, and adults. As a consequence, a broader and deeper range of choices through which to experience their personal interests better serves this public.

Our conversations on how to make our courses complementary began to include discussion of the need for a book such as this. Early in our discussion was the desire to publish a book that not only included our own expertise, but the expertise of others who could inform our purpose. We are indebted to the authors associated with this book. All are highly regarded writers, scholars, and professionals in their fields and disciplines. Their participation in this publication demonstrates the rich rewards realizable through collaboration by professionals and educators to positively impact the quality of arts and cultural experiences that can be accessed in leisure time.

Gaylene Carpenter and Doug Blandy

PART I

Orientation to Arts and Cultural Programming

Successfully designing and delivering arts and cultural leisure experiences is more daunting than it appears to be on the surface. People interested in programming such experiences would be well advantaged by learning about the process from others and by accessing resources relevant to the arts and cultural leisure experiences they intend to produce. Providing these advantages is the purpose of this book. In it, we draw from the experiences of respected arts managers and educators to discuss the arts and cultural experience. We also draw from the professional literature and educators in leisure studies to discuss program and leisure theory. Though this is the first time such a task has been undertaken, the authors we invited to join us did so willingly and with enthusiasm. We take their willingness and enthusiasm as a sign that writing this book on programming arts and cultural experiences was a good idea.

This book is divided into three parts. This first includes three chapters that introduce arts and cultural programs, discuss program theory, and describe the various tasks and functions necessary for programming. We call part I *Orientation to Arts and Cultural Programming*.

Chapter 1 discusses the contemporary popularity of arts and cultural programs and suggests that this popularity is embedded in public interest in the arts and in the initiative demonstrated by arts and recreation agencies offering arts and cultural leisure experiences. The reader will also learn about existing programs in arts and culture and the types of organizations currently offering programs. This first chapter introduces concepts of program theory and leisure behavior and explains how they relate to the planning and implementation of successful arts and cultural leisure experiences.

Program theory is the subject of chapter 2. Approaches to designing and implementing programs are presented, along with recurrent themes of programming models. Examples of program theory in action are provided, and comprehensive programming and its implications for program development are discussed. In focusing on program theory, chapter 2 is essential for programmers who are just getting started or for those who want to look carefully at the theoretical basis behind current decision making in arts and cultural programming.

Chapter 3, the last chapter in part I, examines the programming tasks and functions necessary for delivering quality arts and cultural leisure experiences. It does this within the context of the five phases inherent in the programming process. These phases are program needs assessment, program development, program implementation, program evaluation, and program modification.

Overview of Arts and Cultural Programming

Gaylene Carpenter, EdD
University of Oregon

Every major newspaper in the country has similar special sections providing guidance to the world of arts and leisure. Is it that these two areas are merely contiguous subsets of the field of entertainment, or is it that they are overlapping in a deeper sense, sharing critical components of experience?

~ John Neulinger, 1981, p. 5

 rts and culture are essential in the lives of individuals and in the formation of communities. Opportunities to engage in arts and cultural leisure experiences begin during early childhood and continue through older adulthood. Some people's lives are dominated by their participation in the arts, while others find that participating in arts and cultural leisure experiences enhances their lives only occasionally. Often, communities build their reputations and promote themselves with their arts and cultural amenities. Indeed, the arts and cultural sector is essential to quality of life.

Why a Book on Arts and Cultural Programming?

Given the number and types of organizations and individuals offering arts and cultural programs, those providing the programs often find that their overall knowledge of programming influences their success. For example, a leisure programmer with minimal knowledge of the arts charged with offering a variety of programs for the general public (e.g., community center activities, art activities, recreation activities, and youth sports) may feel poorly equipped to manage programs covering a wide range of arts and cultural experiences. Or an arts administrator who has little knowledge of program theory may struggle with one or more of the various tasks required in producing successful experiences. These apparent voids between knowledge of arts and cultural leisure experiences and knowledge of program theory provide the context from which this book evolved.

This book bridges two different but related disciplines: recreation and leisure and arts and culture. The core of their relationship is their mission to provide choices of leisure-time activities for people to participate in arts and cultural experiences. In this book, conventional wisdom from both disciplines sometimes is discussed separately, but more often the two are integrated in ways to challenge our ways of thinking about arts and cultural programming. Program theory, long embedded in recreation and leisure professional development, is rarely applied specifically to the arts and cultural sector. As such, arts administrators typically have minimal knowledge on managing comprehensive programs that address people's leisure needs and interests. Conversely, recreation and leisure professionals could offer more arts and cultural experiences to their constituents if they knew more about the programming possibilities in the arts and cultural sector.

To provide a context for the rest of this book, this chapter briefly discusses contemporary factors associated with arts and cultural programming, including popularity of the arts, organizational initiative, public education for the arts, venues, and participant expectations. Several examples of

The recreation and leisure field and the arts and cultural sector must not only produce more experiences for their participants but also do so both independently and in collaboration with one another.

Photo courtesy of Gaylene Carpenter

how arts and cultural opportunities have been delineated and several examples of programs in operation are discussed. These examples are followed by a section devoted to leisure theory and concepts applied to arts and cultural programming.

Arts Are Popular

Most people who attend arts events or patronize arts facilities are seeking a leisure experience (Stebbins 2005). Cherbo and Wyszomirski (2000), in illustrating the flourishing arts industry, pointed to several public and industry indexes that measure the popularity of the arts. They noted that 96% of the U.S. population engages in the arts (e.g., views a film, listens to a CD, engages in an artistic hobby, attends a live performance). Americans for the Arts (2007) reports that the nonprofit arts industry generates $166.2 billion U.S. in economic activity every year. This figure represents $63.1 billion U.S. in spending by arts organizations and $103.1 billion U.S. in event-related spending by arts audiences. Arts and cultural opportunities are currently provided by a diverse delivery system addressing a range of individual needs and interests, from public access to recreation that is relatively inexpensive to elite experiences that are quite expensive. Indeed, the range of individual interests related to arts and culture and the diverse delivery system for the arts and culture appear to be key components necessary for facilitating participation for the great number of people.

An increased popularity in cultural tourism has contributed to the growth in arts and cultural programs. Cultural tourists are more likely to produce greater benefits to local economies than are other types of tourists (Getz 1997; Shaw and Williams 2002). This is important when considering that Americans for the Arts (2007) reports that two-thirds of American travelers include a cultural, arts, heritage, or historic activity while on a trip of 50 miles (80 kilometers) or more (one way) from home. Cultural tourists who visited Massachusetts' arts, heritage, recreational, and natural resources, for example, recently spent over $11 billion U.S. in one year (Massachusetts Cultural Council 2006).

The efforts of arts administrators of nonprofit and commercial arts institutions to build up audience constituents have contributed to the growth in arts and culture (McCarthy and Jinnett 2001). Statistics Canada (2000) recently reported a 22% increase in the number of nonprofit performing arts companies (i.e., theater, music, dance, and opera) operating in Canada. In 2002, almost 35% of American adults attended one of several live arts events, choosing jazz or classical music performances,

operas, musicals, plays, ballets, or museum exhibits (Americans for the Arts 2007). The marketing strategies of arts managers appear to be making a difference.

Organizational Initiative Is on the Rise

Administrative initiative to provide for arts and cultural experiences has grown steadily during this past decade. Much of this initiative has come from public and nonprofit arts organizations, whose directors increasingly see the need to both respond to people's interest in arts experiences and respond to artists' interests in promulgating their work. Public and nonprofit organizations have not only traditionally offered arts and cultural programs, but we are also seeing increases in the number and type of arts and cultural programs this decade.

Most public park and recreation agencies have maintained an acceptable level of programming in arts and culture, while many others have increased their number and variety of such offerings. Funk (1987) noted that though the park and recreation field does not have sole proprietorship of the arts, it has helped dispel the perception that the arts can be enjoyed by only an elite, privileged few. These organizations' missions are imbedded in the provision to offer a variety of recreation experiences for all.

Another factor contributing to organizational initiative is the increase in the number of graduates obtaining professional development degrees in arts management over the past 10 years. These young professionals have entered the field with new ideas for programs and services and are seeing their ideas implemented.

Public Education for the Arts

Though arts participation in general has increased in the past decade, the arts in public education have declined. In the not-too-distant past, most North American public schools offered a range of courses in the visual arts, music, dance, and theater. Today, however, limited resources have all but eliminated these educational opportunities, as school officials have had to cut budgets in these areas. Public recreation has traditionally offered arts and cultural programs; given the reduced availability of programs in public education, these public-based arts opportunities are even more essential. Meyer and Brightbill (1956) were early advocates for providing arts programs in public recreation, a trend that continues today (Edginton et al. 2004; Rossman and Schlatter 2003; Russell 2005). Public recreation professionals are aware of the need to provide a variety of program options for citizens. To illustrate, the mission of the Cultural Affairs Division of the Department of Parks, Recreation and Cultural Resources for Arlington, Virginia, reads as follows:

> To use the power of the arts to transform lives, build community and make Arlington a great place. The Division provides programs and services that are focused on meeting the needs and interests of the Arlington community by encouraging the growth and development of the arts. (Arlington Arts 2003)

Staff members in Arlington's Cultural Affairs Division are charged to facilitate programs and services that promote Arlington as an innovative community that values the arts as an essential part of life, to manage arts facilities, to enable artists to produce high-quality work, and to increase citizen access to the arts throughout residential and commercial neighborhoods.

Many nonprofit arts organizations have become active in providing arts education for the children and youths associated with their particular organization. It is not unusual for local theater groups to run summer theater camps or for community arts organizations to partner with community recreation centers to provide summer programs. Larger arts organizations assume major responsibilities for building knowledge and appreciation for performing arts. For example, one of four principles emphasized by the Kimmel Center for the Performing Arts in Philadelphia, Pennsylvania, is to provide vital arts education and community programming to serve the interests of a diverse audience.

Arts educational experiences are not for just the young. Two music festivals in Eugene, Oregon (the Oregon Bach Festival and the Oregon Festival of American Music), have very popular and successful Elderhostel programs designed to educate and entertain adult populations. Riley and

Stanley (2006) remind us that the baby boomers differ from their parents, and their lifestyles and interests will affect the arts. Middle-aged and older adults are choosing to pursue arts instruction and arts experiences.

Venues Are Inviting

Chicago's Millennium Park illustrates how investments made by public agencies to create spaces in which citizens can experience arts and recreational experiences contribute to growth. Referred to as a *cultural park* (Leider 2006), the 24.5-acre (0.1 square-kilometer) Millennium Park is located downtown and has transformed unsightly railroad tracks and parking lots. According to Chicago's mayor, Richard M. Daley, the park generates civic pride, improves quality of life in the city, and reflects Chicago's love of community and affinity for the arts. The park's urban location enables city residents to connect with nature, get to know their neighbors, and engage in sports, environmental, and cultural activities *(Parks and Recreation* 2006).

More and more cities across North America have added attractive or renovated existing venues for outdoor summer concerts in parks, alongside rivers, and in other popular outdoor settings. Private businesses and nonprofit organizations are providing nontraditional spaces as venues for arts and cultural programs and other activities. Music performances in wineries are common, and art walks through downtown and gallery districts are popular. Historic sites are being renovated in ways that will attract arts and cultural activities in commercial establishments.

The Urban Institute's evaluation of the Wallace Foundation's Community Partnerships for Cultural Participation Initiative has revealed some interesting findings on venues (Walker 2004):

- Three out of four of the top locations where people attend arts and cultural events are community venues rather than conventional arts venues. These include open-air parks and streets, schools and colleges, and places of worship.

- Most people who attend arts and cultural events do so in community venues at least some of the time, while a substantial group of participants visits only community venues.

- Community venues tend to attract people who are motivated by social and family interests.

- Certain community venues, such as churches, appeal more strongly to African Americans and Hispanics than to Caucasians as places to experience arts and culture.

- People who attend the largest number of events at community venues also participate in a range of civic activities.

The Krannert Center of Performing Arts at the University of Illinois offers free concerts in their lobby and coffee house.

Photo courtesy of Ragen E. Sanner

Creative arts and cultural programmers need to think outside the box when deciding where to provide experiences. As can be seen in the examples just given, venue selection impacts participation.

Participant Expectations

People in contemporary North American society expect arts and cultural experiences to be available to them during their free time. The middle-aged and older adults of today appear to be more engaged in leisure pursuits than previous generations were. They were lucky enough to have visual arts, music, dance, and theater included in their public education. Many of the current middle-aged adults grew up at a time when urban parks were becoming more common, when most communities had organized recreation and community school programs exploring arts or outdoor activities, and when youth organizations involved more and more children in arts and crafts. It has been suggested that these adults have a leisure astuteness not seen in previous generations because of the existing and developing opportunities in their schools and communities (Carpenter 2004a). Colbert (2001) predicts that by 2015 in Canada, the two largest segments of the market will be the baby boomers, who will be 50 years and older, and their offspring, who will be between 15 and 35 years of age.

Several arts and cultural activities take place outside of organizational contexts and therefore could go unnoticed

> because [they are] institutionalized, not identified with a specific organization, an educational institution, or nonprofit arts organization. This art is happening in a community-based way, in people's homes, in public places, in community halls, churches, temples, mosques. (Cady 2005, 3)

These are the kinds of arts opportunities that relate and contribute to human development through socialization and that build on participant expectations. Leisure socialization plays a role in people's expectations to engage in arts and cultural experiences. Throughout life, individuals undergo the process of leisure socialization (Iso-Ahola 1980) depicted in figure 1.1.

Within a context of social and cultural forces, people interact with social agents (e.g., parents, peers, teachers), who directly influence an individual's leisure experiences (e.g., appreciate art, do art, want to do more art) and encourage participation. Participation shapes the individual's perceived competence in the activity and has much to do with whether or not the individual continually pur-

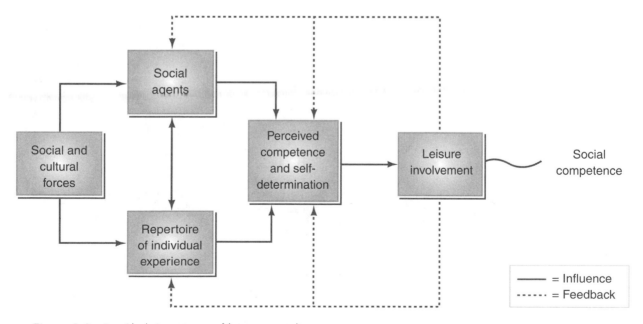

Figure 1.1 Iso-Ahola's process of leisure socialization.

Reprinted, by permission, from S.E. Iso-Ahola, 1980, *The social psychology of leisure and recreation* (Dubuque, IA: Wm. C. Brown Company), 132.

sues that activity. Positive involvement in leisure pursuits, in this case arts and cultural experiences, facilitates the individual's social competence.

The next section of this chapter examines the arts and cultural sector in order to show how the recreation and leisure and the arts and culture disciplines view programming. General and specific examples are given to illustrate a variety of arts and cultural programs.

Arts and Cultural Programming: Conceptualizations

Program theory originated during the early 1900s and has evolved through the body of knowledge associated with play, recreation, and leisure. Programming is the process of planning and delivering leisure experiences to an individual or a group (Carpenter and Howe 1985). Arts and cultural programming, then, is the planning and delivering of arts and cultural leisure experiences for individuals and groups. In this way, arts and cultural programming emphasizes the type of leisure experience that is being made available.

As arts and cultural programming has proliferated, ideas about what constitutes arts and cultural experiences have expanded. Wyszomirski (2002) portrayed the arts and cultural industry as a large, heterogeneous set of individuals and organizations engaged in creating, producing, presenting, distributing, and preserving as well as educating about aesthetic, heritage, and entertainment activities, products, and artifacts. Chartrand (2000) identified a number of cultural industries in the arts industry, and those included parks and recreation, leisure, education, tourism, antiques and collectables, cosmetics, cuisine, funeral, furniture and fixtures, gaming, multiculturalism, native culture, official languages, physiotherapy and psychotherapy, sports, and religion. Both of these conceptualizations that describe programming opportunities in arts and culture will be discussed further. The first comes from the literature in leisure and recreation and the second from arts administration.

Table 1.1 (see page 10) shows the 11 categories that Arnold (1978) delineated for the popular arts: horticulture arts, home economics arts, athletic arts, folk arts, cultural arts, ethnic arts, fine arts, performing arts, communication arts, sensual exploration arts, and child art. Historically, Arnold's categories guided the development of arts and cultural programs in public recreation.

Balfe and Peters (2000) identified five broad categories of art: visual; design, building, decorative (also visual but part of functional things); literary; media; and performing (presented in front of an audience at an event). They then developed a taxonomy that illustrated existing activities and art forms (Balfe and Peters 2000). The following list shows their taxonomy of the arts and cultural sector and includes selected programs and sample activities:

- Visual arts (painting, jewelry making, tattooing, designing, crafting)
- Literary arts (writing poetry, screenplays, or books)
- Media arts (creating computer art, choreography, composing music videos)
- Musical arts (song writing, instrument making)
- Dance and other movement arts (choreography, gymnastics, skating)
- Performances, exhibitions
  - Music (playing a musical instrument or singing; opera, bluegrass, hymns, rap)
  - Dancing or moving (ballet, ethnic, folk, ice dancing)
  - Acting (performing in plays, musicals, mime, or comedy)
  - Literary (reading poetry, storytelling, giving lectures)
  - Multimedia or other (music videos, street performers, circuses)
  - Ancillary activities within all these performing and exhibiting activities (directing, technical assistance, production)
- Media (films, TV, computerized art, animated film, Internet art)
- Selling or renting art objects, media products, and so on (fairs, festivals, shows, stores)

- Collecting, preserving
  - Libraries
  - Archives
  - Museums
- Teaching about arts and culture (theory and appreciation, arts management)
- Administrative, technical, governance, fund-raising work (artists' collaboratives, boards, technical work)

Table 1.1   Popular Arts

Category	Description
Horticulture arts	<ul><li>Parks</li><li>Gardens</li><li>Houseplants</li><li>Growing scenes</li></ul>
Home economics arts	<ul><li>Weaving</li><li>Crafts</li><li>Cooking</li><li>Fabrics</li><li>Decorating</li><li>Design</li></ul>
Athletic arts	<ul><li>Martial arts</li><li>Display arts or gymnastics</li><li>Fencing</li><li>Exhibitions</li></ul>
Folk arts	Participatory level of arts in fairs, festivals, circuses
Cultural arts	Arts participated in by people of various cultures that are distinguishable by their geographical location
Ethnic arts	Performances or exhibitions of cultural arts by performing groups
Fine arts	<ul><li>Painting</li><li>Sculpting</li><li>Photography</li><li>Architecture</li></ul>
Performing arts	<ul><li>Ballet</li><li>Opera</li><li>Theater</li><li>Symphonies performed on stage</li></ul>
Communication arts	<ul><li>Television</li><li>Radio</li><li>Speech</li><li>Some modern dance</li><li>Children's theater</li><li>Extemporaneous theater</li><li>Improvisational works</li></ul>
Sensual exploration arts	Arts experiences designed for the senses, including touch, taste, sight, and smell
Child art	Children's interpretation and experimentation with life

While categories and taxonomies are useful in conceptualizing arts and culture, it is tempting to return to Wyszomirski's description because it allows the programmer to find room to create whatever arts and cultural experience individuals or organizations find of interest.

When it comes to producing effective arts and cultural programs and services for consumers and artists, two key elements contribute greatly to success: knowledge of both program theory and its application and knowledge of contemporary arts and cultural programs and services. Given this foundation, along with professional commitment to providing arts and cultural leisure experiences for all and the capacity to demonstrate leadership and initiative, any one of us can develop and manage opportunities for arts participation. Arts and cultural programs contribute to community and social capital, the economy, sponsoring organizations, and, importantly, the human experience.

Types of Arts and Cultural Programs

The variety of arts and cultural programs available today appears to be greater than it has been at any other time in history. The number of recreation and arts organizations throughout North America is too great to identify every one of them. However, the U.S. Census Bureau's Web site conveys the magnitude and multiplicity that exist (see www.census.gov). Table 1.2 highlights the various kinds of organizations offering arts and cultural programs and services to their members and to the general public. It is meant to give an overview of the types of organizations and the kinds of programs and services being offered. No attempt is made to delineate between public and nonprofit institutions, as programs are not likely to be exclusive to one type or another.

The following discussion highlights several arts and cultural programs and services. Each was selected because it is a contemporary program in operation that helps individuals and communities benefit from arts and cultural leisure participation. Some programs reflect collaborations with other organizations in and out of the arts. Still others demonstrate sole proprietorship. As a collection of stories about arts programming, these samples convey the type and variety of arts and cultural programs and services that are available today.

- Blue Star Camps in North Carolina provide activities that encourage campers to explore and develop their creativity. Camp administrators view art as a fundamental and traditional camp activity and believe that the visual arts are experiential learning at its best (Foster 2003). More than two dozen summer camps from western North Carolina collaborate with business leaders and the local community arts council to celebrate the visual and performing arts created by campers. Art Matters: The Creative Side of the Summer Camp Experience drew record-breaking crowds on its opening

Table 1.2   Arts and Cultural Programs

Organizational type	Sample programs offered
College or university	Theater performances Music performances Special events
Community arts center	Visual arts classes Public art shows Special events Artists' services
Community theater company	Summer theater camp for children Acting classes for adults Public performances
Digital art	Video series Digital showcase YouTube workshop
Museum	Arts education Interpretive and lecture programs Touring exhibits
Parks and recreation	Arts and crafts classes Dance and movement classes Summer concerts in parks
Performing arts center	Classical series Cultural events Touring entertainers and shows
Religious organization	Participatory music groups Holiday and sectarian events Youth arts programs
Symphony orchestra	Public performances Performances for children Talks by conductor Development activities
Youth organization	Summer arts camps Practice space for youth bands Nature crafts Group singing

night. The exhibit was conceived of and hosted by Arts Center, a small grassroots organization in Henderson whose mission is to bring arts experiences to a diverse community in western North Carolina. The event included children's artwork in ceramics, weaving, papermaking, wood burning, photography, blacksmithing, and poetry.

•   Oregon Country Fair (OCF) is a yearly 3-day festival for the public that is supported by a year-round infrastructure of 4,000 volunteers, a staff of 6 full- and part-time employees, and a 12-member board of directors that sets policy and provides direction. As a 501(c)(3), charitable, and educational organization, OCF offers entertainment, handmade crafts, and food in a wooded setting that the organization owns in Veneta, which lies west of Eugene, Oregon. In 2005, 45,000 visitors attended, 700 artisans displayed their work in 250 booths, 61 outdoor restaurants offered culinary choices, and almost 100 entertainers performed on 14 stages. Begun in 1969 as a benefit for an alternative school, the OCF has a rich and varied history of alternative arts and performance promotion, education, land stewardship, and philanthropy (Oregon Country Fair 2006). In addition to the yearly festival, OCF donates $40,000 to $50,000 U.S. annually to other nonprofit community organizations and to local public schools for arts, cultural, and educational programs. It oversees environmental restoration efforts and, in 2006, composted or recycled 33 tons (30,000 kilograms) of landfill waste generated by the 3-day event. General manager Leslie Scott emphasizes that the fair is about fostering social capital through a network of relationships built around thousands of volunteers and the community (Calhoon 2006).

•   Schaumburg Park District (SPD) is a suburban agency near Chicago with extensive program offerings in arts and culture for the public (Schaumburg Park District 2006). The district has received awards from state and national professional organizations recognizing it for its programs and services. Its mission is service oriented: providing versatile leisure opportunities and preserving open space that promotes the well-being of the residents. Arts and cultural programs and services provided during the summer include dance activities and venues for all ages, theater classes for youths, family oriented street theater, and a summer talent show. SPD also operates the Cultural Arts Studios, which comprise the Schaumburg School of Dance (e.g, hip-hop, jazz, ballet, country, Irish), The Theatre (e.g., drama, mime, improvisation, puppetry), the Visual Arts Academy (e.g., ceramics, greenware, specialty art), and the Schaumburg Music Conservatory (e.g., lessons, kindermusik, kid rock, adult chorus). Major events scheduled throughout the summer include the Summer Breeze Concert Series that takes place in a lakeside setting and the Town Square activities that feature bands and orchestras, poets and storytellers, and cultural gatherings for residents (there is even a family ice-cream social). Two major arts programs are the Prairie Arts Festival and the Art and Craft Student Showcase. Noon Times are free midweek entertainments at the community recreation center's outdoor theater. Participants can bring a picnic lunch or purchase lunch on site, and the varied entertainments include comics, jugglers, magicians, and animal acts.

•   Accessible Arts, Inc. (AAI) is a nonprofit arts organization in Kansas City that serves local residents and provides resource information throughout the United States. With a mission to champion the arts for children with disabilities and to advocate access to the arts, AAI states that its core principle is to make the arts accessible to children with disabilities. Founded in 1988, AAI programs and services are wide ranging and focused on arts training for children with disabilities. They include training workshops, technical assistance, art demonstrations, special programs, and a resource center. AAI is an excellent example of the full range of services that organizations offer as part of their overall programs. AAI's Access to the Arts lesson curriculum was specifically designed for K-12, and it includes a video that features children with special needs participating in dance, music, and visual arts. The emphasis is on identifying the effects of the arts in life, encouraging hands-on participation, identifying abilities, working with students who have special needs, and developing strategic adaptations to eliminate barriers and facilitate participation (Accessible Arts, Inc. 2006).

•   Toronto Fringe Theatre Festival (TFTF) is one of the largest fringe festivals in North America, attracting 120 theater troupes from all over the world (www.fringetoronto.com). The festival began in 1989 with 4 venues and 40 productions and grew to 27 venues and 130 productions by 2006. The festival includes performances at dozens of venues that range from theater sites to

coffee shops, a Kids Venue, a 24-hour playwriting contest, and more. One of the unique aspects of fringe festivals is that they create experiences that artists and audiences can share over several days. Toronto's Fringe is one of 23 member organizations of the Canadian Association of Fringe Festivals, an organization that makes Canada number one in fringe festivals worldwide. Fringe festivals throughout Canada boost cultural tourism for the country; TFTF 2005 generated 46,585 in ticketed attendance and well over $300,000 of box-office revenue to the artists.

• Seattle Art Museum (SAM) is located in the economic and cultural capital of the northwestern United States. The Seattle metropolitan area and Puget Sound region are home to the largest concentration of population north of San Francisco and west of Chicago (www.amlife. us/economic_trends.html). SAM allows people to connect with art in three distinct locations: the Seattle Art Museum in downtown, the Seattle Asian Art Museum at Volunteer Park, and the Olympic Sculpture Park on the downtown waterfront. SAM offers a variety of educational activities, programs, and services. According to SAM director Mimi Gardner Gates, innovative technologies play an important role in realizing SAM's vision of connecting art to life in the 21st century (Seattle Art Museum 2006).

• Prison Arts Foundation was founded in 1996 in Northern Ireland and is an example of a very different kind of arts programming for a specific demographic group (Prison Arts Foundation 2006). Its aim is to release the creative self of all prisoners, previous prisoners, young offenders, and previous young offenders using a wide variety of arts experiences, including writing, drama, fine art, craft, music, circus and physical theater, and dance.

• Center of Creative Arts (COCA) is the largest multidisciplinary arts institution in the St. Louis metropolitan area (Center of Creative Arts 2006). COCA is housed in a 60,000-square-foot (5,600-square-meter) building, which is where most of its programs take place. In addition to the building, which includes a 400-seat theater, COCA also includes a gallery where more programs such as exhibitions, gallery talks, and workshops are held. COCA partners with other organizations, such as schools, in some of its programs (e.g., after-school classes). A number of the COCA's classes and workshops for children and adults in theater, dance, circus, and visual arts take place after school and during weekends at locations in and around St. Louis. The center supports a wide variety of programs and services, including a student company called *Ballet Eclectica*, the Family Theatre Series, summer camps, awards and recognition activities, performances, and events. The innovative Urban Arts and Art and Technology programs are designed to engage youths in school, after school, and during the summer. Urban Arts is a multifaceted outreach program of arts instruction, performances, workshops, and residencies. The Art and Technology program fosters literacy, creativity, and technological skills through digital painting, image editing, bookmaking, animation, and Web design.

• The Los Angeles Philharmonic (LAP) was founded in 1919 and is southern California's leading performing arts institution, entertaining an audience of 1 million each year. LAP offers a 30-week season at the Walt Disney Concert Hall, designed by Frank Gehry, and a 12-week summer series at the legendary Hollywood Bowl (Los Angeles Philharmonic Association 2006). Committed to creating innovative music education programs for people of all ages and backgrounds, LAP features the School Partners Program for both elementary and secondary schools, teaching artist faculty of musicians who teach in the schools, Community Partnership Program that includes community and neighborhood concerts, youth concerts and showcases, instrumental competitions for young musicians, professional development training for musicians and teachers, and Upbeat Live program, which involves preconcert talks and events.

• Tourism Mexico features a range of arts and cultural experiences on its Web site (www. visitmexico.com/wb/Visitmexico/Visi_Actividades). Noted opportunities feature archaeology, historical and contemporary architecture, arts and crafts, festivals and traditions, gastronomy, religion and mysticism, and museums. A closer examination of one city, the capital of Oaxaca, shows the myriad of arts and cultural attractions that are available, including the handicrafts traditions of the area; the dozens of temples, churches, and ex-monasteries that depict the customs, music, and everyday presence of people; the year-round festivals such as Puerto Escondido's Festivities, the Salina Cruz Festivity, the Bani Stui Gulal, and the Day of Death; and the numerous museums,

including the Museum of Cultures of Oaxaca, which houses pieces of Mixtec and Zapotec origin (Oaxaca's Tourist Guide 2007).

As these sample programs demonstrate, there are many arts and cultural programs operating around the world. Many organizations offer full and diverse programs, while others concentrate in one or two areas. Several, it seems, partner with other organizations and private businesses, and still more collaborate with one another so they can combine their particular areas of expertise in order to serve their members or the public.

The Leisure Perspective

This chapter began by indicating that arts and cultural programs and services are essential to the lives of individuals and the formation of communities. Opportunities to participate in arts and cultural leisure experiences contribute positively to the quality of people's lives and communities. But what is meant by the term *leisure experiences?* This section of the chapter examines this question and offers examples of how concepts associated with leisure theory inform our thinking about arts and cultural programming.

Arts consultant George Thorn (1999a) linked arts and leisure this way in saying, "You can't prevent the making of art. You can't prevent people from wanting to connect with art. Nothing else can compete with the moment that these two connect. Our job is to create more and more moments!"

Arts and cultural programmers connect people with art during leisure and in doing so create those moments that George Thorn described. When these two connect because of intervention by programmers, we can say that the programmers are doing their jobs; they are the experience makers.

Futurist Alvin Toffler (1970) used the term *experience makers* when referring to those whose primary job responsibilities are to create leisure experiences and environments that enhance the well-being and quality of life of the participants. Experiences, he predicted, can be sold, and there is ample evidence in contemporary society that people will pay to pursue experiences related to travel and sightseeing, recreation places and spaces, and fitness and sport; they will pay for entertainment and spectator and informal and home-based experiences. And, as we have seen in this chapter, people are participating in a wide variety of arts and cultural leisure experiences. Keeping in mind our definition of programming as the planning and

It is your job as an experience maker to ensure that participants have an experience that truly enhances their well-being and quality of life.

Photo courtesy of Trips Inc.

delivering of arts and cultural leisure experiences for individuals and groups, we are indeed leisure experience makers. Next, this chapter will explore leisure: what it means, what it contributes, and how particular concepts associated with leisure apply to arts and cultural programs.

What Leisure Means

According to Russell (2005), leisure has been a part of everyday life from the beginning of human history. Drawing from sociology, psychology, economics, political science, anthropology, media and cultural studies, and the humanities, Russell posits that our contemporary meanings and uses of leisure are best understood when examined historically. She identifies links that connect music, art, and literature with leisure, beginning with the kingdom of Kush (4000 BC), ancient Greece and the works of Aristotle and Plato, ancient Rome, ancient China, Muhammad's early empire, ancient New World societies, medieval Europe, and the Renaissance and concluding with today.

The word *leisure* historically has had and today still has multiple meanings. Yet there are certain current conceptualizations of leisure that programmers can use in creating arts and cultural leisure experiences. In contemporary society, leisure is typically conceptualized in one of three ways: as free time, as an activity, or as a state of mind.

Leisure as Time

Viewing leisure as a person's free, unobligated time is a prevailing conceptualization. It has often been implied that if you stopped people on the street and asked them to tell you what leisure is, they would say it is their free time. The ways in which people in a free society spend their discretionary time are often explored in leisure research.

Discretionary, or free, time makes up one-third of the life span for Americans (Chubb and Chubb 1981). There are 168 hours in a week. Kelly (1996) speculated that if 56 hours are subtracted for sleep and 50 are designated for work and the commute to work, some 62 hours remain for maintaining self and the household. In addition, much of our free time comes to us in childhood and later adulthood—at times before we have developed knowledge, skills, and awareness about what we can do with our free time and at times when we may feel limited by a fixed income and by physical and social psychological challenges.

More than thirty years ago, Best and Stern (1976) noted that the tendency to live linear lifetime patterns rather than alternative lifetime patterns means that most people experience extended lengths of nonwork time during childhood, youth, and retirement. While many people experience variations in this lifetime pattern, the predominant paradigm today still emphasizes that childhood, youth, and retirement are the years for education and free time and that middle adulthood is the stage when nondiscretionary activities related to work and social roles often occur during so-called free time or time away from these activities. The effect of living the linear lifetime pattern is that a person's free time is often available in very short time frames: 1 hour here, 20 minutes there.

Other factors are associated with real or perceived free time. For example, in the U.S. today, teenagers spend 16.7 hours a week online and another 13.6 hours in front of the TV. The public spends $70 billion U.S. a year on gambling, which is three times the amount spent on movies, concerts, sporting events, and theater performances combined (trendSCAN 2004). Sadly, not everyone gets the same amount of free time. The desire to have more free time is often documented from leisure research perspectives (Robinson and Godbey 1997; Schor 1991; Veal and Lynch 1996; Zuzanek and Beckers 1999). There exists a lively debate over whether people are working longer or shorter hours and whether they have more or less free time. For example, while Robinson and Godbey (1997) report that Americans have more free time now than they had 30 years ago, the findings of Schor (2003) indicate that work hours are on the rise. Others note that overworking, overscheduling, and time poverty threaten people's health, families, friendships, and communities (DeGraaf 2003). In one longitudinal study, researchers found that middle-aged adults longed for more free time for leisure than they currently had; they usually desired to have from one-third to one-half more time per week for leisure (Carpenter 1999). Every year for 10 consecutive years, the

overwhelming majority of middle-aged adults indicated that they wanted more free time per week than they currently had available for leisure. Time scarcity, which is commonly experienced by working adults (DeGraaf 1994), affects individuals and those organizations interested in providing arts and cultural programs and services.

Leisure as Activity

This conceptualization of leisure is about what people do during leisure. The range of activities people can choose from is perhaps greater than it has been at any other time in history. This well-accepted view of leisure is predicated on the fact that activities and leisure are somewhat synonymous. Like the view of leisure as free time, the concept of leisure as activity is quantifiable. Activities can be observed and measured so that participation patterns can be gathered. Programmers can create new activities and modify existing activities in ways to encourage participation.

Earlier in this chapter, table 1.1 and the taxonomy of art forms depicted the works of Arnold (1978) and Balfe and Peters (2000), while table 1.2 offered a sample of arts and cultural programs arranged by organizational setting. These provide an overview of the kinds of arts and cultural programs that offer leisure activities. As such, they are good examples of what is meant by leisure as activity.

Leisure as State of Mind

A third conceptualization of leisure is that it is a state of mind; it feels like what the individual experiencing it says it feels like. Following are four excerpts in which participants recall their most memorable recreation experience and describe what the arts or cultural leisure experience felt like. These personal accounts were published along with several others in a special publication of *Leisure Today* called *Recreation Dimension—The Human Dimension* (Gray and Ibrahim 1985). Interestingly, the feelings experienced with arts and cultural participation were similar to those generated by activities requiring physical exertion, thus conveying that the feeling, or the state of mind of the participant, is not particularly altered by the type of activity. What follows are the words used by four arts and cultural participants who described their leisure experiences.

Gaining a New Perspective

The director chose me to do it . . . there were people that I respected who came to me and told me that they had the feeling, they sat in the audience and knew that I had them right there in the palm of my hand. It was important coming from my peers . . . who had experienced the feeling themselves; they knew exactly what it was and when it was happening. It's a nice, warm feeling to know that people appreciate what you are doing—that all your work was not in vain, that you've done it right. I think it's pride. I was proud that people enjoyed my work. (An actor in a theatrical play)

Painting at Banff

If I couldn't paint, things would be pretty boring for me. It's probably the most important thing in my life, and I really can't imagine my life without it. I get a lot of enjoyment from music and other cultural things, but painting is my life. That's what I do, and everything else is sort of in context to that. When I travel, those experiences are all reflected in my paintings. When I read, when I listen to music, anything I do is all related back to that. (A winter painting experience)

Attending a Ballet

When the performance was over, I found myself . . . shouting, applauding with tears of joy in my eyes, and I was not aware that I was in the middle of thousands of people who were also applauding. I had the feeling that my world had just been completed. I left the performance knowing that I would never be the same. (A young man at his first ballet)

Reliving a Musical Journey

We were going to one of the big concert halls. . . . It was just like a skating rink. There were no seats there, no ice, just people standing [and] talking. And all of a sudden before the concert started, somebody began to cheer, you know, hip, hip, hurrah, and I looked over to that part of the gallery and thought maybe this is a rowdy crowd or something and we got in the wrong place . . . I guess, and I didn't know what was going on, but it came time for the performance and the conductor walked in and all those people stood there so quiet, you could hear a pin drop. Maybe there were three or five out of the four or five hundred who found a place and sat down but the rest of them just stood there silently for 45 minutes, while they listened to Beethoven's "C Major Mass." (A retiree describing a music experience)

When viewed as a state of mind, leisure is subjective. When leisure is viewed as time or activity, whether or not an experience is leisure can be measured quantitatively, as with time, or can be observed as behavior directed toward certain activities. Leisure as a state of mind yields personal meanings that are attached to the experience, and one person's leisure experience is not necessarily another's. Leisure is defined as a psychological condition by the meaning it holds for the individual (Russell 2005). Thus leisure is contextual (Kleiber 1999): The meaning that people attach to leisure depends on the place, the time, and the people. Whether an experience is leisure, then, is solely defined by the individual (Russell 2005).

Leisure Behavior

Conventional wisdom tells us that leisure is characterized by feelings of freedom and choice; leisure includes choosing to do nothing. Neulinger (1974) identified the defining criterion of leisure as perceived freedom (Mannell and Kleiber 1997). Perceived freedom is the state in which people think that what they are doing is done by choice and because they want to do it (Neulinger 1981). In addition, the desire to participate and keep participating in a leisure activity is intrinsically motivated (Neulinger 1981). Perceived freedom and intrinsic motivation are essential to the leisure experience.

Leisure behavior typically is perceived as pleasurable and as contributing to human development and social civility. Our free time provides the context in which we can exercise choice and experience feelings of freedom inherent in leisure. Activities can be designed to encourage the realization of leisure. But neither the free time nor the activity itself guarantees that the individual will experience leisure (as a state of mind).

Leisure is goal directed—that is, when pursued, leisure is undertaken for a reason. Arts and cultural programmers may create a situation for specific reasons that participants may or may not find motivating, as the intention to participate comes from within the participants themselves. McCarthy and Jinnett (2001) proposed a three-stage participation model through which individuals move in deciding to participate in arts experiences. Individuals may or may not be aware of this process, but even so, the model depicts the components that programmers can manage to facilitate participation. For example, if ticket prices are relevant to potential participants, programmers can take that into consideration when determining the cost of the tickets. As depicted in figure 1.2 (see page 18), the model of McCarthy and Jinnett considers a person's background, beliefs, and perceptions regarding arts participation; the practicality of participating; and the actual experience itself.

Similarly to Iso-Ahola's process of leisure socialization discussed earlier in this chapter, McCarthy and Jinnett's model takes into consideration early socialization with respect to the arts. Both of these models acknowledge the importance of sociopsychological factors, family influences, and previous experiences and how they contribute to individuals' perceptions regarding participation.

What Leisure Contributes

The Academy of Leisure Sciences (2006) issued a white paper as a way to widely distribute information on the economical, physiological, environmental, psychological, and social benefits of

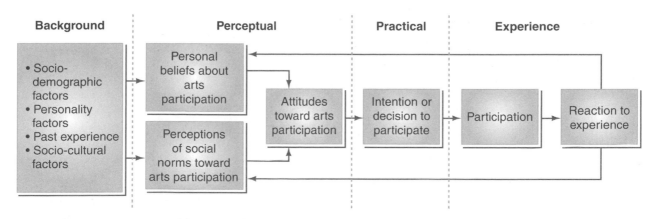

Figure 1.2 The participation model proposed by McCarthy and Jinnett.

Reprinted, by permission, from K.F. McCarthy and K. Jinnett, 2001, *A new framework for building participation in the arts* (Santa Monica, CA: RAND Corporation), 24.

leisure. Before that time, Driver, Brown, and Peterson (1991) edited an extensive volume of leisure research related to the benefits of leisure. This research contributes important information that arts and cultural programmers can use to promote programs and services, to justify expenditures related to programs and services, and to report the beneficial effects programs and services have on organizations and individuals.

The economic benefits of leisure have been studied frequently and are of interest to economists, leisure and arts administrators, and those in travel and tourism. Each year, people spend billions of dollars of their discretionary money purchasing entertainment and recreation goods and services, participating in arts and sports experiences, and visiting vacation locales.

Research has also focused on leisure as improving or meeting desired conditions of individuals, groups, and societies (Driver, Brown, and Peterson 1991). This latter area of leisure research has been extensive and has contributed to an understanding of leisure from several disciplines (e.g., psychology, sociology, social psychology). It also relates well to programming and providing arts and cultural leisure experiences for groups and individuals. Following are several examples that illustrate leisure researched from different disciplines.

Mannell and Stynes (1991) noted that the psychological benefits of leisure can be placed in three broad categories:

- Development of the self, including self-actualization; identity affirmation; interpersonal and leadership skill development; cognitive, social, and emotional development in children; and spiritual development
- Experiential learning, skill and knowledge acquisition, and environmental attitude change
- Short-term, transient experiential outcomes such as flow

The sociological perspective views the leisure behavior of individuals and groups as occurring within the context of society. Here, researchers are interested in patterns of behavior, social interactions, and relationships; behavior norms; institutions influencing leisure; and the like. Kelly (1996) reminded us that leisure is activity chosen in relative freedom for its qualities of satisfaction. Given this, the number and variety of leisure options are vast: "When leisure is defined as a quality of experience and as the meaning of activity, then it may be almost anything, anywhere, and anytime for someone" (Kelly 1996, 3).

Kelly (1996, 13) further noted that because leisure is an important phenomenon in society when measured by time invested, money spent, and values expressed, "We need to know as much as possible about anything that important to so many people."

The social psychology of leisure is the scientific study of the leisure behavior and experience of individuals in social situations (Mannell and Kleiber 1997, 25). The sociopsychological perspective is concerned with how people come to perceive time or behavior as free or discretionary. According to Mannell and Kleiber (1997, xv), the question is "how do people's personalities and the social

situations that they encounter during their daily lives shape their perceptions, experiences, and responses to leisure?" In social psychological theory, leisure behavior and experiences associated with perceptions, emotions, beliefs, attitudes, needs, and personality characteristics (i.e., internal psychological dispositions) are examined within the context of individuals' lives related to other people, group norms, and media (i.e., situational influences).

Applying Leisure Concepts to Arts and Cultural Programming

This portion of the chapter presents selected theories associated with leisure as they apply specifically to arts and cultural programming. These include leisure repertoire, seeking change and familiarity through leisure, serious leisure, flow, and leisure constraints. These discussions are meant to convey concepts related to leisure behavior and to suggest how these concepts may relate to programming arts and cultural leisure experiences. There is a vast body of knowledge in the literature regarding leisure behavior, and the discussions presented here should not be viewed as all-inclusive. Rather, they should be viewed as representations of the kind of information about human leisure behavior that has relevance to arts and cultural programs and services because it betters our understanding of leisure and leisure behavior.

Leisure Repertoire and Seeking Change and Familiarity

Iso-Ahola (1980) developed two models that offer insight into programming arts and cultural leisure experiences across the life span. The first model depicts the concept of leisure repertoire and is shown in figure 1.3.

An individual's leisure repertoire is the number of leisure activities available to or participated in by the individual. As people age, especially as they reach middle adulthood, their leisure repertoire peaks. Presumably the leisure options grow as people develop awareness and skills as children, youths, and young adults. Then, in later adulthood, perhaps due to declining health or more focused interests, people find the number of options in their repertoire reduced.

Figure 1.4 (see page 20) shows Iso-Ahola's second model, which describes changes in people's tendencies to seek familiar or new forms of leisure over the life span. Older people are more like young children than adolescents and young adults in their preference for familiar experiences through leisure (Mannell and Kleiber 1997).

The trajectories in these two models superimpose rather well, suggesting a connection between the leisure repertoire and the desire for novelty or familiarity in leisure. For

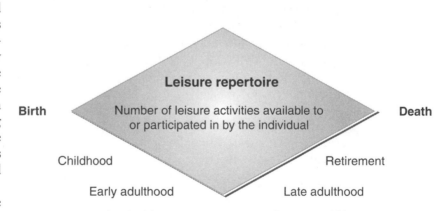

Figure 1.3 Individual leisure repertoire as a function of life span.
Reprinted, by permission, from R.C. Mannell and D.A. Kleiber, 1997, *A social psychology of leisure* (State College, PA: Venture Publishing, Inc.), 249; adapted, by permission, from S.E. Iso-Ahola, 1980, *The social psychology of leisure and recreation* (Dubuque, IA: Wm. C. Brown), 174.

programmers deciding about arts and cultural programs and services, these models can be very informative regarding individuals' needs and interests. The models also lend credence to offering varied programs for youths and young adults, as they are building their repertoires and desire new experiences. Conversely, programmers should consider fine-tuning programs to specific interests of adults, who are growing older and have less interest in the unfamiliar.

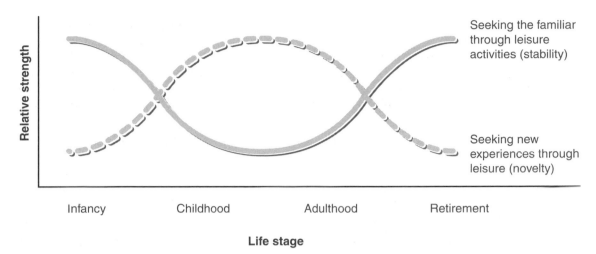

Figure 1.4 Changes in tendencies to seek familiar or new forms of leisure over the life span.

Reprinted, by permission, from R.C. Mannell and D.A. Kleiber, 1997, *A social psychology of leisure* (State College, PA: Venture Publishing, Inc.), 253; adapted, by permission, from S.E. Iso-Ahola, 1980, *The social psychology of leisure and recreation* (Dubuque, IA: Wm. C. Brown), 176.

Serious Leisure

The concept of serious leisure was originally advanced by Stebbins (1982). Serious leisure is the systematic pursuit of an amateur, a hobbyist, or a volunteer activity that participants find so substantial and interesting that they launch themselves on a career centered on acquiring and expressing its special skills, knowledge, and experience (Stebbins 1992). Amateurs pursue leisure experiences that are typically equated with a profession. A person participating in a community theater program is somewhat like a professional actor but is not drawing a salary and is instead engaging in serious leisure behavior. Hobbyists, though lacking the professional alter ego of amateurs, still may need to prepare for small publics who take an interest in what they do (Stebbins 2005). For example, there may be a group of individuals who have a passion for model trains and who meet to work on their displays and share their hobby with others at public events. Volunteers typically dedicate hours of their personal time in service to others and to organizations. They do so in a variety of ways, performing different roles and assuming different responsibilities.

Often contrasted with casual leisure pursuits, serious leisure pursuits require perseverance, personal effort to obtain special knowledge and skill, commitment to regular participation, and commitment to follow a leisure career in the pursuit. For example, an amateur musician needs to know the pieces and to practice before performing to audiences. Hobbyists and volunteers spend many, many hours of their free time engaging in their chosen leisure pursuits. Individuals engaged in serious leisure pursuits report finding deep fulfillment in their activities. Programmers offering arts and cultural leisure experiences often depend on individuals engaged in serious leisure pursuits to provide casual leisure experiences to others. Amateurs, hobbyists, and volunteers frequently facilitate a wide variety of arts and cultural leisure experiences that many nonprofit and public organizations would not be able to afford to offer without them. Their leisure passion enables programmers to offer more, and their abilities need to be tapped by leisure programmers.

Flow

The model emphasizing the state of flow has been widely applied to leisure programming. The concept of flow was originated by Csikszentmihalyi in the mid-1970s (1975). Since then, it has received a lot of attention by researchers and professionals from many disciplines. It is a model of optimal experience that relies on a match between a person's abilities and the challenges presented by an activity or environment (Kleiber 1999). When experienced, this conscious state engages the individual in intrinsically rewarding activities that "are just fun to do" (Csikszentmihalyi 1993, xiii).

Assuming that we are designing arts and cultural experiences in which people can experience leisure (i.e., state of mind), it becomes important for programmers to understand flow and how it can be managed. Flow is realized when an individual's feelings of competence match well with their feelings associated with the perceived challenges presented in the experience. Any activity has the potential of creating a flow experience for the individual, but relaxing moments of leisure and entertainment are less likely to create flow than actively involved activities that stretch physical or mental abilities.

> Certain activities are more likely to produce flow than others because (1) they have concrete goals and manageable rules, (2) they make it possible to adjust opportunities for action to our capabilities, (3) they provide clear information about how well we are doing, and (4) they screen out distractions and make concentration possible. (Csikszentmihalyi 1993, xiv)

When imagining and producing arts and cultural leisure experiences, programmers can design programs and services that address these criteria. In doing so, they will be facilitating the opportunity for their participants to experience flow.

Leisure Constraints

The literature associated with leisure constraints has addressed both nonparticipation and the desire to participate in specific kinds of leisure. Jackson and Scott (1999) noted that the notion of leisure constraints involves much more than the choice to participate. They suggested that the formation of preferences, the derivation of enjoyment, specialization, and the choice of facility are among many factors that need to be addressed. In a recent synthesis of the literature on leisure constraints, Jackson (2005) presented the hierarchical/negotiation model, which depicts the commonly accepted views of the factors influencing our understanding of how to address leisure constraints (see figure 1.5).

The following are examples of potential constraints related to participating in arts and cultural leisure programs. Each constraint potentially inhibits participation, but if it is addressed and removed or minimized, a desire to participate can be facilitated:

- A perception of the arts as being for the elite
- Cost that is seen as prohibitive

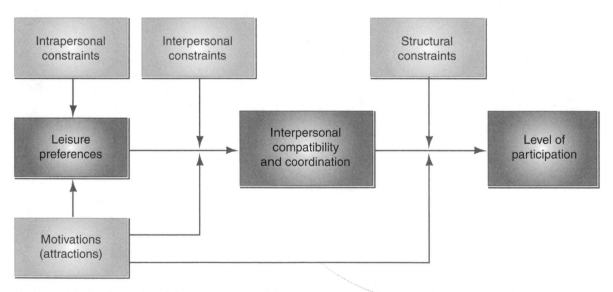

Figure 1.5 The hierarchical/negotiation model.

- An activity site (i.e., facility or venue) that is viewed as unattractive, poorly maintained, or inaccessible
- Hours of operation that are not conducive to using public transportation
- Other arts and cultural activities that take place at the same time or that are less expensive
- Lack of awareness or skill to participate in a specific activity
- Lack of sufficient time or interest to participate

The people who are responsible for managing arts and cultural leisure experiences must address these and any other constraints during the program planning processes discussed in chapter 3.

Summary

This chapter introduced arts and cultural programming from two distinct but related aspects: arts and cultural programming and leisure. The discussion began by addressing why this book in arts and cultural programming was written and what this book accomplishes. This was done by providing information on contemporary factors associated with arts and cultural experiences and by outlining the kinds of arts and cultural programs and services being offered. Several specific examples of arts and cultural programs and services were provided. Then different concepts of leisure were explored. Lastly, contemporary meanings associated with leisure, definitions of leisure, and leisure concepts were applied to arts and cultural programming. The next chapter looks at program theories as they relate to arts and cultural programming.

Programming Approaches

J. Robert Rossman, PhD

Illinois State University

Photo courtesy of Ragen E. Sanner

Programming arts and cultural leisure experiences is one of the most satisfying professional experiences you will have in your career. When you design and implement activities, events, services, and performances, you provide opportunities for the general public to engage in and enjoy arts and culture. There are several approaches to programming; using the appropriate one to organize your programming efforts will contribute to your success.

This chapter describes approaches to designing and implementing programs. Recurrent themes of programming models that apply to arts and cultural programming and the outcomes of various approaches to programming are discussed and compared. Examples of how each approach might operate in the real world are provided. Later in the chapter, comprehensive programming and its implications for program development are discussed.

A program is a plan or procedure for developing opportunities for individuals to participate in arts and cultural leisure experiences. The word *program* is robust and is often used to describe the entire inventory of an agency's programs and services as well as an individual program or service. Three categories of opportunities are usually produced—activities, services, and events. Programming is considered a management activity focused on assessing participant needs and desires and organizing a program of arts and cultural experiences to meet those needs and desires.

Published programming models outline approaches for action. They are frameworks that describe how a programmer operates, and each of them makes assumptions about the roles that the patrons and the programmer will play in delivering program services. They are grounded, action-oriented models that guide professional behavior.

Programmed Services

Over the past 40 years, recreation and leisure service providers have developed a variety of approaches for programming—in other words, for organizing and delivering services designed to provide leisure experiences. This body of knowledge is useful to all agencies responsible for organizing experiential services that provide a variety of engagements to their participants. This notion of producing experiences was recently given additional credibility in the book *The experience economy: Work is theatre and every business a stage* (Pine II and Gilmore 1999). These authors assert that the service economy is being replaced by the experience economy, which is made up of organizations that provide patrons with experiences, or series of memorable events that engage the participant in a personal way (Pine II and Gilmore 1999, 2). Learning techniques for producing programmed experiences is essential for community arts professionals.

Implementing personalized programs often requires developing new ways to include patrons in arts and culture. For example, Illinois State University sold tickets to a preperformance dinner with maestro Keith Lockhart, conductor of the Boston Pops Orchestra. The Ford Center Theatre in Chicago sold tickets for a backstage visit following performances of *Wicked*. To provide memorabilia of visits to a special exhibition featuring the Swiss artist Alberto Giacometti, the Hong Kong Museum of Art provided patrons an opportunity to have their photo taken and computer enhanced. The resulting photograph was an elongated image of the individual—a picture stylized as if it was a work of Giacometti! Programs developed as experiences almost always engage patrons in novel ways.

A program is a designed opportunity for an arts or a cultural experience. Providing designed experiences for individuals is somewhat tricky because experience itself requires the participant to be engaged. This requirement results in one of the programmer's major dilemmas: the amount of freedom the participant will be allowed in determining the outcome of the event versus the degree of intervention the programmer will exercise in determining that outcome. The services a programmer develops will range from direct services to enabling services. In providing direct services, the programmer arranges most of the program, and the participant basically only attends and participates. At the other end of the continuum are enabling services, in which the programmer does much less to organize the event and instead enables participants to organize and operate their own experiences. At various points across the continuum of services, the ratio of programmer effort to participant effort in providing a program will change.

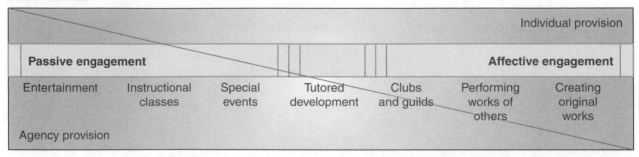

Figure 2.1 The continuum of engaged experience.

Experience is not possible without engagement. At the very least, the participant must take in and process information in order to have an experience. More active engagement includes processing information, interacting with the environment, and affecting the outcome of the experience. Figure 2.1 illustrates the continuum of engagement options. It includes the types of services provided, the degrees of engagement required, and examples of services likely to be produced. A few points on the continuum are designated in this figure; once you understand the continuum, you should be able to identify many more.

Individuals prefer different amounts of engagement for a variety of reasons, including their level of education, interest, or skill in a specific art; the amount of time they have to devote to an activity; their access to ongoing art opportunities; their age, health, and income; and so on. In some cases, individuals participate exclusively in one modality. For example, a patron of the opera participates only as a member of an audience and is only entertained by performances. In other cases, individuals may participate across the entire spectrum of engagement modalities. For example, an individual interested in dance may attend performances, take classes, engage a private dance instructor, perform choreography, and create choreography for some music. When developing an inventory of programmed services, the programmer needs to be concerned about producing a complete range of engagement opportunities for participants.

Categories of Programmed Services

There are three categories of services a programmer develops and operates: activities, services, and events. Activities are focused occasions of interaction. They are the most intensely programmed experiences and are the basic building blocks of service. They include instructional classes, workshops, and other similar programs. Activities usually require individuals to register to participate, and the programmer will need to provide the individualized attention expected by those registered for a program.

Services are specific personal functions related to the arts that are performed for a fee. Often, patrons could provide a service for themselves but are willing to pay to have someone else perform the service for them. An example of this is the continuum of options for experiencing a museum exhibit. Patrons could prepare themselves and engage in self-guided tours of the exhibit. This method is the least expensive way to participate. However, patrons may prefer to pay for a prerecorded audio tour in which an expert has done the investigative work and shares this knowledge with the patron via the audio tape. A third level of service is a group or a personal tour conducted by a member of the museum staff, in which participating patrons have the opportunity to ask questions about the works being exhibited. These alternatives result in three levels of service, each of which is offered at a different price and each of which provides an increasing amount of the staff's attention to the patron.

Events are collections of activities and are usually offered with a theme. A community arts festival is one example of an event. The duration of an event can vary widely, lasting a day, a weekend, a week, a month, or sometimes a season. In some cases arts are the central theme of an event and in others arts are a supporting amenity to an event with a different focus.

Patron Motivation

There is a range of motivations for participating in activities during personal free time. Understanding these motivations will help the programmer design services that meet patron expectations. Excluding serious artists who intend to make a career of the arts, why do individuals participate in arts and culture? Researchers in leisure have demonstrated that individuals believe they are having a leisure experience when the engagement provides the following three feedbacks. One, the individuals perceive that they have freely chosen the activity and have continuing choices within the activity. Two, the activity is autotelic, and the engagement itself provides motivation to continue participating, without adding the incentive of external rewards. And three, the participants perceive that they play some role in determining the outcome of the activity; that is, they can positively affect the outcome. When these perceptions are operationalized by participating in an activity, the activity is usually described as fun, relaxing, or pleasurable and is labeled as a leisure or recreation experience.

A wide range of activities provides these outcomes and is described as leisure participation. Both sports and arts activities can be structured so that participants readily experience these perceptual outcomes, and, not surprisingly, sports and arts are major areas of leisure participation. But the list is long and includes gardening, outdoor recreation activities, cognitive activities, water sports, literary activities, and many others. Humans seek autotelic activities, and the various activities just reviewed are simply different conduits though which these outcomes are accessed. The availability of an activity, an individual's skills and abilities, and an individual's previous socialization into various activities account for a good part of the variation in participation and the specific activities any one individual pursues.

The previous discussion might lead to the assumption that the engaging qualities of participation are contained in the activities themselves. For example, you might assume that a class on oil painting will always provide these perceptual outcomes. But this is not the case. How participation is structured and how a program is operated make a difference in the outcomes an experience provides. The participants who are recruited into a program and their beginning expectations affect their overall satisfaction with an activity. An individual's experience and perceived competence in a specific activity will also determine perceptions of the program. Thus a programmer needs to be concerned with who is recruited into a program, how the program is operated and evaluated, and how these evaluations are used to determine the program's future.

Approaches to Programming

How programs are designed, where ideas for programs originate, and how meaningful outcomes for program services are identified influence the service delivered. Over the past 40 years numerous approaches to programming have been developed. Edginton and colleagues (2004) identified 33 approaches in the literature on leisure service. Some of the more recent approaches have been built by combining and subsuming previous ones. In reviewing these, we will first discuss the program development cycle and then discuss some of the issues raised by these various approaches that programmers must deal with in organizing and operating program services.

Cyclical Nature of Program Development

Since 1985 (Carpenter and Howe), the notion that program development is cyclical has been established though the work of numerous authors (Farrell and Lundegren 1991; Rossman and Schlatter 2003; and others). As the concept of a program development cycle has evolved, the number of steps involved in developing programs has increased. Although programming cycle diagrams depict a linear progression of step-by-step development, they also acknowledge that while the process is generally linear, it includes frequent iterations between adjacent steps. When implementing program services, the programmer generally progresses through the cycle, with the caveat that iterations addressing issues raised in previous steps are frequently undertaken for further clarification.

The various stages of program development and the order in which they should occur are illustrated in figure 2.2. Different authors emphasize different steps in the model. While some offer

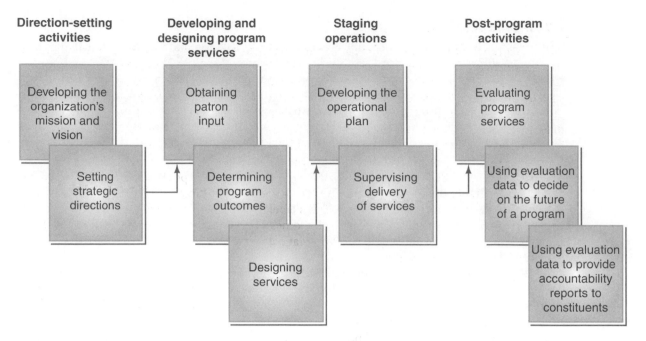

| Direction-setting activities | Developing and designing program services | Staging operations | Post-program activities |

Figure 2.2 The program development cycle.

only a single technique for accomplishing a step, others offer multiple techniques for implementing each step. The collective literature makes clear that these are the steps that leisure programmers currently believe must be completed in order to develop successful programs. Furthermore, the current literature suggests that there are multiple options for implementing each step. Programmers need to learn several options for completing each step so they can implement an appropriate program development strategy for a specific program.

Operational Issues of Programming Approaches

The model of action outlined by the program development cycle seems relatively straightforward to implement. But how the programmer executes each step will influence the quality of a program and its effect on patrons. There are a number of different approaches to this enterprise, and a programmer needs to be well versed in how to implement each step of the program development cycle.

As discussed previously, the steps of the program development cycle have cumulated over the past 40 years. Concurrent with this developing model, different authors have emphasized different overarching approaches that programmers should use in organizing program services. The following discussion outlines six recurrent approaches from these models and describes the issues of each approach and their effects on program development. Programmers should be aware of how each of these issues will affect their work.

Direct Versus Enabling Services

This continuum of service was discussed earlier in this chapter. It is mentioned here to remind you that determining what mix of programs to offer along this continuum is an ongoing issue that the programmer needs to resolve. The notion of serving can create a trap for a programmer. Over time programmers may tend, under the rubric of providing service, to provide more and more of the service for patrons. We call this *event creep*; the programmer does more of an event each time it is operated. Remember that this programming strategy will not allow patrons to increase their own abilities, and this delivery strategy will not serve patrons who desire services that facilitate opportunities for affectable engagement. To keep from falling into this trap, the programmer must consciously avoid it while nurturing and developing programs over time.

Prescriptive Approach

The prescriptive approach is a default method for programming and was the original approach used to develop services (Danford and Shirley 1964; Murphy et al. 1973; Edginton et al. 2004). In the arts, it was often a high-culture approach predicated on an assumption that experts knew which specific arts should make up a community arts program. The approach, as designed and taught, does not require the programmer to consult patrons. Implementation is a matter of designing programs the programmer knows should constitute a community arts program, publicizing their availability, and operating them. Thus, much of the literature developed with this model provides technical information about how to organize and manage services.

The approach arose from early professional models of practice that assumed that a knowledgeable professional would prescribe programs for a given community. Program ideas came from the broad expertise of the arts programmer or were prescribed from a generally accepted portfolio of community arts programs as determined and implemented by those in the profession. With this method, it was assumed that there is a generally known mix of program services that should constitute a community arts program.

In the prescriptive approach, programmers develop very specific goals for developing program services and then design services to meet these objectives. This approach requires programmers who have broad knowledge about the arts and previous experience in operating community arts programs.

This approach developed in an era when it was thought that program managers were experts in their fields and knew best about the services to offer their patrons and about how to operate these services. Although developed at a time when populist participation in program development and decision making were not valued as they are today, the method does place decisions about which program to offer in the hands of experts. Because the approach depends on experts in arts and cultural experiences to be the source of programming ideas and development, it includes a built-in mechanism for ensuring quality programming. Professional expertise is often critical to raising the performance standards of arts programs. Self-directed groups can become complacent with performance levels and delude themselves into believing that they are producing higher quality output than they actually are when examined by someone who is truly knowledgeable. Art is not like sport; it does not have the feature of competition to provide a continuing gauge of performance.

When implemented as designed, the prescriptive approach does not demand sufficient consultation with boards, patrons, or others to meet today's expectations for participatory program development. Furthermore, it does not incorporate the patron input that has been made possible with modern techniques of marketing surveys and focus groups. It does remind the programmer that there are performance standards apart from the normative standards that may be developed in a given group; part of the programmer's responsibility is to manage the dynamics of a group so that it incorporates these standards into its value system.

Traditional arts programs involve senior citizens and oil paintings.

Photo by Josh Alder, courtesy of CVALCO

Community Process Approaches

A collection of programming approaches envisions the programmer as a community catalyst who works with art groups in a community to develop program services to meet their needs (Korza 1994). Often the group to be worked with varies in the model. Edginton, Compton, and Hanson (1980) proposed working with community leaders. A more grassroots effort that focused on working with the community residents, who were the recipients of the services, was envisioned by Edginton, Compton, and Hanson (1980); Kraus (Edginton et al. 2004); and others. Carpenter and Howe (1985) suggested working with other agencies to synergistically produce program services of a higher quality than those possible for any single agency to produce. A newer version of this basic method is the servant leadership movement, in which programmers adopt a code of serving that guides their interactions with patrons in a way that helps the patrons reach desired goals. In this model the programmer assumes both leading and following roles as needed to implement a group's wishes (Jordan, DeGraff, and DeGraff 2005).

The theoretical roots of these approaches grew out of the urban unrest of the 1960s and the methods of social engineering that developed to improve life in urban ghettos. Community process approaches empowered residents to control their own destiny, including guiding the development of their own recreation services and facilities. Working with indigenous patrons, community developers identified and articulated a community's needs and then worked with the community to obtain the resources necessary to provide for those needs. Various techniques were used to obtain the required resources, including advocacy, fund-raising, and organizing the community to provide labor and other resources needed to develop the services and facilities.

In implementing a community process approach for program development, the programmer must assume various roles, including enabler, advocate, and encourager, that are needed to coalesce a group's efforts and move the group members to the actions needed to obtain the social and physical resources required for reaching their objectives. Community process advocates believe that their interactions with a community help build the social capital of the community. Operating in this modality is time consuming for the programmer, and there is some question about the degree to which every group needs this kind of facilitation.

An enduring legacy of this movement is patron involvement in decisions that determine the strategic directions of a programming organization. Institutionalized structures that have evolved for obtaining this kind of input are advisory boards, policy boards, and boards of directors. It is generally accepted that successful arts and cultural programs are often integrated into a community through the visible participation of community leaders in guiding the organization. Thus, to succeed with this approach, program managers need small-group process skills that enable them to successfully interact with these kinds of boards. They need to both glean from the group the desired programming directions as well as obtain the group's ongoing commitment to support the arts organization in the community.

Investigative Approaches

Investigating the services desired by target populations is an obvious method for developing program services and was also one of the first proposed (Danford and Shirley 1964). It has received ongoing revision throughout the development of programming approaches (Tillman 1973; Edginton, Compton, and Hanson 1980; Edginton et al. 2004; Farrell and Lundegren 1991; Rossman and Schlatter 2003). Various mechanisms have been used to obtain this input, including, in the earliest days, suggestion boxes, oral communication from patrons, and written evaluation forms. Cynically, at one point this method was called *give them what they want*.

However, as social scientists perfected surveying techniques, the methods for obtaining participant input became more sophisticated. In the 1960s and 1970s, community needs assessments included systematic random surveys of community populations with attitude and interest surveys that investigated the programs and delivery features desired by residents. In the 1980s and 1990s, the questions asked and the frameworks used to analyze the results were further refined with concepts from marketing.

Systems theory and marketing were the two frameworks used to formulate investigative approaches for programming. Systems theory suggests that there are three components to a system:

inputs, processes, and outputs. All systems approaches to program planning provide techniques for implementing each component and view systematic needs assessments as critical inputs to program planning. The process stage is implemented by analyzing the results of the survey. This is followed by the output of the system: the recommendations for program development that flow from the data analyzed. One problem with planning studies completed in this manner is the overwhelming amount of data often generated from the survey and the lack of a suitable analytical framework for organizing the results into meaningful recommendations.

Marketing concepts provided more focus to investigative planning studies. The notions of identifying target groups and market segments gave programmers identifiable cohorts with similar needs that could be managed. The market mix itself, including product, price, promotion, and place, also provided a more manageable list of program features that could be addressed in program development.

Systematically investigating the population of potential patrons for programs and the program features they desire has become a standard operating procedure for most arts organizations. One disadvantage of this method is the frequency with which it needs to be repeated to make certain that data are current and credible. Although frequent investigation is a desirable practice, many organizations simply do not have the financial wherewithal to conduct these surveys as often as they should be conducted.

Although surveys can provide good information about patrons' current desires, they are limited by the patrons themselves. That is, patrons are often limited because their only frame of reference for recommending programs is what they have experienced previously or have seen available elsewhere. Thus, these surveys are not likely to provide the programmer with ideas for innovative programs. Other methods are needed to develop creative, new services.

Nevertheless, systematic random surveys remain a useful tool for program development. They are an important method for obtaining reliable input from the targeted population and for investigating patron desires regarding programs.

A second widely used method for investigating patron desires is the focus group interview. Developed by marketers, this technique allows for more direct interaction with small groups of patrons to ascertain their views about program services. In the hands of individuals skilled in group process techniques, focus group sessions can yield useful information for developing new or tweaking existing programs.

Cafeteria Approach

The cafeteria approach is more eclectic than the methods already discussed and was one of the earliest models of program development (Danford and Shirley 1964; Murphy et al. 1973; Farrell and Lundegren 1991). In providing a cafeteria of offerings, the agency makes a conscious effort to present a comprehensive variety of programs. The basic method is to make certain that new programs are offered each program cycle. The programmer promotes and expands the programs that succeed and eliminates those that fail, replacing them with new experimental courses. This is a conservative approach that usually leads to success by generating a varied selection of programs that have worked elsewhere.

The cafeteria method facilitates a broad view of the agency's inventory of programs, as it encourages the programmer to operate from a system-wide level. This paradigm of operation dovetails nicely with marketing notions of program life cycles. Programs cycle through five stages—introduction, takeoff, maturation, saturation, and decline. In the cafeteria approach to program development, there is a natural flow of a new program being introduced, grown, matured, and then removed when it is no longer sufficiently enrolled. The programmer's challenge is to manage the inventory of programs so that the programs are well distributed among the varying stages of the life cycle, thus ensuring that at any one point a few new programs are being introduced, a few old programs are being eliminated, and the majority of programs remain reliable and sustainable.

One deficit created by the cafeteria approach is the tendency for programmers to ignore an individual program. Because of the broad, system-level view encouraged by the approach, the programmer does not often focus on the minutia of how a program is offered and operated. Thus,

how the program affects patrons is not usually a part of the evaluation paradigm used with this method. Rather than nurture the program, the programmer is tempted to simply replace it with a different program. But, how a program is operated contributes much to its success, and the suitability of its operation needs to be examined before it is abandoned.

An important message to programmers from the cafeteria approach is that programs may not last forever, and some will need to be eliminated. Once implemented, programs tend to gain their own inertia, and programmers are reluctant to cancel them. This hesitation comes from two sources. One is the affinity that programmers gain for a program and the professional pride they take in its continuance. The other is the tenacity of the small but committed core of participants all programs seem to acquire over time. This group often makes it difficult to cancel the program even though the overall number of people participating in the program does not make it economically justifiable to continue.

Interaction Approach

The interaction approach (Rossman and Schlatter 2003) focuses on how an experience is produced for the patron within the interactions of the program. Rather than being concerned about the macroissues of developing programs within an organization, it examines the microissues of producing a participant's experience.

The approach was developed from symbolic interaction theory, a branch of social psychology that examines how experience is created in ongoing episodes of social interaction. It directs the programmer's attention to the events that produce the participant's experience and the overall outcomes that are achieved through this interaction. The method assumes that experience is produced through patrons interacting with their environment in what is called a *situated activity system*. The situated activity system comprises six elements: the people interacting in the system, the objects they interact with, the rules that guide their interactions, the physical venue where the program occurs, the relationships that exist among the participants or those they build through interaction, and, finally, the movement of the interaction through time. The role of the programmer is to plan, organize, and orchestrate interactions within a situated activity system so that patrons achieve the desired experience as a result of participating in the program.

The interaction approach differs from the other approaches in the level at which it deals with programs. It deepens the programmer's responsibility so that the programmer is concerned with participation and outcome in addition to delivery of services. Since the positive benefits that agencies claim result from their services depend on the patrons' experiences, this concern is well focused and should have the attention of the programmer.

The interaction approach helps the programmer stay focused on the intended end of her work. Implementing the steps of the program development cycle is hard, can involve working with a lot of different people and organizations, and can be time consuming or even frustrating. In order to keep motivated, often it is useful to reflect on the intended end of the effort. In designing and implementing opportunities for arts and cultural participation, it is easy to lose track of the purpose: to provide patrons the opportunity to experience the arts and culture. The interaction approach requires the programmer to constantly examine his efforts in the context of this intended end product.

The interaction method does not have built-in features to deal with some of the system-wide issues that the other approaches take into account. There is no requirement to scan for the comprehensiveness of an agency's services. There is no prescribed method for investigating patron desires. There is no method for working with patrons in developing programs in order to meet their needs. However, the focused operational planning suggested by the approach is a useful framework for planning events and for reviewing the adequacy of program plans for all services.

Best Practices in Programming

Work completed in developing approaches to program planning has resulted in a series of best practices for implementing programmed experiences that provide opportunities to engage in arts and cultural leisure experiences. The cumulative results of this work provide comprehensive guidelines to help programmers focus on their work and to alert programmers to the issues they must resolve

as they organize and operate program services. Agencies that program arts and cultural experiences face the same issues and can benefit from the work completed in leisure programming. From the work just reviewed, what are the best practices that can be derived?

First, there is a program development cycle, and those who consistently adhere to this cycle succeed more often than those who don't. There are steps to follow, a variety of techniques available for implementing each step, and a general order for completing the steps to achieve success. The cycle imparts organization and process to programming.

Second, a well-prepared programmer knows the steps of the program development cycle and has developed a kit of techniques for implementing each step. Part of good programming is having sufficient experience and wisdom to know how to approach a programming problem and to create a program that meets an identifiable need for a targeted population. Different techniques will be needed depending on the group being served, the agency providing the service, the potential programming partners, the specific arts activity, and the program's current location in the program life cycle.

Third, there are enduring issues that must be dealt with in programming. These issues exist because they have no set answer or correct position. The programmer needs to be aware of these issues and understand them when recommending the development of a specific program. Following is a brief summary of each issue.

When developing a program, programmers must be aware of how much of the organization and content of the program they want or their patrons want them to provide. They operate on a continuum between direct service and enabling service—that is, between delivering the complete program and enabling participants to provide most of the program.

Programmers should be experts in their fields and be able to make sound recommendations for developing arts and cultural programs. They should also know that some patrons desire to be involved in strategically planning the program services of an agency. They should understand that this involvement may constitute a critical commitment to the arts on the part of the patrons that they must nurture in order to gain the visibility and credibility needed to ensure the sustainability of the arts organization and thus arts and cultural opportunities in a community. Therefore, programmers should use the prescriptive approach judiciously to provide impetus for new programs and to create standards where needed to ensure the artistic credibility of the arts organization and its programs.

Although there is an objective sensibility to the quality of art that is shared by those well trained in the arts, there are many features of the arts that are truly a function of individual choice. A programmer must work with patrons to help them sort out their preferences and implement programs that build their organization and the social fabric of their community.

Similarly, programmers must commit themselves to querying their patrons about the types of programs and program features desired. These investigations provide current data and send an important message about the openness and responsiveness of the arts organization to its patron base.

While keeping within the degrees of freedom permitted by the agency's mission, the programmer must be committed to offering a broad range of arts and cultural opportunities. Furthermore, the programmer needs to be committed to truly managing the organization's inventory of programs by perpetually introducing new programs, nurturing continuing programs, and canceling programs no longer serving the organization. (Comprehensive programming is discussed further in the next section of this chapter.)

Programmers must remain concerned about what goes on in their programs. What happens to patrons as a result of participating in the arts and cultural programs is the ultimate question of performance and accountability. Techniques that focus on engaging individuals in the interaction of a program are available to help programmers implement well-planned experiences.

Although programming can be complex, it is a known process, and there are a variety of techniques for implementing each step of the process. Programmers need to be well versed in this process and its techniques so they can match programming techniques with specific patrons, programs, and collaborating organizations in order to deliver comprehensive services that satisfy patrons and grow and sustain opportunities for arts and cultural experiences in a community.

Developing Comprehensive Program Services

If an agency is to fully serve its target population, maximize its revenue, and meet its organizational goals, it needs to develop a comprehensive inventory of program services. Regardless of the resources available for developing services, it is always more efficient to keep them fully utilized and deliver services at their maximal capacity.

Offering comprehensive services is useful in two ways. First, patrons are served best when the agency presents a complete range of services. Second, comparing the agency's current offerings with comprehensive service offerings provides the agency with an analytical framework for searching for new program opportunities.

In actual practice, programmers are constantly searching for new program ideas. Sources for these ideas include information from colleagues about programs that are succeeding elsewhere, promotional literature and Web sites of other organizations, participant input collected through surveys and focus group interviews with target populations, and observations of what is happening in general throughout society.

There are several dimensions of comprehensiveness that a programmer needs to address. These are variables across which a variety of services can be developed. Collectively, they will result in a matrix of potential services that probably cannot be fully developed; however, the resulting matrix of potential programming opportunities is a useful tool for heuristically contemplating possible services.

Time Frames

Some of the most basic units of analysis for offering programs are the time frames in which services can be offered. Comprehensive programming requires offering services across a variety of time frames. Following are various time frames to be considered.

Annual Time Frames

Many arts agencies operate throughout the year; others operate seasonally. Regardless of its length, the season should be fully programmed while operating. In planning a season (annual or other), one of the first steps is to examine a calendar for the obvious dates for holding events and the obvious

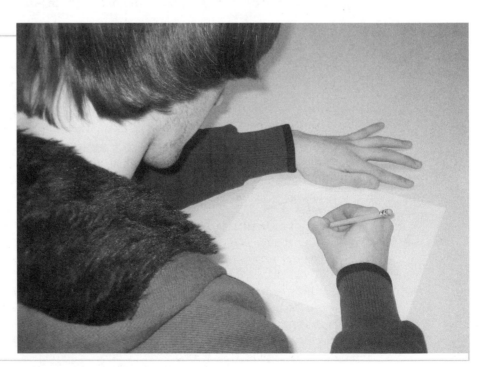

Develop programming that keeps participants interested in the outcome of their work.

Photo courtesy of Ragen E. Sanner

dates to avoid. Some of these will be national dates, while others will be locally observed holidays and events. For example, in the United States, Thanksgiving is a nationally observed holiday that has an accompanying season that is usually programmed. Holidays such as Kwanzaa, Chanukah, and Cinco de Mayo are celebrated by smaller portions of the population. Depending on its patron base and community, a specific arts organization may or may not program events during these holidays. Scanning the calendar should give some structure to the season's overall schedule of programs.

Programming Seasons

Although the majority of the arts are performed indoors, the programs being offered often differ by season. Some arts organizations operate throughout the year, while others operate during specific seasons. For example, summer theater festivals operate in the summer and are often held outdoors. There is an opera season that is mainly a winter program, although it begins at the end of fall and runs into early spring.

Often, the seasons of the year dictate who is available for participation and create a natural rhythm of expectations from patrons. For example, during the school year youths are available only in the late afternoon, evening, and weekend. In the summer, they are available during the week. Thus some programs need to be organized around seasons simply because of participant availability. Programmers should contemplate how their offerings might vary by season and plan accordingly.

Other Time Frames

Using other time frames to review and plan program offerings is also a useful analysis tool. Examining the adequacy of program offerings on a monthly, weekly, daily, and hourly basis often reveals unfilled blocks of time deserving further program development.

Using the arts to deepen other programs is another strategy that programmers can implement. Programmers need to examine popular events to see if it is possible to piggyback on them and infuse arts and cultural experiences into them. For example, holding an arts exhibition depicting football during the 2 weeks preceding the Super Bowl would provide a local arts contribution to an existing national event. Or, an arts organization might add a live band concert to a Fourth of July fireworks celebration. Developing these kinds of programs sends an important message about the ubiquity of art and exposes the arts to new audiences who are not frequent consumers of the arts. Making arts and culture accessible is an important function of community arts organizations.

Arts Program Areas

The arts generate a diverse set of programming opportunities. Visual arts, performing arts, graphic arts, and, more specifically, music, painting, sculpture, drawing, drama, and so on provide a wide variety of programming opportunities the programmer can develop. The mission of some arts organizations, like an opera company, is dedicated to the development and presentation of a single art form. Such a mission restricts the number of program areas available to the programmer. However, other arts organizations, like a community arts organization, may be dedicated to arts and culture in general, thus allowing for the development of many art forms. Comprehensive arts organizations provide the programmer with an almost unlimited inventory of possible programs. Comparing current program offerings with what could be offered is one method of examining the comprehensiveness of the agency's offerings while concurrently identifying possible new programs to develop.

Organizational Formats

There are a variety of ways to organize a specific program. This variety of organizational formats creates a dimension for additional program development. For example, oil painting can be offered as an instructional class for skill development, a focused instructional class of shorter duration like a weekend workshop, a special exhibition of oil paintings, a competitive event, a drop-in event of scheduled discipline time with tutoring feedback, an oil painting club in which members exchange

Make sure that participants are taking the class because they want to and not just because it fits their schedules.

Photo courtesy of Hult Center for the Performing Arts/Eugene

advice and feedback, or a drop-in activity in which individuals continue to develop their abilities on their own. Each format will best suit a different cohort of individuals for any number of reasons.

Often, the programmer can expand the number of programs offered simply by scheduling the same program in additional formats. There is a temptation to believe that individuals register for a program because of their interest in its content. For example, we assume that individuals register for sculpturing because they are interested in sculpture. However, individuals often register for a program because it fits their schedule. That is, they select a program in a stepwise fashion, looking first at programs that fit their schedule and second at programs that are conveniently located. From the programs that fit these criteria, they make their final selection based on content that interests them. It is often not the case that they look at an interest area first.

So, one proven strategy for program development is to expand the inventory of programs by offering the same activity with different organizational formats. These new formats will likely attract some of the same participants, but they may also attract new participants who can now access the program because it is offered in a different scheduling format.

Age Groups Served

Arts are for all age groups, but often it does not work well to have all age groups participate concurrently. Scheduling the same activity for each interested age cohort is an obvious program distribution method and a way to expand offerings. For example, painting classes can be taught to age groups ranging from preschoolers to teenagers to middle-aged adults to senior citizens with additional age groups in between. Each age cohort is distinct and requires different programming approaches.

Gender

Sports are for the boys and arts are for the girls! Or so the conventional wisdom said. Although no one differentiates programs by gender these days, the different genders do tend to gravitate toward specific art forms. If both genders are to be served, especially within the preteen and teenage cohorts, the programmer must make a conscious effort to provide offerings that accommodate each or both genders as needed. An agency's cumulative program offerings should attract both genders.

Ethnicity

Although some art forms are universal, others are specific to ethnic groups. Providing ethnocentric art is one way of celebrating diversity in today's society. Offering ethnocentric art from the cultures of indigenous subcommunities is especially important in a heterogeneous community.

Participant Skill Level

Skill and ability in art are not evenly distributed throughout the population. Thus, programs should serve the range of artistic abilities and cultural interests, from beginning to advanced. In some cases skill level can be designated directly by the program title, such as by naming classes *beginning sculpture* or *advanced sculpture*. In other cases, skill level may be accommodated by totally different strategies, such as by engaging individuals who are interested but have less talent as volunteers, docents, board members, and so on. And, depending on the art form, there may be many jobs that need to be done, such as the many involved in a theater production. The programmer needs to ensure that a sufficient range of opportunities is available, so that individuals with diverse abilities can find a program that fits their interests and talents.

Summary

Constantly striving to provide a comprehensive inventory of services accomplishes several desirable outcomes for the programming agency. First, it produces a complete set of opportunities for the agency's patrons. Second, it helps the agency discover its voids in service and implement new programs accordingly. Finally, it ensures that the agency is using its resources in the most efficient manner and is thereby being a good steward of its resources.

Programming Tasks and Functions

Gaylene Carpenter, EdD
University of Oregon

G iven that arts and cultural programmers are essentially experience makers, those who are better able to manage the wide range of tasks inherent in programming will in all likelihood be those who produce the better programs and services (i.e., experiences). Though it is good to realize that practice will make you a better programmer, it is still worthwhile to be aware of the things that programmers need to think about and do in order to produce successful arts and cultural leisure experiences.

This chapter summarizes programming tasks and functions and discusses the factors associated with these functions that are somewhat unique to programming. This overview of programming tasks and functions will give you an idea of the processes that the programmer must manage, while the discussion of the factors associated with programming will provide you with a sense of the multifaceted nature of arts and cultural programming. Other chapters in this book will go into much more detail on these subjects and are written by authors who are experts in those aspects of arts and cultural programs and services.

Once programmers become aware of theoretical approaches to programming, they frequently temper their style of organizing and managing accordingly. No matter which model you prefer, key functions emerge. The model, whether it is linear, cyclical, or interactive, does not alter the tasks and functions that need to be performed in order to make arts and cultural programs and services available.

The term *comprehensive program* refers to *all* of the activities, events, classes, resources, and services an organization makes available to various groups and individuals. Generally speaking, professionals who manage arts and cultural programs are responsible for programming more than one activity or service concurrently. They typically manage these experiences by working with other paid and volunteer staff members. A comprehensive program usually involves a wide range of visual, literacy, performance, cultural, historic, and media arts opportunities designed to encourage participation.

Comprehensive programs typically operate throughout the year and include several face-to-face experiences, services, and drop-in or walk-through opportunities. These experiences may be performances, exhibits, amusements, social occasions, special events, classes, fund-raisers, excursions, and any combination thereof. They may take place in a variety of venues, including theaters, galleries, museums, gardens, community centers, downtowns, youth centers, universities, schools; the list could go on and on. Often the experience occurs in a setting that is unassociated with the

sponsoring organization (e.g., a group of actors affiliated with an inside theater doing an outside street performance).

The programs and services that may be offered are as diverse as arts and cultural leisure experiences already are, and as the creativity of the programmer allows. Yet as diverse as the programs and services may be, similarities exist among them. The following list is of programming commonalities shared by two quite different arts organizations—the Oregon Bach Festival and the Maude Kerns Art Center:

- Several full-time staff members
- Seasonal staff members
- One megaevent per year
- Series of ongoing activities
- Social activities
- Volunteer recruitment and training
- Free and fee-based offerings
- Sponsorship support
- Volunteer recognition
- Fund-raising events
- Long-range program efforts
- Membership plans and privileges
- Policies and procedures for participation
- Marketing strategies
- Legal and financial counsel

One organization is an international performing arts organization (the Oregon Bach Festival), and the other is a community arts organization (the Maude Kerns Art Center). Both are nonprofit organizations operating in the same midsize city. Given the preceding list, they may appear to be similar, yet in actuality they offer very different programs to their constituents (see www.bachfest. uoregon.edu and www.mkartcenter.org). The number and variety of activities that each manages demonstrate the multifaceted nature of arts and cultural programming.

Tasks and Functions, Functions and Tasks

It is useful to think of functions first and then think of the various tasks that need to be performed in order to realize a given function. For example, the function of assessing consumer needs requires the programmer to identify and complete tasks associated with collecting and documenting the necessary information. As the programmer moves on to another function, such as developing a program, the tasks inherent in that function need to be accomplished as well—usually before the program or service is actually provided. Throughout this chapter, we will refer to the functions associated with arts and cultural programming as *needs assessment*, *program development*, *program implementation*, *program evaluation*, and *program modification*. This five-phase model was developed by Carpenter and Howe (1985) and will be used to organize our discussion of tasks and functions. This model suggests that programming is a cyclical phenomenon in which, in contrast to linear models, phases overlap in a circular, interdependent manner.

We will begin our exploration of the program planning process by first examining two job announcements for programming positions in arts and culture. The first is a sample posting for a Program Coordinator position with a nonprofit arts organization. The second position, an expressive arts programmer, was posted by Arlington County, Virginia, a public employer.

Job Description

Program Director

The person hired will be responsible for managing cultural programs consistent with the educational and outreach mission of this arts organization. Responsibilities for this full-time appointment include providing professional oversight and direction to existing arts and cultural programs, researching and initiating new programs and services, and managing a 20-person part-time program staff of activity coordinators and instructors. The successful candidate must demonstrate an ability and interest to collaborate with staff and volunteers in other community organizations whose responsibilites include cultural arts programming. Minimum qualifications include a bachelor's degree in arts management, recreation, or education (graduate study encouraged), strong interpersonal and communication skills, competent management skills including previous experience doing arts and cultural programming; and computer skills that include creating marketing and interpretation pieces used in promoting programs for the organization.

Job Description

Expressive Arts Programmer

Responsible for coordinating community arts programs to include development, design, budget management, implementation, evaluation, analysis, and program leadership (including direct, hands-on program facilitation with participants) of community expressive arts programs that serve a diverse community in a variety of settings. Duties also include the recruitment, coordination, oversight, and training of staff, volunteers, and interns. The spectrum of programs range from classes for leisure and skill development, to summer camp for youth, to specialized programs that use the arts to help build assets within our participants, and to provide preventive and intervenient programming for at-risk populations. The communities served are diverse in age, culture, socioeconomics, language, and abilities.

The position requires the ability to apply a variety of expressive arts media/modalities, with an emphasis on drama, music, and movement, in the design of community-based arts programs for all ages. The employee must have good organizational skills and strong interpersonal/communication skills in order to interface effectively with a diverse community.

The work involves a high level of collaboration with other program leaders within the agency (i.e., Neighborhood Recreation Areas, Bilingual Outreach, Office for Teens, Therapeutic Recreation, and the Senior Adult Office). This position in the Recreation Division is part of a team of recreational art program staff and requires the ability to work well in both team situations and in a self-directed manner.

As can be seen, the two jobs require applicants to possess specific programming capabilities and the ability to perform related tasks and functions. A careful reading of both positions conveys a necessity for the new hires to be skilled at needs assessment, program development, program implementation, program evaluation, and program modification.

Needs Assessment in Arts and Cultural Programming

Knowing constituents' needs and interests is an integral part of programming. It is often the first function required. It sets the tone for the rest of the programming process. Needs assessment generates ideas for programs and services and assures that the organization has a system to incorporate participant input into program decisions. Needs assessment does not just happen; it must be approached systematically, and the information gathered must be applied to programs as they are being developed. (See chapter 6 for more information.)

Malcolm Knowles (1970, 1980) conceptualized a model for assessing needs that, when applied, would produce program objectives. In applying his idea, Knowles urged programmers to visualize how needs, when examined through a filtering process, would help programmers translate needs

into program objectives. His well-accepted model has been applied to a variety of programming situations for more than 25 years now. Knowles noted that needs assessment enables programmers to consider how individual, organizational, and community needs are filtered through institutional purposes, feasibilities, and clientele interests to produce program objectives. Individual, organizational, and community needs are at the top of the filtering system. Though certainly not static, they do not vary greatly from year to year. Institutional purposes, feasibilities, and clientele interests tend to vary more frequently.

Individual needs include basic human needs such as physical, ascribed, and felt needs. These needs are at the core of the human experience and, from a developmental perspective, vary across the life span. The basic human needs include physical needs (to maintain the body), personal growth needs (to experience self-fulfillment), security needs (to be secure both physically and psychologically), new experiences needs (to experience novelty or risk), affection needs (to share and care), recognition needs (to receive attention or respect), and learning needs (to gain competencies or master skills).

Ascribed needs may be felt by individuals, but they initially come from external sources. For example, if someone suggests to you that you should go to an opera performance and you accept their suggestion as a need of yours, then you have an ascribed need. Carpenter and Howe (1985) noted that organizations are often masters at convincing individuals that they need one or another particular leisure experience. When it comes to youth programming, many arts organizations are influential in ascribing the need for involvement. Clever marketing can be very effective in ascribing needs to groups of people. As such, ascribed needs often become felt needs. Felt needs are those the individual actually feels; they come from inside the person and motivate participation. For example, a person who loves opera and has moved to a new city will likely seek operatic experiences on their own.

Organizational needs are aligned with the purpose, core values, and mission statements of the organization. These needs stem from the organization's reason for being. They are defined by key individuals who are possibly founding members and, later, as the organization evolves, by those in leadership positions. Organizational needs do not change dramatically, though they may be revised through long-range planning.

Community needs are defined in part by organizational needs when determining whom the organization is designing programs for, such as a specific demographic. Youth organizations, for example, will design arts and cultural experiences for children and teens. In this way, the notion of community becomes narrowed to the population that the organization is serving, and so the needs of that particular community are what must be included. *Community* can also refer to the larger social community in which the organization functions and to which the organization may or may not respond by creating arts and cultural experiences. The array of community needs stemming from this broader definition is often too challenging for one organization to address. When this is the case, arts organizations often partner with other community-based organizations in order to meet community-wide needs.

Once individual, organizational, and community needs are identified, they are screened through institutional purposes, program feasibility, and constituent interests. Institutional purposes are short-range goals that are set by the organization and that are consistent with organizational needs. For example, a local YMCA may want to reach middle schoolers during summer months by creating a hip-hop camp. The institutional purpose relates to the goal of reaching out to middle schoolers, and the means to accomplish this goal is a summer camp that emphasizes music for that age group. Program feasibility is about whether or not the organization has the capability (i.e., human and nonhuman resources) to provide such a program. In this example, the YMCA very likely has the capability to provide the hip-hop summer camp, given its existing camp facilities, ability to produce a themed camping experience, and existing infrastructure to advertise the program. In order to run the camp, the YMCA may need only to recruit leaders with knowledge of hip-hop. Assuming that the interests of the constituents, in this case the middle schoolers, indicate that the constituents would like to participate in a hip-hop camp, programmers can identify program objectives and feel fairly confident that the summer hip-hop camp will be a successful arts program.

Utilize arts and cultural programming designed to keep youths motivated to participate.

Photo courtesy of SouthEast Effective Development (SEED)

Program Development

Before the programmer can successfully negotiate all that goes on during program development, the needs assessment must be completed because it provides a foundation from which decisions are made. During program development, the programmer fully engages in decision making, deploying and redeploying existing resources (both human and nonhuman), and overseeing multiple, logistical sources of information. The decision-making process is largely what drives the function of program development. Tasks inherent in program development require continual reshuffling of the deck, so to speak, as frequently a decision made for one task influences another task and decisions cannot be made in isolation.

The following tasks must be accomplished during program development:

- Determine program objectives
- Determine program format or pattern
- Develop program policies and procedures
- Determine and address scheduling needs
- Secure necessary facilities or venues
- Manage budget, finances, and sponsors
- Address leadership and staffing needs
- Recruit and train staff if necessary
- Develop promotional and marketing strategies
- Address legal issues and necessities
- Procure and distribute resources
- Address safety and security considerations
- Partner and collaborate when needed

Tasks in program development are not accomplished in isolation; rather, they affect each other in multiple ways. Program development is constantly *in process* and as such is a dynamic rather than

a static function. Programmers probably spend more time in program development than they spend in any of the other phases of programming.

In the next section, four of the tasks required for program development are discussed in order to illustrate their dynamic nature: determining program objectives, determining program format or pattern, developing program policies and procedures, and addressing leadership and staffing. These tasks were selected for discussion because they may raise additional questions for the programmer and therefore require additional decision making.

Determining Program Objectives

Identifying program objectives is an important early task because once determined, these objectives will guide the programmer in making decisions. Program objectives should be identified for all constituent groups (e.g., participants, leaders, observers). Programmers may use multiple-option programming in developing objectives (Sheffield 1984), as this technique enables people who have different motivations for participation to all realize their reasons for participating. Sheffield noted that people's motivation to attend activities varies; they desire different outcomes for their participation. Called *goal structures*, these outcomes are competitive, individualistic, or cooperative. Professionals can design programs to meet any or all three of these goal structures. For example, a literary event can meet participants' desires by including (1) a contest for the best short story (competitive goal) for those who want to achieve their goal when others do not, (2) an open forum for creative writing (individualistic goal) for those whose success in participating is not related to others' goals, and (3) a city-wide history project (cooperative goal) in which one participant can't meet the goal unless all do. Using multiple-option programming acknowledges that individuals have differing motivations when attending arts and cultural programs.

Determining Program Format or Pattern

Determining the program format involves choosing among the various available program patterns. These patterns set the tone for the experience. Widely accepted program patterns include physical, educational, cultural, social, environmental, or personal-development patterns or any combination of these. Specific arts and cultural experiences may also determine which program formats are the most appropriate for the activity undertaken. For example, music education programs that typically take place indoors may make experimenting with the environmental format by moving outdoors unrealistic. On the other hand, that same music education program may be enhanced if offered in an unanticipated way. As this music education program may offer less potential to include physical activity in the overall experience, the programmer may want to consider how music

Combine movement and music to enhance the enjoyment of the participants and the audience.

and movement could be combined to alter the experience for the participants. Integrating more than one program pattern into a single activity often results in a more enjoyable experience for participants.

Developing Program Policies and Procedures

Different programs require different policies and procedures. Some require many and others require few. Policies and procedures for any given program or service typically emanate from organizational philosophy and principles. Philosophy and principles do not change often, and when they do, it is usually during times of organizational change. Policies and procedures change frequently, and typically they vary with different types of programs and services. As a result, those who have programming roles in organizations frequently need to devise and revise policies and procedures. The following is an example of how policies and procedures arise from philosophy and principles:

- Philosophy (the fundamental beliefs of the organization): Individuals should have opportunities to experience making art.
- Principle (a specific statement about organizational beliefs): Skilled facilitators and artists who can create meaningful art-making experiences for individuals will be recruited and hired.
- Policy (guidelines for implementing principles): Programs for skill development will be offered to individuals who have little or no previous experience in making art.
- Procedure (program practices that assure policy realization): Two new programs will be designed for those who have little or no previous experience in making art.

As can be seen, program procedures not only emerge from organizational philosophy but also become rather specific about the tasks programmers must perform during program development. In this example, the programmer must find skilled staff (facilitators and artists) to facilitate the program and should direct promotional strategies toward individuals with little or no experience in art making.

Addressing Leadership and Staffing

The task of recruiting effective leaders and supportive staff is one with major ramifications to program success. We have all seen the master artist who does not communicate well enough to be a positive asset to the program. Does this mean that we should not encourage the artist to participate? No, but it does mean that we may need to create a process by which that artist can do better. Leadership and staffing tasks involve more than recruitment; they are also about the growth and development of the paid and volunteer staff members who lead the programs. The importance of accomplishing this task applies equally whether we are working with organizational employees or volunteers. Leadership recruitment, development, and acknowledgment are vital for a successful program.

That being said, there are different strategies programmers can take in making leadership and staffing decisions. The chosen approach frequently clarifies the leadership needed to implement the program. Carpenter and Howe (1985) identified three approaches for addressing leadership and staffing: synergetic, facilitative, and consultative or contractual. The synergetic approach is used most often when organizations collaborate to produce an arts and cultural leisure experience. The approach is desirable when the program would benefit from more than one person or organization having a say on how to design the program. Several people or organizations working together can offer better arts and cultural leisure experiences to a constituent group than any one individual or organization can offer working alone. The idea of working with others is frequently valued in nonprofit and public organizations, as financial resources are often restrictive. Also, these days granting agencies reinforce synergetic programming by making it a requirement in grant applications.

Using a facilitative approach works very well for many arts programs. This leadership approach assumes that the staff can work with program participants in a way that lets the participants guide

their experience. Programs that enable self-directed participation need only to have staff available should a participant have a question or some other requirement. Museum programming and public parks producing concerts are two examples of when the facilitative approach is most applicable. This approach works best when the program staff assumes a minimalist role after carefully setting up the arts environment to allow participants to move through the experience at their own pace. Unobtrusive observation and facilitation can then be available should the participant desire them.

The consultative or contractual approach is being used more frequently in part because nonprofit and public organizations often find that it is more cost effective to hire someone to do a specific program or aspect related to a program than it is to hire full-time staff to do the same. Usually consultants do not receive a benefits package in addition to their fee; employees of organizations do, and that costs money. Occasionally an outside firm is able to absorb additional costs perhaps related to insurance or to facilities, and that, too, can save on the cost of producing the program in house. Consultative or contractual arrangements can be quite effective in sponsorship development and marketing efforts.

Programming Realities

Keeping in mind that comprehensive arts programming involves a wide range of visual, literacy, performance, cultural, and historic arts, the programmer also needs to remain cognizant of certain programming features that come into play during program development. Before moving on to discuss the next phase in programming, it is important to mention two realities inherent in program development. The first is how decisions made during program development affect each other, and the second relates to characteristics of comprehensive programs that should be addressed during program development.

Interactive Quality

The nature of program development requires programmers to be able to multitask and, at the same time, to expect that once a decision is made, it will be influenced by other task-related decisions. Programmers talk about the *interactive quality* that continuously permeates program development. This interactive quality refers to that fact that making a decision related to one or more tasks will affect other tasks that are still being resolved. For example, an organization's policies and procedures can influence program objectives, a selected venue can influence legal agreements, grant monies available can predetermine leadership decisions, and securing the best artist to facilitate a program can dictate when the program takes place. The programmer may find that the downtown location chosen for an activity requires extra security, and thus the location influences the budget, which in turn affects the number of leaders and artists who can be brought in, which then shapes the entertainment and any number of other task-related decisions that need to be made. This interactive quality is the best illustration of how program development is a dynamic rather than static process.

Program Characteristics

Today more than ever, programs vary in where they take place and what they seem to offer. Locales are more diverse than they have been in the past, and in many instances creative programmers purposefully seek nontraditional sites. Whether organizations offer activities or events or services or any combination of these also appears to be more varied. Given the vast array of programs and services that exist along a varied continuum of educational, informational, entertainment, and amusement opportunities, the doors to innovative programming are wide open.

Generally, programmers try to maintain certain desirable program characteristics that have to do with balance, diversity, variety, and flexibility. Balance means providing an opportunity for enjoying and participating in visual and performance arts. A balanced program includes literature, music, drama, dance, and other forms of art-making expressions. Balance also assures that people of all ages and cultural backgrounds have the opportunity for arts experiences. Diversity is achieved through various organizational forms. A diverse program enables a person who is interested in

a particular activity to choose whether to participate formally or informally. It provides services that call for varying degrees of skill so that those who are interested may find a level at which they can participate. Variety is introduced into programming as a means of heightening or sustaining interest through featured events, city-wide or collaborative events, novelty programs, or festivals. These programs are offered less frequently than the ongoing activities and services are offered. Flexibility is about responding to the changing desires of participants, attendees, and audiences. New activities and services should be added to meet new interests, and others should be discontinued when their popularity wanes. Arts programs with these characteristics generally serve a greater number of people and, as such, afford variety and richness to individuals' leisure experiences.

Program Implementation

This phase of programming is when the program takes place. Program implementation is the actual provision of the arts and cultural leisure experience. It is at this point that we connect the making of art with the people wanting to connect with art (Thorn 1999b). Once programs and services are implemented, we can see the effects of the decisions made during program development.

The vast number of programs that are implemented every day cover the spectrum of arts and cultural leisure experiences. It is plausible to assume that these experiences were created from needs assessments and then developed within the context of an organization as discussed earlier in this chapter. The examples given thus far also support this assumption. There are two programming concepts that programmers should consider when implementing programs and services. One relates to the total experience while the other relates to the life cycle of the experience. Both concepts are in operation during program implementation, and, most importantly, both can be managed to improve the overall experience for constituents.

When implementing programs, we should think about exactly when the program starts and exactly when it ends. We typically designate a starting time and an ending time, but often participants think about and even plan for the program before its official start; at other times, they think about the program well after it has finished. We can call this notion *programming with the total experience in mind.* The literature related to the multiple phases in the total experience is historically found in leisure and recreation (Clawson 1963; Clawson and Knetsch 1966), and it continues to interest researchers and theorists today (Hultsman 1998; Rossman and Schlatter 2003; Stewart 1992). Briefly, the number of phases can range from 3 to 5. Core phases include anticipation, participation, and recollection; additional ones include preparation and travel to and reflection and travel from. When programming arts and cultural experiences with the total experience in mind, we want to give some thought as to how we manage the various inherent phases. The following are ideas we can consider before and after program implementation:

- Anticipation
  - Implement marketing and promotional strategies that encourage anticipation.
  - Consider adding spontaneous involvement for participants in long lines for ticketed events.
- Preparation and travel to
  - Make direct contact with constituency groups.
  - Form partnerships with businesses that might have a connection to the program.
- Participation
  - Manage the program life cycle.
  - Meet and exceed the constituents' expectations.
- Reflection and travel from
  - Ask participants for feedback (i.e., program evaluation).
  - Sell souvenirs and promotional products with the organizational logo.

- Recollection
  - Create and circulate a contact list that encourages attendee communication.
  - Facilitate reunions among interested participants.

The program life cycle is another concept that relates to arts and cultural programs during the implementation phase. Viewing leisure programs as commodities, Crompton (1979) originally adapted the product life cycle found in business literature to leisure programs. Predicated on the notion that programs, like people, have natural life cycles, this concept of the program life cycle has been successfully applied in leisure and recreation (Carpenter and Howe 1985; Crompton 1979; Edginton et al. 2004). The program life cycle consists of five stages that all programs are said to move through: introduction, takeoff, maturation, saturation, and extension, decline, petrifaction, or death. When applied to programs, the life cycle is influenced by the number of participants in relationship to the leadership intervention required. Early on when a program is in its beginning stage, the number of leaders or staff in attendance is typically greater than the number of participants. The cycle can be applied to a one-time program (i.e., an art fair) or to a program series (i.e., art classes).

When a program initially begins, there are typically fewer participants than there are staff members necessary to facilitate the experience. Introducing a new program serves to generate interest and support; it involves promotion, often to new constituents. During takeoff, awareness of the program and interest in participation increase, and so the program is likely to show enrollment growth. During maturation, the program may still grow but does so at a slower rate. Program attendance typically is at its highest, and other organizations may try to emulate its success. At this point, the focus can shift from promoting involvement to getting participants to favor this program over competitors' programs. The degree to which participants derive satisfaction from the leisure experience affects the program's continued existence (Carpenter and Howe 1985).

During the fourth stage, saturation, the programmer may need to alter the shape or duration of the program life cycle while implementing the program. At this point, the program is relying on repeat business and is somewhat vulnerable to dropouts. The program may be revitalized in order to minimize dropouts and maintain audience interest. Revitalization can be done in many

New leadership can help revive a program by bringing new ideas and energy to the project.
Photo by N.K. Hoffman, courtesy of the Young Writers Association

ways, perhaps by changing the program format or pattern, the leadership, the venue, or the other program components. If the program cannot or should not be regenerated, it will enter decline. Programmers should not fret when a program declines, because if it had a good run, it may be time for it to be done. If the decline comes too soon, the programmer should question the needs assessment and decisions made during program development, as early decline suggests flawed program planning. Once in decline, if not regenerated, the program will become petrified and then die.

Arts and cultural programmers cognizant of the total experience and the life cycle of programs are in a very good position to manipulate the inherent experience and life cycle components to the betterment of the program. As far as total experience goes, programmers may not be taking advantage of all that they could to design and promote their programs and services. As far as the program life cycle goes, programmers may be spending too much time and energy on arts and cultural programs that should cease to exist. Now we move on to program evaluation.

Program Evaluation

In its most basic sense, evaluation is the process of judging the merit, worth, or value of something (Carpenter and Howe 1985, 150). A primary purpose of program evaluation is to judge the effectiveness of the leisure experience in order to make needed changes. The presumption is that we want arts and cultural programs and services to be effective—that is, that we want to produce worthwhile experiences for our patrons and our organizations. Howe (1993, 19) argues that a program's value also includes efficiency as well as effectiveness: "If a program is efficient, it uses resources prudently and is worthy of continued investment. If a program is effective, it is enjoyable, meaningful, and satisfying for the participants."

Whether evaluation is stimulated by competition for shrinking resources (Carpenter and Howe 1985), by an increased expectation for accountability (Dreeszen 2003), or by the desire to make decisions based on systematically gathered information (Henderson and Bialeschki 2002), it is an essential phase in programming arts and cultural leisure experiences. Besides providing evidence of program success, data realized through program evaluation are essential to the program needs assessment. They also provide substantive support for program modifications. (See chapter 6 for more information on program evaluation.)

Program Modification

Based on the premise that an experience can always get better, program modification is confirmation that in the cyclical programming model the ending is just the beginning. Good programmers always want to build on the information obtained in program evaluation to improve their arts and cultural programs for their consumers and organizations. As such, program revisions should be expected.

During this phase of programming, legitimate modifications can only be made using information gained in program evaluation. If our evaluative work was narrowly defined and conducted, our support to make major changes in our programs will also be narrow. Thus program evaluation and program modification are closely entwined. However, to actually have a phase that encourages modification demonstrates that we accept the fact that programs will be revised because programmers have carefully examined them (i.e., evaluated them) and used what was discovered during evaluation (i.e., modification). Often programmers gloss over evaluation, usually because they are stressed for time, and are never able to use findings that could improve their programs.

There are several outcomes inherent in program modification. Keep in mind that a comprehensive program will have many experiences (activities, classes, and so on) and that evaluating all aspects of the program includes evaluating staff, venues, and so on. The following are suggested outcomes that may or may not be relevant to all program aspects in any one program:

- A program that is positively evaluated may require few or no modifications.
- A program with a mixed evaluation should be modified accordingly before it is offered again.
- A program with a negative evaluation, indicating problems that cannot be remedied, should be terminated.
- A program in demise is a natural occurrence (see the discussion on the program life cycle) and should not be perpetuated if it is no longer satisfying participants.

Arts and cultural programmers rarely work in isolation when designing and providing programs. One person rarely makes a modification without first consulting others (i.e., staff members, key volunteers, sponsors). When there are different opinions regarding the importance of evaluative data in making a program modification, collaboration and open communication are essential.

Summary

This chapter identified various tasks and functions that are inherent in programming arts and cultural leisure experiences. These tasks and functions were examined within the context of a programming model that emphasizes a cyclical approach and includes five phases: program needs assessment, program development, program implementation, program evaluation, and program modification. The multiphase nature of program planning was highlighted throughout the chapter. Discussions in this chapter focused on certain aspects related to program needs assessment and program development; future chapters in this book address specific tasks in program development (i.e., program financing, marketing, managing, and so on).

PART II

Applying Program Theory to Practice

Part II provides readers with foundational theory and then applies that theory to contemporary practices in arts and cultural programming. The contributors provide a variety of theoretical perspectives related to program management, audience development, assessment, documentation, budgeting, and marketing. The way in which they merge their sophisticated understanding of this theoretical context with knowledge about best practices is remarkable. Arts and cultural programmers who carefully consider the material in part II can feel confident in their understanding of the breadth and depth of the approaches to arts and cultural programming that apply to small, medium, and large organizations and venues.

In chapter 4, James E. Modrick explains the ways in which programs can be divided into several parts and how the development and implementation of planning strategies are integral to each part. Strategies for program execution are provided. He concludes by discussing methods for bringing the parts of a program together to form a cohesive experience for both planners and participants.

In chapter 5, Kristin G. Congdon provides a comprehensive overview on how to cultivate program audiences. Her approach to cultivating audiences is accomplished through an inclusive rather than exclusive view of audiences. In this regard she discusses tolerance, diversity, and the importance of reaching audiences through collaborative approaches to planning and implementation of programs. This chapter also provides important information on risk management.

In chapter 6, Karla Henderson provides an overview of the evaluation and documentation of arts and cultural programs. In doing so she provides guidance on conceptualizing an evaluation process and models through which evaluation can be acomplished. Timing associated evaluation is also considered.

In chapter 7, Chris Burgess assists programmers in developing reasonable and responsible budgets. Frameworks and models are provided. The role of fund-raising within an overall budget strategy is considered. Strategies for analyzing a budget in relation to program needs are presented.

In chapter 8, Francois Colbert provides an overview of marketing arts and cultural programs. He offers convincing evidence on the importance of marketing and offers a definition of marketing within the arts and culture context. Strategies for monitoring marketing planning and implementation are included.

Pulling the Pieces Together

Managing Programs

James E. Modrick, MA
Indiana University

The opening quote by Dolly Parton identifies the fundamental paradox associated with managing programs in the context of leisure. This book presents arts and cultural programming from a leisure perspective. Such programming requires the programmer to design a rich and an engaging experience that involves a modest investment of time and effort on the part of the participant. Designing such an experience is challenging and labor intensive. This work is the ultimate task of management: working with and through others and getting all the elements aligned for the purpose of achieving organizational and participant objectives.

This chapter follows two distinct approaches to engaging the public: encountering participants where they are through community-based arts programs and attracting people to where you are through easily accessible engagements. Essential elements in these approaches are based on the principles of universal design and inclusive practice. Managing such programs means creating environments with and for the participant that are intuitively engaging through multiple means of participation.

Applying universal design and inclusive practice to program management is not an academic exercise but a practical one. The applications of universal design and inclusive practice come from the author's many years of experience with VSA arts festivals, which are events that include people with disabilities. While the specific example and experience involves including people with disabilities, the intent of this chapter is to extend the application of inclusive practice and universal design to program management principles and practices. VSA arts, which was founded as Very Special Arts in the mid-1970s, is an organization committed to expanding opportunities in the arts for people with disabilities. In the early 1990s the organization moved away from the notion of *very special* to avoid unintentionally demeaning people with disabilities. Also, the expression no longer fit as universal design and inclusive practice became central to the work of VSA arts. *Special* describes self-contained environments designed exclusively for a particular population, such as people with disabilities, while the intent of VSA is to engage people with disabilities in mainstream arts programming. As such, VSA festivals broaden the programming perspective beyond disability to include everyone. This programming recognizes varying ability and activity levels.

This chapter explores program management by focusing on the planning of the event (including the process of developing the event), the various activities or practices within the event, the location of the event, and the people involved in the event. It also discusses promotion, performance, and participation and in the end combines these elements as the essence of effective and efficient management.

Planning

Planning is essential to any endeavor, but it does not just happen. It is strategic, organized, and purposeful. While no one can foretell the future, effective planning allows the programmer to be ready for the future by anticipating and preparing for as much as can be anticipated. Planning involves thinking and acting on a defined process, which includes considering the practice and activities of the event, the sites of the activities, and the required volunteer and paid personnel (Korza 2003; Yeoman 2003).

Planning for ease of access and engagement requires taking into consideration multiple points of access, use, and engagement. This is why I suggest an ideal of universal planning that draws from the principles of universal design.

The performing artists of the Inner Harbour African Drum Ensemble from Georgia perform at the Start with the Arts Family Festival. Art form should fit venue, and nothing attracts attention in open-air venues better than drumming does.

Photo courtesy of VSA Arts, © 2006 Scott Suchman

The principles of universal design originated in the fields of architecture and product design, which is why their application in planning might be considered an intellectual exercise. The notion of multiple means of engagement, access, and intuitive use that underlies the principles of universal design is a way of thinking (Center for Universal Design 1997). Universal design is more than a set of principles or a collection of rules; it involves habits of mind that can be applied to virtually any field. These habits of mind are incorporated into the planning process, since planning is not only a principle but also a central practice in management. Working from the perspective of engagement, access, and use creates a planning process that is more effective, efficient, and inclusive of people and points of view.

Define the Program Objective

When applying universal design, a clear understanding of use is essential. Begin with the end in mind. What are you trying to do and how do you know it is worth doing? Answering these questions provides the basis for everything that follows. Therefore, central to the planning process is deciding what you want to accomplish through your leisure program.

While date, place, and budget will constrain the overall plan, defining the program's objective in the beginning is crucial. Defining what you want to do and how you want to do it allows the planning process to be driven by these objectives rather than by the limitations of space and money. It also maintains the connection with your mission statement, which should not be lost in all the planning. Everything needs to be done for a reason.

There are many things to consider when planning. The nature of the arts engagement and the audience participation, the roles of volunteers and staff members, the decision to attract the participants to your space or put your program in their familiar venues, and the way to create the space for the exchange between artist and audience are all part of this primal conversation. This conversation should also delineate the measurable outcomes that will ultimately define your success.

Involve a Planning Committee

Another element critical to the success of any planning process is the planning committee. This is the group of people who define all of the elements discussed throughout this chapter and who assist with the overall program management. They are key individuals who provide connections

to essential agencies: municipal representatives, fire and public safety representatives, cultural representatives, and the like. Keep the promotional plan in mind by engaging television and radio representatives. They will be much more likely to promote the event if they have been involved in its development.

A principle of inclusion that comes from the community of people with disabilities is the expression *Nothing about us without us*. While this statement refers to involving people with disabilities in developing an accessibility plan, there is a lesson embedded within it that applies to the development of any program. Creating something meaningful for an audience means engaging the targeted population in the planning process. As a program manager, you should include both younger and older participants as well as the artists in the planning process (Korza 2003, 118). No one person can ever represent a general population, but if you really want to know what is engaging and how it is experienced, nothing replaces the wisdom of simply asking people from multiple interest groups.

Create a Timeline

The best way to begin planning is to work backward from the actual event. Once the date is established, setting up a timeline of critical milestones is a process of working backward to the present time. The amount of time required for planning depends on the complexity of the event; a good minimum timeline is 1 year. However, if the event requires significant fund-raising, a longer time frame is needed. Once the date and place are established, the next critical milestones include setting the scope of the program, projecting audience, determining staffing needs, and implementing the promotional plan.

For example, VSA arts produces two similar events that have differing timelines due to their relative complexities. The annual Start with the Arts Family Festival has a 12-month planning calendar, although the planning of each festival tends to overlap with the subsequent year's planning. The International VSA Arts Festival, which is produced every 5 years, has a planning process that lasts a minimum of 3 years. Most of the additional time needed for the international festival has to do with coordinating participants from many locations. For both events the fundamental elements of the timeline remain the same, with the decision on date and place coming very early and the promotion and logistical plans rarely covering more than 12 months (see tables 4.1 and 4.2).

The timeline is an essential tool for program management. It maps the event and defines the modes of information exchange. It names the point in the process of developing the event where the organization is currently located and outlines what pieces of information are needed to move to the next point in that process. Additionally, it lets the manager know where problems may arise and provides the structure from which contingency plans can be developed.

Address Budget Issues

Beyond the timeline, there is a second essential map for the program manager: the budget. Budgeting is the conversation that moves program planning from the visionary to the practical. Whether funds are earned, contributed, or provided through in-kind donations, it takes money to make events happen. The budget is also a statement of priorities that indicates the essential elements of the program and matches the funding available to the allocated expenses (Korza 2003, 123).

The budget needs to include expenses for the event location. These include space rental plus equipment costs for staging, electrical, sound support, lighting, and storage. The second major budget area comprises personnel and staffing expenses. Payments to the artists should be an early and essential conversation within the planning process. Far too often the perception is that artists should just be content with having the opportunity to perform or present their work. Artists are professionals and should be treated as any other staffed position involved in a leisure program (Korza 2003, 128-129). Creating art is meaningful, and while artists appreciate the opportunity to present their work, they should also be reimbursed. Finally, the budget needs to include the promotional plan. Expenses should be broken out for designing, printing, and placing promotional materials. The budget also needs to include costs such as insurance and legal requirements and, if at all

Table 4.1 Sample Timeline for Annual Festival

	Place	Program	Personnel	Promotion
Event + 11 mo	Confirm location	Set program scope	Set staff assignments	
Event + 10 mo		Call for artists	Set volunteer needs	Announce date and place
Event + 9 mo	Develop site plan and layout			
Event + 8 mo		Schedule program		
Event + 7 mo		Select artists	Recruit volunteers	
Event + 6 mo		Contract artists		Design print materials
Event + 5 mo	Arrange equipment and staging needs			Print materials
Event + 4 mo		Finalize program		Design displays
Event + 3 mo			Schedule volunteers	Banners and displays designed and in production
Event + 2 mo				Create press materials
Event + 1 mo	Confirm equipment and staging	Confirm artists and program	Train volunteers	Contact press
Month of event	Set up and break down			Schedule press

From VSA Arts, 2006, *Program development files* (Washington, DC: Author).

Table 4.2 Sample Timeline for International Festival

	Place	Program	Personnel	Promotion	Purse
Year 1					
Event + 35 mo	Confirm location	Set program scope			
Event + 34 mo		Call for artists	Hire program staff	Announce event	Set fund-raising goal
Event + 33 mo	Develop site plan and layout				
Event + 32 mo					Develop proposals
Event + 31 mo				Design print materials	
Event + 30 mo					Set foundation goal
Event + 29 mo					
Event + 28 mo					
Event + 27 mo					
Event + 26 mo					
Event + 25 mo					
Event + 24 mo		Select artists			

(continued)

Table 4.2 *(continued)*

	Place	Program	Personnel	Promotion	Purse
Year 2					
Event + 23 mo	Invite internationals				Recruit sponsors
Event + 22 mo					
Event + 21 mo					
Event + 20 mo					
Event + 19 mo					
Event + 18 mo		Confirm artists		Schedule press conference	Set final budget
Event + 17 mo					
Event + 16 mo					
Event + 15 mo					
Event + 14 mo				Create press materials	
Event + 13 mo		Finalize program			
Event + 12 mo				Hold press conference	
Year 3					
Event + 11 mo	Finalize site plan		Hire logistics staff		Finalize sponsors
Event + 10 mo				Announce date and place	
Event + 9 mo	Arrange for equipment and staging		Set volunteer needs		
Event + 8 mo					
Event + 7 mo				Design print materials	
Event + 6 mo			Recruit volunteers		
Event + 5 mo				Print materials	
Event + 4 mo		Confirm program		Design displays	
Event + 3 mo			Schedule volunteers	Banners and displays designed and in production	
Event + 2 mo				Create press materials	
Event + 1 mo	Confirm equipment and staging		Train volunteers	Contact press	
Month of event	Set up and break down			Schedule press	

From VSA Arts, 2006, *Program development files* (Washington, DC: Author).

possible, include a small contingency fund for unanticipated expenses that arise the day of the event.

Select a Location

There are few early decisions that have as wide-ranging influences on the planning process as the selection of the event location. This decision begins with the fundamental questions of a cultural or community venue, an indoor or outdoor setting, and variety of artistic performances or activities. If the intent is to actively engage the audience through performance or movement, then the space needs to fit that intent. No amount of marketing or planning will make up for a mismatch of intended activity and venue.

Site selection needs to reflect the objectives of the event and fundamental intent. You need to present the art in a setting that shows respect for that work, yet when programming a leisure experience you also want to catch people where they are and engage them in an intuitive way. VSA arts festivals have done both: They have included artistic performances both in performing arts centers and in shopping centers or train stations. Some art forms, such as drumming, lend themselves to open-air settings, while others, such as concert piano, present unique challenges for certain settings like train stations. One model is not necessarily better than the other; they are just distinct and so expectations need to be clear. For a meaningful connection to be made, you, your artists, and your audience need to be on the same page regarding the questions of who, what, and where for the actual program. A planning committee and a process that includes each of these perspectives will go a long way toward an effective program.

Within each of the prior considerations, the program manager must also address access and participation issues involving getting the audience and the artists to the location. For leisure programming, the goal is to make participation as intuitive and accessible as possible, addressing the Americans with Disabilities Act as well as the principles of universal design (National Assembly of State Arts Agencies 2003).

Organize a Detailed Schedule for the Event

The planning process includes not only a timeline leading up to and following the event but also a detailed timeline for what will occur within the event itself. Developing this timeline is a matter of determining the activities and performances that will take place and scheduling them to accommodate the flow of participants. The challenge is balancing the audience for each event with the choice of events in which the audience can participate.

The detailed schedule also allows the program manager to assess supply needs as well as address the logistics of getting the supplies to the places where they are needed when they need to be there. The detailed schedule of performances and activities is a critical data set for the actual execution of the program, but at this stage it provides the requisite information to align fiscal resources with required staff and materials. The detailed schedule is much more than the printed program. It should be a very detailed accounting of setup and supply needs and include the time needed for preparation and resets between activities as well as a flowchart showing movement of materials and people to and from the location.

Organize the People Involved in the Event

The final element to the planning process is addressing the people who will be involved in the event. This encompasses defining the roles for paid staff, short-term contractors, and volunteers. The roles of each must be distinct. The distinction between the work of staff and the work of contractors is critical. If contractors are provided the same resources that staff members are provided, then they will be legally recognized as staff, not contractors. Beyond that, distinction between staff and volunteer roles is essential to avoid confusion.

Once the staff and contractor positions, which will be limited by budget allocations, are established, the program manager must determine what volunteers are needed for executing the program. After

this framework of staff, contractual and volunteer positions, is placed around the needs for human resources, appropriate descriptions for various functions can be developed. Defining volunteer functions is particularly important. Volunteerism is more than doing a good thing. The volunteers' responsibilities within the event must be clearly articulated in writing. This means developing a job description for each volunteer position, including a description of the responsibilities and the reporting structure for that role. An organized approach to the volunteer effort will create a better experience for these essential people.

The timeline should also incorporate the recruiting, training, and orienting of volunteers for the event. These tasks will take time, but working through local service organizations can provide focused and consolidated efforts. Recruiting volunteers is a very effective way of creating word-of-mouth promotion for the event. Having volunteers is far more than just having help with logistics. Volunteers are an essential audience for the event and participation.

Think About Safety

You are proposing to gather a large number of people and move them around within a defined space. Audience members and artists will need to get to specific locations, and before the event even opens there will be significant amounts of equipment to move and set up. Depending on the event location, there may be other issues concerning people and traffic that need to be considered. All of this means that there are essential public safety and security concerns that need to be addressed.

Moving audiences and artists is a larger issue than simply moving people from activity to activity: It also involves addressing fire code requirements, emergency service delivery, and, in the worst case scenario, site evacuation. Since September 11, planning for the community experience in the United States has also had to fulfill the requirements of the U.S. Department of Homeland Security for public protection and security. All of these concerns can be addressed only by allowing for time to do so in the overall plan, and they underscore the importance of having representatives from these agencies on the planning committee to ensure that they know the purposes of the event. This new reality of public programming is not only being recognized in the planning process but also becoming increasingly evident in the leisure research (Godbey et al. 2005, 154-155).

Document the Event

Planning does not end when the event concludes. Time for follow-up and sessions for lessons learned by all involved should be part of the process. An effective program manager recognizes that there is a huge difference between defining success and assessing the overall experience on those measures of success. Recall that you began the planning process by answering questions about what you wanted to accomplish and why it was important to accomplish it. Now there are a couple of new questions for you to consider. Did you actually do what you thought you would do, and is it still worth doing? You will want to document what worked and what you learned. A tendency for program managers is to be overcritical. Rather than list the things that did not go as planned, capture the circumstances when expectations or plans went astray, and then note what was done in those circumstances to move forward. This documentation will inform your future planning.

Program Execution

The great thing about a planning process that works well is that eventually it turns into something. Planning for the event is no longer needed because the anticipated event arrives! At this time we enter the moment of execution.

Throughout the planning process, the emphasis of management is on anticipating needs and establishing systems for managing those needs. Once in program mode, the emphasis shifts to managing immediate and short-term needs. The time for making decisions becomes rather short, and the effectiveness of those decisions depends on the quality of information and options available to the manager.

Before the actual program takes place, create the buzz that will attract your participants. This is accomplished through promotional efforts. There are several elements to consider in the planning process, particularly timelines and people involved in planning the event. Along with those is promotion through public service, public relations, or paid advertising.

The timeline for promotional efforts presents distinct challenges for leisure programming, since the decision to participate may be a last-minute decision. For that reason, the timeline needs to include some work in advance and then a significant promotional push as the event arrives. As the event nears, the challenge is to create a top-of-mind awareness for those who make the last-minute decision to attend. Patience must rule, as the significant resources for promotion are reserved to influence the last-minute decision to attend.

Promoting the event should involve all media: print, newspaper, television, radio, and Internet. Small fliers distributed through common community sites such as grocery stores and pharmacies are often part of the general awareness campaign. They can be distributed and posted well in advance of the event, often with the message to save the date. Newspapers often have calendar listings of events that are coming up, and they are cited most often as the source of information for the last-minute decision maker. However, when creating the timeline, it is essential to pay attention to lead time for calendar listings. Newspaper space for the calendar is usually committed before advertising space, which means that if you wait until the week of your program to send in your notice, the notice will be too late. Television

Area children engage in journaling as an arts start at the Start with the Arts Family Festival. Programs should keep connected to their mission, which in this case involves the arts as a reflection of learning and education.

Photo courtesy of VSA Arts, © 2006 Scott Suchman

and radio can be difficult to attract and afford. An effective strategy to attract their attention is to involve them in the planning process. This involvement does not need to be limited to on-air personalities, although they are key people to try to engage. Often the station will have a public service director who can get the station to broadcast information about the event as part of its requirements for making public service announcements. The Internet and related networking communications such as e-mail and text messaging are new and growing media, particularly for younger generations. Tapping these resources absolutely requires involving the younger generations if the messaging is to be effective.

Promotion is the first place where budgetary issues arise. Advertising is expensive no matter what media are involved. Relying solely on public service announcements will create challenges. Having the patience for people to make last-minute decisions to attend without investing in promotion is a recipe for indigestion. Finding the right mix is the management task. For arts and cultural leisure programming, television and radio advertising are generally out of the question, a fact which only reinforces the importance of involving these media in the planning process in order to gain free airtime promotion. Print media, both promotional flyers and print advertisements, are investments that will pay off with attendance. They can also be structured in a way that can provide some

information on potential attendance. Bear in mind that developing flyers and print advertisements includes graphic design, which needs to be incorporated into the budget.

The execution of the actual performance, activity, or event is what reveals the quality of the planning process. The management challenges become evident through the shortened time frame. In program mode, you are essentially managing the flow of people and activity. Artists, performers, support personnel, and participants themselves need to get to the places where they are going.

When the challenges are logistical, program management becomes about communication. Communication is the exchange of essential information, and a quality planning process prepares for information management. All the work of planning goes into creating a collective understanding of what should be happening during the event. The list of things that should be happening makes up the information base for the event. Program management becomes a process of tracking, understanding, and attending to things that are happening during the event; this process is facilitated by a continuous flow of communication about what is going on. Using communication as a means of information management encourages an exchange that focuses on essential facts. This exchange allows the manager to concentrate on and attend to any gaps between what is happening and what should be happening.

The ultimate test of the planning process and of the quality of the program itself comes in the form of dealing with the unanticipated complications. No matter how comprehensive your planning process, no matter how many what-if scenarios you consider, no matter how much of the overall environment you attempt to control, the cruel truths of Murphy's Law will come to pass when you execute the event. There will be gaps between what is happening and what should be happening. Something will go wrong, and quite likely it will do so at the most inopportune time. Effectiveness will show through having a variety of contingency plans in place or at least in mind. There should be not only a plan B but also a plan C and plan D if possible. The more that you anticipate in advance and the more effective that your communication and information management are during the event, the greater will be your capacity to have and implement contingencies.

In managing the event, your ultimate responsibility is for the well-being of the participants, including the audience members as well as the artists. At a very fundamental level, we are referring to safety and security needs. The event site and the movement of participants need to support the concept of low-effort engagement. To be effective, the environment must provide a sense of comfort and ease. Safety and security should be evident but not omnipresent. The assistance of emergency and public protection personnel from medical, fire, and police agencies is essential. At some point, it becomes their job to ensure safety and security, but a successful event requires a

Young artists demonstrate the fruits of their creativity with family and friends as a result of well-planned and managed leisure arts programming.
Photo courtesy of VSA Arts, © 2006 Scott Suchman

coordinated and cooperative effort. You are going to need these agencies, and these agencies are going to need you in order to fulfill their roles.

While much of leisure programming focuses on the experience of the audience, we cannot ignore the experience of the artists themselves. Artists remain the center of the arts experience. Without their creative talent and skill, there would be no art. Artists need to be considered in the mix of matching individual desires to program outcomes. In order for the programming experience to exert the greatest effect and influence, the artists need to feel engaged throughout the planning and program. Because of all the logistical concerns, it is very easy for the individual artist to begin feeling like nothing more than a part of a program or a piece of equipment that needs to be manipulated. The artists can also start to feel like a novelty being put on display. These attitudes need to be actively guarded against, and the voices of the artists must be heard and respected.

Once you are fully engaged in managing the program, doing that counterintuitive thing of managing a leisure experience, it is important to remember why you chose the path of arts and cultural leisure programming. These are programs that are fundamentally about arts participation and community engagement. The quality of this shared engagement experience is of paramount importance. It is the quality of each experience that builds interest in future participation. Program management is about delivering and maximizing this experience.

Pulling Together

The ultimate task of the program manager is to align all the elements of planning and programming—all the people, places, and performances—in a common direction that achieves the program objectives. Without such alignment, the various elements move in different directions and the intuitive engagement and participation are lost. The underlying objective and function of a leisure perspective are not achieved. Managing for aligned efforts and planning for an organized structure create the seamless integration required for an effective program.

This seamless integration does not happen by chance. It takes the purposeful collaboration of many individuals and organizations. These individuals need to be engaged in meaningful ways that allow them to understand the objectives of the program. They need to be able to see how their contributions and decisions help achieve success. In short, the process needs to be inclusive and accessible. Collaboration needs to involve the individual voices and choices from planning through participation. Within this process lie the social function of community and the purpose of the arts in society.

How will you know when you've pulled everything together? Part of your answer will come through program evaluation, but more will come through communication and observation. As the program manager, you need to pay attention to multiple measures of success, just as you create programs that permit multiple means of engagement. Beyond all that can be measured, there are ways of understanding the overall alignment in the program at any point from planning through execution. Success for these program efforts occurs when participant desires match your desired outcomes. Clearly this involves matching the desires of the audience members with your program outcomes, but it also includes matching the desires of programming partners throughout the planning process. When their desires meet your organizational objectives, management alignment and program success become more likely.

Summary

While this chapter deals with program management from a leisure perspective, the programs being managed are about arts and culture. An aspect of any arts and cultural program is advancing the art being presented. Leisure programming is an essential part of public participation in the arts and culture in your community. Ultimately, the planning and the programming are about bringing artists and audiences together for an exchange that is at the very essence of why this work is pursued. This exchange of energy and engagement between audience and artist is the function of

the arts in society. All that leisure programming does is create access to this exchange in an intuitive, low-effort means. It opens the door for further and richer participation in the arts and in the community.

Leisure takes time, effort, and energy. It takes a lot to look easy. Planning, preparation, and alignment of information and actions are the elements of effective management. Whether your program seeks to engage your organization in a public space or to attract the public to your institution, attending to the practices of universal design and inclusive collaboration from planning through programming will help create a successful endeavor.

Cultivating Program Audiences

Kristin G. Congdon, PhD
University of Central Florida

As an arts educator, I have spent decades working with diverse groups of people in various settings, including museums, public schools, universities, correctional facilities, recreational centers, and other community-based locations. While it has always been important to reach all segments of society with arts programming, cultivating the creative side of our citizenry has never been more crucial.

Richard Florida (2002) and Bill Ivey and Steven J. Tepper (2006) believe that the United States is in danger of becoming divided based on the way in which its citizens live their cultural lives. According to Ivey and Tepper, the number of cultural organizations grew dramatically during the 20th century, and today there are about 50,000 in the United States. During this time, the organizations we considered to be our best arts organizations "were heavily influenced by national standards; while venues remained local, the art was decidedly not" (Ivey and Tepper 2006, B7). We were trained to want the best. The established arts world, elite tastes, record companies and film studios, and foundations and public arts granting organizations promoted this desire. We were encouraged to appreciate quality art: to see the best and listen to the best. However, Ivey and Tepper (2006) point out that many of our experiences were passive; we sat in auditoriums, movie theaters, concert halls, and stadiums.

The change that is taking place in the 21st century is one that involves actively engaged participants. We now want to be more active players in our experiences. Florida's book title refers to this transformation as *The Rise of the Creative Class* (2002), and Ivey and Tepper (2006) describe it as "a revitalization of folk culture" and a "participatory culture" (B7).

These changes are important to cultivating audiences because, according to these authors, programming will serve us all better if it involves more active engagement. In order to relate to the evolving culture, cultural facilitators should look at expanding the topics that can be explored as well as diversifying the traditional elite arts. Technology, which has made it possible for more people to engage in creative pursuits from the comfort of their own personal spaces, should be used to reflect the manner in which everyday people in the United States now function. All kinds of people are making their own music, Web sites, and films. They are communicating with others about needlework, scrapbooking, cooking, gardening, sports, and just about everything else imaginable. Even when participants are "not producing art themselves," they are developing "the skills and expertise to be connoisseurs and mavens—seeking out new experiences, learning about them, and sharing that knowledge with friends" (Ivey and Tepper 2006, B7).

We now have an unlimited number of creative topics to explore, and we are not confined by what our community organizations offer. In order to survive and attract audiences in the 21st century, community organizations must recognize that they play different roles in their constituents' lives and must adapt programs to the new ways of living that affect people every day. Not everyone is interested in opera, classical music, and so-called *high* or *elite art*. Today people are looking for the unconventional as well as for new territories and new identities to explore. Categories of art have been broken down, and status is no longer easily connected to particular arts activities. Ivey and Tepper (2006) claim that we are looking for another way of experiencing culture, and they suggest that a "new kind of cosmopolitanism underlies the mixing and matching of different cultural forms" (B7). Even when we enjoy the elite arts, we tend to want to branch out so that we can experience the classical in a new way. A classical music fan may also listen to ethnic music, pop, country, and most every other genre.

Florida (2002) recognizes that a new kind of creative energy is forming from these new ways of exploring culture. The creative class wants to live in regions of the country that attract diverse populations and to sample a variety of arts and leisure experiences. Its members look for places to live where artists, writers, collectors, and other actively creative people live. They want to exchange ideas and to mix, match, and recreate their lives from a smorgasbord of choices. Audiences are interested in emerging artists, new art forms, diverse ways of creating, and more democratic participation. As a result, community-based organizations needing to bring in large audiences cannot take risks by focusing too narrowly. Most members of the creative class work long hours and choose wisely about how to spend their precious free time. And people who work several service jobs have little time to imagine leisure activities. Because they have limited time to explore their options, they more easily "rely on the cultural fare offered to them by consolidated media and entertainment conglomerates" (Ivey and Tepper 2006, B8).

The audience-building task of community-based arts managers and programmers is both challenging and exciting. The answers to success lie in (1) incorporating technology; (2) expanding aesthetic ways of thinking; (3) exploring new roles for traditional performances, exhibitions, and other leisure activities; and (4) finding new ways to involve audiences in participatory experiences. As we examine these ways of building and sustaining audiences, we must look at several aspects of developing programs.

Risk Management

When arts managers are developing their programs, they must consider the potential risks to the staff members, visitors, environment, and artwork at each and every step of planning. If planning a festival, tents must be secured and traffic patterns must be evaluated. If installing an exhibition, the safekeeping of the artworks must be intricately planned for. If programming a concert in the park, policy issues like alcohol consumption and smoking must be addressed. The well-being of groups and individuals should be considered with each decision that is made. Sometimes it is not easy to spot a potential risk, so when making decisions it is important to ask, Does this present a risk to anyone or anything?

Sculptures, for example, may be dangerous when placed in parks or on an organization's property. Ordinarily sculptures are designed to be looked at—but what happens if children decide to climb one or to use it as a skateboarding ramp? Or, if part of a sculpture is mobile, could it unex-

Martin Zagbo, from the Ivory Coast of Africa, performs at the Florida Folk Festival.
Photo courtesy of Kristin Congdon

pectedly hit anyone or anything? If an outdoor fountain is being designed for a park, are its walls high enough that children cannot fall in or its water shallow enough so that drowning is impossible? Can the elderly move safely through the festival grounds? Can a concert be loud enough to be heard throughout the park without creating hearing impairments for individuals sitting near the speakers? Can any piece of a costume, used with an exhibition in order to create a feel for a particular culture, create a risk? For example, when designing the education program for a show on motorcycles at the Orlando Museum of Art (OMA), the curators decided that while providing old motorcycle jackets for audiences to try on was safe, providing helmets was not safe due to the possibility that they might transfer lice from one person to another (Rosoff 2006).

Communities disagree about what they identify as indecent language or visual imagery. Perhaps the most noteworthy case involves Robert Mapplethorpe's much-debated photographs. In 1989 the Corcoran Gallery of Art in Washington, District of Columbia, canceled a Mapplethorpe retrospective, and shortly thereafter the Museum of Art in Cincinnati, Ohio, had four photographs removed from its walls based on the premise that they were obscene. But child nudity and homoerotic images are not the only targets that can create a brouhaha. In 2002 the Jewish Museum in New York presented the exhibition, *Mirroring Evil: Nazi Imagery/Recent Art*. Showing the work of 13 artists, this exhibition explored the use of National Socialist imagery. It shifted the perspective from the more commonly seen view of the victims to that of the perpetuators of the

violence. According to Camhi (2002), the images that were displayed "share in varying degrees the lure of an aesthetic that once mobilized a nation, with disastrous consequences" (AR36). Although the Mapplethorpe exhibition, *The Perfect Moment*, had already been shown and was well received in Chicago and Philadelphia, the photographs were censored in Washington out of fear that they might anger a politically sensitive and volatile government (Hess 1989). In contrast, the New York exhibition was shown to purposely place viewers in the active space of evil. The two shows were controversial for different reasons.

Sometimes the controversy is not about visual imagery. In numerous other examples, it focuses on how money is spent, how art is presented or performed, or when a program takes place. Program planners should consider the effect they want to achieve and anticipate the community response. If controversy occurs, is it useful and desired? Sometimes the desired effect can be to shock or disturb in order to jar an audience into thinking about a relevant topic. If a minority group or interest might show a negative response, is putting on the program worth the potential alienation that might occur? If the plan is to risk angering certain community members in order to make a point, can the anger be tempered by sending out early press releases, writing text panels, and providing educational programs that explain the choices that have been made? Involving prominent citizens in the planning and decision making of a cultural organization can lead a community to think about an issue before responding negatively. If a program is not appropriate for children, this information should be made clear to parents. In museums and galleries showing multiple exhibitions at once, notices should be clearly posted by potentially controversial spaces so that parents can prevent children from seeing work that may be inappropriate for them.

More mundane issues must also be considered. Is adequate parking available? Do people need to walk a long distance or cross a busy street? Is the parking area safe with good lighting? Should a security guard be hired to make sure that people get to and from their cars or public transportation without mishap? If the public is fearful of traveling to an organizational space, generating a diverse audience will be very difficult. Program planners should either make the public feel safe or move the event. In the long run, organizations have a moral responsibility to work with others on the health and safety of their neighborhood spaces.

Issues regarding fire hazards can also complicate well-meaning planning. If an organization wants to rent or buy a space for presenting plays or films, it should have a fire marshal tour the building early on in order to find out how many people can be seated. If the number is too small to make the event financially successful or if costly renovations are mandated in order to accommodate the desired number of people, these drawbacks might quash the project. If firecrackers or fire will be used in any fashion, the organization must consult with the fire marshal to assure that regulations can be adhered to. Bathroom facilities must also be considered. If a festival is being planned and large numbers of people are expected, portable bathrooms may be a necessity. Knowing that most people prefer flush toilets when they are available, questions should be asked about the sewer systems and how much these systems can handle. Likewise, if the festival is scheduled over a number of days and people come for the entire event, as they do for the Florida Folk Festival in White Springs, limited camping spaces must be prioritized and alternative housing must be found. Clearly established policies on the use of limited resources can help ward off angry visitors.

If your event is scheduled to take place outdoors in either extreme heat or extreme cold, provisions need to be made to relieve participants who may not be able to tolerate the weather. Spaces where the public can warm up or cool down are needed. Outdoor heaters and misters can offer temporary relief. Free water should always be available. A first aid kit should be handy, and whenever there are large crowds, medical staff should be visible and ready to handle any broken bones, heart problems, or other medical emergencies.

There are other safety issues to address. Some issues need to be revisited as time goes on. For example, at one time the Florida Folk Festival presented a recurring act by a cracker cowboy who used to entertain in sideshows. He was so good with his whip that he would call a stranger up on stage and snap a short stick right out of the individual's mouth, causing the audience to gasp with pleasure. He was always a crowd pleaser, but as he aged, concerns were raised. Although there was never an accident, his act was probably curtailed at an appropriate time.

Food is often served at public programs. If a person gets sick from eating this food, an organization might be held liable. While programmatically it might be best to hire a neighborhood cook or baker, such a decision should be weighed with the understanding that insurance generally comes with restaurant caterers and not with a local cook. If a decision is made to hire the local person for food preparation, insurance can be purchased.

Every cultural organization should have policies on how to handle a complaint, an injury, or extreme weather. Policies will vary according to the locale and to the function of an organization or event. It is a good idea to ask for copies of policies from established organizations in your area and from similar organizations around the country to help you develop your policies. You can learn a lot by asking others. Policies and procedures should be reviewed and updated on a regular basis.

Tolerance and Diversity

Knowing your community is the best way to begin your plan to build and sustain an audience. Knowing how to work within evolving individual and group differences is important (Lippard 1997). If you are working in a place that welcomes diversity, then you will have a lot more latitude in what you are able to do. If your programming efforts are based in a homogeneous community, then connecting with established values and ways of thinking is advised. When audiences can see how a certain musical performance or theater production relates to them, they are more likely to be interested and accepting. When community members embrace multiple kinds of expression, they have more opportunities to test and shape their own lives. Mary Catherine Bateson (1990) believes in having multiple models for how to live your life "so that it is possible to weave something new from many different threads" (16).

Begin by involving your community in decision making. Boards of directors and advisory boards can help you reach audiences with whom program staff members aren't familiar. A diversified staff will also signal openness and create a comfort zone for more members of the public. Diversity should not be identified as just ethnicity; it should also address age, economic class, ability, and sexual orientation. People feel welcome when they can identify with staff members, and having a diverse staff helps ideas flow within the organization, making an organization with a diverse staff richer and more innovative than an organization with a more homogenous staff.

Staff should ask questions about the organization and programming decisions when they are being discussed to make sure that at every level difference is accommodated. (The term *difference* as it is used here does not mean bringing in hateful or disruptive groups unless disruption is a desired outcome, as it might be when inviting the Guerrilla Girls, a feminist, activist performance group that points out discrimination in the arts.) It is a good idea to discuss the target populations that you want to attract to your programs. Maybe an orchestra sees that it isn't attracting youth or a new immigrant population and thus creates a goal to involve these groups. Once potential audiences are established and goals are identified, programming and marketing strategies are easier to develop. For instance, if the goal is to attract African Americans, an organization may do well to advertise through carefully selected churches, beauty salons, and barbershops instead of only going through the mainstream media. If the goal is to continuously attract Cubans to a park or community center, setting up places to play dominoes and drink Cuban coffee might help. Many communities have local newspapers that are read by gays and lesbians, Hispanics, or African Americans. Sending press releases, in appropriate languages, to these publications can be a good marketing strategy. Bilingual flyers can also be useful. Web sites should be easy for the elderly to read as well as include languages that address target groups.

Sometimes events can be planned around a recreational or an occupational activity. In 1987, Doug Blandy and Kristin Congdon facilitated an exhibition at Bowling Green State University called *Boats, Bait and Fishing Paraphernalia*. Local experts were hired to curate various aspects of the exhibit. As a result of their participation, the event drew a record crowd, attracting many people who had never been to a gallery (Blandy and Congdon 1988). More recently, the OMA had an exhibition on *The Art of the Motorcycle*, which drew in motorcycle enthusiasts who came again and again to study the bikes and learn about the history of the motorcycle. Many of these visitors had never been to the museum before (Rosoff, personal communication July 6, 2006).

If you are trying to attract people from the working class, it is a good idea to think about when they might be available to participate. Will they be more likely to come if a family meal or child care is part of the event? When members of Group Material, an activist arts group in New York City, began their project in 1979, they decided that their target audience would be everyone who elite culture had dismissed or taken for granted. They wanted to question possible exclusionary practices in the art world as well as the dominance of a market economy. In order to meet their goals, they rented a storefront space and worked to establish a dialogue with people who were not art professionals. They wanted to make art relevant again by reestablishing it in everyday activities. Gearing their programs to people from the working class, they were open during evening hours and from 12:00 p.m. to 10:00 p.m. on weekdays. They invited all kinds of people to display work and, unlike galleries of the time, made no hierarchal distinction among the items displayed or the individuals involved (Avgikos 1995). In this case, disrupting the established way of doing things was seen as positive.

Sometimes an organization is formed to serve a specific audience, as is the case with Project Row Houses in Houston, Texas. For this project, 22 shotgun-style houses in a historic African American neighborhood were renovated. These structures now serve as a positive presence in the African American community. The project, which is coordinated by artist Rick Lowe, is both communal and collaborative. Numerous local, state, and national organizations have contributed, and neighborhood people have pulled weeds, planted gardens, and repaired houses. The buildings are used as residences for single mothers, educational spaces for children, galleries, and studios. Programs have centered on memories, collections, hairstyles and fashion, storytelling, and incest and have included blues and jazz, barbecues, and tributes to Martin Luther King Jr. This neighborhood, once neglected and ridden with crime, is now seen as one of Houston's musical and cultural hubs and as the beginning effort in revitalizing an entire community. While Project Row Houses is local, its message and influence are national (Congdon 2004).

Some artists create art in order to envision a more tolerant community. For example, in 1998 Danny Deveny, a former member of the Irish Republican Army, worked with Marty Lyons to create huge political murals at the Douglas Fairbanks Theatre in New York, which was showing *A Night in November*, a one-person play about the conflict between the Northern Irish Protestants and the Catholics. Working in the style of social realism, these artists did what was once unimaginable: They placed Catholic and Protestant imagery on the same walls (Hayt 1998).

Taking time to understand a group's rituals and religious beliefs can be helpful not only in knowing what kinds of programs to develop but also in knowing when to schedule events. For instance, you wouldn't want to schedule a theater production on Passover if a portion of your audience is Jewish.

Almost all U.S. states have state folklorists. These people can help you identify traditional artists in your area who represent diverse cultural groups. Planning some music, art, storytelling, food, or history event around new immigrant groups, recreational aesthetics, or occupational folklore can help you diversify your programs. State folklorists often work for arts councils, but universities and state historical agencies also host them. The magazine *Teaching Tolerance*, published by the Southern Poverty Law Center, is an excellent resource on how to introduce diversity to children. (Teachers can receive free copies by contacting the Southern Poverty Law Center at 400 Washington Avenue, Montgomery, Alabama 36104.)

As with risk management, every organization should have policies that address discrimination and sexual harassment. When unfortunate conflicts arise, it is crucial that they are handled in a well-structured manner that has been approved by the organization. If appropriate policies are not in place, events could worsen, get blown out of proportion, and be aired in public, which can damage an organization's ability to function effectively.

Encouraging Access

In the last several decades a major effort has taken place to incorporate special populations into cultural activities. Welcoming special populations involves much more than making sure your pro-

grams are presented in places that are wheelchair accessible (although this aspect of planning is extremely important). Interpreters for people with hearing impairments, large print, good lighting, and microphones for clear audio are all advised. Following the guidelines set out by the Americans with Disabilities Act (U.S. Department of Justice 1996) is the law in the United States. This legislation treats the discrimination of people due to disability the same way it views the discrimination of anyone due to race, religion, or gender.

Driving the way in which cultural programming now incorporates special populations is a new approach to the way that disability is perceived. Doug Blandy (1991) explains that instead of seeing disability as a characteristic that limits people, the emphasis is now on seeing disability as a characteristic of a human-made environment that is limiting. In other words, changing the spaces we live and work in and the way in which programming is done can eliminate many disabilities, and people will be able to move, communicate, and comprehend effectively.

Sometimes changing an environment to adhere to the Americans with Disabilities Act can be difficult and expensive. Most people with disabilities are understanding of this fact and are willing to

Be sure to consider ways to provide access to all participants.
Photo courtesy of Ragen E. Sanner

work with organizations to find ways to facilitate accessibility. In the late 1990s, a visitor using a wheelchair at the Florida Folk Festival had trouble getting to the main stage due to the sandy ground. He contacted the Florida Folklife Council for help. Working with administrators at the Stephen Foster Park, which hosts the festival, and park administrators at the state level, they built wooden ramps on various trails surrounding the main stage. These walkways are now used by everyone and are a welcome addition to the park.

Besides adapting our environments to make cultural programs more accessible to everyone, suggests Blandy (1991), we should avoid using designations like *outsider art*, *mad*, or *l'art brut* to describe people's artwork. These are pejorative words and phrases that create a sense that there is only one way to be normal or to view the world. As Blandy states, "such designations emphasize disability rather than ability, dis-similarity rather than similarity" (139). The results of such labeling are counterproductive to the goals of most cultural organizations.

Program planners can go above and beyond the law in letting people who are often overlooked in cultural activities feel included. For instance, performances and exhibitions can make visible the work and circumstances of such people. In 1992, the Smithsonian Institution in Washington, District of Columbia, a city that has a large homeless population, curated *Etiquette of the Undercaste* in an attempt to encourage a dialogue about the problem. Although the exhibition created controversy over using taxpayer dollars on a topic that many people thought should be relegated to places other than museums, the administrators stood strong in their belief that cultural institutions should not ignore troublesome issues or hold them at a distance (Adams 1992).

While the Smithsonian exhibition made the homeless population its subject, other programs work directly with special populations. In Seattle, Washington, the Seattle Children's Museum includes art, music, drama, and creative writing produced by youth offenders. Hosted by the Experimental Gallery and traveling to various schools in the city, this showing communicates the grim realities of young adults who would otherwise remain invisible to the outside world (Zibart 1998). Instead of displaying the work of children who have little voice, Tim Rollins collaborates with these children. In 1982 he founded Kids of Survival (K.O.S.) and the Art and Knowledge

Workshop, a joint art program for teenagers in the South Bronx who are learning disabled and emotionally handicapped. Wanting to test out theories that he had learned in a graduate program in art education at New York University, Rollins established new ways of working with youths. Believing that the school system was antiquated and that "people in the South Bronx are as talented, innovative and creative as the people in any other community," he set out to help some of the most troubled youths achieve economic parity (Rollins 1990, 136). He accomplished this by paying 10 teenagers who were labeled uneducable and unemployable. Instead of being viewed as problems, these young people are now viewed as talented artists, and their work is collected by prestigious museums around the world.

Uniqueness of Arts and Cultural Expressions

The kinds of activities that people participate in have vastly expanded. In 1955, *The Guinness Book of World Records* began recording events like the quickest time for pushing an orange with the nose through the John F. Kennedy air terminal (24 minutes, 36 seconds), the greatest number of jumping jacks performed (33,000), and the most snow angels created at one time (1,791 in 2002 in Bismarck). The popularity of this book and people's participation in these odd kinds of activities have grown since 1955. The Web site alone gets 14 million hits a month, and the book has sold more than 3 million copies and has been printed in 23 languages (Watson 2005). People are clearly interested in extreme activities. The book by Susan Sheehan and Howard Means, *The Banana Sculptor, the Purple Lady, and the All-Night Swimmer* (2002), documents several passionate individuals and their leisure-time activities, demonstrating how odd our hobbies can be. One man sets out to have the best collection of precanceled stamps, while another aspires to eat at every McDonald's in the United States; other people fly kites and collect postcards. In their book, Sheehan and Means point out that the publications on magazine stands make visible the ubiquitous nature of unusual hobbies and pastimes.

Thankfully, communities, like individuals, have their idiosyncrasies. For public art to speak specifically to a community, arts planners must understand the symbols inherent in various group aesthetics and communication systems. When an artist, a musician, or a storyteller incorporates visual or audio hooks that are locally understood, some degree of heightened emotionality and connection can be made. In this way, community is not only reflected in but also created by artwork. For example, the *Cincinnati Gateway* by Houston Conwill, an accessible public artwork that creates a narrative about the social possibilities of the area, was accepted by the community far better than was Richard Serra's *Titled Arc*, which caused years of controversy in New York City before it was torn down. While some people responded to *Titled Arc* as an excellent piece of art carefully placed in a courthouse plaza, others felt that it was distasteful and that it might impede local police due to the fact that it was so large. Some critics even labeled it as a place that could enable terrorist activities (Doss 1995).

Arts programmers are often referred to as *cultural workers*. They promote cultural democracy, as they recognize the power that cultural expressions have to create dialogue, to root a community in tradition and history, and to explore possibilities for ways of being and solving problems.

Aesthetic approaches can vary from cultural group to cultural group. This doesn't mean that all Cubans or all avid bowlers will think, see, or appreciate the same kinds of things, but it does suggest that tendencies toward certain ideas can be identified among cultural groups. For example, many Amish cultures view embellishment and ostentation as a sin. Since originally buttons were used as ornamentation, a preferred way to fasten an Amish blouse or shirt might be a hook and eye (Bender 1989). In contrast, *rasquachismo* is a Chicano aesthetic that favors elaboration and flamboyancy. "Bright colors . . . are preferred to somber, high intensity to low, the shimmering and sparkling to the muted and subdued" (Ybarra-Frausto 1991, 157). Patterning can be piled onto patterning, and every inch of space can be filled with something to look at. "Ornamentation and elaboration prevail, joined to a delight for texture and sensuous surface" (Ybarra-Frausto 1991, 157).

One of the most popular pastimes in the United States is gardening, and the way in which gardens are created often signifies a cultural preference (Lippard 1997). In many African

This Japanese American memorial garden has been designed to appeal to that culture's aesthetic preferences.

Photo by Cari Garrigus, courtesy of CVALCO

American neighborhoods in Los Angeles, food is grown between flowers and shrubs. Although originally this was done for economic reasons, the practice is now medicinal, spiritual, and aesthetic (Robinson 1987). Should an arts organization landscape its yard in this manner, it would be putting out a welcome sign to a specific cultural group. At the same time, it may be signaling to others that the organization does not belong to them. Aesthetic choices represent a community's hegemony of taste, which generally advantages one group's perspective over another's (McEvilley 1992).

Gardening was also used as a catalyst to organize rebellious Los Angeles youths in the 1960s and 1990s. A high school biology class in the south central part of Los Angeles grew healthy food as well as produced and sold a salad dressing that provided scholarships for some students (Lippard 1997), thereby extending the way in which a garden communicates identity and possibility.

Often traditional cultures evolve their ways of doing things. Mexican cut paper, called *papel picado*, is used to frame an altar space or a place for ritual activities. It is now being made in plastic. The plastic is more durable than the tissue paper is, and it still functions to let spirits pass though the spaces (Carmichael and Sayer 1991). Change and innovation are alive and well in traditional cultures. Cultural organizations need to recognize this fact and incorporate it into their planning processes.

Providing Experiences for All

A 1996 study by the National Endowment for the Arts (NEA) found that U.S. adults born after 1945 are less interested in the established arts. Attendance at concerts of classical music has declined, as have opera and musical theater *(Orlando Sentinel* 1996). In response, cultural organizations across the United States have worked hard to increase audiences by programming for various age groups, diversifying content, partnering with other organizations, and adapting local context.

Sometimes it helps to think of cultural programming in expanded ways. One example of how an organization can explore art's power to affect a population occurred in 1988 when the Museum of the City of New York curated an exhibition on drug addiction and used former addicts as docents. A number of the attendees had drug problems, and the docents were able to immediately place them in treatment programs (Virshup 1988). Increasingly, the arts are being used to help troubled youths. A 1996 White House study, Coming Up Taller, reviewed 218 programs in 36 states and in

the District of Columbia and found that cultural programming can help reduce crime (Blumenthal 1996). In order to encourage first-year students at Long Island University to feel more comfortable in their new environment, a semester-long orientation includes discussions on artwork, asking students what effect art has on them. The course stimulates discussion and builds community (*Chronicle of Higher Education* 1997). John Malpede, the performance artist who founded the homeless theater group LAPD, claims that if art is to serve the public, artists need to place themselves in collaborative efforts with people they wouldn't normally be with (Lippard 1997). In doing so, new ways of exploring creative ventures are possible.

Many other attempts to expand audiences have been successful. In Philadelphia, an antigraffiti network engages graffiti artists in painting murals on the walls they have trashed (Barboza 1993). In New York City, troubled girls from Brooklyn take photographs of themselves at the International Center of Photography in Manhattan as a way of exploring possibilities (Kennedy 2006). In Cambridge, Massachusetts, diverse groups of women create oral history quilts as a way "to learn how to interact respectfully with others" (Cohen 1999, 1).

Where an event is held directly relates to the audience it will attract. Florida (2002) points out that our growing creative class is drawn to organic, indigenous, street-level culture: "Much of it is native and of-the-moment, rather than art imported from another century for audiences imported from the suburbs" (182). He goes on to say that German films and Senegalese music can be embraced, but visitors enter a space with an understanding that they are going into a cultural community and are not just attending an event that has been bracketed in its organizational form. Discussing the participatory nature of street-level culture, Florida remarks, "You may not paint, write or play music, yet if you are at an art-show opening or in a nightspot where you can mingle and talk with artists and aficionados, you might be more creatively stimulated than if you merely walked into a museum or concert hall, were handed a program and proceeded to spectate" (183). There is an appealing fluidity to moving from one space to another or from one event to another. It is like being at a smorgasbord, as you can do more than one thing in a single visit. For this reason, many cities have adopted days of the week or the month when galleries have openings, musicians play, dancers take to the streets, and poetry is read.

Cities can have an audio identity, as music can be associated with a certain place. For instance, you find the "blues in Chicago, Motown in Detroit, [and] grunge in Seattle" (Florida 2002, 228).

Sometimes when a traveling exhibition or program comes to town, it can be localized to attract more people. For example, when the OMA displayed the work of Grandma Moses, it also curated an exhibition featuring local grandmothers who painted. Connections can be made to various groups in other ways. For instance, a symphony can play the *1812 Overture* at a Fourth of July event (Florida 2002). An arts programmer who wants to do a show on lowriders in a conservative cultural community that is well schooled in the Renaissance might make a connection between the paint on the cars and the 15th-century Italian technique of glazing transparent color that was used "to paint the body of Christ as a physical being filled with light" (Hickey 1997, 69). While this connection is not enough to build an entire program on, it could pique someone's interest, and it demonstrates an aesthetic interest that reaches across time and space.

All kinds of spaces are being designed to incorporate creative learning. More and more children's playgrounds are being constructed to encourage learning about physics, geography, local history, and the environment. Working with children, Deborah Ryan from the University of North Carolina at Charlotte designed three nonpatriarchal playgrounds aimed mostly at serving African American children living in poverty. In one playground, the children can simulate the sounds of a storm or crawl inside a bear cave that makes a growling noise with a tube fashioned from a concrete pipe (Seligmann and Cohen 1993).

Florida (2002) claims that the United States is becoming nationally, economically, politically, and culturally divided. He believes that all these aspects of division are linked. He further states, "The real need is to bring more people into creative work—to create more markets and opportunities to tap the creative capabilities of far greater numbers of people" (xvii). In order to do this, cultural organizations need to keep the programming diverse, use technology in creative and expansive ways, and foster talent. In Florida's mind, reaching out to all populations is not only an economic but also a moral imperative.

Partnerships and Collaboration

Partnerships are important to audience development because multiple organizations working together have the power to draw on more constituencies and interests. Organizations who partner are able to share resources such as equipment, time, and expertise. Some communities, like Charleston, pull together the entire arts community for an annual festival that attracts people from around the world. Since 1989, Eatonville, Florida, has partnered with various central Florida organizations to ensure the success of its annual Zora Neale Hurston Festival of the Arts and Humanities.

Another example from central Florida centers on the recent closing of the muck farms due to overfertilization of the fields. When the farms shut down, thousands of farmworkers were displaced. The Crealde School of Art received a grant from the Florida Humanities Council to document the last harvest so that the 40 years that these farmworkers, who were often invisible to the rest of the community, spent providing inexpensive fruit and vegetables would not be lost. Crealde partnered with the Farmworker Association of Florida, the Florida Folklore Society, and Valencia Community College to make the documentary successful. No one organization could have done it alone (Congdon 2004).

When the Cultural Heritage Alliance (CHA) was formed at the University of Central Florida in 2003, it immediately established itself as a partnership organization. Established organizations were identified as possible partners, and general partnership agreements were signed. Without its partners, CHA would be a small organization and have little effect. Its partners include the Florida Folklore Society, the Department of State, the Florida Folklife Program, the Orange County Regional History Center, the Crealde School of Art, the International House of Blues Foundation—Orlando, and the City of Orlando Families, Parks and Recreation Department. Almost all CHA programs are done in partnership since the missions of all these organizations overlap. CHA's success is largely due to the strength of these partnerships. Information on the Cultural Heritage Alliance can be found at www.heritagealliance.ucf.edu.

When we think of partnerships, we generally think of working with other people. But our understanding of partnerships should extend beyond an anthropocentric view. Laurie Anne Whitt and Jennifer Daryl Slack (1994) point out that a community needs to include sites where humans and things other than human can come together. Our shared circumstances create an interdependency that is useful to consider when cultivating cultural audiences. "Geographical and ecological features of community are rarely incidental to political and cultural struggle: they contextualize—enable and constrain—relations of power" (Whitt and Slack 1994, 6). These relationships, in the broadest meaning of the word, should be considered when programming. It matters how we work with the environment in terms of where we play our musical instruments, how we construct public art, and how we landscape our organizational spaces. Even how we think of nature can make a difference. For example, Acoma poet Simon Ortiz believes that a wilderness does exist. For him, this wilderness is our modern cities (Lippard 1997). Our choices and ways of understanding our environment involve not only building audiences and community context but also ethical considerations and ways of seeing.

Environmental changes can profoundly affect artists. The increasing shortage of native plants for southwestern Native American basket makers has greatly affected their traditions (Whiteford 1988). Shortages are also troubling the African American basket makers living north of Charleston, South Carolina, where development has destroyed their sea grasses (Congdon 2004). Both groups have been making baskets for centuries, and both are working with various organizations, environmental groups, and politicians to ensure that their creative heritage can survive. Partnerships are extremely important for cultivating new audiences, exploring new content, and preserving heritage.

Summary

To successfully cultivate program audiences, arts facilitators should use multiple approaches. Established operas, ballets, symphonies, and museums must rethink their communities and their changing lifestyles and tastes. Collaborating with other groups, recognizing the environment and

its effect on culture, expanding into new and different spaces, and building vibrant communities with an active street life are all important.

CASE STUDIES

Kristin G. Congdon

Folkvine.org

Folkvine.org is a Web-based project that is collaborative and grounded in several communities (the artists' communities, the Folkvine community, and the evolving Web community). It was established by a group of faculty members and students in the Cultural Heritage Alliance (CHA) at the University of Central Florida in partnership with artists from central Florida and increasingly in partnership with the state. Funded by the Florida Humanities Council and later by the Department of State, Division of Cultural Affairs, it highlights folk artists whose creative expressions have been embraced by their communities.

The Folkvine team created the Web sites on the ten Florida folk artists in a manner that expresses each artist's aesthetic and key messages. For example, Taft Richardson's bone sculpture is about resurrecting what has been discarded, neglected, or demolished: animal bones, neighborhood environments, children, and plant life. His site is about a journey of resurrection. Ginger LaVoie's Hawaiian quilts are about Polynesian culture, place, spirituality, and storytelling, and Ruby Williams' produce stand and folk paintings are all about nourishment and folk wisdom. Each site is intended to be a poetic reflection of the artist and his or her community.

At www.folkvine.org, a Florida visitors' center displays postcards that lead to the artists' sites. Each site is rich with art and films of the artists and their communities. Some sites include interactive activities such as creating your own clown name or designing your own mask. Context and story are important to understanding each artist's creative life.

Along with the postcards on the counter at www.folkvine.org are tour guides centered on humanities topics like place-making imagination and social economy. These guides demonstrate to the Web surfer that while a clown-shoe maker and a produce stand owner may not seem to have much to do with each other, in fact they do relate (Congdon 2006). They each create give-and-take meaning from their environment and build wealth on social connections.

Besides connecting diverse artists on a Web space, Folkvine.org explores Web-based ways of programming in the humanities. Folkvine.org also holds public events in real space that are planned around each of its artists. The artists make the guest lists for their events, and in some cases Folkvine team members spend a day with an artist gathering names and addresses of invitees. This might mean walking the streets to identify neighborhood people with their addresses. The events take place in spaces selected by the artists, who know best where their community will feel at home. Refreshments are carefully selected, and activities that coordinate with the work of the artist are planned for participating children. At two events, the program was produced in Spanish as well as in English (a challenge for some of the Folkvine team members). Evaluations of the Web site and the program are both written and handled more informally with a video camera.

Folkvine.org targets artists who are admired by their communities but have not had much exposure outside their local areas. Since Folkvine.org posted its first artist site in 2003, artists have received increased recognition and opportunities, and their communities have gained exposure. The Florida Folk Heritage Award, granted by the secretary of state, has been given to Ruby Williams for her paintings and to the Scott family members for their clown shoes. Through Folkvine.org, the Florida Humanities Council has extended its audiences beyond its normal constituency.

While many of the Folkvine team members question their right to represent selected artists, they also understand that Folkvine.org is inventing a new kind of community. It is not an accurate, true depiction of anyone, as the creativity of Folkvine team members is mixed with the creativity of the focal artists. To recognize this situation, previously invisible team members were placed on the Web site as bobblehead dolls that make comments through the tour guides. As the Web site

evolves and team members have more time to reflect on what they have created, they gain new insights about creativity, place, and art making.

Motorcycle Stories

In 2005, the Cultural Heritage Alliance (CHA) at the University of Central Florida partnered with the Orlando Museum of Art (OMA) to develop a Web site that collects stories about motorcycle riding. The site was designed to create excitement about the forthcoming OMA exhibition, *The Art of the Motorcycle*, a recreation of the 1998 landmark exhibition at the Guggenheim Museum in New York City. Coordinated by Chantale Fontaine, CHA's Web designer, the site was set up before the exhibition opened in January of 2006.

Two Web sites were established due to the different needs and expectations of the two organizations' audiences. While OMA, who serves a relatively conservative audience of all ages, had to be careful about the images and language it was presenting to the public, CHA was more interested in capturing everything that could be posted. Because OMA works with many children and wanted to use the Web site in its educational programs, it carefully read each posting before making it public. A few additional narratives were posted on the CHA site. Still, the differences in the two sites were overwhelmingly minor. It is likely that the storytellers made a conscious effort to censor themselves. Even so, the stories seem to ring true to the diverse motorcycle groups that responded.

Besides confronting censorship issues, project planners faced another challenge in dealing with university rules about research with human subjects. The university required that the project go through the Institutional Review Board process and a release form was mandated. While Fontaine was able to structure the site so that a release form could be signed by each participant, it quickly became clear that some writers were not interested in the formality of filling out a form. The project planners therefore recognized that the stories posted would not be as plentiful as they might have been without the release form, but they also understood the two organizations' ethical mandates.

Both OMA and CHA agreed that they would not edit the text unless it was so poorly worded that it didn't make sense. This decision was based on two factors: limited resources to do the editing and a desire to keep the narratives authentic. Minor editing was necessary in only a few cases. Many participants were technologically skilled enough to post a photo, which made the site more exciting to surf. If a photo was not sent, Fontaine supplied one from the CHA collection to keep the project more visually enticing.

OMA placed a computer kiosk in its rotunda so that visitors could write a story in response to the exhibition or read stories by others as a way of enhancing their museum experience. The Web site was also incorporated into a University of Central Florida course taught at OMA on contemporary aesthetics.

The big surprise was how widespread the interest in the Web site was. The project planners had thought that the narratives would come mostly from people in central Florida because OMA advertised the site in its newsletter. But narratives came from all over the United States and from several other countries.

Although the exhibition has ended, the Web site continues to exist as a testimony to the lives of motorcyclists. There are stories about daredevil stunts, motorcycle tours, gearheads' masterpieces, families, and brushes with the law. The site can be found at http://sfdm.cf.edu/~motorcyclestories/home.php.

Creating the Web site for *The Art of the Motorcycle* brought up many questions about representation, censorship, and function. While many cultural organizations use the Web to advertise their programs, they don't always design the sites to function independently of the programs. If a Web site needs monitoring, as this one did, it can be time consuming to keep up. A host organization may need to consider the availability of resources a project will need to keep it functioning into the future.

Evaluating and Documenting Programs

Karla A. Henderson, PhD
North Carolina State University

ll professionals want their work to count and to make a difference in people's lives. We want people to enjoy life and to be the best that they can be. Therefore, we want our leisure and arts programming to be rewarding for participants. We also hope that our staff members feel productive in their work and enjoy themselves. Making a difference through arts events and programs is a goal that must be measured and documented for a plethora of reasons, even though doing so is sometimes uncertain and difficult. Evaluation aims to measure the outcomes of programming efforts in order to determine the value of arts and cultural programming and the ongoing improvements that should be made. Evaluation requires that we listen and then "stand up and speak."

Evaluating Programs

Evaluation is the broad term used to describe a combination of perspectives and techniques found in programming of any nature. Evaluation aims to document information from a range of perspectives. I am reminded of the issues surrounding perspective by a story that my sister sent me regarding the differences between people who are rich and people who are poor:

> One day the father of a very wealthy family took his son on a trip to the country with the express purpose of showing him how poor people live. They spent a couple of days and nights on the farm of what would be considered a very poor family. On their return from their trip, the father asked his son, "How was the trip?"
>
> "It was great, Dad."
>
> "Did you see how poor people live?" the father asked.
>
> "Oh, yeah," said the son.
>
> "So, tell me, what did you learn from the trip?"
>
> The son answered, "I saw that we have one dog and they had four. We have a pool that reaches to the middle of our garden and they have a creek that has no end. We have imported lanterns in our garden and they have the stars at night. Our patio reaches to the front yard and they have the whole horizon. We have a small piece of land to live on and they have fields that go beyond our sight. We have servants who serve us, but they serve others. We buy our food, but they grow theirs. We have walls around our property to protect us. They have friends to protect them."
>
> The boy's father was speechless.
>
> Then his son added, "Thanks, Dad, for showing me how poor we are."

Evaluation is assessment and documentation that enable professionals to get perspectives from others to assess the programs developed and the amenities used. Sometimes the results are as anticipated and at other times new and useful information is garnered. Evaluation enables arts managers and programmers to make enlightened decisions about future offerings and financial expenditures.

What's in a Definition?

Evaluation is the systematic collection and analysis of data based on criteria to make judgments about the worth or improvement of something (Henderson and Bialeschki 2002). Effective evaluation means using assessment and documentation together with identified focused questions and supporting evidence to make decisions. There are many other definitions of the term *evaluation*, all with slightly different interpretations. Generally, however, the goal of evaluation is to compare what is to what should be.

I like comparing evaluation to solving a crime. For example, when a robbery occurs, detectives solve the case by using criteria, evidence (or data), and judgment (or decisions). The criteria are the questions that need to be answered: What happened, what was stolen, who stole it, and what was the motive? The evidence includes information such as statements from witnesses, an inventory of what was missing, and physical data like fingerprints. From the questions asked and the evidence collected, the detective can make a judgment about what was stolen, who took it, and why it was stolen. With those judgments, an arrest can be made. If the detective does not have enough evidence, the judgment (i.e., arrest and conviction) is difficult to make. These same principles apply to evaluation.

Leisure and arts professionals continuously engage in intuitive evaluation. We notice that the orchestra was out of tune, that not enough art materials were ordered, or that we should have marketed this event more widely. The informal evaluations that participants and professionals make in leisure and arts organizations are always present and are useful. However, when decisions are made concerning where to place limited resources, something more than intuitive judgment is necessary. Formal systematic evaluations should be conducted regularly within organizations. These evaluations provide a rigor for when outcomes are complex and evidence is needed to make reliable, valid, useful, and informed decisions.

The major purpose of evaluation is, therefore, to inform decisions. The best decisions are based on systematically gathered evidence that relates to a particular purpose or standard for decision making. Evaluation provides information that leads to *action*. Developing an evaluation system, gathering resources, and conducting regularly scheduled formal evaluations create more efficient and effective operations, staff activities, and leisure programs that increase recreational, educational, and personal benefits for children and adults (Henderson and Bialeschki 2002). Several characteristics of evaluation should be kept in mind:

- Evaluation is a process. It consists of three dimensions: determining criteria, collecting and analyzing evidence, and making judgments.

- The goal of evaluation is to facilitate decision making by ascertaining value. Decisions should be based on sound judgments and not on personal or intuitive biases. Evaluation should lead to decision making for a specific situation or context.

- The most common way to evaluate is to measure how well objectives are met. However, this approach is only one of many ways to conduct evaluations.

- Evaluation within an organization should be ongoing. An organization's evaluation systems should address personnel (staff), program, policy (administration), place (areas and facilities), and participant outcomes.

- Evaluation does not necessarily occur only at the end of an event. Evaluation may occur as an assessment to determine what should be. It can be formative (i.e., ongoing) to examine processes or summative (i.e., at the end) to ascertain outcomes.

- Responsive evaluation is based on the premise that evaluation should respond to issues within an organization. Evaluation should be relevant to an organization and its decision makers as well as to the people (e.g., participants, staff members) affected by the decisions. To reemphasize, evaluation should result in action that improves programs.

Rationale for Assessment and Documentation

We conduct evaluations for many reasons. Each organization has its own purposes for undertaking assessment. Regardless of the purpose, evaluation requires formal and systematic data collection that includes criteria, reliable and valid evidence, and an open perspective for understanding phenomena and examining how to improve programs, facilities, staff, and administrative procedures in leisure and arts management (Henderson and Bialeschki 2002).

Some professionals fear evaluation because they are afraid of the results. If everything appears to be fine, evaluation seems like more work being added to an already overburdened schedule. Evaluation, however, is not meant only for crises when changes *have* to be made. When evaluation is done systematically, crises can often be avoided.

Evaluation occurs not for a single reason but for a combination of nonmutually exclusive reasons that lead to better arts and cultural programs (Henderson and Bialeschki 2002):

- Evaluation creates accountability. Accountability is the capability of an organization to justify its activities, expenditures, and services. Often projects are evaluated for accountability when an external unit such as a city manager or funding agency requests the evaluation. Accountability, however, should be an ongoing concern of any organization regardless of who is watching.

- Evaluation sets a baseline. This approach to evaluation is usually described as a *needs assessment*. Assessing a baseline can also provide a starting point for measuring change and planning for future action.

- Evaluation assesses whether goals have been met. The most important prerequisite for this evaluation approach is that appropriate and measurable objectives have already been articulated. Assessing goals should determine if the stated objectives are operating and if other objectives may be more appropriate.

- Contemporary evaluation in leisure and arts management determines the effects of a program, a facility, or an administrative procedure. Impact evaluation asks what differences a program has made and how the program will affect people both now and into the future. Outcomes are defined as the benefits or changes that occur.

- In simple words, evaluation demonstrates what works and what doesn't. Evaluation allows professionals to increase the utility and success of future programs and also allows individuals to share procedures that might be useful for other professionals in similar situations.

- Evaluation facilitates organizational improvements related to quality control and future action. This is probably the most practical reason for evaluation. Professionals assess staff members, programs, policies, or participants in order to revise their existing operations. For example, site improvements might be sought by appraising existing facilities and physical property for adequacy, accessibility, safety, attractiveness, appropriateness, availability, and functionality.

- Evaluation allows organizations to comply with external standards set by government or by other funding

Organizations should have a system in place for evaluating programs.
© PhotoDisc

agencies or professional bodies. Often these evaluations are performed for additional purposes that directly aid the organization, but they may be done simply to meet accreditation or licensing requirements.

Thus, evaluation is important for many reasons. Doing evaluations, however, requires some expertise in using evaluative research methods, writing specific and measurable objectives, selecting appropriate measurement techniques, and committing to use the resulting information for the reasons just described.

Evaluation takes time, and the implications of the results may not always be clear. Managers of arts and cultural programs should not begin an evaluation unless they have a sincere desire to use the results to improve their organization. Further, evaluation should be undertaken only if the benefits outweigh the costs. Keep in mind that the best evaluations in the world cannot provide a definitive picture of the future, reduce the costs of goods and services, or choose the best course of action. This decision is up to the stakeholders in an organization. Better decisions, however, can be made based on evaluations.

Evaluation: A Trilogy

As described, three elements must come together to result in an effective and efficient evaluation: criteria, evidence (data), and judgment (Henderson and Bialeschki 2002). To determine criteria is to determine the purpose of an evaluation and the specific questions that will be explored. Depending on the goals of an arts and cultural program, the criteria may be quite evident. If a program has a set of good objectives to serve as the criteria, the evaluator can then decide how to gather the evidence and move on from there. If, however, arts and cultural programmers are not sure what needs to be evaluated and do not have set objectives, then determining the criteria may be more difficult. For any program or facility, measuring everything with any degree of depth is impossible. An evaluator must be able to articulate what is practical to measure. A difference exists between a criterion that asks how many people participated in a program and one that identifies the participants' satisfaction with the program. Sometimes programmers have one set of criteria that they think should be measured while stakeholders (e.g., boards of directors or patrons) have something else in mind. Thus, it is essential to identify what questions you wish to address or what criteria you wish to evaluate *before* collecting data.

Evidence means data. Data are pieces of information that are collected to answer the questions posed in the criteria. In gathering evidence, the timing (i.e., needs assessment, formative evaluation, or summative evaluation), type of data (i.e., qualitative or quantitative), sample size (i.e., entire population, probability sample, or convenience sample), sample composition (i.e., demographics), and data handling (i.e., data collection, coding, analysis) must be determined. The evidence relates directly to the criteria that were established. If poor or unclear criteria were set, designing measurement instruments may be difficult. Data collection and analysis are not tricky to learn, but applying them appropriately based on criteria requires effort.

Judgment is determining the value of something based on the evidence that was collected using the previously determined criteria (Henderson and Bialeschki 2002). Judgments specifically refer to the conclusions and recommendations that are made for any evaluation. A programmer for an arts and cultural program might have collected excellent data, but without the final step of making conclusions and recommendations, the evaluation is incomplete. Conclusions come from answering the questions posed as criteria. Recommendations are proposed courses of action that are based on the conclusions and the context of the organization. Recommendations must be practical, financially feasible, and consistent with the organization's mission.

When to Evaluate

The timing of an evaluation relates to three areas: assessment, formative evaluation, and summative evaluation. Evaluation may be done at the beginning of a program or year (assessment),

during the program or year (formative evaluation), or at the end of the program or year (summative evaluation):

    a. Assessment almost always examines some type of need and is the foundation for further planning.

    b. Formative evaluation examines an organization's process or efficiency and addresses how to improve programs while they are in progress.

    c. Summative evaluation measures the product, referred to as *outcomes*, *impacts*, or *effectiveness*, and is used when an arts manager wants to prove whether a program worked the way it was planned.

Thus, the criteria developed for an evaluation will depend on its timing and on whether it will be used for planning the program, improving the process, or measuring the product.

Needs assessments are often conducted in community programs. Assessments may answer questions such as, What is the socioeconomic profile of the community? What are unmet needs? Where do people's interests lie? What arts programs are currently available? Assessment implies that the arts and cultural programmer wants to find out where to begin. This may involve assessing the potential participants, the resources available in a community, or the need for training a new staff member. To collect data for a needs assessment, a plan must be devised. The plan usually includes defining what the organization needs to know, developing a timeline and plan of action, generating goals, collecting data about what is, analyzing data for discrepancies between what is and what should be, and developing ways to initiate the desired programs.

Formative evaluation is usually undertaken when examining an organization's processes. Formative evaluation involves systematically examining the steps in the development and implementation of a program, the organizational structure, or the organizational policy (Henderson and Bialeschki 2002). Formative evaluation occurs while a program is in progress and examines the process as it is occurring. Feedback is provided early so that revisions can be made and weaknesses pointed out while making changes is still possible. Questions asked during a formative evaluation might include, Are some marketing efforts better than others at attracting registrants and audiences? Are the participants progressing toward their individual goals?

When people think of evaluation, they usually think of summative evaluation, which occurs at the end of a project and measures the results. Summative evaluation examines effects and effectiveness at the conclusion of a program or at the end of the year. Formative evaluation can occur within any stage of a process, whereas summative evaluation occurs only at the process termination. A common form of summative evaluation is to examine the input and activity resources, such as how comfortable the arts venue was or how effective the leaders were. Summative research focused on outcomes or impact is more complicated when evaluating what people experienced and how an arts and cultural program contributed to individual or community quality of life.

What to Evaluate

Henderson and Bialeschki (2002) proposed that evaluations should focus on the 5 Ps: program, personnel, place, policies (administration), and participant outcomes. These five areas are not discrete and tend to overlap. For example, an arts and cultural program is of little use unless it somehow influences a participant. The policies of an organization may affect the program. The place, in terms of the area or facility, will affect the job of the staff members or personnel. Seldom do we evaluate any one of these aspects without also acknowledging how it relates to the others. In leisure and arts services, the 5 Ps apply, but generally the areas of focus are program and participants.

Every organization needs an evaluation system that encompasses all 5 Ps. Having a master plan for how evaluation fits into an organization is important. Using a system means that not every aspect of an organization needs to be evaluated every year. In fact, for available time and money, focusing on quality evaluations that can be used in critical decision making might be far more useful than evaluating everything. Programmers need to determine which of the 5 Ps to evaluate

You must determine if program participants will be a part of the sample.

Photo courtesy of Shawna Gribskov, Pacific Winds Music

and how often to evaluate them. For example, staff evaluation is usually done once a year, while facilities should be monitored every day for risk issues. A specific program like a popular children's painting class might need to be formally evaluated every other year. Note, however, that a system for formal evaluation does not mean that intuitive evaluation isn't ongoing. Also, an extenuating circumstance might require a program to be evaluated more often than planned.

In addition to considering which of the 5 Ps to evaluate and how often to evaluate them, the system should take into account the what, why, when, who, and how of each evaluation. After determining the reasons for performing the evaluation and the Ps that might be evaluated, issues like the following must be considered:

- What will be the timeline (how often and when during the year)?
- What sample will be evaluated (all participants, a random sample)?
- Who will be in charge of the evaluation (an outside evaluator, the division head, the event manager)?
- Who will use this information (program leaders, the board of directors)?
- How will the evaluation be conducted (methods and instruments)?
- What resources are needed to carry out the evaluation (personnel, facilities, funds, supplies)?

Evaluation requires careful planning. Trying to assess everything usually results in poor conceptualizations of projects or data overload without useful interpretation. Further, evaluation involves time and money. Evaluations also carry political overtones that must be understood by staff members, participants, and funders. Thus, to have a system in place means that you have established appropriate reasons for evaluating and are planning to use the information to make good decisions.

Evaluating Personnel, Policies, and Places

Many different staff members work in leisure and arts organizations. These staff members may be full time, part time, or seasonal. Volunteers are considered to be unpaid staff (Tedrick and Henderson 1989). The benefits of staff evaluation include improving job performance and providing feedback for the personal development of staff members, regardless of whether they are young and holding paid positions for the first time, have been in the profession for 30 years, or are occasional

volunteers in the organization (Henderson and Bialeschki 2002). Evaluation is important in the personnel process, and midyear (formative) evaluations as well as end-of-year (summative) evaluations are generally used. The personnel evaluation should examine the relationship between the criteria stated in the job description and the performance of the staff member. Feedback to staff, however, should occur both informally on an everyday basis and formally as part of an established performance review.

Evaluation is also used for policies, procedures, and administrative issues such as the way that the organization is structured and operated. Budget analysis is another way to examine policies and administration. For example, cost-benefit analysis and cost-effectiveness are econometric models that are used to evaluate leisure services. Cost-benefit analysis relates the costs of a program or an operation to its benefits, which are expressed in dollar figures. Social and cultural benefits derived from arts and cultural programs, however, are hard to quantify. Cost-effectiveness is easier to measure because it is the ratio of costs to revenues generated. Performance-based program budgets are another common way for organizations to evaluate how money is spent in relation to the program outcomes. Economic impact is another example of a policy or an administrative area that might be measured in an arts program. Economic impact describes the revenue activity generated by a particular event such as a festival or an arts and crafts fair.

When places or facilities are evaluated, the emphasis is usually on use as well as safety. Preestablished standards are often helpful in evaluating risk-management and safety concerns in the facilities, equipment, and landscapes of an organization. Routine checks in the form of walk-throughs, scheduled maintenance procedures, and maintenance logs can serve as a formal evaluation system for facilities and equipment.

Evaluating Programs and Participant Outcomes

Leisure and arts professionals probably most often associate evaluation with program evaluation. Programs are most often assessed in terms of participant outcomes. Evaluation is seen as one of the prime components of any programming model when programs such as cultural arts are examined along with assessment, objectives, and implementation. Evaluation, however, may occur not only at the end of a program but also throughout the program or even at the beginning of the program. Evaluating programs at all stages of their development may help assure that they achieve the desired results (Carpenter and Howe 1985).

Recently, the logic model has emerged as a potential framework for thinking about program evaluation as well as assessment of participant outcomes (W.K. Kellogg Foundation 2001). The premise of the logic model is that program components should lead to program outcomes. The model provides a picture of how an organization does its work in terms of the theory and assumptions underlying a program. The model suggests that a logical sequence of events occurs (Baldwin, Caldwell, and Witt 2005). The model also provides a means for integrating planned work and the intended results of that work. Stated another way, it provides a means for examining how program planning and implementation relate to participant outcomes.

Figure 6.1 shows a logic model for Learn to Draw, a hypothetical adult program that teaches drawing. The program components include six classes, knowledgeable staff to conduct the program, a drawing studio, and marketing of the classes. A short-term outcome is called a *proximal outcome*. It is the first step toward achieving other outcomes. In this case, adults learn basic drawing skills and meet other people who are interested in drawing. These outcomes lead to distal (future) outcomes, such as the adults drawing on their own or signing up to take another arts class. Finally, the effects of the drawing program might include a greater appreciation of community arts opportunities and an improved quality of life for the participants.

The logic model links directly to evaluation. It increases the potential for programming effectiveness by focusing on the questions that have value for the stakeholders. The model lends itself to questions asked for both formative and summative evaluations (W.K. Kellogg Foundation 2001). It also enables an evaluator to ask questions about the context of the program (e.g., What aspects of the arts program most shaped our ability to do the work? Were the instructors good teachers?).

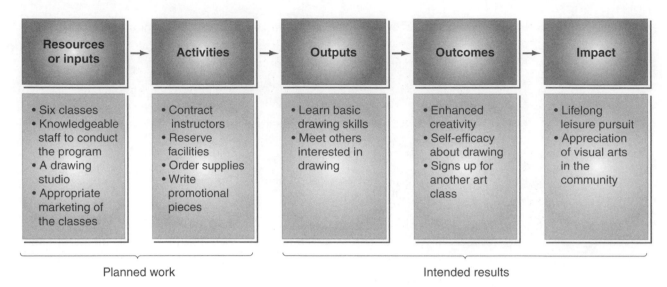

Resources or inputs	→	Activities	→	Outputs	→	Outcomes	→	Impact
• Six classes • Knowledgeable staff to conduct the program • A drawing studio • Appropriate marketing of the classes		• Contract instructors • Reserve facilities • Order supplies • Write promotional pieces		• Learn basic drawing skills • Meet others interested in drawing		• Enhanced creativity • Self-efficacy about drawing • Signs up for another art class		• Lifelong leisure pursuit • Appreciation of visual arts in the community

Planned work   Intended results

Figure 6.1 A logic model for Learn to Draw, a drawing class for adults.

It addresses the quantity and quality of the implementation (e.g., How many people participated? How did people find out about the program?). Further, the focus on outcomes includes criteria such as effectiveness, magnitude, and satisfaction (e.g., What is our assessment of what resulted from the arts program? How satisfied were the participants? What have we learned about doing this type of program?).

Another way that I like to think about program evaluation is by examining levels of program evaluation adapted from the work of Bennett (1982). Seven levels of program evaluation are presented in figure 6.2. The first four relate to how the organization designs a program (the program components) and how the participants respond (the proximal outcomes). The last three relate to distal outcomes that can result in larger social effects (Henderson and Bialeschki 2002).

Following are short explanations of what program evaluation involves at each of the seven levels:

1. Inputs—resources available and expended, such as money, paid staff and volunteer time, facilities, and equipment

2. Activities—strategies, techniques, and organizational processes that are used, including publicity, actual activities, and program delivery

3. People involvement—outputs, usually measured in terms of volume of activity pertaining to statistics and demographics describing the number of people, the characteristics of the people, and the frequency and intensity of involvement

4. Reactions—responses from the participants, including degree of interest, like or dislike for activities, satisfaction, expectations, appeal, and opinions

5. KASA (knowledge, attitudes, skills, aspirations) outcomes—

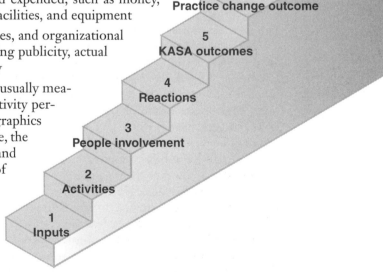

Figure 6.2 Seven levels of program assessment and evaluation.

Adapted, by permission, from K.A. Henderson and M.D. Bialeschki, 2002, *Evaluating leisure services: Making enlightened decisions* (State College, PA: Venture Publishing, Inc.), 48.

benefits and changes that individuals or populations achieve during or after participating in program activities

- Knowledge—awareness, understanding, problem-solving skills
- Attitudes—feelings, changes in interest, ideas, beliefs
- Skills—verbal or physical abilities, new skills, improved performance
- Aspirations—desires, courses of action, new decisions

6. Practice change outcome—adoption and application of knowledge, attitudes, skills, or aspirations to leisure or lifestyle

7. End results—social, economic, environmental, and individual consequences; how people are helped (and hopefully not hindered) by the program

These seven levels show how different aspects might be part of program evaluation. Leisure and arts professionals are interested in how well they are designing and implementing programs, and this information can be evaluated in the first four steps of this model. For an organization to function efficiently and effectively, these aspects must be considered. The logic model, however, suggests that the significance of any social program depends on the outcomes associated with KASA, practice change, and quality of life. Evaluators must be aware of what exactly they are measuring when evaluating a program. For example, the number of people who participate in an arts program does not necessarily relate to whether or not the participants learn a skill.

Thus, a big challenge in program evaluation is ensuring that the arts manager knows what levels or outcomes are being measured. Most program evaluations do not measure, or cannot measure, all seven levels. Outcomes related to practice change and quality of life occur at a much later time than that measured when a program concludes. A manager of an arts and cultural program must determine what levels can be measured given the program goals and the time, money, and measurement instruments available.

We have now demonstrated how program evaluation and participant outcomes are linked. The goal of providing arts and cultural leisure experiences is to produce positive benefits and to measure outcomes based on involvement in the activities. Participant outcomes include what individuals know, think, feel, and can do and how individuals behave or change as the result of a program. Ultimately the goal is to improve quality of life for both individuals and communities. Achieving this ultimate outcome requires periodically assessing all levels and in particular determining what participants think, feel, and experience.

To effectively measure participant outcomes, evaluators must employ several steps. First, they must determine the criteria or outcomes being measured. Then, the data that are needed to measure the outcomes must be identified, collected, analyzed, and compared to the criteria. Finally, the findings must be used to form conclusions and recommendations. For example, a programmer who wants to know if summer concerts in the park create greater community cohesion might determine that the desired outcome is increased attendance. The measurement used might be attendance over the course of the concert series, together with a short survey administered randomly on the last night of the series. The staff could then make judgments about the value of the program in relation to the outcome of attendance and perceived community cohesion. Other positive outcomes might benefit individuals attending the concert series, but in this evaluation, the focus was on determining specific goals that can be measured.

Different populations may need to be examined with different tools. For example, evaluating youth programs may be more difficult than evaluating adult programs. Youths may have shorter attention spans. Measurement is also complicated by the rapid developmental stages that children undergo. Changes in aspects such as social skills may not be the result of an arts program as much as they are the result of maturation. Data collection must also be age appropriate. Evaluations should be sensitive to diversity. For example, individuals who speak English as a second language may understand the wording of instruments differently and therefore may not score in the same ways as would people who speak English as their first language. People with disabilities may also interpret instruments differently than the evaluator intended if their needs are not considered.

Evaluating outcomes is not as easy as evaluating inputs, activities, and reactions. There are no magic formulas for evaluation. More funders today, however, want to see that programs make a difference in people's lives. Therefore, applying the logic model and focusing on all levels of evaluation are important to consider.

Additional Thoughts About Evaluation and Documentation

All evaluations must be completed with honesty and integrity. Political and ethical issues can arise during evaluations. If arts programmers are honest with themselves and the people they work with, fewer problems will result (Henderson and Bialeschki 2002).

Evaluation is political because it often supports or refutes the views that people hold. The simple fact that people are involved makes evaluation projects political. Politics encompass personal contacts, value-laden definitions, controversial recommendations, subtle pressures to please, and advocacy for certain results. According to Patton (1978), to be innocent of politics in evaluation is to become a pawn.

Several considerations should guide the evaluation process to make it less political (Henderson and Bialeschki 2002). First, understand the program well before undertaking an evaluation. Understand the strengths and the limitations of the organization. Second, before claiming any conclusions about the evaluation, provide evidence. Judgments must link directly to the criteria and the data uncovered. When drawing conclusions, be careful not to go beyond the actual findings. Third, make the purpose of any evaluation clear to all involved *before* beginning the evaluation. Keep that purpose clear throughout the evaluation process.

Make sure the instruments used in data collection are age appropriate.
Photo courtesy of SouthEast Effective Development (SEED)

Ethics have to do with what is right and wrong and how a professional conforms to the standards of a given profession. Ethics in evaluation primarily involve being as open as possible (within the constraints of privacy) about a project. People (participants or personnel) have the right to know that they or their programs are being evaluated. In addition, participants also have some right to confidentiality concerning the information that they wish to divulge.

An arts manager or programmer has ethical obligations to the staff members and participants. Be careful not to promise too much from an evaluation: Be realistic about an evaluation project's value and limitations.

Staff members performing evaluations have the responsibility to assure anonymity and confidentiality if needed. Anonymity means that no one, including the people collecting the data, knows the names of the people participating in an evaluation, such as the individuals completing a survey. Confidentiality says that the evaluator will know who participated in the evaluation, but no one else will. An evaluator may also want to present statistics in categories that are broad enough that no one can figure out how a particular individual might have responded.

Coercion is an ethical concern in some evaluation projects. People should never be forced into participation. Involvement can, however, be a prerequisite that is understood by participants before they begin a program.

Another ethical aspect relates to participants having a right to know the results of an evaluation project. Sharing results with participants as well as other professionals is the best way to assure that good programs and evaluation processes are developed. An arts and cultural programmer may want to send the results to the participants, post the results on a Web site, or hold a meeting to explain what the evaluation project revealed. Sometimes this procedure is referred to as *debriefing*, but providing results need not be that formal. The bottom line is that people who have given you information should have access to the compiled results if they are interested.

Some evaluation issues might be considered moral as well as ethical since they relate primarily to the individual evaluator. These concerns relate to biases and unintentional mistakes in conducting an evaluation project that may affect the results (Henderson and Bialeschki 2002). For example, choosing an inappropriate or inadequate sample may affect the outcomes of a study. Careless data collection that uses an inappropriate instrument for the respondents or poorly written questions is a moral concern. Staff members performing an evaluation must be honest about their skills and either get help or do an evaluation project that is appropriate to their competence level. Allowing biases, prejudices, preconceived perceptions, or friendships to influence the evaluation outcomes and pandering to the stakeholders are further issues to avoid. An evaluator must also avoid being predisposed to any particular outcome when beginning an evaluation project.

There are several aspects that must be considered when the evaluator actually gets to the judgment phase and presents the conclusions and recommendations. For example, ignoring negative results is a problem, as is discounting some findings or not letting all the information out. All the details of the study should be reported, including information suggesting that a procedure may not have gone particularly well. The possibilities of negative results should be discussed ahead of time with the stakeholders of an evaluation in order to avoid moral conflicts and embarrassment that might arise later. Although dragging out an evaluation is not morally wrong, an evaluator has a responsibility to complete an evaluation project in a timely manner. The bottom line is that a professional must do the best possible evaluation. Thus, shortcuts must be avoided. Proper sampling and analysis are imperative.

Posavac and Carey (1992) offer several ideas when addressing political and ethical issues in evaluation. First, an evaluator must realize what can and cannot be done, admit limitations, and adjust. Second, patience is necessary and planning is essential to avoid pitfalls. Third, the evaluator must focus on practical questions and feasible issues. The evaluation questions must be focused and the criteria clearly defined. Finally, a self-evaluation orientation must be adopted for the work. The evaluator is the one who ultimately knows whether the appropriate decisions were made. Staff members performing evaluations must continually monitor themselves and always strive to do the right thing.

So Now What?

Evaluation is an ongoing process. This chapter only scratches the surface in its discussion of the skills, competencies, and knowledge needed to perform effective evaluations in arts and leisure organizations. Evaluating anything is not easy, especially when the evaluation is formal and systematic. A programmer must be confident that an evaluation system or project can make a difference in an organization. Many people are fearful of evaluations, so the value of evaluation cannot be overarticulated. Evaluation should be viewed as a constructive process even though the data may not always be as positive as hoped. Some people have little faith in evaluations because in their previous experiences the evaluations did little good or the resulting recommendations were never carried out. Arts and cultural programmers are challenged to make sure that evaluations are *used*.

Any professional going into an evaluation project needs to do so with good intentions and an open mind. Each evaluation undertaking will be different, so the same method or the

same instrument cannot be used in every case. Organizations that have good goals or established standards will likely be able to complete evaluations with greater ease than can those organizations that do not. Further, evaluations need to work within the resource and time constraints that are built into any organization. Sometimes nothing can be done about time and money constraints, and in some cases doing no evaluation is better than doing one that is poorly designed or that collects limited or even incorrect data. Though identifying criteria, using models, and determining types of data are not very exciting, these design steps are crucial in setting up effective evaluations.

For a project to be successful, good methods and measurement tools must be used. Sometimes measuring evaluation criteria is difficult, especially when assessing higher levels of outcomes. Nevertheless, the evaluator must try to conduct solid evaluations while at the same time being careful not to promise more than the evaluation can deliver.

Evaluating Arts and Cultural Programs

The following list, taken from Henderson and Bialeschki (2002), summarizes considerations for a professional who is evaluating arts and cultural programs:

- Make sure that you have the skills and knowledge necessary to do the type of evaluation needed. If not, get help or get someone else to do the evaluation.

- Be clear about the purpose of the evaluation. Make sure that stakeholders are also clear about those purposes.

- Make sure that the expense of an evaluation in terms of time and effort is comparable to the value received from doing the evaluation. This cost-benefit analysis may be difficult to quantify, but the concept should be kept in mind.

- Remember that evaluation may occur not only as a summative evaluation (occur at the end of a process) but also as an assessment or as a formative evaluation.

- Do not allow biases, prejudices, preconceived perceptions, or friendships to influence the evaluation outcomes. Further, do not let the whims of some stakeholders prevent you from doing the type of evaluation that you think needs to be done.

- Make sure that when you go into an evaluation you understand thoroughly the organization and its context and limitations.

- Select and use research methods and measurement instruments that are specifically related to the criteria. In other words, spend time at the beginning of the project carefully planning what to do.

- Continually think about how the criteria, evidence, and judgment phases of the project fit together. Each succeeding component should be a natural outgrowth of what has gone before.

- Collect data carefully. Careless data collection results from using the wrong instrument and poorly written questions that are inappropriate to respondents.

- Avoid bias in sample selection. In addition, think carefully how you will motivate people to participate in the evaluation. Before you begin to collect data, think about the sample size, the sample representativeness, and the desired response rate.

- Beware the possibility of the Hawthorne effect, which occurs when people act differently just because they are glad you are paying attention to them by doing evaluations.

- Consider data analysis before beginning the project.

- Base your conclusions and recommendations only on the data that you collect from the project. Do not claim more than you have evidence to support.

- Address all the results of an evaluation and not just those aspects that are positive. While you may have to handle negative results carefully, you have an ethical responsibility to address them. Be careful that you do not discount any findings.

- Be open to finding unexpected results as you conduct an evaluation. The real value of some evaluation projects is what you learn that you didn't expect to learn.

- Write a concise, complete, well-planned evaluation report. Unless you communicate the results to others, the study will do little good. This report also requires that you write specific recommendations.
- Get results disseminated as soon as possible after completing an evaluation. Nothing kills the enthusiasm for an evaluation like having it drag on for months or even years.

Reprinted, by permission, from K.A. Henderson and M.D. Bialeschki, 2002, *Evaluating leisure services: Making enlightened decisions* (State College, PA: Venture Publishing, Inc.), 357-359.

Summary

I hope this chapter provides you with a framework for thinking about evaluating leisure, arts, and cultural programs. A single chapter, or a single book for that matter, will not make you an expert on assessment, evaluation, and documentation. Becoming a good evaluator requires education, practice, and a healthy dose of common sense. I hope this chapter offers a beginning point for exploring education and for applying evaluation processes to the arts through practice and common sense.

Economics of Programming

Arts Financial Management From Macro to Micro

Chris N. Burgess
College of Charleston

Before an arts manager can truly begin planning on a specific programmatic level, there must be an organizational understanding that allows programs to mesh not only with mission ideals but also with financial realities and expectations. Ultimately, the failure to research and understand an organization's economic history can place a program at a significant disadvantage before it begins. In effect, a program might be destined for failure simply because of a lack of financial due diligence taking the larger organizational context into account.

This context might manifest itself in many ways and incorporate a variety of tools, some of which are utilized within this chapter. The purpose here is to present not only the basics of program economics but also a framework through which cultural organizations might plan and implement programming that is directly related to mission ideals and is the product of fiscal analysis based on real data as well as on larger economic indicators.

Chapter Framework

I will begin with a concise study of project budgeting by examining a specific grant proposal format. Then I will move into a larger economic perspective in which programming is viewed through a broad lens and multiple aspects of an organization's finances are integrated into programmatic decision making.

We have a variety of tools at our disposal when engaging in economic examination. The primary methods include the following:

- Earned-to-unearned income splits
- Expense breakdowns—programming, administrative, fund-raising
- Ratio interpretations
- Longitudinal trend analyses and budgetary projections

These methods allow us to analyze organizational finances from top to bottom by using a diverse array of economic indicators. In the United States this analysis is not limited to organizational insiders but might be undertaken by anyone with access to the organization's Internal Revenue Service (IRS) Form 990. The 990s of U.S. nonprofits are freely available at www.guidestar.org (2007) and are rapidly becoming major sources of information for not only the organizations themselves but also donors, grantors, board members, peers, volunteers, and media members.

Organizations classified under the 501(c)(3) IRS code are required to file a yearly 990 federal tax return if their annual gross receipts are greater than $25,000 U.S. The 501(c)(3)s are nonprofit organizations that are granted tax-exempt status in return for providing services that benefit the public good. As there is no specific arts classification under the 501(c)(3) coding, arts organizations are generally included under the education category. The other four primary categories are religious, charitable, scientific, and literary. This classification is one of the reasons why we often see an arts organization declare its educative role in its mission statement.

The information contained in the 990 goes to the heart of organizational finances: expense breakdowns, income analyses, and balance sheets. The 990 is the nonprofit's statement of financial position, particularly for external stakeholders who do not have access to internal information or audited financial statements. As a result, identifying funding sources and making case statements are now simply formative steps in a program budgeting process that necessarily includes holistic organizational financial awareness.

In this chapter I will illustrate how the 990 can be used to examine an organization's finances as well as demonstrate how organizations must embrace financial analysis tools as part of their programming, for both budgetary and strategic reasons. In essence, if you and I can take a random 990 and perform a comprehensive financial analysis within a matter of hours, organizations must strive to do the same and much more. Such analysis and interpretation of data are critical components of not only programmatic success but also organizational solvency and survival.

Finally, the hope is to illustrate not only the readiness of economic data for analysis but also the increasing importance that responsible financial management is granted by all members of an organization. For example, what is the fiscal difference between staging Beethoven's Ninth Symphony and

The number of participants affects economic, artistic, and aesthetic factors and should be taken into consideration when planning.

Photo courtesy of Derek Campbell

presenting a more contemporary piece by a composer such as Steve Reich, between producing a musical with 15 cast members and putting on a drama with 3, or between organizing a show of emerging visual artists and taking part in an expensive traveling exhibition featuring a popular artist? Further, and perhaps even more importantly to some, what are the implications on an artistic, aesthetic, or audience level? There is a balance that must be reached both in these aspects and in the financial interests of the organization. This balance will underlie the discussion throughout this chapter.

Program Budgeting

When contemplating programming and finances, the tendency is to think in terms of budgeting on a specific level, such as a program or project, as well as to think of potential income sources. Later in this chapter we will deal with programming in a larger organizational context. At this point, however, we will look deeper into various aspects of project budgeting, beginning with identifying and cultivating donors beyond the individual constituency base. The underlying theme behind all donor prospecting is research. For instance, there are foundations that are very specific in the types of initiatives they seek to fund.

Finding the Right Donors

Organizations can use multiple research tools to narrow the search for prospects and heighten the likelihood of submitting successful grant applications. For instance, using a simple search on the Foundation Center's Web site (Foundation Center 2006) culls the following information on two well-known foundations: the Lilly Endowment and The Andrew W. Mellon Foundation. This search illustrates the information that is readily available.

The Lilly Endowment considers proposals across three program areas—community development, education, and religion—but 60% to 70% of grant funds go to the state of Indiana due to the Lilly company's historic involvement with Indianapolis (Lilly Endowment Inc. 2006). The Andrew W. Mellon Foundation offers grants across six program areas—higher education and scholarship, scholarly communications, research in information technology, museums and art conservation, performing arts, and conservation and the environment—and has a much broader geographic reach than that of the Lilly. Yet the categories are quite subcategorized and sometimes are closed to new applicants except under certain circumstances.

Thus, identifying donors, particularly foundations, involves identifying not only the prospects but also the limitations of the granting programs themselves. This research is vital, as once a logical match is found within the vast universe of granting organizations, the probability of success increases and greater organizational efficiency is achieved.

Private foundations are not the sole source of program funding, as there are numerous businesses that seek to establish themselves as conscientious corporate citizens, and they help create this image branding through either corporate foundations or programs for direct giving. For instance, in 2006 American Express awarded $1.3 million U.S. in grants through its Performing Arts Fund to 12 institutions in 12 different cities across the United States (American Express Performing Arts Fund 2006). In most cases, these donor companies have a definitive focus to their philanthropic activities. Other businesses, however, might have more of a cause-related marketing perspective and thus might be open to new ideas in advancing these causes while also reaching target markets. In many cases, both approaches are available to the nonprofit, in that the philanthropic arm of the corporation might be separate from the marketing arm, or the two branches might simply have different objectives. Ultimately, connecting with your local business environment is a major step in building a thriving donor base.

Creating the Budget

When formulating a budget for your project or program, you must be as specific and detailed as possible. No detail is too small, particularly when applying for funding. The excerpted form in figure 7.1 is based on multiple grants seen in the cultural sector and serves as an example of how granting organizations might expect a project budget proposal to be put forth.

Applicants must also expect to submit a project description that narrates an overall summary of the project and outlines the expected effects on the potential target audience and the results desired. The description should fully explain the project as well as its importance to the community. What are the benefits? Who is the target audience? Why? How does the project differentiate itself from the others competing for limited dollars? What makes it special? These are all aspects to address when constructing the project summary. Before embarking on project budgeting, it is important to have a clear understanding of what goals are in place and what resources are needed to obtain them.

In most formats, the project description is followed by the income and expense sections, with categorical breakdowns for each integrated into the budget. In the sample grant form in figure 7.1, probably the most important facet of the income section to understand is the differentiation between cash and in-kind donations.

In-kind donations are goods, services, or other commodities that are contributed to the organization and can be assigned a fair market value. There are many examples of these donations; essentially, they cover anything and everything beyond cash—materials, volunteers, equipment, and so on. The grant application in figure 7.1 is asking the applicant organization to account for both the cash match and the full in-kind match.

Any income source listed within the in-kind section must also be detailed within the expense section, or there is a risk of misstating the project's actual financial condition. Nonprofits must remember that even while a gift of materials does not cost the organization money, it is still a gift that must be acknowledged in financial records and is an expense that must be noted. The income and expense will balance each other out, but recording the transaction offers a more precise characterization of the organization's revenue spread and expense breakdown for the program or project.

For example, if an organization receives paper valued at $100 U.S. that fully covers its paper needs for the proposed program, it should not only recognize the $100 U.S. as an in-kind gift in the income section but also note a $100 U.S. expense for paper. The paper is being consumed for the project and has a value of $100 U.S. that would have been spent had the in-kind gift not been received. Ultimately, the gift and expense cancel each other, and a true economic picture emerges of both the income and the expenses associated with the project. In some cases, the expense outweighs the value of the in-kind gift. This is normal and should be portrayed honestly on the project

INCOME	
1. Amount requested:	$
2. Total match for this project (be as specific as possible).	
Cash (refers to the cash donations, grants, and revenues that are expected or received for this project)	Amount
Total cash a. $	
In-kind: Donated space, supplies, volunteer services (these lines must also be listed as direct costs under *Expenses* below; identify sources).	
Total donations b. $	
Total match for this project (2a + 2b) $	
Total Income (1 + 2a + 2b) $	

EXPENSES				
1. Direct costs: Salaries and wages				
Title and/or type of personnel	# of personnel	Annual or average salary range	% of time devoted to the project	Amount
Total salaries and wages a. $				
Total fringe benefits b. $				
Total salaries, wages, and fringe benefits (a + b) $				

2. Direct costs: Travel (include subsistence)			
# of travelers	To	From	Amount
Total travel $			

3. Direct costs: Other expenses (include consultant and artist fees, contractual services, telephone, copying, postage, supplies, materials, publication, distribution, transportation other than of personnel, equipment or space rental, and other project-specific costs.

Total other expenses $	
Total project costs (1 + 2 + 3) $	

TOTAL INCOME _____ = **TOTAL PROJECT COSTS** _____

Figure 7.1 A sample project budget form for grant application.

budget. You may, for instance, receive $100 U.S. in paper but end up needing to purchase $100 U.S. more. In this scenario, a $100 U.S. in-kind gift of paper is noted under income and a $200 expense for paper is entered under expenses with a budget note that $100 was an in-kind donation. These entries may sound confusing; however, the organization is presenting as explicitly as possible the income received as well as the expenses involved in the project. Herding cats it is not, but sometimes it might feel that way to those constructing the project budgets.

The expenses section is important as much for what it contains as for what it does not contain. There are two basic costs for a project budget: direct and indirect. Direct costs relate directly to a project activity and include expenses such as salaries, transportation, materials, and so on. Indirect costs do not directly relate to the actual project activity but instead are associated with the administration or management of the organization. These costs are often called *overhead costs* and are not always allowed by funders. Examples might include the cost of a copy machine or utility bills. In cases where indirect costs are allowed, an indirect cost rate and indirect cost base is obtained from the finance director of the organization and applied to the grant.

Also notable is the allowance for fringe benefits that is included in the project budget proposal. This rate varies widely across organizational types and is accessible from the finance director or accountant. It covers expenses such as social security, state unemployment insurance, workers' compensation, and insurance. Once it is determined who is involved with the project and what percentage of their time will be directed toward it, the rate is applied to the final salary amount.

Finally, the expense section includes other types of direct costs, such as transportation or any additional expenses that directly relate to the project. The hope is to balance total income and total costs, thereby illustrating not only the need for the grant for fulfilling project goals but also the organization's financial diligence and awareness.

A Broader Lens—Building a Financial Management Toolbox

Before we move forward, take some time to examine table 7.1, which contains financial data for a fictional performing arts organization. Given this information, what can you conclude about the organization's fiscal status? How can the data be utilized in your analysis? Are some of the data categories more valuable than others to your inquiry? What recommendations might you put forth? What other information should you seek to further explain the organization's financial situation?

Even seemingly simple chores, such as office tasks, must be taken into financial consideration.

© Photodisc

Table 7.1

	Current ratio	Earned to unearned income split	Total assets to total liabilities	Revenue	Expenses	Expenses breakdown
1999	.95	40%–60%	1.5	$8,337,470	$7,679,951	Programming: 82%, Administrative: 12%, Fund-raising: 6%
2000	1.45	45%–55%	2.5	$10,276,771	$8,587,314	Programming: 85%, Administrative: 10%, Fund-raising: 5%
2001	1.99	50%–50%	3.0	$9,491,694	$9,392,584	Programming: 87%, Administrative: 9%, Fund-raising: 4%
2002	2.42	52%–48%	6.0	$10,838,145	$9,245,621	Programming: 85%, Administrative: 12%, Fund-raising: 3%
2003	2.01	33%–67%	5.0	$11,017,186	$10,988,036	Programming: 75%, Administrative: 17%, Fund-raising: 8%
2004	1.56	35%–65%	4.0	$10,264,125	$11,657,365	Programming: 68%, Administrative: 25%, Fund-raising: 7%
2005	1.24	28%–72%	2.1	$9,121,147	$10,798,689	Programming: 65%, Administrative: 32%, Fund-raising: 3%

Why should you seek out this additional information, and where might you look for it? How might the financial information that is presented in table 7.1 influence potential donors? Should this information be freely accessible? What are the potential drawbacks or benefits to such access? What are the implications for the organization? How does such information affect or reflect programming decisions? All of these questions, addressed in the discussion to come, affect the future financial behaviors of nonprofits across the cultural sector.

At this point, you are not expected to fully understand or interpret the financial data seen in table 7.1; the data are presented to set the stage for what is to come. All of the information offered is easily compiled from organizational 990s and is often used by potential donors and grantors to gain insight into an organization's financial status. Indeed, as this information becomes more readily available to public inspection, it is critical that nonprofits place significant emphasis on understanding their financial situation and how this situation is perceived by others. Moreover, it is vital that the information presented in financial documents such as the 990 is as comprehensive and representative as possible. As recently illustrated by the National Overhead Cost Study (NOCS), which was conducted from 1999 to 2004 by researchers from the Urban Institute and from Indiana University, nonprofits have been somewhat ineffective or even disingenuous when tracking costs such as fund-raising or administrative overhead in their pursuit of high programming expense allocation percentages (National Overhead Cost Study 2004b, 2004c).

Economic Analytical Tools and Concepts

All of the financial information that was presented in the previous section can be used to gain insight into the financial status of an organization. The different pieces of information are valuable tools for

the financial analysis and the responsible financial management of nonprofit organizations. First, we will look closely at the earned-to-unearned income split, a critical and often undervalued indicator, before moving on to expense breakdowns and ratio analyses. Finally, we will pull the financial data together when considering the utility of employing broad trend analyses for understanding overall financial management and programmatic effectiveness.

The Money Mix—Earned and Unearned Income

Earned income is revenue that the organization brings in through program activities, concession sales, merchandise sales, and other income generators directly related to the goods or services of the nonprofit. Unearned income is revenue that the organization brings in through donations, investments, endowments, or other sources in which program services and activities are not directly involved. In some cases, organizations include investment income as a category separate from earned and unearned income in an attempt at greater precision. Nevertheless, the basis remains the same, at least in general terms. A ticket sold falls under earned income and a contribution solicited goes under unearned income in the parlance of financial management.

Memberships can cross both categories. In this chapter they will be viewed as unearned income when members receive a tax deduction for the amount given that exceeds goods received (in which complimentary admission to programs is not included); they will be viewed as earned income when membership and admission are intertwined. This ambiguity relates directly to organizational discipline, as program activities and ticket policies necessarily differ by cultural form. Also, some ambiguity is inherently embedded in the unearned-to-earned income dichotomy simply because many categories overlap. Nevertheless, a good illustration of an earned-income membership line item is that of an aquarium membership package that includes admission to the venue and should accordingly be considered as part of earned income. An example of an unearned-income membership can be seen in the donor clubs of a symphony, in which membership has its benefits but does not include complimentary admission to season offerings as part of its perks. Rather, the social or logistical elements of the membership are the primary selling point.

As a result, the earned-to-unearned income split becomes an important indicator of not only organizational financial stability but also organizational priorities, strategies, and effectiveness. For instance, while there are no universally accepted benchmarks within these categories applicable across the nonprofit sphere, a 2002 study funded by the Pew Charitable Trust revealed that in fiscal year 1998 arts and cultural organizations averaged an earned-to-unearned income split of 54% to 46% (Cohen, Filicko, and Wyszomirski 2002). Put simply, an organization with this split and an annual budget of $1 million U.S. would see $540,000 U.S. in earned income and $460,000 U.S. in unearned income over a fiscal year. The same research showed that performing arts organizations average 59% to 41% earned-to-unearned income, while museums and other visual arts organizations average 49% to 51% (Cohen, Filicko, and Wyszomirski 2002). While not conclusive or longitudinal enough to extrapolate definitive conclusions, the splits are illustrative and likely are a realistic economic indicator for nonprofits. At a minimum, they provide logical points of comparison though additional factors such as the nature of the discipline or mission involved inherently have major impact on the data and must be taken into consideration in any financial analysis. For instance, one would not expect a theater company in which earned and unearned income are pursued relatively equally to have a comparable split with an arts education organization whose programming is largely offered free to the community. The nature of the mission has a direct impact on the split seen.

So, what do these splits mean for programming and program budgeting? For instance, what about the organizations that consistently fall woefully short of the general benchmarks? Or, for that matter, what about those organizations that steadily exceed the benchmarks? What are the factors involved? How is organizational programming affected? How do we know? Why do we care? The following example allows us to consider some of these questions.

A recent newspaper story on a midsized regional symphony orchestra made reference to an organizational earned-to-unearned income split of 30% to 70% for the current fiscal year and hinted that this split was part of a longstanding trend. Following the appearance of this news piece,

an organizational official agreed to an interview as well as to provide financial documentation with the understanding that the organization and interviewee would remain anonymous, a condition immediately agreed to and honored herein. Questions posed to the orchestra in the summer of 2006 revealed that the split was not only accurate but also reflective of at least the past 3 fiscal years. The orchestra was showing signs of moving even more toward a reliance on unearned income. Indeed, a 20% to 80% split was forecasted for the upcoming year, largely due to leveling ticket sales accompanied by increasing expenses. This plateau in ticket sales was not simply the result of program stagnation, as attempts were made to both expand and narrow offerings. There seems to be an overall leveling that cannot be surmounted. Indeed, the programming changes have in large part precluded what could have been a substantial decline.

Yet, ticket revenue is not a synonym for earned income but is only one aspect of earned income, so the next logical step for an organization in this position is to determine what percentage of earned income is made up of ticket sales and what percentage comes from other sources such as sold services (in which the organization is hired out) or program advertisements. A look at years past for the orchestra indicates that these latter aspects generally made up 8% to 10% of organizational earned income. Thus, during those years, ticket sales accounted for only 20% to 22% of overall revenue. But do these numbers represent a problem? And if they do, is this problem organizational or programmatic or both? What if the split is reversed? Is this latter situation any better on an organizational or a programmatic level?

In short, the answer to the first question is that it depends, but these numbers are likely problematic for the organization, particularly over the

Planners must take into account the type of music that an audience is accustomed to and wants to hear.

Photo by Steve Smith, PhotOregon, courtesy of Raychel Kolen, Eugene Symphony Association

long run. However, it is not our intent here to establish a broad set of earned-to-unearned income benchmarks that are applicable across the cultural sector. Each discipline has specific characteristics that make such generalities somewhat specious. For instance, comparing an orchestra with a ballet of the same size generally does not allow for substantive conclusions, particularly if the dance company has an academy through which it draws earned income. Even if the dance organization is running a split that is exactly opposite that of the orchestra, we should not automatically assume that it is more economically viable or financially responsible. It is simply utilizing a business model that differs from that which the symphony uses, largely because of discipline parameters, and is subject to somewhat different economic factors.

Thus, comparison is more complicated than simple numerical extrapolations. While it is helpful to have sector benchmarks for performing arts organizations, organizations engaged in such financial analysis must look within their discipline for points of comparison. For instance, the orchestra should examine its peers, both financially and regionally, to see how it compares. Moreover, it should not assume that a similar organization running a split that heavily emphasizes earned income is better off financially, as running such a split potentially brings about its own set

of problems. Such an organization might be constrained programmatically, in that when earned income is the dominant revenue stream, any change can upset that balance. For instance, moving away from seasons loaded with warhorses such as Beethoven and Mahler toward seasons featuring more contemporary or obscure fare might have substantial repercussions on the orchestra's finances if the change alienates some in the audience.

Whatever the case, and surely this discussion could go on for many more pages, it is logical to conclude that relying too heavily on any source of income, whether earned or unearned, places cultural organizations in general at financial risk: Any shift in macro- or microeconomic factors, however slight, can significantly affect them. Nonprofit organizations are particularly susceptible to economic fluctuations in that they are hit twice, so to speak, whereas for-profit organizations are more often hit only once.

In an economic downturn, the entertainment industry, of which nonprofit cultural institutions are an integral part, often sees attendance weaken as discretionary income declines. For outlets such as movie theaters or music stores, an economic downturn means a loss of sales. For nonprofit organizations, this downturn means a loss of sales and a possible decline in contributed dollars as well. As a result, the nonprofit organization's two revenue streams are likely to fall at the same time, particularly when the donor base is largely made up of ticket holders. Thus, paying particular attention to both internal and external economic indicators is critical to the success of the nonprofit organization.

Expense Breakdowns

A primary indicator that has gained attention as organizational 990s have become more available is the expense breakdown, in which programming, administrative, and fund-raising costs are calculated as a percentage of overall expenses. Funders have long made use of this breakdown when making their decisions, but never before has this information been so readily within the reach of the entire donor base of an organization. As a result, the expense breakdown has taken on new significance, as potential donors sometimes use it as a major factor in their funding decisions.

New benchmarks are emerging to assist the donor in the decision-making process, though the guiding rationale behind these benchmarks is not always apparent. For instance, the Better Business Bureau's (BBB) Wise Giving Alliance, a merger of the National Charities Information Bureau and the Council of Better Business Bureau's Foundation and Philanthropic Advisory Service, offers the following recommendations in the Finances section of its Standards for Charity Accountability (Better Business Bureau Wise Giving Alliance 2003):

> This section of the standards seeks to ensure that the charity spends its funds honestly, prudently and in accordance with statements made in fund raising appeals. To meet these standards, the charitable organization shall:
>
> - Spend at least 65% of its total expenses on program activities.
> - Spend no more than 35% of related contributions on fund raising. Related contributions include donations, legacies, and other gifts received as a result of fund raising efforts.
>
> From the Council of Better Business Bureau, Inc., 2003.
> Available: www.give.org/standards/newcbbbstds.asp

Note that the administrative section is excluded from the BBB's benchmarking recommendations and is presumably contained within the two categorical benchmarks in some capacity. Most standards promoting the 65% to 35% breakdown appear to consolidate the administrative and fund-raising numbers (National Overhead Cost Study 2004c). However, in the Wise Giving Alliance standards the administration category reemerges later when the BBB recommends that a full expense breakdown be provided on organizational financial statements.

Other attempts at benchmarking not only have different standards but also break out the administrative category, just as is seen in the 990. For instance, some mention 75% to 80% as the target for organizational programmatic spending (Ruppel 2002), while others go lower with a 70%

threshold (Ruegg and Venkatrathnam 2003). Some seek to further differentiate the breakdown through an organizational typology lens. For instance, the National Overhead Cost Study (2004c) divided the nonprofit sector into five categories:

- Human services
- Arts, culture, and humanities
- Education
- Health
- Environment and animals

Interestingly, of these categories, the arts, culture, and humanities subsector spends the least on programming, which accounts for 72% of organizational expenses (National Overhead Cost Study 2004c). However, even when using these five categories to narrow the nonprofit arena, the study cannot detail on a more minute level how programmatic expenses are broken down across disciplines, much less across the general nonprofit cultural sector.

Both academic research and qualitative observation make it clear that, regardless of category, there is the potential for nonprofit organizations to overemphasize programmatic spending in their expense breakdowns, as donors often equate resource allocation with organizational effectiveness and financial efficiency. There are several problems that emerge from this tendency. First, the expense breakdown cannot be viewed without a critical eye. The expenditure of funds does not equal programmatic effectiveness. Second, this emphasis, combined with somewhat nebulous reporting guidelines, can lead organizations to understate administrative and fund-raising numbers and inflate programming numbers, thereby providing inaccurate, and sometimes misleading, numbers. This is a troubling possibility that must be addressed through more consistent guidelines that allow for broader comparability of organizations.

Expense breakdowns cannot be viewed in isolation. An expense breakdown for a given year in and of itself tells very little about the organization's overall financial health or programmatic spending strategies. For instance, a spike in administration costs could simply be the result of staff turnover, while a decline in programming expenditures might stem from artistic or logistical retooling. There are many reasons explaining the expense breakdown of a particular year, and if you are inside the organization, you should be easily able to do so. But for those external to the organization, such information is not as apparent. Thus it is critical that a longitudinal analysis in which multiple years are covered be undertaken and the organization compared to others within a peer group. Identifying peers for comparison might involve choosing like-sized organizations across a particular region and discipline or using a tool such as the Charity Navigator Web site (Charity Navigator 2007), which provides a wide range of financial analysis data. Regardless of the method utilized, this comparison is vital to understanding an organization's financial status across a wide range of indicators.

Finally, contextual information regarding program efficacy and audience response is of substantial importance, as is ratio analysis, particularly in terms of fund-raising effectiveness. Ultimately, the expense breakdowns are important but not the primary economic analysis tool for nonprofits, even when looked at longitudinally through a peer analysis. The expense breakdown is simply one aspect of a larger process.

Ratio Analysis

Using specific ratio analysis is a critical aspect of arts financial management as a whole but will be highlighted somewhat briefly here due to the primary emphasis on programming. Granted, all financial management issues affect programming at some level, but some ratios are more important to understanding not only the financial state of a cultural organization but also its programming effectiveness beyond a qualitative basis. Expense breakdowns have already been discussed in terms of how they represent organizational spending across particular categories; it is also important to understand other types of quantitative analytical tools, particularly the current ratio and fund-raising efficiency.

Current Ratio

The current ratio is found by dividing current assets by current liabilities. It gauges the ability of an organization to pay its debts over the course of a year. A current asset is an asset that can be turned into cash or consumed within the year, and a current liability is a liability that can be expected to be paid within the year. In short, the current ratio is a basic liquidity measurement.

When measuring this ratio from a 990, you can use lines 45 through 53 (cash, savings, accounts receivable, pledges receivable minus doubtful allowance, and so on) as current assets, while lines 60 through 63 (accounts payable, grants payable, deferred revenue, and so on) might be used as current liabilities. This is most assuredly not to say that these totals will give an exact representation of the ratio, but they will provide a substantive glimpse for the outsider analyzing the organization. Also take note that the IRS is considering changes to the 990 form that will slightly affect the numbering scheme detailed throughout the chapter. Unlike the expense breakdowns discussed earlier, for which there is a lack of a definitive expense threshold across sectors, the current ratio should be a minimum of 2:1. In other words, current assets should be twice as great as current liabilities. This is a standard benchmark across multiple industries and should be adhered to where possible, though again, there can be variations across sectors that should be taken into account.

As a general rule of thumb, an organization below this threshold faces potential liquidity problems and thus potential programmatic problems, as cuts or changes to programming are likely. Ultimately, ratios that decline over time are significant red flags for an organization. Recall the data introduced at the beginning of this section in table 7.1 for the fictional performing arts organization. Figure 7.2 illustrates two trends that were determined from these data, both of which are fairly clear. From 1999 to 2002, the current ratio was on an upward trend. Thus, even though this ratio was below the 2:1 threshold until 2001, there was a definite move upward and thus a greater basis of financial stability.

The key for the organization is to understand the ratio trend. Is the ratio on the upward track because the organization is generating new revenue streams through programming or because the organization has substantially reduced expenses, thus allowing for an increase in current assets? Perhaps both of these reasons are in play. The organization must know what's going on behind the number. Ultimately, the interpretation of the number is more important than the number itself. Understanding the movements of the ratio, and thus revenues and expenses, over time and in comparison to peer organizations brings forth holistic and strategic insight in which financial interpretation can influence programmatic and administrative decisions.

Continuing the analysis, we see that the ratio peaks in 2002 at 2.42 and, instead of leveling, begins a new downward trend that lasts through 2005. At this point the organization is on the verge of experiencing liquidity problems, as a downward trend not only reflects difficulties in the ratio of assets to liabilities but also speaks of potential problems with cash flow. As liabilities come due and there are fewer current assets available to pay them, the organization will need to undertake various corrective measures like cutting costs—including programming—or securing alternative sources of income such as lines of credit. Whatever the course of action, the ratio must be stabilized and reversed, particularly since it is below the minimum threshold and moving even lower.

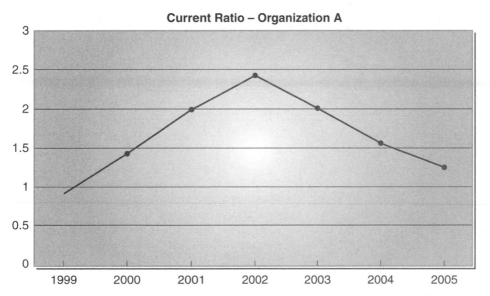

Figure 7.2 A longitudinal current ratio.

Clearly, such a situation will affect all levels of the organization, particularly programming, as revenues and expenses come under intense scrutiny.

A very high current ratio is not necessarily a positive sign, though there is no specific maximum threshold for the current ratio. Rather, the interpretation is more subjective and is based largely on logic and context. For instance, an organization with a 20:1 current ratio is in very good financial shape to pay its bills because of its highly liquid state, but this high liquidity poses a potential problem. It is possible for an organization to be too liquid. Yes, in most cases an organization's current ratio should be greater than 2:1 as a matter of responsible fiscal management and stability, but a very high current ratio should force an organization to question its asset management. The organization with a 20:1 ratio might be better served by moving some of its current assets into longer term investments or into programming. Again, though, a broader time element and peer comparison will be helpful in identifying not only economic patterns that can place data in context but also organizational priorities and management tendencies.

Fund-Raising Efficiency

The next aspect of a ratio analysis, fund-raising efficiency, is less formalized in that, again, definitive sectoral thresholds are not in place. However, this is not to say that certain expectations are not ingrained. The ratio itself is an efficiency measurement by which we might quantitatively gauge the fund-raising efforts of an organization. Once we have this measurement, we might then apply qualitative elements to explain the results.

For instance, quantitatively a ratio might reflect poorly on an organization, yet with further investigation, we may discover that the organization is in the midst of a major fund-raising campaign in which developing long-term giving is the goal. Thus this campaign is leading to higher fund-raising costs for the year studied. Moreover, ratios often reflect the type of fund-raising employed. An organization that relies solely on grant writing will most likely have a better efficiency level than one that combines grant writing with other fund-raising activities. Generally speaking, writing grants does not cost a great deal of money. Remember that efficiency is not the same thing as the amount of funds raised. An organization may be demonstrating a good fund-raising efficiency but still not be raising enough money to survive. Again, this is where longitudinal analysis and contextual information are both critical and must be used in tandem rather than in isolation.

Calculating fund-raising efficiency is rather simple. It can be approached from two directions, both of which provide interesting insights. This calculation is the focus of the next section.

Calculating Fund-Raising Efficiency

Fund-Raising Costs/Total Contributions or Total Contributions/Fund-Raising Costs

These two mathematical formulas lead to two different ways of approaching fund-raising efficiency. The first method provides us with a cents-on-the-dollar approach. For instance, an organization spending $25,000 U.S. on fund-raising that brings in $750,000 U.S. sees the following: $25,000/$750,000 = 0.03. The organization is spending 3 cents on fund-raising for every 1 dollar it brings in. The second approach reverses the numbers: $750,000/$25,000 = $30. It shows that for every $1 U.S. the organization spends on fund-raising, it brings in $30 U.S.

The calculations say the same thing mathematically, but sometimes constituents understand or can relate to a particular format or both formats together more easily. In either case, the ratios are seemingly very good, with the organization seeing a high return on its fund-raising dollars. As a result, more funds are available for programming and program expansion. The ratio is a valuable method of illustrating to a potential funding source how much of the donation is to be spent on programs, and therefore a good ratio might be highlighted in grant applications or project proposals.

There is no definitive benchmark to apply to fund-raising efficiency, but the goal is to have as low a number as possible from a cents-on-the-dollar perspective while also making sure you are hitting your fund-raising targets. This is where contextual information is once again important.

A low fund-raising efficiency ratio is of little value if goals are missed and revenue is negatively affected. Moreover, as mentioned in the section on expense breakdowns, there is a question of expense allocation that must be considered. Are all fund-raising expenses truly accounted for in the efficiency ratio? In most cases the answer is unclear, and so it is important to supplement the ratio—indeed, all ratios—with other elements of the financial analysis toolbox.

Trend Analysis

Trend analysis is a vital aspect of assessing the financial status of an organization. In this section, we will look at trend analysis in the larger organizational perspective as well as examine how this analytical tool is critical to departmental and programming budgeting. Indeed, trend analysis is an integral component of budgeting and economic planning across an organization—though it is not always utilized or is sometimes simply ignored. Moreover, the analysis allows us to move beyond basic glimpses into revenue and expenses into broader studies of economic patterns and indicators.

In effect, the purpose of trend analysis in general is to avoid viewing financial data in isolation and to instead constantly compare these data to data from previous years in an effort to gauge organizational and programmatic fiscal effectiveness. Like the other financial analysis tools discussed throughout the chapter, the trend analysis is a quantitative measurement device that cannot be used exclusively. It should be used as part of the toolbox and should be combined with qualitative feedback gained from programmatic implementation. Within the cultural sector, financial analysis tools are critical to responsible management but are also part of a larger skill set and administrative approach.

Whether applied on an organizational, departmental, or programmatic level, trend analysis is essential to effective planning and budgeting. Consider the following scenario: A marketing and development department of a midsized performing arts organization is asked by the executive director to submit its budget for the following year. The department faces a variety of strategies.

One, it can simply follow an incremental approach and ask for a percentage increase based on basic economic conditions or accepted organizational culture. Two, it can follow the zero-based budgeting process, in which all department initiatives are put in competition with one another and revenue is projected from zero across all line items. Finally, it can employ a combination of these two approaches, in which conducting a trend analysis allows the department to better understand its efficacy over time in expending marketing and fund-raising dollars as well as to identify any potential patterns in ticket purchases, audience satisfaction, or donor tendencies. Ultimately, this analysis and interpretation of data is critical for the department in determining not only its budget request but also its justification for expense and revenue projections. Consider tables 7.2 and 7.3, which depict financial data for a nonprofit performing arts organization named *Theater Hypothetical*.

The trend analysis provides a detailed glimpse into the organizational finances over a particular length of time. It also allows us to identify any emerging trends as well as any problem areas that might be of concern. For instance, a quick look at the trend analysis for Theater Hypothetical establishes a few key items. The earned-to-unearned income split is flipped from the performing arts standard we saw earlier, but the split is very consistent across the 5 years. A peer analysis should be conducted to gauge how the theater compares with similar organizations. Nevertheless, the consistency does allow for the reasoned conclusion that the split is not so much of a concern for Theater Hypothetical. Still, further analysis of the numbers for the ticket sales reveals a significant programmatic opportunity to raise revenue and lower the historical dependence on donors.

This recognition is likely to take on added importance as we notice that within the section displaying unearned income, most line items are flattening or actually declining, a portent perhaps of future problems. Moreover, the Donor Clubs line item seems to have peaked in 2001 and 2002 and now shows signs of leveling at a much lower point, a situation that can be interpreted in a few ways. The simplest explanation is that donors are not satisfied with the benefits received in exchange for the dollar thresholds. A more complex possibility, backed up to a certain degree by the concomitant decline in ticket sales, is a potential disconnect from the audience that is as yet unrecognized or unresolved.

Table 7.2

		2000/01	2001/02	2002/03	2003/04	2004/05
Unearned Income	Grants	123,687	146,215	135,400	143,600	143,365
	Indiv. Contrib.	51,362	62,111	74,503	50,234	38,562
	Bus. Contrib.	50,231	47,541	42,352	38,400	19,023
	Donor Clubs	318,081	343,248	292,484	242,129	243,851
	Sponsors	187,000	234,521	248,649	261,220	262,011
	Special Events	83,892	74,009	82,689	62,154	47,154
	League Giving	186,000	187,000	200,000	190,000	180,000
	Totals	1,000,253	1,094,645	1,076,077	987,737	933,966
Earned Income	Sold Services	75,000	55,000	52,500	58,700	25,000
	Program Adv.	18,754	18,659	15,843	11,234	13,012
	Ticket Sales	625,873	687,268	712,413	656,206	629,711
	Merchandise	12,012	10,145	9,875	10,188	9,241
	Concessions	5,006	4,121	4,875	6,982	6,241
	Totals	736,645	775,193	795,506	734,140	683,205
Total Revenue		1,736,898	1,869,838	1,871,583	1,731,047	1,617,171

The "League Giving" line item is a reference to peripheral guild or league organizations that sometimes exist which act as separate organizations that fund-raise specifically for the nonprofit. Orchestra Leagues for instance are common.

Another trend that seems to be developing is that individual contributions, business contributions, and special events proceeds are declining. Business donations in particular are a concern, as this line item has declined steadily over the 5 years being measured. This fact is important for two reasons: (1) Budget projections must take these types of trends into account when determining revenue targets for the upcoming fiscal year, and (2) identifying consistent problem areas allows for strategic and targeted action.

Table 7.3 Earned to Unearned Income Splits

	Earned %	Unearned %	Ticket Sales as % of Total Revenue
00/01	42.4	57.6	36.0
01/02	41.0	59.0	37.0
02/03	42.0	58.0	38.4
03/04	42.4	57.6	38.3
04/05	41.7	58.3	39.3

Nonprofits often use a demographic approach to fund-raising. In this approach audience access is the primary selling point to entice corporations to contribute or act as sponsors. This is a strong strategy and one that is often helpful. However, it should not be a stand-alone tactic. Businesses also want to see two other aspects in play. The first is a willingness to expand the business model. Rather than asking a corporation for a sponsorship of season programming, the organization can develop a program specifically with that business in mind and build promotional events that benefit both the nonprofit and the for-profit organization. The second is strong financial management. It is often said that people give to winners, and in the nonprofit world, this is most assuredly the case. An organization that exhibits excellent money management builds confidence in the community that contributions will be managed responsibly and ethically. An organization that is constantly going to the street with requests for donations in the face of a shutdown builds a self-perpetuating cycle in which crisis management is the

operational norm. This culture is noticed by donors of all levels and may lead to substantial distrust.

It is critical that programming administrators and implementers view analysis trends with an analytical eye. In our theater example from table 7.2, ticket sales have been largely consistent but are exhibiting signs of weakness, particularly over the last 2 years. Marketing and programming must work together to understand the cause of this developing trend, especially in light of the declining unearned revenue base, and develop countermeasures. Again, this is why each revenue stream must be considered in combination with the other. Programming cannot live in isolation from marketing or fund-raising; the two must work together to maximize revenue as well as audience satisfaction. Too often, an organization introduces programs or productions without understanding how they fit into a larger strategic and financial plan. This is a situation that should be addressed on an organizational level as part of the nonprofit's basic corporate culture.

It is not that finances should drive programming; rather, the more factors that are considered when designing seasons and new programs, the better the chance of survival and success. And at the end of the day, isn't a successful and creatively active organization the goal we all strive to fulfill? A nonprofit does no one any good if it cannot stay in business or if it struggles to such a degree that its programming becomes ineffective or invisible.

People outside of the organization can also conduct a trend analysis by using the data from 990s. Using the lines detailed in table 7.4, anyone interested in a nonprofit organization can perform a broad trend analysis to gauge the organization's financial health from its own reported numbers.

Table 7.4

	Year	Year	% change
Total Contributions, Gifts, Grants (Line 1d or e)			
Program Service Revenue (Line 2)			
Total Revenue (Line 12)			
Total Expenses (Line 17)			
Net Assets or Fund Balances (Line 21)			
Program Services Expenses (Line 44b)			
Management and General Expenses (Line 44c)			
Fund-raising Expenses (Line 44d)			
Total Cash (Lines 45 and 46)			
Pledges Receivable (Line 48c)			
Grants Receivable (Line 49)			
Inventories (Line 52)			
Land, Buildings, and Equipment (Line 57c)			
Total Assets (Line 59)			
Total Liabilities (Line 66)			
Unrestricted Net Assets (Line 67)			
Temporarily Restricted Net Assets (Line 68)			
Permanently Restricted Net Assets (Line 69)			
Analysis of Income Producing Activities (Line 105)			

Throughout this chapter we've noted the potential inaccuracies sometimes contained in the 990, but just as with the other financial management tools discussed thus far, this method of analysis should be combined with other quantitative and qualitative data in order to develop a more cohesive financial picture of the organization. The longer the time period that you choose to analyze, the more accuracy you might claim in determining financial strengths and weaknesses. As a result, 5 years is the general recommendation, though the 2-year percentage analysis provides significant insight when you are seeking to understand the differences between two years' fiscal outcomes. Put simply, the 2-year analysis is a quick way of determining what went right or wrong on a short-term financial basis through a line-by-line examination while a longer analysis allows true trends to show themselves over time.

Summary

As demonstrated by the broad range of financial concepts presented here, organizational programming involves a wide array of economic tools and approaches, whether you are building project budgets or creating seasons. Understanding that programming is integrated into a cohesive and expansive financial management process that employs multiple economic tools is critical to the development of a cultural organization and its programmatic efforts over the long term. Too often programming is viewed only through budgetary lenses within a narrow time frame, with little consideration given to other economic data that might be used to better inform programmatic decisions on both artistic and strategic levels. Hopefully, the tools and approaches presented in this brief analysis of economic factors affecting programming will help organizations not only broaden their reach and strategic thinking but also embrace responsible financial management ideals across all organizational levels.

Program Marketing

Francois Colbert, MBA, MSc
HEC Montreal

This chapter looks at planning program marketing. It describes marketing and marketing for non-profit organizations, particularly cultural enterprises, and discusses competition, quality of customer service, brand management, and market positioning.

What Is Marketing?

The purpose of marketing is to optimize the interaction between a business and its clients and to maximize their mutual satisfaction. Marketing consists of four elements: the consumer's need, the satisfaction of that need, the connection between the business and the consumer, and the desire to achieve financial equilibrium (or to optimize profits, in the case of a for-profit organization).

Marketing is a tool that companies use to realize their mission. Program marketing must therefore reflect the needs set out in the organization's mission statement. When the marketing objectives are derived from the company's global objectives, the program marketing emerges from the company's global strategies.

There are two ways to look at marketing: in terms of satisfying market needs and in terms of achieving a corporate mission. In the first case, the company tries to determine consumers' needs and then offer the consumers exactly what they want, even if doing so means modifying its product or other business variables (even its mission, if necessary). Companies that operate this way are said to be *market oriented* and are profit-making operations. In the arts and leisure sectors, this type of market orientation exists in forms such as the profit-based companies that offer a strictly commercial product like Broadway shows and Hollywood films. Cultural enterprises that are product oriented, on the other hand—usually nonprofit organizations—take an artist's vision as their starting point and look for a consumer group that is interested in that vision. Companies in the leisure sector start from their mission statement and offer a product that corresponds to their objectives.

Marketing as it applies to nonprofit organizations, particularly cultural enterprises, can be defined as the art of making contact with market segments that are likely to be interested in the product. This process involves adapting the marketing variables—price, distribution, and promotion—in order to put the product in contact with a sufficient number of consumers, thereby achieving the objectives that were set based on the company's mission (Colbert et al. 2007).

We can use a model to demonstrate how a company markets a product. The two models shown in figure 8.1 illustrate the marketing process for a market-oriented company and for a product-oriented company.

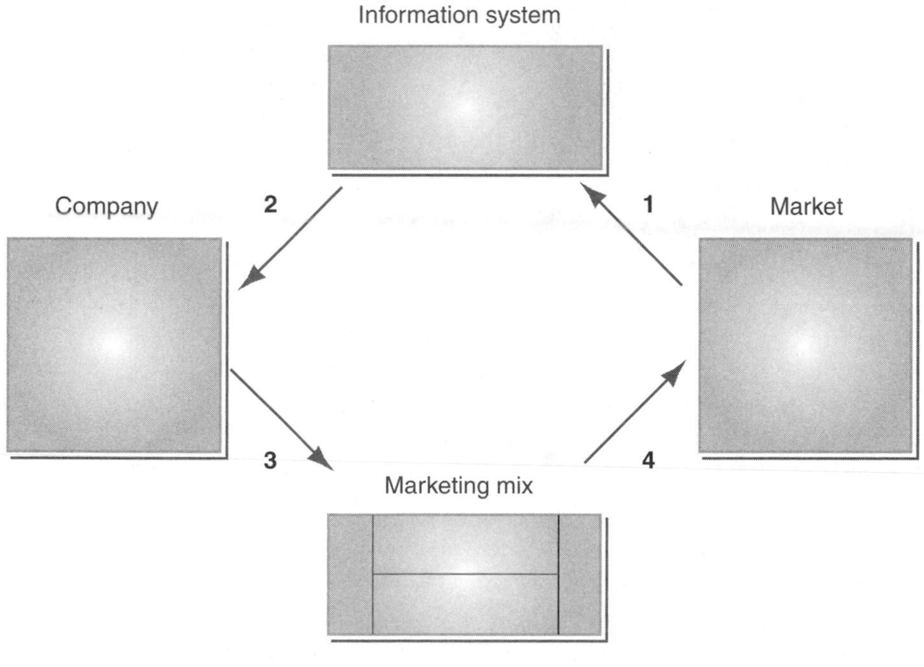

The traditional marketing process begins when the needs to be met are defined by the information system. The company then decides whether or not to broach the market in question based on the resources at its disposal.

Marketing for cultural enterprises and nonprofit leisure organizations, however, begins within the company itself and is based on a work proposed by an artist or on the mission of the organization. For artistic enterprises, the mission and the artist's vision may be one and the same, particularly if the company was created around the artist. For example, since many dance companies are founded by

Figure 8.1a   Traditional marketing.

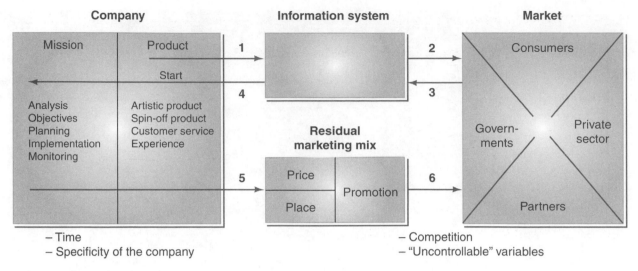

Figure 8.1*b* Cultural marketing.

choreographers, the mission of those companies is to perform the choreographer's works—moreover, the company is often identified by the choreographer's name. In contrast, multiproduct organizations (festivals, repertory theaters) have founders who establish their missions but are based on an artistic vision, not the creation of a single person.

Why Marketing?

As we saw in chapter 1, the leisure sector has expanded remarkably over the past 40 years, especially in the area of culture. This incredible market growth has resulted in an impressive supply of products and services: In the orchestral milieu alone, the American Symphony Orchestra League includes almost 1,000 ensembles, 200 of which are youth orchestras (Noteboom 2006). Consumers can choose from an incredibly vast selection. In large centers, it is impossible for one person to see or buy everything available, even with an unlimited budget and unlimited time. To succeed, therefore, companies must clearly identify the consumers likely to be interested in their product and devise a strategy to ensure they receive a share of consumers' disposable income. In our modern societies, cultural and product-based enterprises can no longer be content to simply *offer* their products; they must *sell* them. In other words, the companies must be sure they are understood and accepted by their potential clientele. They must work at developing their client base in order to ensure sufficient income—not only for the company but also, in the case of cultural enterprises, for the artists they represent.

The Market

Cultural enterprises (and nonprofit organizations in general) can target up to four different markets: end consumers, governments, sponsors and patrons, and partners (coproducers, distributors, or specialized media). A specific marketing plan must be crafted for each of the company's markets.

Each market usually consists of several segments. A market segment can be defined as consumer subgroups that share similar characteristics, express similar needs and desires, and respond to the same marketing strategies. Each segment requires an adjustment to one or more variables in the marketing mix. If it is not possible to adjust at least one variable, there are not two segments, but one.

Competitors and Competitive Advantage

In each market segment, there is at least one competitor vying for the same clientele. To counter the competition and attract consumers, companies should have something in their arsenal that is superior in the eyes of their clientele. In marketing terms, this superior element is called the

The unique niches within the cultural industry allow programmers to find a marketing edge because their programs can be so different from the other programs available that they don't have to work to set themselves apart.

Photo courtesy of Gaylene Carpenter

competitive edge. The competitive edge is a characteristic that is unique to a given company; it is something competitors don't have or can't get.

Certain enterprises, for example, have an advantage in terms of product manufacturing. A company may have a very low production cost that its competitors can't match because they don't have the same advantage. This low production cost allows the company to offer its product at the lowest price on the market. Some companies control the distribution market; others find such a credible spokesperson that they can trump anything the competition can come up with. Others offer a product that is clearly superior by virtue of its quality, unique nature, or prestige quotient. Still others are known for their peerless customer service. In a highly competitive world, it is crucial that a company set itself apart by offering consumers an indisputable reason to choose them over one of their competitors.

The cultural industry has an advantage that other sectors of the economy do not have. Since artists generally strive to set themselves apart from their peers by finding a unique creative niche, the cultural company's competitive edge is simply the product offered—the artist's work. For organizations that offer entire seasons (theaters and museums) or extended programs (festivals and community organizations), effective programming can constitute a competitive edge by offering the public artists or shows that are out of the ordinary. Companies that are unable, for any number of very good reasons, to distinguish themselves through their products (in the eyes of the consumer) must absolutely find an advantage in one of the other elements of the marketing mix.

Serving the Audience (Quality of Service)

Consumers have become extremely demanding about the service they receive. Once obtained, consumer loyalty cannot be taken for granted; companies have to actively retain their existing clients. In highly competitive markets, clients who receive poor service may go elsewhere to find what they are looking for. This is certainly the case for the leisure sector as well as for the cultural industry. Why should clients continue to subscribe to a theater whose directors aren't interested in giving them good service? The temptation is strong to switch to a competitor who offers an equivalent artistic product.

Poor customer service can ruin the quality of the artistic or leisure experience, decrease the buyer's satisfaction, and ultimately tarnish the company's brand image. The organizers of a festival (or any other organization) who neglect this aspect risk losing their clients the following year. The role of customer service is to maximize the client's experience with the company and to manage

the client's expectations of that experience. Good customer service can set a company apart from its competitors and enhance customer loyalty. It is much more expensive for a company to attract a new client than it is to retain a client the company already has.

An efficient company that is interested in its clients' well-being examines its moments of truth. These moments occur every time a client comes into contact with the company, perhaps by telephone, over the Internet, at the box office, at the cloakroom, or at the bar. The company analyzes these moments of truth and looks for ways to increase client satisfaction at each point. It tries to put itself in the consumers' shoes in order to understand consumer expectations. Remember that often the only contact clients have with a company is through their relationship with frontline employees: telephone operators, service representatives at the counter, box-office clerks, ushers, waiters, guides, and so on. It is often this contact that determines whether or not clients accept the company's offer—whether they buy again. The careful selection and training of frontline employees, including volunteers (chapter 4), is a luxury no company can afford to deny itself. At Northern Stage, a major British theater company, the communications department hires people for their attitude and willingness to converse with the clientele and not just for their ability to sell tickets (Raines and Gee 2006).

The company should pay similar attention to all its other markets. A poorly treated sponsor, for example, will be unimpressed and unlikely to continue offering its support. Obviously, however, the best customer service in the world cannot compensate for programming that is of no interest to the client. That is why the product is at the center of every marketing strategy.

Marketing Planning and Program Marketing Planning

Programming starts with a plan that is focused on the product. That plan, which determines all the other variables in the marketing mix, is also based on knowledge of the clientele and the company's target segments, the sales objectives and customer service objectives, a position statement, a contingency plan, and a formal procedure for evaluating results.

Purpose of the Marketing Plan and Programming Plan

Marketing planning requires the manager to answer a series of questions related to the components of the marketing model to ensure that the marketing plan has a solid foundation. The five questions are as follows:

1. Where are we and where are we going? (Analysis of the situation)
2. Where do we want to go? (Setting objectives)
3. What efforts are we prepared to make? (Human resources, financial resources, technical resources)
4. How do we plan to get there? (Marketing mix, strategic orientations)
5. How should we proceed? (Implementation, tactical choices)

The same questions have to be answered with respect to programming. A good program cannot be prepared if the objective is not clearly understood or if quality resources are insufficient.

These five questions are not answered linearly. On the contrary, it is virtually impossible to construct a marketing plan without going back and forth among all five questions. Marketing planning is first and foremost an iterative process that must constantly evolve in order to reflect changes in the environment and in competitors' reactions. It is not unusual for a cultural enterprise to revise its marketing plan throughout the year based on incoming results. Similarly, a long-term plan usually has to be revised on an annual basis. A long-term plan is not intended to keep the manager in a straitjacket until it ends; it must be revised periodically to take into consideration the company's results and to address any new elements that could not have been foreseen at the time the plan was drawn up.

The marketing plan is an extremely useful exercise that gives companies a clear idea of the direction they should take. It is also a process that forces managers to look at all facets of each of the five questions in a structured way.

Steps in the Process

A marketing plan involves several steps. It is an iterative process. Taking stock of the company's current situation and envisioning where the company will end up if nothing is changed are essential. It is based on the vision that a pertinent objective can be set. This exercise doesn't have to be exhaustive; it should be simple but enlightening. Expending excessive effort is not necessary to arrive at a clear idea.

Once we know where we are and where our current strategy will take us (unless we change that strategy), it's time to decide on a goal. Although the marketing objective is based on the company's mission and objectives, it must also take into account the company's financial, human, and technical resources (see chapters 4 and 7).

Once a marketing direction has been set based on the company's requirements (mission, objectives, and resources), the manager is ready to tackle the three major steps in the marketing plan: the positioning (or repositioning, as applicable), the addressing of other variables in the marketing mix, and the monitoring of activities.

Objectives

Companies define their objectives over the short, medium, and long terms. The definition of *term* varies depending on the organization. One company's short term may be 1 year, while another's may be 3 months. Similarly, *long term* might mean 10 years for one company and 5 for another. It is up to the manager to decide on a horizon that best suits the company's current situation.

It is essential that a company set measurable objectives—measurable in terms of quantity rather than quality. "Increase sales" is not an objective that can be easily measured at the end of the term. It will be easier to determine if the objective has been met if it is expressed as a figure: "Increase ticket sales by 20%." For more examples of measurable objectives, the reader can look at the Examples of Marketing Objectives sidebar that follows. This does not imply that companies shouldn't set qualitative objectives, however. It is useful to be able to qualify what the company wants to achieve. What we are trying to do here is stress the importance of the operational aspects of any marketing action. Once the global objective has been set, it can be broken down based on target markets or on the types of clientele the company is seeking to attract.

Examples of Marketing Objectives

- Increase our subscription sales by 10% over the next 2 years.
- Raise our subscriber retention rate from 60% to 75%.
- Double the number of tourists who visit our museum between May and September.
- Generate a minimum of $1 million U.S. at the box office for each new film on the market.
- Increase our audience rating (market share) by 50% over the next 3 years.
- Persuade 20 new bookstores to stock our new releases.
- Add one new territory to our distribution network every year for the next 5 years.
- Increase our brand awareness among the general public by 20% to 30% over the coming year.
- Find five new sponsors willing to commit $1,000 U.S. each.

Strategies and Tactics

A *strategy* originates in an overview of all the means to be used to achieve a final objective (e.g., to increase the number of active members to 300), while a *tactic* is a specific adjustment to an element of the strategy at a given point in time (e.g., to invite a well-known personality to be a spokesperson for the organization). A manager can devise and implement several tactics to help achieve the desired results of the company's strategy without changing that strategy in any way.

We may sometimes prefer to use the term *means* rather than *tactic*, as these two terms can often denote the same thing.

Strategies and tactics can be determined both for the company as a whole and for its marketing function in particular. All marketing strategies and tactics, however, are based on the company's overall strategy.

Positioning and Brand Management

Every company can be viewed as a brand, even if its brand is no more than its name. The artists it represents and the shows it offers enhance its brand in the mind of its clients, which assures its place on the market. This phenomenon is called *product* or *brand positioning*.

Positioning and Repositioning

Since the notion of positioning or repositioning is central to every marketing strategy, the marketing plan must be based on the firm's strategic vision. The term *positioning* can be defined as the place a product occupies in the consumer's mind as compared with products offered by the competition. Repositioning is any modification of the product placement following further analysis of the situation. Managers must reflect on the kind of product they are offering, the market segments they are targeting, and the place their product (when compared with the products offered by their competitors) occupies in the minds of the consumers in those segments.

Positioning forces the manager to think strategically: to look at the product, the market, and the competition as three interrelated and interdependent elements. This *analysis* raises several questions: Where are we in the market? How is the market evolving? How big is it? If we continue applying the same strategy, where will we end up in the market? How are we perceived in comparison with our competitors? What are our company's strengths? Is there something we do better than our competitors do? In other words, do we have a competitive edge? Do we have a positive public image? Are our intentions clearly understood? If we had to invent a slogan that would define us immediately in the eyes of our clientele, what would it be?

The positioning exercise should be done for each of the company's target markets. In fact, the positioning exercise is just as crucial for the company's sponsors, governments, and various partners as it is for the clients.

Remember that consumers base their judgments on their perceptions—regardless of whether those perceptions are valid. That is why it is so important to put yourself in the client's shoes. What might seem clear to you in terms of positioning or public message may be perceived quite differently by the people you are trying to convince. The following example illustrates this concept of perception.

Example of Perception

The Powerhouse Museum in Sydney, Australia, surveyed the general public to find out how people perceive museums. When asked to identify the characteristics of an ideal leisure activity, respondents gave the following answers: a relaxed atmosphere, entertaining, a good place to take the family and friends, friendly, fun, an exciting place to be, great value for money, plenty of room to move. In their minds, museums did not share these attributes. They described museums as educational, places of discovery, intellectual experiences, challenging, thought provoking, absorbing, fascinating, innovative, places where you can touch the past—even though the museum directors were convinced that their institutions were fun, exciting, good places to take the family, and offering great value for money. The survey results revealed a significant difference between what museums thought they were offering and what potential consumers thought the museums offered. Since the consumers' perception of museums didn't correspond to their description of an ideal leisure activity, they tended to look elsewhere for the perfect leisure experience (Scott 2000).

What do people think about your organization?

Segment Positioning

Companies may wish to adapt their strategy to the needs of a single market segment. This type of strategy, called a *concentrated marketing strategy*, is used primarily by small organizations whose limited resources and very specific mission make it advantageous for them to target a particular segment. In certain cases—a troupe specializing in theater for young audiences, for example—positioning is done for segments that are defined by sociodemographic variables. In other cases, positioning is based on geographical considerations. A municipal parks and recreation department, for example, must consider the citizens of its specific municipality. In most cases, however, organizations position themselves according to segments that are based on what consumers want; we call this strategy benefit segmentation.

In segment positioning you must answer questions like this based on sociodemographic variables. Positioning a product according to the benefits it offers and the segments it targets allows managers to determine which products are their main competitors as well as which products are their potential allies.

Every positioning strategy is the result of careful analysis of the attributes and benefits sought by consumers. Without this analysis, positioning is just a theoretical exercise that does little to support the company's strategies. It is therefore important to understand exactly the criteria on which consumers are basing their choices and to remember that clients are not buying the price (even though the price is a significant variable) but the experience offered by the company. Market studies are useful but not indispensable at this point; the manager's experience and thorough analysis of the market can provide equally sound results.

Competitive Positioning

Managers who have a clear understanding of the segments targeted by their product are better able to position that product. In many cases, however, different products can appeal to the same segments and provide the same benefits. This is where competitive positioning, or product differentiation, comes into play. In such cases, managers must offer their clientele an additional benefit to distinguish their product from that of their competitors. The image management of certain personalities in show business is an interesting example of this phenomenon, which involves creating an event that will set one star apart from all the others. By seeking to differentiate themselves, these personalities are looking for a competitive edge, something that potential clients will not be able to do without.

During the life of a company, it will inevitably happen that a product will have to be modified; sometimes even the company mission must be changed. This situation, which arises when consumer tastes and preferences shift or new competitors arrive, requires repositioning.

Branding

Branding is an important facet of the marketing strategies of most commercial enterprises. Clients in different markets recognize a product by its brand and use brands to differentiate products. A

brand can be a name, symbol, logo, or drawing: The Disney Mickey Mouse ears, for example, constitute a brand that is recognized around the world.

All companies have a brand name, even if it is just the name of their business. The name of a well-known company evokes images in the minds of clients (consumers, donors, and so on)—images that they associate with a particular product. Even people who have never been to La Scala in Milan or the Museum of Modern Art (MoMA) in New York have a pretty good idea of what they would find there.

The purpose of the brand is to identify the products of one company and differentiate them from those of another or, simply, to distinguish one company from its competitors. The brand presents a condensed version of the benefits the company offers; it can represent a response to consumer expectations. For example, when Pavarotti fans buy one of his CDs, they know exactly what to expect. Some people also (consciously or otherwise) adopt a brand—of clothing, for instance—as a sign of belonging to a specific group.

There are five characteristics associated with a brand: perceived quality, brand awareness, loyalty, association with salient elements, and association with identifiable tangible and intangible assets (Caldwell 2000):

• *Perceived quality*—The various markets and market segments have an idea of the quality of a brand even if they have never used or consumed the product. The definition of quality may differ according to the segment: A knowledgeable music lover and a person who is unfamiliar with classical music may use different criteria in their definition of quality. Or, similarly, the quality of a festival may be defined differently by people looking for an event with atmosphere compared with those who purchase a ticket simply because they want to hear the artist being featured. It is important to differentiate *quality* as defined by specialists (critics, other artists) from *quality* as defined by the general public.

• *Brand awareness*—The greater the percentage of the population that can identify a brand (with or without assistance), the stronger the brand. Promoting a well-known brand is often easier than proposing a new one.

• *Loyalty or satisfaction*—The number of repeat purchases or the rate of subscription renewals can measure this factor. The more loyalty consumers demonstrate toward a particular brand, the stronger the company.

• *Association with salient elements*—Markets may associate a brand with the quality of a museum's collections or the work of an artistic director.

• *Association with tangible and intangible assets*—The architectural features of the Sydney Opera House constitute an important element in the market's perception of its brand. This performing arts center is known around the world for the original design of its building; in fact, the Sydney Opera House serves as the logo for Australia's tourism department.

There is no doubt that the higher a brand scores in each of these areas, the more it is perceived as a strong, clear brand with a high market value. Remember that we are not talking about *objective* strength and worth but are talking about *perceived* strength and worth. Experts may judge a brand to be superior, but if consumers do not perceive that superiority, the brand cannot be considered strong. Similarly, clients can have a false impression of the characteristics of a brand because, as we mentioned earlier, marketing works with clients' perceptions, which do not necessarily reflect objective reality. When clients have the wrong impressions, it is up to the company to launch a promotional campaign to clarify the situation.

Program Marketing Planning

The elements described before form the basis for defining the marketing mix. Now that the presenter or event organizer has a good understanding of the market, he can decide on a particular program for each segment targeted; this means he first has to define its product, then the corresponding other three variables of the marketing mix: the price, the distribution, and the promotion variables. Let's talk about those variables.

Product

Marketing defines *product* as a set of benefits evoked by the consumer (Colbert et al. 2007). This definition forces us to look at the product from the client's point of view. When consumers buy a book or a CD, they obtain tangible merchandise; when they see a movie, a show, or an exhibition or participate in a municipal recreation activity, they obtain a service. But what they are really buying is not the product or service but the experience of consuming. This experience varies depending on what the consumer wants—wherein lies the interest in defining this experience as a benefit obtained by the consumer.

The importance of the client's point of view cannot be stressed enough. Even in a product-based approach, managers must put themselves in the consumers' shoes in order to understand the consumers' thoughts, priorities, and values. This reasoning is what lies behind the statement that it is impossible to sell consumers something that they don't want. A company may practice false representation, but consumers rarely make the same mistake twice. The key to successful marketing lies in putting ourselves in our clients' place in order to understand and serve them. If we start from the consumer's point of view, we will be in a better place to define a strong position or to reposition, to build a solid brand, and to develop customer service that will set our company apart. We will also be able to see that certain populations will never be interested in our company unless we modify our product, which is something that most nonprofit operations, particularly cultural enterprises, have no interest in doing (see chapter 6) except in the event of repositioning by the artistic director.

Programming as a product includes at least two dimensions: (1) the programming offered as a global entity and perceived as such by potential clients and (2) each of the proposed works or services. Marketing managers must be able to manage both dimensions concurrently. On the other hand, a product mix such as that of a festival or theater season must be based on a strategy designed to maximize effects in terms of both interest and sequence. The choice of works and the order in which they are presented constitute a delicate balancing act: Events that are less accessible and more challenging to consumers must be interspersed with lighter, more popular works. This process is generally referred to as *product portfolio management*.

Three Other Variables in the Marketing Mix

Once the company has clearly developed its positioning (and product being offered) in each of its target markets and segments, the manager can focus on the other three variables in the marketing mix: price, distribution (place), and promotion. This exercise starts by thinking strategy and then moves on to defining the tactics (or means) that will be used to achieve the expected results of the strategy. Thus the first step is to decide on a direction, and the second step is to devise the means to reach the goal in that direction.

The positioning exercise the company has already carried out indicated what benefits the clients expect to obtain from the product and how the company's product differs from what competitors have to offer. This knowledge makes it easier to come up with ways to attract the target clientele.

Price

The first thing to do is define a direction for the price by asking, What results do we want our pricing strategy to achieve (for further information, the reader may refer to the Examples of Pricing Strategies sidebar)? Naturally, every organization wants to maximize its income by determining the price that the consumer is prepared to pay. To do that, however, it needs to implement several strategies: preferred pricing (e.g., for gala events or benefits), student pricing, last-minute pricing, and discounts. The tactic used will correspond to the exact price that is set.

The price of a product is not just a question of the amount of money needed to participate in an event. Rather, the price can be defined as including the monetary worth, the expense of going out, the consumer's effort (the time spent researching and consuming the product or service), and the perceived risk of dissatisfaction (Colbert et al. 2007).

Often a leisure activity or cultural product is offered free of charge or, more precisely, at no financial cost to the consumer. As just stated, however, consumers must nonetheless pay a certain

price to take part in the event, particularly in terms of the risk of disappointment and the potential waste of precious leisure time. Clients must always sacrifice something in order to attend an event, be it money, time, or both. There is also a sort of risk involved in that consumers cannot test the product before experiencing it. There is definitely always a price to pay, though it is not always monetary. There really is no free lunch.

Companies can enhance the perceived value of their product through effective promotional strategizing, good product positioning, or unique customer service. Consumers may then be more prepared to pay a higher price—in terms of monetary cost, time spent, or risk involved.

Setting a price for a product is often the most difficult decision a manager will have to make. The fair price is the price the consumer is prepared to pay. Although that definition does nothing to help managers in their day-to-day work, it once again shows the importance of putting yourself in the consumer's shoes before making any marketing decision. Setting your price too high may discourage consumers; setting it too low will deprive the company of precious income and will send a message that the product being offered is of inferior quality.

Examples of Pricing Strategies

- Maximize income in all price categories.
- Project an image of prestige.
- Attract students.
- Encourage people to try the product.
- Aim for maximum market penetration.
- Follow the market leader.
- Offer the lowest price on the market.

EXAMPLE 1 Let's consider the market segments of a theater company. We can define two major client groups based on the time and money components of the price variable: People who have time to go to the theater but who have a lower income, and people for whom price is no object for the small amount of leisure time they have (Colbert, Beauregard, and Vallée 1998). If the company's objective is to maximize box-office receipts, the company must consider the needs of both segments by implementing a differentiated pricing strategy. This strategy could consist of setting as low a price as possible for the cost-sensitive segment while charging a premium for clients who view price as secondary and are prepared to pay a supplement in exchange for a certain advantage, such as the option of exchanging their ticket for an equivalent seat on another evening.

As for the tactic or means used to achieve the expected results of the strategy, we need to look at the exact amount that will be charged for a single ticket or subscription. In the case of subscriptions, the company could offer a 25% discount to attract its price-sensitive clientele and announce a flexible subscription format (strategy) at 25% *above* the regular price (tactic) for clients interested in the option of exchanging their ticket for another evening. In the same way, the price for student tickets (strategy) could be set at $10 U.S. (tactic), and last-minute tickets (strategy) could be sold at half price (tactic). The company might even increase prices by 20% (tactic) if the show is held over (strategy), since public approval will automatically increase the show's value.

EXAMPLE 2 Another example comes to us from the Ravinia Festival in Chicago. The Ravinia has opened a private restaurant with a membership fee that gives members access to a parking lot in the vicinity of the main festival gate. The company president can invite guests to the restaurant before concerts and to a brief presentation of the works on the evening's program. After the concert, members can mingle with the musicians or singers over dessert and refreshments (Lapierre 1999). People who pay this premium consider that the value added to the product is worth the additional cost.

Distribution (Place)

Distribution refers to the delivery of the good, service, or product to the consumer. Distribution may be the tour of a performance company or traveling museum exhibition, the venue of a festival

or community activity, or the delivery of a book, CD, or film (in a movie theater or on DVD). Delivery is achieved through a series of distribution intermediaries. Organizations that deliver their product in a fixed location (such as a summer camp, festival, theater, or museum) and have no desire to move their product elsewhere can use the easiest method of product distribution: direct distribution. Producers of a touring show or traveling exhibition are obliged to do business with a distributor (hall, museum, or exhibition center); sometimes they even use the services of a booking agent to sell their show to distributors in the targeted territory.

The distribution variable usually is broken down into three components: distribution channels or networks, physical distribution, and commercial location. Distribution channels or networks involve choosing and managing relationships with intermediaries (e.g., agents and distributors) used to reach the consumer. Physical distribution includes the logistics of transporting works of art or personnel and tour equipment to destinations or points of sale.

The commercial venue, whether it is a performance hall, museum, festival, movie theater, or summer camp, is often a crucial strategic decision. A shrewd choice can give a company a significant competitive advantage. For example, a bookstore whose clientele consists primarily of students would do well to locate near a campus. It would do even better to occupy the only locally available location for a bookstore, as competitors would be forced to open farther away from campus, and thus their location would discourage students from using them. Libraries, theaters, and museums, on the other hand, greatly enhance their power of attraction when located in the same area: Consumers are willing to travel greater distances in exchange for being able to choose from a wider selection. This is, of course, the principle behind shopping centers, which offer all the products consumers could desire under one roof, saving them several trips to multiple locations.

A significant aspect of direct distribution is the quality of customer service. What clients are looking for above all else is a complete consumer experience when they visit the site of the organization. The satisfaction they gain from an artistic presentation must not be marred by shoddy customer service.

Once again, the strategic decision for distribution is based on the direction the company wants to take (for more examples, see the Examples of Distribution Strategies sidebar below). A touring company may organize its own bookings with potential distributors or may hire an agent to do the bookings. A publisher may decide to sell directly to the consumer without going through an intermediary (perhaps by creating a book club) or may follow the usual channel of agent to distributors to bookstores. The tactic used will correspond to the people or organizations that serve as intermediaries and to the support the company plans to offer them (e.g., advertising material or reimbursement of unsold tickets). The physical distribution strategy for a touring company will depend on the possible arrangements in the different cities where the company will be performing, while the tactic will consist of the means of transportation and hotels. Strategy related to location will be the choice of venue for an event, and the tactic will lie in the organization of the premises and customer service.

Examples of Distribution Strategies

- Maximize control of the network.
- Maximize the number of points of sale.
- Optimize customer service.
- Minimize distribution costs.
- Choose the most prestigious retailers.
- Eliminate the need for intermediaries.
- Open a store in every city with a population of 25,000 or more.
- Provide 24-hour delivery.

Promotion

Promotion is concerned with the communication between a company and its clients (its four markets). This communication has four purposes:

1. To inform clients of the existence of the organization and its programming and tell them how they can access it

2. To periodically remind consumers of the program and the organization

3. To persuade consumers of the superiority of the company's offer (positioning) as compared with the competition

4. To establish a relationship with the client

Four promotional tools are available to get the company's message out to the public: paid publicity or advertising, personal selling, free publicity, and sales promotion. There are many means of communication available for each of these options: publicity and advertising (newspapers, magazines, radio, and television), public relations, billboards, direct marketing, annual reports, intranet, Internet, derivative products, personal sales, employee uniforms, and so on. Since any contact between a company and its market constitutes communication, even the company's personnel cannot control what others say about them.

For small nonprofit enterprises with limited financial means, the two final tools in the list—free publicity and sales promotion—are the best ways to advertise their product. Companies try to get the media to talk about their programming and organize press conferences and public appearances by their artists. They sell promotional items, hold contests, reduce prices, and give demonstrations. They offer reimbursement policies, deferred refunds, and loyalty programs. They even dress their personnel in the company colors. In short, they do anything that entails little or no immediate financial outlay.

Since all the promotional tools serve the same cause, it is vital that the company have an integrated vision of all aspects of its communication. The employee in charge of press relations must be aware of instructions given to box-office personnel; the person who canvasses for sponsors must be up to date on the ins and outs of the company's publicity campaign in the media. All forms of communication must be consistent; they must present the same image and pursue the same goal in an organized fashion. Nothing is more frustrating for clients than to see an offer advertised and then discover that the information they need is not available on the company's Web site or that the person who answers the company telephone doesn't know anything about the offer.

Even a cultural enterprise can avail itself of the most expensive promotional strategy—personal selling—without investing vast sums of money but instead using a little imagination. Boston's Handel and Haydn Society devised a campaign called *Help Build Our Audience* that encouraged subscribers to invite one guest or more to one of the society's fall concerts for a mere $5 U.S. per ticket, with subscribers acting as hosts for the evening. This approach combined person-to-person sales with a preview of the orchestra and maximized customer service (Kinzey 2005/2006).

Communication Objective

Since promotion is a communication tool, it is important to distinguish between a marketing objective and a communication objective. A marketing objective is expressed in terms of the results to be achieved for all four variables in the marketing mix, while a communication objective focuses on the message the company wants to send to the market. If, for example, the marketing objective is to increase sales by 20%, the communication objective could be to increase the company's brand awareness by the same amount (see page 124 for more examples of communication objectives). The message is not to persuade consumers to buy the product but to increase the number of people who are familiar with the company. If the number of potential consumers who know about the company goes up, sales will usually follow.

The choice to increase brand awareness is a strategic decision on the part of the company. At the tactical level, the company may prefer to use one form of media over another, to advertise on a certain day, and to use a particular format. The company can decide on the graphics, choose which firm to use for promotional material, and so on.

Examples of Communication Objectives

- Project an image of prestige.
- Ensure 80% media coverage at launching.
- Promote easy access to venue.
- Project a youthful image in order to renew clientele.

Direct Marketing and Relationship Marketing

Direct marketing is a time-honored technique that started when companies began mailing catalogs to target client groups. With the advent of e-mail and the Internet, companies have found a way to communicate with clients without having to go through the media.

Sending promotional e-mails to a specific clientele costs much less than it costs to place an advertisement in one medium. Moreover, if the distribution list is carefully prepared, it can be used to target clients who are potential consumers and to avoid annoying people who have no interest in what the company has to offer.

Direct marketing also allows companies to use what is now commonly called *relationship marketing*, a method that attempts to adapt the product to reflect what the clients want (see the example of the Steppenwolf Theatre in the Example of Direct Marketing sidebar). It fosters individualized relationships, treating clients personally so that they will feel they are part of the organization, which encourages their loyalty. Sometimes what seems like a small gesture will greatly enhance a client's satisfaction with the company. Relationship marketing does not require organizations to change their artistic product in any way; it is rather a question of quality customer service.

Marketing communication managers must take special care in setting up the company's Web site on the Internet. Now that a company's Web site is its calling card, it is crucial that the site be designed with the client in mind. It must be easy to navigate and to find the information being sought. The information must be complete without being overwhelming or weighty. An effective Internet site must be tested by existing clients and updated regularly. In addition to keeping clients informed, a Web site gives companies a forum for establishing a dialogue with various target groups. Companies can set up online customer service and organize virtual communities, discussion groups, chat rooms, or even blogs.

Example of Direct Marketing

Chicago's Steppenwolf Theatre systematically requests the e-mail address of anyone who buys a ticket or a subscription. In doing so, the company has accumulated almost 50,000 addresses over the past few years. This database is an invaluable tool for promoting current or upcoming shows, particularly when the company needs to react quickly to a decline in ticket sales. In just a few hours, the company can draw up a promotional offer, draft an e-mail message, identify the appropriate segment in its databases, and send out a mass e-mailing at minimal cost (Ravanas 2006).

Monitoring the Effectiveness of the Marketing Program

Any marketing plan must attempt to prepare for the unforeseeable and be able to determine if its objective has been reached. Managers need to ask themselves the following questions: How will I measure my progress and decide if I am still in line with my objective? At what point should I start thinking that I might be headed for disaster? What can I do to stay informed? What methods should I use to adjust my aim?

This is where the importance of a good marketing information system (MIS), particularly an internal data system, becomes apparent. The MIS is a fundamental component of the marketing process. It is a set of tools that provide managers with the information they need to make informed decisions.

An MIS includes three types of data: internal data, secondary external data, and primary external data. Internal data come from within the company: sales reports, financial reports, client reports, the opinions of museum security guards or theater box-office personnel, and so on. Secondary external data are published by public or private agencies in the form of reports available in libraries, on the Internet, or from the agencies themselves. Primary external data consist of information that the company has compiled directly from the consumer. This compilation, called a *market study*, *survey*, or *market research study*, can be conducted by the company itself or by a specialized outside firm hired for that purpose.

Companies must have a means of monitoring the progress of their sales on a regular basis (see chapter 6). For some, a regular basis is once a week; for others, it is once a month. The most basic monitoring tool is a statement that compares current sales with those of the previous year. Another method is monitoring the geographical provenance of the clientele. In certain cases, companies have to subscribe to specialized periodicals or consult statistics published by specialized firms in order to stay on top of market trends.

Regardless of the method a company uses to monitor its marketing results, the company has to be prepared for the unforeseeable and, most importantly, decide in advance what steps it will take to relaunch a campaign that isn't getting off the ground. The company may choose to set aside a budget for extra advertising, offer free tickets to certain target groups, or reduce its expenses. The method used is not as important as planning for the unexpected and being prepared for the worst.

Summary

In this chapter, we have seen that marketing is not restricted to promotion alone. It includes managing the product, brand, customer service, distribution, and price. The marketing process also relies on market analysis and an appropriate system for monitoring results.

PART III

Arts and Cultural Programs in Context

We have come to the third and last section in the book. This section may perhaps be the most enjoyable for readers. For Arts and Cultural Programs in Context, we called upon experts in various arts and cultural program settings to share successful programs with our readers. In addition, we organized these programs by type based upon key contexts where arts and cultural leisure experiences exist and are emerging. As such, the reader will find chapters on festivals, special events, community arts, cultural programs, museums, and performing arts. The authors for each chapter also included case studies taken from actual arts and cultural organizations and, in many cases, written by a professional arts manager or leisure specialist.

Tom Delamere discusses festivals in chapter 9 by first defining the term and then exploring the unique characteristics of these increasingly popular forms of programming. Trends and challenges are presented along with innovative approaches to festival programming. Elements requiring extra attention by festival programmers are provided and differentiating between programming and packaging is considered.

In chapter 10, Gaylene Carpenter provides an overview of special events programming by focusing on the growing number and type of arts and cultural experiences offered. Cultural tourism as well as convention tourism are introduced as contexts in which special events in arts and culture occur. Various types and locales for arts and cultural programs are also explored so the reader is introduced to exhibits and openings, public outdoor performances, education, and culinary special events.

Lori L. Hager explores community arts in chapter 11. Key historical moments in the community arts field are explored first. This is followed by a discussion of contemporary principles and practices in this area of arts and cultural programming. She also offers an overview of challenges faced by professionals working in community arts settings. Trends in community arts programming are also included in this chapter.

In chapter 12, Doug Blandy examines cultural programming within the context of cultural democracy. He presents informative discussions related to orientations to cultural programming and to cultural competence. Using a folklore orientation to cultural programming, he examines processes related to conceptualizing, designing, and implementing cultural programs. His chapter concludes with a discussion related to ethics and cultural programming.

Janice Williams Rutherford assists programmers in understanding arts and cultural programming in museum settings in chapter 13. Viewing museum programming as enhancing leisure experiences, she discusses museum theater and living history as means for connecting with museum participants. Arts and cultural programs designed as family activities are explored along with community discussions that can relate to timely topics of interest. She concludes her chapter by providing the reader with challenges facing museum programming.

In chapter 14, Steven Morrison focuses on performing arts programming. He begins by detailing challenges and trends in arts and cultural programming experienced in performing arts settings. He explores the need for structuring the programming process and nonprofit influences on programming decisions. Programming as a function of strategic planning is considered as are strategies for making good programming decisions.

In chapter 15, coeditors Carpenter and Blandy examine the future for arts and cultural programming. This chapter allows the coeditors to do some imagineering about what might be in store for managers in arts and leisure settings who plan to continue designing and implementing arts and cultural leisure experiences. Based in part on forecasting the future, a task that at times can be both challenging and incorrect, the authors thought long and hard about social and organizational factors that would play a role in the not too distant future. Given their collective best guesses and those of others regarding future impacts and realities, the chapter was titled, Imagining the Future of Arts and Cultural Programming. But since knowing the future is often impossible, this last chapter should at least get the discussion about the future off to a good start!

Festivals

Tom Delamere, PhD
Malaspina University-College

Maybe you and your family
and friends could have your
own arts festival. And include
whatever you like to do.
Such as drawing, or painting,
or dancing, or dressing up,
or singing, or cooking. There
are many ways of saying who
you are and how you feel.
Ways that can be so helpful.
Ways that don't hurt yourself
or anybody else. You know,
that's how you can tell when
you're grown up inside: You're
sure that what you're planning
and doing are things that can
be a real help to you and your
neighbor. I'm proud of you,
know that. I hope you do.

Mister Rogers

So, where's the Cannes Film
Festival being held this year?

Christina Aguilera

There is incredible diversity in both the number and the types of arts and cultural programs that are based in the festival setting. There are festivals celebrating music, festivals devoted to all manner of visual and performing arts, and cultural and heritage festivals. There is artistic and cultural capital that is created and utilized at festivals and is reflective of the diverse nature of our communities. This capital enriches our communities on many levels: socially, economically, environmentally, and even politically.

After reading this chapter, you will understand the importance of the festival as a source of community identity and community development. Additionally, you will be able to describe the trends and issues that challenge festival programmers and identify both positive and negative effects of festivals. Finally, you will understand the complexity and diversity of festival programming. You will be able to discuss various types of festivals and the application of programming elements to make the festival unique and memorable and to enhance the participant experience.

Defining *Festival*

Festivals breathe life into our communities. First and foremost, they are celebrations of some aspect of the community that is special to the residents of that area. Often the terms *festival* and *special event* are used to denote the same occurrence, when, in fact, they carry separate meanings. A key

point of distinction is the temporal nature of the two activities. A special event is a one-time-only activity, whereas a festival possesses more enduring qualities. A festival is generally recurring; that is, it is a fixture on the annual calendar. The Kronos Quartet may perform a concert in your community during a special event, or it may perform a concert in the Ottawa International Chamber Music Festival as part of a festival. The festival may occur annually (or less frequently), and it has ongoing roots in that specific community. Both the festival and the special event are open to the public (though some special events may be closed) and both may have a fixed date or fixed dates, but only the festival has an ongoing link with the community. That link is what separates the festival from the more commonplace event.

Many of our communities take their identity from their festivals and become well-known for that reason. When people think of Newport, Montreux, or New Orleans, they think of jazz. Edmonton, Alberta, when not billing itself as the "City of Champions" (to celebrate Stanley Cup and Grey Cup victories), is known as "Festival City" in recognition of its many summer festivals. Nova Scotia bills itself as "Festival Province" and promotes itself to tourists on the basis of the many celebrations held there during the tourist season.

The notion of utilizing the festival as a tourist attraction is not a new one. Local chambers of commerce and economic development offices have viewed arts and cultural festivals as a means of expanding the tourist season or even of creating a new tourist season. However, implementing a festival based solely on anticipated tourism is a recipe for failure. For the festival to succeed, it must have tangible roots in the community. If local residents do not support the festival, it will wither and die regardless of the amount of tourism it draws to the community. Tourists will not go where the local residents do not go—if local residents are not involved in the festival, as performers, spectators, or volunteers, no amount of tourism will save the festival. All festivals depend on community support for their very existence, and it is this two-way synergistic relationship between festival and community (community deriving identity from the festival and community support breathing life into the festival) that improves the quality of life for us as individuals and for our communities.

Unique Characteristics of Festival Programming

The following programming aspects, while applicable to all types of festivals, are those of which the arts and cultural festival programmer should be specifically aware. Organizers planning for a successful festival will need to plan for these factors. These selected characteristics also differentiate festival programming from other elements of leisure programming by their scope and scale.

Scheduling

The schedule is one of the most important aspects of festival programming. It is the main element of the program and the means by which the program is implemented. The pace, the flow, and the feel of the festival are all dictated by the schedule. The schedule is a tangible manifestation of the plan of the festival for both the organizer and the spectator.

The calendar dates chosen for individual festivals are important not only in avoiding conflicts with other attractions but also in building a critical mass of activities and developing relationships with other festivals whose elements may complement those of your festival. The timing of the festival during the calendar year may also relate to the content or intent of your event.

Within the festival itself, the organization of the schedule of events affects programmers, performers, and patrons. Schedule program elements too closely, and the audience may be numbed by the constant stimulation. A loose schedule, with too much time between activities, may result in boredom. It is important to build time into the schedule to set up and tear down between acts, to keep acts on schedule, and to keep the audience entertained between activities.

Volunteer Management, Recruitment, and Retention

Volunteers are the lifeblood of any festival. Volunteers are often devoted fans of that activity, and successful festivals are the ones that treat volunteers well and have a loyal corps supporting the

festival endeavor. Volunteer burnout is often a significant concern for festival organizations that are becoming increasingly reliant on volunteer support (Delamere and Hinch 1994). A rule of thumb in North America is that 20% of the volunteers do 80% of the total volunteer work. With good volunteers frequently taking on more than one volunteer position, there is a fear that the available pool of volunteers is being depleted. This problem is being compounded by the growing number and size of festivals across the continent. As much as the festival organization needs volunteers, the individual volunteers have specific goals that need to be met through their activities with the festival.

Effective volunteer management should be in place to ensure the best possible fit between the needs of the festival organization and the motivations, needs, and expectations of the volunteers. The volunteers believe strongly in the festival, its goals, and the art form that it celebrates. By giving volunteers the responsibility and the tools to accomplish mutually valued goals and by taking great lengths to honor and appreciate volunteer contributions (see figure 9.1), festival organizers can strengthen their events and ensure that volunteers return in subsequent years.

Risk Management and Crowd Management

Risk management is defined by van der Wagen (2001) as the process of identifying, assessing, and managing risk. Risk takes on many forms at a festival. If your festival is being held outdoors, then the threat of inclement conditions or a natural disaster needs to be accounted for. Financial risk is always present, especially when the bulk of the revenues are generated during the festival itself while expenditures are made throughout the year. Legal risk and liability issues arise whenever spectators are involved, and these issues can also occur between festival organizers and performers if contractual obligations are not met. In this post-September 11 world, safety and security are a clear priority at the larger, more visible festivals. With an increasing reliance on computer-based systems (for lighting, sound, fireworks, registration, ticketing, and so on), it is essential that these systems run efficiently and risk free.

Crowd control is a critical concern that often falls under the responsibilities of the risk manager. As many major festivals (especially music festivals) are held outdoors where there is no reserved

Figure 9.1 The Volunteer Recognition Wall at the Edmonton Folk Music Festival.
Photo courtesy of Tom Delamere

seating, special procedures must be put into place to ensure orderly entrance to and egress from the seating area. Wristbands and seating escorts help mitigate crowd-related crises (see figures 9.2 and 9.3; Sonder 2004). At festivals offering beverage tents or beer gardens, proper security plans should be in place to thoroughly screen patrons, to discourage overconsumption, and to deal with underage or rowdy patrons (Getz 1997; Delamere and Rollins 1999).

A good site and logistics plan can assist greatly in managing spectators and festival operations. Signs directing staff members and spectators toward festival elements such as the festival itself,

Figure 9.2 The mad dash to claim a seat.
Photo courtesy of Tom Delamere

Figure 9.3 Running down a rain-soaked hill to get to the best spot.
Photo courtesy of Tom Delamere

parking, public transit, site entrances and exits, concessions, lavatories, first aid, lost and found, wheelchair access, crafts, recording and memorabilia sales, and recycling stations can ease traffic flow in and around the festival site as well as facilitate access for police, fire, and ambulance services (Yeoman et al. 2004).

Festival Effects on the Host Community

There is a bigger picture that festival programmers should be aware of: the effect that their festival has on the host community. As much as the programming and packaging of the festival create an atmosphere for the performer and the spectator alike, there is a larger symbiotic relationship between the festival and the host community. The festival has both intended and unintended positive and negative outcomes that affect relationships within and outside of the community (Delamere 2001).

Given the tendency of festival funding agencies to focus on the bottom line, the tangible economic effects are often given higher priority (Delamere, Wankel, and Hinch 2001). Other effects may be less tangible and more difficult to measure—not impossible, just more difficult. Understanding the need for a balance among economic, social, environmental, and political goals and outcomes is essential in promoting a sustainable approach to developing the festival within the community (Delamere, Wankel, and Hinch 2001; Delamere 2001). Governments and festival organizations, in order to foster good public relations and to prepare before acting, should more fully understand the effects of their programs on the host community (Rollins and Delamere 2007). Perhaps it is time for programmers and festival organizers to be cognizant of a quadruple bottom line inclusive of economic, social, environmental, and political effects.

Festival Style

> "Anyone can make the simple complicated. Creativity is making the complicated simple."
>
> *Charles Mingus*

Getz, in his book *Event Management and Event Tourism* (1997), suggests that the term *style* possesses three meanings that are particularly important to festivals and festival programmers. The first definition, that style is a manner of expression and design, suggests that a festival can contain distinct elements that lead to a readily identifiable style and set the festival apart from others. In the second definition, style is identified as an excellence of artistic expression that allows individual festivals of the same type (i.e., jazz festivals) to differ from one another. The third meaning of style is that of fashion: the variations in popularity that festival types (street performers, folk music) cycle through, or what is hot versus what is not. Creativity and creative program elements lay at the very core of style.

The key elements of style, as they relate to the total festival experience, serve as the unifying thread for the programmer. From the initial building blocks of the core festival, activities, and celebrations, these elements can be engineered by the programmer and festival organization to influence the experience of the festival patron.

Sensory Stimulation and Entertainment

- Sound quality and lighting
- Staff costuming and activity demonstration
- Parades
- Display of interesting and unusual artifacts
- Performing arts
- Site and facility tours
- Free performances as part of the festival offering

- Planned spontaneity
- Other unique promotions

Games and Humor

- Involving the audience in games and activities
- Participatory drama
- Literary humor
- Visual and other sensory humor

Belonging, Sharing, and Other Emotional Stimulation

- Evocation of shared cultural values
- Bringing diverse groups together
- Interaction with heritage arts and culture

Ritual

- Commemorative activities
- Opening and closing ceremonies

Authenticity

- Genuine reflection of cultural values
- Accurate presentation of sites and artifacts
- Faithful re-creation of events, sights, and sounds

Commerce

- Sale of arts, crafts, performer goods
- Souvenirs of the festival

Hospitality

- Greeters, staff, and volunteers
- Gifts or mementos to guests
- Quality of the host-guest interaction

Education

- Clinics and workshops
- Seminars and discussions
- Question and answer

Adapted, by permission, from D. Getz, 1997, *Event management and event tourism* (Elmsford, NY: Cognizant Communications Corporation), 168.

Merchandising

Good merchandise, coupled with a good logo, can extend the reach of the festival considerably. Certainly, the sale of festival-related merchandise on and off the site can generate additional revenue for the festival organization. Merchandising is significant not only as a revenue source during tight fiscal times but also as a means of branding and marketing the festival. Branded merchandise helps raise a lasting awareness of the festival in the eyes of the consumer. Items that can be branded or merchandised include clothing, pins and buttons, jewelry, stationery, packaged food and beverages, art works (including posters), and other unique souvenirs and collectables (Getz 1997).

The acquisition of a festival poster, program, or T-shirt turns that item into a collectible. When gazed upon by the festival patron in subsequent years, it will engender positive memories associated with that festival. The merchandise becomes a souvenir, but the experience lives on (Yeoman et al. 2004). For me, the poster and T-shirt from the 2004 Montreux Jazz Festival carry that special significance (see figure 9.4). The Montreux festival freshens its image every year by commissioning a different artist to create the logos and designs used for that year's celebrations. While visiting

friends in Switzerland, I traveled to Montreux for a day during the festival and was taken by both the music and the Burton Morris art work for the 2004 festival. Many Swiss francs later, I (and many of my friends in the Nanaimo, British Columbia, jazz scene) owned souvenirs of that celebration.

Festival programmers can make sure that their event includes appropriate space and time for sellers to display wares. Musicians, for example, may wish to display and sell T-shirts and CDs, and this aspect of festivals can also reinforce patrons' memories of the experience (Sonder 2004). Hearing a musician, purchasing a CD, chatting with the musician at a workshop, and having the CD autographed can create memories that last a lifetime. Visual artists can display and sell prints of their works at an art exhibition. Crafters and artisans can share their skills and talents with an appreciative audience. Merchandising serves not only as a potential revenue stream but also as a conduit that connects the performer or artist to the audience member, thereby further enhancing the festival experience.

Figure 9.4 A festival poster from the 2004 Montreux Jazz Festival.

Photo courtesy of Tom Delamere

Trends and Challenges

Given the complexity and diversity of arts festival types, it is important to consider the trends and challenges that festival programmers and organizers face. Note that challenges are not viewed here as being wholly negative. On the contrary, challenges should be viewed in the positive sense whenever possible. Challenges are opportunities that can refine and strengthen festival operations.

Staying Fresh and Relevant

For any festival organizer, keeping the festival fresh, interesting, and relevant is an ongoing challenge. The entertainment marketplace is crowded with options. Festivals are competing not only with each other but also against virtually every other form of entertainment on which consumers can spend their hard-earned dollars. With more and more festivals and more and more entertainment options arising, festival organizers are competing for ever-shrinking pieces of the consumer-dollar pie. Staying fresh and relevant is fraught with potential pitfalls. If resources are used to attract new and trendy performers and installations, the festival programmer may risk alienating a loyal fan base. Similarly, if the programmer sticks with the tried and true year after year, the festival could stagnate without refreshing its audience.

The Funding Question

"I'm all in favor of getting grants for musicians. Or any other good brand of Scotch."

Pepper Adams

Funding is scarce. Whether from the National Endowment for the Arts or the Canada Council for the Arts, federally funded programs for arts and cultural activities face increasing taxpayer and political scrutiny. All levels of government (local, state or provincial, federal) are being held more accountable for program spending, and often in economic crises, it is funding for leisure activities that is targeted. Festival organizers, faced with greater demands from the funding agencies to show an economic impact, may have to alter their festivals' goals in order to gain ongoing access to those funds. There are pressures to increase admission fees, to attract sponsors, and to charge more for associated amenities and services, actions which may run counter to the mandate under which the festival was created. Doing more with less is more than a mantra—it is a reality!

Building Partnerships

"Jazz is not dead, it just smells funny."

Frank Zappa

One way festival organizers deal with scarce financial resources is to work together in order to pool and more effectively utilize those resources. The annual summer jazz festivals hosted in major cities across western Canada have chosen to not compete but instead to work together to attract top-level talent. In 1987 the organizers of the Edmonton, Vancouver, Victoria, Calgary, Winnipeg, and Saskatoon jazz festivals banded together to form Westcan Jazz. This umbrella organization allows the festival organizers to synchronize the dates of their events (which run from late June through early July), coordinate their festival programs, and share artist fees and travel expenses (Historica 2007). By working together to attract talent for multiple dates rather than bidding against each other for talent or single dates, the festivals use their energies and financial resources to strengthen the group. By pooling marketing resources, organizations like Westcan Jazz can achieve greater market penetration by effectively targeting their audiences.

Differentiating Between Programming and Packaging

Programming may be thought of as the presentation of a leisure product or service in relation to the way in which it might be used, while packaging can be seen as the bundling of products, services, or experiences that can be purchased separately and offering them together as a single product at a single price. From a festival-related perspective, for example, the booking and scheduling of individual performances or exhibits can be considered programming. Alternatively, packaging would consist of the sum of all the related actions and activities that provide the total experience for the patron: the entertainment together with the venue, concessions, amenities, ambience, experience, risk management, guest services, and price.

It is the total festival package, together with the programming of elements within the package, that has great appeal for the spectator. The following list presents reasons why festival packaging and programming are important for the spectator or consumer:

- Value
- Convenience
- Consistent quality
- Ease of budgeting and planning

- Appeal to special interests
- Added excitement

Adapted from D.W. Howell et al., 2006, *Passport: An introduction to the tourism industry*, 4th Canadian ed. (Toronto, Canada: Thomson Nelson), A. Morrison, 2002, *Hospitality and travel marketing*, 3rd ed. (New York, NY: Thomson Delmar Learning), and M. Sarbey de Souto, 1993, *Group travel*, 2nd ed. (Albany, NY: Delmar Publishers Inc.).

Additionally, there are key reasons why packaging and programming are important from the point of view of the festival's champions and organizers. Many of these factors should be considered on a continuing basis by event organizers and may also be trumpeted by festival boosters trying to get the inaugural festival off the ground:

- Increased off-peak business, attract tourists
- Increased customer/spectator satisfaction, value-added features for the customer
- Appeal to newer market niches
- Ability to capitalize on emerging market trends
- Enhancing the appeal to special interest groups and specific market segments
- Accuracy of forecasting and increased efficiency
- Increased per capita spending and lengths of stay, improved cash flow
- Public relations and publicity value of novel, unique packages
- Usage of complementary facilities and services
- Develop partnerships
- More frequent and repeat use

The planners of the opening ceremonies at this guitar festival planned well so that the participants were kept entertained, fed, and provided with ample opportunity to dance from start to finish.

Photo courtesy of Ragen E. Sanner

Adapted from A. Morrison, 2002, *Hospitality and travel marketing*, 3rd ed. (New York, NY: Thomson Delmar Learning), D. Getz, 1997, *Event management and event tourism* (Elmsford, NY: Cognizant Communication Corporation), and D.W. Howell et al., 2006, *Passport: An introduction to the tourism industry*, 4th Canadian ed. (Toronto, Canada: Thomson Nelson).

In either case, the end product of creative programming and packaging may be utilized to attain start-up and ongoing financial and technical support from granting and sponsoring agencies.

Innovative Programming in Arts and Cultural Festivals

As noted, one of the challenges that festival organizers face is that of staying fresh and relevant. Programming is essential in this instance and is being effectively utilized in various arts and cultural festivals, as evidenced in the following three examples. Each festival is using programming to achieve product differentiation and make for a far more memorable experience in the minds of the festival patrons.

Bumbershoot (Seattle, Washington)—Embracing All the Arts

Many arts and cultural festivals are genre specific (e.g., a folk festival, a jazz festival, or a specific type of art or literature festival), but Seattle's Bumbershoot is all that and more. Billed as Seattle's Music and Arts Festival, Bumbershoot knocks down walls and erases boundaries. Taking an umbrella approach to music and the arts, Bumbershoot attracts music, film, comedy, spoken word, dance,

visual arts, performance arts, and literary arts (Bumbershoot Info 2007). Admission to the festival site in downtown Seattle is based on a 1-day or a 3-day pass; admission is not charged for individual venues. Seating is on a first-come, first-served basis, providing pass holders a great deal of choice and value for their dollar. The link connecting the festival, the arts, and the community is strong:

> Into its fourth decade, Bumbershoot continues to change, evolve, refresh, and redefine itself for the next generation of festival lovers. At the same time, the festival continues to honor the basic principle that celebrating art as a community is a fundamental necessity. (Bumbershoot History 2007)

Edmonton Heritage Festival—Celebrating Diversity Across Cultures

In Edmonton, Alberta, the annual Edmonton Heritage Festival brings together more than 70 cultures from around the world. This ethnocultural festival attracts nearly 400,000 visitors to Hawrelak Park in Edmonton's beautiful North Saskatchewan River valley, and the mission of the festival is "to promote public awareness, understanding, and appreciation for cultural diversity through an annual summer festival, and to provide educational events, programs, and/or projects on a year-round basis" (Heritage Festival Edmonton 2007). The various ethnocultural communities at the Edmonton Heritage Festival come together to display traditional cuisine, entertainment, arts, crafts, and interpretive materials. In this increasingly complex world, with conflicts occurring at many a turn, the Edmonton Heritage Festival helps us celebrate diversity and learn and understand more about each other and our heritage. This celebration of the multicultural heritage of Canada and Alberta serves as an example of the reach and the power of community-based (both geographic and sociocultural) celebrations.

Lane Arts Council (Eugene, Oregon)—Keeping ArtsWeek in Mind Throughout the Year

If you google the term *ArtsWeek* you will get almost 200 hits on community arts festivals from around the world. What, then, makes the Lane Arts Council and its ArtsWeek celebration both successful and unique?

As an advocacy organization supporting the arts in Lane County, Oregon, the Lane Arts Council states that its mission is to "create an environment where the arts flourish with freedom and respect" (Lane Arts Council 2007). The council creates this environment in many different ways, and by embedding the festival in its ongoing programs, the council uses creative programming to achieve its mission. First is the ArtsWeek festival, which is held annually in early June and focuses on the arts and artists in Lane County. Many arts organizations would stop at this point, focusing their efforts on that one major event on the annual calendar. Not the Lane Arts Council. Through its First Friday ArtsWalk program, it keeps the main festival (and the arts) in mind throughout the year. On the first Friday of each month, a free walking tour of participating art galleries and visual arts attractions is held in downtown Eugene. The routes for the walk and the attractions change monthly, providing an ongoing stimulus for participants and fostering return visitations. Additional programs include YouthArts, which connects community artists and youths and families in schools and communities throughout the county, and ArtsAdvocacy, which operates through Creative Conversations meetings with city cultural staff members and consultants and through other training, education, and information dissemination initiatives (Lane Arts Council 2005). The Lane Arts Council keeps a strong focus on its mission; its programs bear this throughout the entire year.

Elements Requiring Extra Attention by the Programmer

Earlier in the chapter we considered programming elements that are unique to festivals and that may differentiate festivals from other forms of programming. There are, however, even more specific elements that the arts and cultural festival programmer should pay attention to. These elements further differentiate the arts and cultural festival from other festival types.

Opening and Closing Ceremonies

The opening and closing ceremonies are cornerstones of many a festival. Often steeped in tradition, the opening can set an exciting and anticipatory tone for the remainder of the festival. A solid opening night can garner favorable press, which may increase ticket and admission sales. Closing ceremonies are often more solemn, poignant affairs. They bring closure to the celebration and allow all involved (organizers, volunteers, performers and artists, and patrons) to pause and reflect on what has been. At the Edmonton Folk Music Festival, for example, the last performance on the closing Sunday night is a rendition of "Four Strong Winds." Festival volunteers and staff members join the remaining performers on the main stage while a candlelight procession weaves its way throughout the audience. The visual and sensory spectacle inspires awe and warmth and is a very powerful means of bringing the festival to a close.

Concessions

One of the trickier areas of festival programming is food and beverage operations. Licenses must be procured, policies set, contracts let, and inspections conducted. These tasks vary depending on local rules and regulations. Will the food and beverage concessions be operated in house, provided by local vendors, or contracted out to a major food service company such as Sodexho or Aramark? A range of customer options should be provided (e.g., both vegan and nonvegan), and the ingredients must be known and accounted for in order to prevent any potential allergic reactions. For culinary festivals, the food and beverage side is the focal point of the celebration, and more often than not, the menu will fit with the theme of the festival (Yeoman et al. 2004). Remember that a menu is not unlike the local recreation program guides that are distributed seasonally in the communities where we live. The local program guide offers a comprehensive listing of leisure opportunities for local residents; each main dish on the culinary festival menu is potentially a separate activity that can be combined with other program aspects (wines, hors d'oeuvres, desserts, aperitifs) to provide an unforgettable leisure (dining) experience for the patron.

Alcohol use at festivals has received increased scrutiny in recent years, mostly in a negative context. In Parksville, British Columbia, the annual Sandcastle Festival (featuring sculpted sandcastles) was suspended and cancelled for awhile following a riot that began when a late-night crowd was dispersed from the festival's beer garden. A group of 1,000 (100 of whom were eventually arrested) roamed the streets of the sleepy retirement community of Parksville; thugs threw bottles and rocks at the Royal Canadian Mounted Police, smashed windows, ruined trees and gardens, and looted liquor stores. The mayor of Parksville even stood on the corner of a major intersection and proclaimed the Riot Act (Delamere and Rollins 1999). Given the need for an increased presence of police and protective services (as a preventative measure), many programmers are questioning the increased costs associated with providing alcoholic beverages at their events.

The beer garden or beverage tent is interesting to a certain extent. Approached responsibly, it can be a civilized add-on to a festival and a good source of additional revenue. Often, though, patrons are herded like cattle into a restricted space and down as much alcohol as possible in the short time available before the next performer takes the stage or the beer garden closes. Contrast this with my experience at the Jazz Parade in Fribourg, Switzerland. There, beer and wine kiosks are scattered throughout the square at Place Georges Python and the surrounding streets within the gated festival site. Patrons can make their purchase and wander freely between the main stage and side stages with their beverage in hand. This civilized, adult approach to alcohol sales and consumption results in fewer negative incidents and allows for much greater freedom of movement, thereby enhancing the festival experience for the patron.

Summary

Programming is increasingly important in community-based arts and cultural festivals and special events. In this chapter we discussed various elements of festival programming and worked to understand the issues that festival organizers face in building toward the future. Through the

presented case studies and practical examples, you can see the challenges that festival programmers must address not only in establishing new events but also in continuing to renew and refresh longstanding successful festivals.

CASE STUDIES

Our Musical Philosophy—Diversity in Programming: An Interview With Terry Wickham

Programming and producing a folk music festival is a daunting task. Fans of folk music are among the most impassioned; they are as diverse as the term *folk music* itself and have certain music and performers that they may want or not want to see. Meeting this wide range of audience needs often makes for a difficult programming landscape that any festival producer needs to be aware of.

Enter Terry Wickham, the longtime Producer and Artistic Director (AD) of the Edmonton Folk Music Festival (EFMF). Since its inception in 1980, the EFMF has become one of the most successful and well-attended folk music festivals in North America and one of the few that regularly sells out in advance. The 2006 EFMF is the 17th consecutive year that Wickham has produced the festival.

Wickham's (and the EFMF's) programming philosophy has evolved over the years; as the EFMF has grown, the audiences, performers, and producers have changed. Remaining responsive, current, and even trendsetting while respecting tradition is no easy task. Wickham's programming philosophy is as follows:

> Firstly, I am looking for the "best" . . . although that can be subjective, there is general consensus that, for example, Ry Cooder is a great guitarist or Emmylou Harris is a great singer or Bruce Cockburn is a great songwriter . . . etc. We set our sights high (others can judge whether we get there).

> Secondly, we are 50% Canadian and 50% other countries. Also, 50% are new to the festival (keeps it fresh) and 50% are repeats (gives us tradition).

> Thirdly, I look for balance . . . Celtic, blues, world beat music, singer/songwriters, bluegrass, headliners, etc. Enough for the young crowd, enough legends, high-energy dance bands, and laid-back acoustic, etc. Some local. . . .

> The biggest change was the introduction of headliners (now being copied by Calgary and Winnipeg) and the introduction of world music. Obviously increasing ticket sales (i.e., audience feedback) . . . has led to bigger budgets making the above changes possible. . . . "If you build it they will come."

> I take suggestions from everywhere, including musicians . . . in fact I listen to musicians, songwriters very carefully . . . musicians also tell other musicians that Edmonton is a very good festival to play. . . .

Providing a balance of performers in any given year is critical to the success of the EFMF, and this point is also true for other types of creative and cultural arts festivals. A delicate mixture of performers or attractions allows a producer or an artistic director to maintain a stable audience base while expanding to embrace new audiences. This does not necessarily mean catering to the flavor of the month or sticking with the tried and true. Many festivals are striving to continuously reinvent themselves in order to remain fresh, vital, and alive. What this means is not only being willing to take risks but also taking educated, justified risks. In so many instances, the talent is the festival program, but the festival itself takes on a life and a spirit that is contributed to by the performing talent, the audience, the location, the community, the tradition, and the new.

As Terry Wickham is fond of noting, "the proof of the pudding is in the show, audience reaction and ticket sales . . . there are no committees involved in booking, it is the decisions of the AD . . . if the board doesn't like the lineups . . . they get rid of the AD!"

Birth of the Blues in Nanaimo—Championing Your Festival: An Interview With Bill Lucas

Bill (Billyboy) Lucas is the Chair of the Nanaimo Blues Society, and he is a man possessed. His passion for the blues began in the late 1960s, when in his teens he saw blues greats Buddy Guy, Muddy Waters, Howlin' Wolf, and John Mayall. At the time a new resident in Nanaimo, British Columbia, Lucas attended the first Nanaimo Adventure Games, where he felt the excitement and the vibe from the younger generation. While Lucas was watching local Maple award-winning blues artist David Gogo perform at one of the Adventure Games social events, a lightbulb appeared over Lucas' head, causing him to ask, "Why not have a blues festival?" Bill let the idea bubble for a year or so and asked a few questions around town (no one said no), and the Nanaimo Summertime Blues Festival was born.

Having a champion for your festival is often critical to getting it off the ground and giving the festival its initial impetus. This champion may be an individual with a great idea or a specialized interest who can rally others to achieve their goals. Often the champion is a combination of personality and passion, a person with a vision who believes so strongly in an idea and a community that he is willing to go to great lengths to gain support. For Bill Lucas, that vision is expressed in a number of ways. Through his leadership, the Nanaimo Blues Society (2007), under whose auspices the Summertime Blues Festival is run, maintains year-round visibility in the community. They hold dances and concerts outside of the festival season, operate portable kiosks in local shopping malls, and participate in the Silly Boat Regatta, all with a goal of staying visible in the community, forming connections, and raising awareness. Often the champion becomes the very public face of the festival and is closely identified with the event. Lucas is at every dance, every concert, and every mall session. Cross promotion is also gained through his activity with Nanaimo's community-based campus radio station, CHLY 101.7 FM (2007), for which he hosts the Friday Night Fish Fry and Stormy Sunday Blues. When people stop Bill in the street to thank him for his passion and energy and for the Summertime Blues, he makes a special point of thanking them, creating a positive energy and a currency that is worth its weight in gold. All this is not done without cost, though. For all his passion and energy, Lucas is very aware of the potential for burnout, a fate that has felled many festival leaders who are passionate about their activities.

The vision of the Nanaimo Blues Society is expressed clearly through its goals and objectives:

- Share our love of the blues by producing a music festival in beautiful Nanaimo.
- Showcase Nanaimo's rich and diverse musical community.
- Celebrate Nanaimo's image as an event and cultural center.
- Stage a music festival that will attract tourists to downtown Nanaimo.
- Foster mentorship among musicians.
- Generate and stimulate local economy (Nanaimo Blues Society 2007).

To illustrate its social conscience, the Summertime Blues Festival has remained a free event. There is no beer garden, and no liquor is served on site. This policy was set for two key reasons: (1) to keep the event accessible for families and to appeal to people of all ages and (2) to maintain good relations and not compete with the many downtown bars and taverns who are in that business.

Passion. Persistence. Purpose. These are characteristics of a champion. Along with the people and partnerships that develop, their visions also grow to fruition. This, in turn, helps to create and maintain vital, vibrant communities to live in or visit.

Special Events

Gaylene Carpenter, EdD

University of Oregon

A s an area of arts and cultural programming, special events are important to include in this book for two reasons. First, the number of special events in general is growing by leaps and bounds, and arts and leisure organizations are contributing to that growth. Second, arts and cultural organizations as well as recreation and leisure organizations can play an even bigger role than they are already playing in meeting the increased demand for special events.

Many people do not realize that museums are not only facilitating special events but also increasingly employing special events professionals. The Kresge Art Museum at Michigan State University recently recruited for a special event and communications coordinator (Michigan State University 2006). The position called for a person to develop and implement special programs and events, to disseminate museum information through public relations and marketing, and to design, implement, and evaluate special events in coordination with staff and volunteers. These tasks are clearly associated with programming. This position in special events could be for any number of arts or recreation organizations—not just for a museum.

This chapter begins with a brief overview of the events industry, clarifies the term *special events*, and concludes with an examination of how arts or recreation organizations are presently involved in programming special events. Several kinds of events are discussed, as are ways in which recreation and arts programmers can be more involved in producing these events. You will also find two case studies in this chapter. One examines events from the perspective of an executive director of a professional association; this person creates and uses arts programming concepts. The other looks at the events of a large regional art museum. These events are designed for nontraditional participants and foster collaborations with other organizations.

Special Events

Fifteen years ago, special events were just that: special events. They were one-time activities that highlighted, recognized, or culminated an ongoing comprehensive program. Today other forms of events are also prominent, and our understanding of special events is expanding. Conceptually, the term *special events* means much more and includes other terms such as *event marketing*, *event tourism*, *convention events*, *development events*, and *fund-raising events*, just to name a few. The past 20 years have been growth years for special events, and it is predicted that these events will continue to grow (Getz 2005; Goldblatt 2002). Both arts organizations and recreation organizations are adding to the growth in special events.

Arts and recreation professionals not only are producing a wider range of special events themselves but also are taking advantage of opportunities when conferences occur in their cities and counties. Programmers are typically charged with planning and implementing special events as part of their ongoing job responsibilities in managing a comprehensive program. In addition, arts and recreation professionals who are active in their organizations will likely participate on teams charged with recruiting conferences to their city or region or on program committees charged with planning and conducting educational sessions for professional conferences. Arts and recreation programmers who facilitate comprehensive arts and cultural programs and services may also engage in planning and conducting special events in collaboration with each other.

What is meant by the term *special event?* The different types, the diversity of formats, and the continuing promulgation of events confound the possibility of a definition that fits everybody's perception. Getz (2005) and Goldblatt (2002), who have written texts on event management that have been widely used for the past 20 years, offer us some insight into special events. Though the two authors do not agree on a specific definition of *special event,* there is a degree of commonality in their perceptions. Goldblatt suggests that a special event is a unique moment in time celebrated with ceremony and ritual to satisfy specific needs (6). Though Getz posits that we "will never be able to come up with a universal, standardized definition nor a classification of what types of events are special" (16), he offers two definitions. One emphasizes the planning organization of the event, while the other emphasizes the event participant:

- A special event is a one-time or an infrequent event that occurs outside of the normal program or activities of the sponsoring or organizing body.

- To the customer or guest, a special event is an opportunity for an experience outside of the normal choices or beyond everyday experience (Getz 2005, 16).

For the purposes of this chapter, our working definition of *special event* is placed within the context of the definition of programming given in chapter 1. Managing special events involves planning and delivering leisure or educational experiences for individuals and groups. Like program planning, managing special events requires overseeing multiple tasks and functions related to the development, implementation, evaluation, and modification of the event. Within this book, we find ourselves agreeing with Goldblatt that special events are celebratory. We also see value in the approach of Getz in that these events typically emerge from an organizational context (arts or recreation) and frequently are viewed differently by the sponsoring organization and the event participants.

Listing the kinds of special events that take place will help our understanding of them. Because of the diversity in the events industry, several typologies of events have been suggested. Two widely accepted views are from Getz (2005) and Goldblatt (2002). Table 10.1 lists the categories of events that they have suggested. The Getz list includes hallmark, mega-, media, corporate, cause-related, publicity, periodic, and one-time events. Goldblatt notes that event management as a profession requires public assembly for celebration, education, marketing, and reunion. From this perspective, he identifies the 10 subfields of events as civic events, expositions, fairs and festivals, hallmark events, hospitality, meetings and conferences, retail events, social life-cycle events, sports events, and tourism events.

Arts and Cultural Events

Figure 10.1 (see page 146) depicts the kinds of special events that take place in arts and cultural programming. These include events that are presented by nonprofit arts organizations and public recreation and leisure organizations. Think of these events as being similar

Table 10.1 Categories of Special Events

Getz (2005)	Goldblatt (2002)
Hallmark events	Civic events
Megaevents	Expositions
Media events	Fairs and festivals
Corporate events	Hallmark events
Cause-related events	Hospitality
Publicity events	Meetings and conferences
Periodic events	Retail events
One-time events	Social life-cycle events
	Sports events
	Tourism events

145

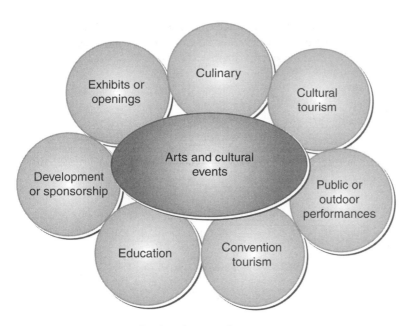

Figure 10.1 Arts and cultural special events.

to or overlapping with established forms of special events and, as special events, as being somewhat unique to our arts and cultural programming purposes. Indications are that we will see growth in the number and types of special events. In the next several sections, we will examine special event areas that are particularly relevant to arts and cultural programming. These include cultural tourism, convention tourism, exhibits and openings, development and sponsorship special events, public or outdoor performances, educational events, and culinary events.

The first two areas for discussion are closely linked to the tourism industry. Both cultural tourism and convention tourism offer the potential for arts managers and recreation professionals to develop arts and cultural leisure experiences for tourists or to partner with tourism organizations to offer collaborative experiences. Following our exploration of these two tourism-linked event opportunities, we will discuss other special events with less direct association with the tourism industry (i.e., exhibitions and openings, development and sponsorship events, public outdoor performances, educational events, culinary events).

Cultural Tourism

Cultural tourism has many meanings. McKercher and du Cros (2002) see cultural tourism as special-interest tourism, as people motivated to travel for reasons that differ from those of other tourists, as being experiential, or as being cultural because of the activities undertaken. Cultural tourism is growing in popularity (Moscardo 2000; Walle 1998).

> [Cultural tourism] was regarded as a specialized, niche activity that was thought to be pursued by a small number of better educated, more affluent tourists who were looking for something other than the standard sand, sun, and sea holiday. It is only since the fragmentation of the mass market in the 1990s that cultural tourism has been recognized for what it is: a high-profile, mass-market activity. (McKercher and du Cros 2002, 1)

Cultural tourists often produce greater economic benefits for local economies than do other types of tourists (Getz 1997; Shaw and Williams 2002). As such, many recreation and arts organizations are marketing their programs to these new constituents. Cultural tourism not only offers visitors opportunities to experience the arts and cultural fabric of local areas and organizations but also brings about communication between visitors and locals (Carpenter 2004).

Convention and visitors' bureaus (CVBs) consider arts and cultural amenities as points of commerce and market those amenities to specific demographic groups. Programmers need to communicate with staff at visitor and convention bureaus so that they have information about arts and cultural programs and services that they can share with convention and visitor groups. Frequently, specific programs are developed for groups with certain arts and cultural interests. For example, if a professional association of archeologists is holding its yearly conference in a city with a museum of natural and cultural history, staff at that museum should plan something to entice conference attendees to that museum during their stay. Many parks are historic sites where special events, including reenactments, take place. Cultural and heritage organizations, such as museums, performing arts organizations, festivals, humanities organizations, and historic preservation groups, have partnered with CVBs, tour operators, state travel offices, hotels, and air carriers in order to create initiatives (Craine, 2005).

In providing cultural opportunities for tourists, professionals in arts and recreation are finding ways to collaborate with other community professionals to create experiences that will attract the savvy cultural tourist. An example from Philadelphia illustrates the convergence of culture, heritage, and place.

Neighborhood Tourism Networks in Philadelpia

Collaborators from the many neighborhoods of Philadelphia provide unique cultural tourism programs that are promoted through the visitor association of greater Philadelphia. The Neighborhood Tourism Network (NTN) takes visitors beyond the colonial icons of the center city's historic district in order to introduce them to where Philadelphians live, work, and play (Philadelphia and the Countryside 2007). NTN is made up of 17 organizations that represent historical and ethnic associations throughout the city in partnership with the Greater Philadelphia Tourism Marketing Corporation. The wide variety of visitor experiences includes Taking a Stand for Freedom (first-person accounts and musical presentations of African American experiences); Voices of Chinatown; Latin Soul, Latin Flavor; Philadelphia's Civil Rights Struggle; Mummers and Mozzarella (South Philadelphia); The Sound of Philadelphia (musical heritage); Exotic Cuisine and Esoteric Culture (West Philadelphia); Philadelphia's Jewish Heritage; Mural Arts Program; and various walking tours.

People who are creating events for cultural tourists are doing so in part because this subset of the general tourist population has specific interests. Like other tourists, cultural tourists are traveling with certain interests in mind—specifically, the arts and cultural activities available in a specific locale. Cultural and heritage attractions are expanding in popularity, and there is more interest in authentic experiences as opposed to traditional resort holidays (Getz 2005, 132). Cultural tourists can experience anything from folk art to a festival honoring a famous author. Cultural and heritage assets are traditionally one of a kind (Craine 2005) and thus are very unique to an area.

Convention Tourism

The convention industry has grown in the last 50 years and is recognized globally for its economic contribution to tourism (Spiller 2002). Today, the convention industry is one of the most buoyant sectors of the tourism industry (McKercher and du Cros 2002, 6). Convention tourism encompasses a wide range of formats, including meetings, conferences, conventions, seminars, workshops, training sessions, and the like, and is part of the more broadly defined tourism and hospitality industry. Spiller (2002) notes that some of the growth in convention tourism equates with the general expansion in tourism. She also notes that both the United States and Canada ranked in the top 15 countries for international congresses (i.e., conventions) between 1974 and 1999.

The terms *conference* and *convention* are defined as a meeting of two or more people or as an assembly of people discussing a common subject or sharing a common purpose (Polivka 1996). These terms are closely associated. Polivka (1996) notes that the National Directory of Occupational Titles and Codes designates *meeting management* as the official title of the profession that employs people who plan meetings, conferences, conventions, and so on. He then discusses the various position titles that meeting planners hold. An arts programmer engaged in planning meetings, workshops, and similar activities would fit into the category of meeting manager.

What does convention tourism mean to us in arts and cultural programming? Let's begin to answer this question by examining selected findings from a recent market report in order to see how they could impact arts and cultural programming. Each year, Meetings Media polls meeting planners, including association planners, corporate planners, and independent planners, in order to track data associated with the industry. Recent findings identified five trends (Davidson 2006) which follow in italics. How arts and cultural programmers can respond to these trends is briefly discussed.

- *Planning cycles average 10.8 months.* This duration allows plenty of time to promote local arts and cultural leisure programs. Because arts and cultural programmers typically plan months

and sometimes years in advance, they can create new experiences for convention visitors or can make meeting managers aware of an organization's comprehensive programs and services that can be accessed during a convention.

• *On average, 17% of meeting planners booked special venues for their meetings.* This means that meeting managers may be looking for nontraditional sites for their attendees—sites other than convention and conference centers and hotels. Appropriate spaces in arts organizations can be attractive booking sites. Though many arts organizations are unable to accommodate large functions, many are able to host smaller, special functions associated with the larger convention. Convention professionals report that the small meetings they routinely plan include seminars, committee meetings, board meetings, and training sessions (Russell 2006). These types of meetings should work well in most of our venues, and with our arts or recreation amenities included as an added value, meeting planners are likely to be interested in pursuing such an option.

• *On average, 19% of meeting planners found recreation facilities to be important in booking hotels.* Thus leisure programmers could create and market enticing recreation packages. Recreation organizations that have fitness centers, walking paths, and activity classes could make them available at special rates for meeting attendees.

• *Typical activities incorporated into meetings included golf, spousal programs, team-building activities, attractions and theme parks, spa activities, casinos and gaming, sporting events, skiing, cooking programs, and festivals (and in that order).* Both arts and recreation organizations could identify collaborative programming opportunities in many of these activities. Potential meeting attendees and their families are often persuaded to attend if there are attractive pre- and postconference recreation or vacation opportunities (Crouch and Weber 2002). Arts and recreation organizations can work with professional associations and local CVBs to plan and facilitate attractive on-site experiences and pre- and postevents for conferences.

• *The top four off-site venues used by meeting attendees were restaurants, unique attractions, historic buildings and landmarks, and museums.* Here again, arts and cultural organizations have a role to play in promoting convention tourism. They could set up special exhibits that would attract meeting attendees. They could also partner with local restaurants to offer discounts for visiting before, during, or after the convention.

As mentioned, there are other areas of arts and cultural special events besides cultural tourism and convention tourism. At least five other types of special events are currently offered to various

Conventions can include activities such as cooking programs.
Photo by Georgia Freedman

publics by arts managers and recreation professionals. In addition, programmers can anticipate that more forms will emerge in the future given the continued popularity of special events for providing participant enjoyment and meeting organizational needs and interests. Special events already among those being currently provided include exhibitions and openings, development and sponsorship events, public outdoor performances, and educational events. Culinary special events are emerging as a uniquely programmable option in arts and leisure settings.

Exhibitions and Openings

Museums, galleries, and community arts organizations frequently program special events related to exhibits, show openings, and lectures or arts performances. These events are usually promoted to the general public though occasionally they may be by invitation only and provide development and sponsorship perks for those individuals involved.

Museums traditionally have had meeting spaces available at their facilities, and more recently these museums have been encouraging staff members to actively promote these spaces for use in outside meetings and functions. More and more often today, plans for building new or renovating existing museums specifically include spaces for various programs, meetings and conferences, weddings, seminars, and other activities. These spaces are being included because in general museums are doing more and more programming (see chapter 13) and because they can attract new audiences and revenue streams. Creating spaces for nontraditional museum activities encourages nontraditional participants to come to museums. These participants may serendipitously realize an interest in the museum and return to view the museum's collections and partake in its other programs. Museums also earn fees for site usage and receive percentages of on-site catering revenues that are generated by meetings.

In other instances, museums initiate or facilitate larger, off-site events. The Museum of New Mexico initiated one of the earliest known off-site exhibitions called the Southwest Indian Fair and Arts and Crafts Exhibition. Even today this special event continues to promote and preserve Native American arts (Vradenburgh 2005) and attracts 80,000 people. It is held during the summer in August. According to its sponsor, the Southwestern Association for Indian Arts, it envelops the town's central plaza and surrounding streets and generates more than $100 million U.S. in revenues to the state and region (Southwestern Association for Indian Arts 2006). This event initiates related events such as gallery openings and art shows. This is a fairly typical outcome in that large exhibitions frequently make it possible for smaller organizations to produce allied programs, activities, and services.

In many communities, community arts organizations collaborate with galleries, museums, recreation and cultural services, and other community arts organizations to offer art walks. These typically occur on the same day of each month, perhaps on the first Friday or the last Thursday. Galleries and museums use special events like this to showcase artists. Performance artists entertain participants inside the arts venues and on street corners and other public spaces along the walk. These collaborative events enable various arts organizations to join efforts in facilitating such events while increasing public awareness of the arts. Art walks have become quite popular in a number of cities.

Another example of collaboration in special events involves the arts and cultural experiences held in conjunction with the Olympic Games that take place worldwide every two years. Perceived primarily as a sporting event, the Olympic Games have included the arts since the Stockholm Games of 1912 (Alliance for the Arts 2006). Categories for competition in the 1936 Berlin Games included painting, graphic arts, and commercial arts. More recently, the 2006 Winter Games in Torino, Italy, featured special events called *Italyart* as part of the Cultural Olympiads accompanying the sporting events. Italyart experiences included drama, dance, art, literature, and cinema (Torino Olympics 2007). Professionals in Vancouver, British Columbia, the site for the 2010 Winter Games, are currently planning a wide variety of arts events, including an Olympic Arts Festival, an Olympic Museum Exhibition, Olympic National Team Artists, an Olympic Flame Relay, and the Olympiad Cultural Program that includes cultural activities, festivals, educational programs, and conferences (Alliance for the Arts 2006).

Development and Sponsorship Special Events

More and more frequently, nonprofit arts and cultural organizations and public parks and recreation organizations are finding that they need to generate more income, especially as other funding sources have dwindled. Finding creative and effective ways to recruit and keep donors and sponsors, both of whom support our organizations, is an increasingly important aspect of programmers' jobs.

It is not unusual to find professional staff members whose responsibilities include facilitating programs that encourage donor contributions. Examples of these events include galas (festive occasions that typically include food and entertainment) and other fund-raising events. In addition, special events are a way to thank and recognize sponsors (businesses and private individuals who contribute money to programs).

Creating arts and cultural programs to generate income is one reason why more programs, services, and special events are being offered today. Another reason is that other programs and activities are being designed for development and fund-raising. Today we see symphony orchestras developing programs ranging from high-profile galas planned at upscale restaurants to garden walks and parties in people's backyards. We see music arts organizations conducting auctions to generate money to purchase instruments for their youth programs. We see representatives from sponsoring organizations and significant donors invited to meet with elite or well-known actors performing in local, community theaters. You name it, and we see it because special events are enjoyable and effective ways to thank individuals and businesses for supporting arts and cultural programs.

While developing special events in order to recognize and recruit donors and sponsors may not seem unusual to us today, it was not that long ago that the prevailing thinking did not involve engaging in such activity. The thinking was that if we open our doors and perform it or present it, participants and donors will come. As we saw in chapter 1, this is not the case given the number and variety of things people can do with their free time. Knowledgeable arts and recreation programmers know that they are competing for people's free time and are acting accordingly in order to communicate the value of their programs and services. They also know that they are competing for people's discretionary dollars and for businesses' sponsorship choices. Development and sponsorship special events are a way to recognize donor and sponsor contributions to arts and recreation organizations.

Public Outdoor Performances

A form of arts and cultural programming that has wide public appeal and seems to be gaining strength can be seen every summer in many cities and counties across the United States. This

Outdoor performances allow the public to experience a wide variety of music and art.
Photo courtesy of Gaylene Carpenter

programming encompasses the live, outdoor performances presented by nonprofit arts organizations, public recreation organizations, and private enterprises. People have come to expect free or inexpensive outdoor concerts and performances by popular and emerging local entertainers. The purposes of these special events range from public service to generating income to creating public awareness of ongoing comprehensive arts and cultural programs to bringing large numbers of community people from all walks of life together in an open, richly cultural setting.

These public outdoor special events are quite diverse and appear in smaller as well as larger geographic areas. Recently, Akron, Ohio, with a population that exceeds 217,000 and makes it the 82nd largest city in the United States (Akron, Ohio 2007), offered a full range of special events throughout the summer, including summer concerts (i.e., Music by the Lakeside, Friday Night Concert Series, Pops 'N More in the Park). In the same year, Fargo, North Dakota, with a population of approximately 90,599 (Fargo, North Dakota 2007), offered a weekly downtown Festival Market, a school Centennial event, museum events and exhibits, and a country music festival during the summer months. Both cities had arts and cultural events to offer every week throughout the summer.

Special events such as these may occur indoors as well as outdoors. Indoor venues serve as locales for such events during times of the year when the weather may be an issue. Indoor venues are also used when sponsoring organizations want to bring patrons to their site. Jazz at the Corcoran Gallery of Art is an example of this kind of program. These noontime jazz concerts are held midweek, presumably on days when gallery attendance is lower. Providing special events that encourage participation during low-usage times is a good way to divert public attention to other arts and cultural programs and services.

Organizers of these special events are finding it more and more challenging to create arts and cultural experiences that are unique. Though holding repeat performances by popular artists is a good strategy for creating successful special events, providing the unusual is a current programming trend. The public can tire of similar programming, and many arts and cultural programmers are finding a wide variety of performers and entertainment options. Special performances such as Taiko drumming and Shakespeare in the Park offer unique experiences. Drumming circles may interest those who prefer participative rather than observational music experiences (World Rhythm Festival 2007). Living-history reenactments and tattoos are attracting more participants and larger audiences. Art fairs and festivals are examples of other large, popular events. The John Michael Kohler Arts Center in Sheboygan, Wisconsin, has a mission to encourage and support innovative explorations in the arts and to foster an exchange between a national community of artists and the public (John Michael Kohler Arts Center 2006). Its Outdoor Arts Festival, held each summer, features more than 100 artists arriving from California to New York. The arts center is using the festival as a special event that addresses its mission.

To conclude this section on performance-related special events, let's think ahead of our times, so to speak. In what ways might the conceptualization or delivery of special events be reconceived in nontraditional ways? What kinds of arts and cultural experiences that are considered innovative today might be reconfigured to be on the cutting edge of tomorrow?

Consider the connection between fashion shows and arts and cultural leisure experiences. Recently, two fashion shows were presented as special events demonstrating how items destined for landfills could be used for fashion and how other items of fashion could be created from sustainable rather than synthetic products. Recycled junk was presented at an event open to the public called *Junk to Funk* that was held in the Pacific Northwest (Junk to Funk 2007), and a fashion show featuring clothes made from corn products was produced for the Biotechnology Industry Organization meeting in Chicago (Springen 2006).

Educational Special Events

Special events emphasizing education are becoming increasingly popular arts and cultural leisure experiences. The interest in educational programs is emerging for two reasons. First, with the decline in arts opportunities offered in public schools, many arts and recreation agencies began growing their educational programs. Second, adults are showing interest in lifelong learning opportunities,

and arts and recreation organizations are responding to offer more educational programs. The range of educational special events is well developed today, and many people believe this area will continue to grow given programmers' initiative to do more.

Arts organizations such as museums and community arts centers have long provided special events, both passive and participatory, teaching children and adults about the arts. Performing arts organizations such as opera companies and symphony orchestras routinely present special events for children in the public schools. Most contemporary organizations offer free events along with ticketed events in keeping with their mission statements, which frequently emphasize access and education. Recreation agencies typically offer a wide range of programs and special events, many of which we have already discussed in this chapter.

Often, educational opportunities take place in conjunction with larger arts and cultural special events. Many of the well-regarded folk festivals, such as the Philadelphia Folk Festival (2006), include opportunities for participants to learn from the experts. In the 2006 Philadelphia Folk Festival, learning experiences in music (e.g., harmonica, fiddle, dulcimer) and dance (i.e., contra, swing, jam, square, Cajun) as well as opportunities to observe artists (e.g., clay, glass, jewelry, leather) were offered throughout the 3-day event. The Chautauqua Institution, located in the state of New York, focuses on art, education, religion, and recreation (Chautauqua Institution 2007). The institute offers a full range of events, primarily throughout the summer months. Its programs provide communities with a wide variety of lectures and discussions on arts and cultural history. Also, other U.S. states have organizations that partner with the institute to offer Chautauqua events around their state. In Oregon, for example, the statewide Council for the Humanities supports and initiates these programs:

> The Oregon Council for the Humanities seeks to improve the quality of life for Oregonians by providing programs that enrich minds and broaden perspectives, foster positive human relationships, encourage civility and good citizenship, and bring together the diverse peoples who make up our statewide culture. (Oregon Council for the Humanities 2007)

These events are educational and include a variety of lectures and discussions that encourage people to share information, participate in dialogue, and revitalize their sense of community. Arts and recreation organizations can help support educational programs such as these by partnering or cosponsoring these special events in their communities.

The Monterey Museum of Art, located in Monterey, California, has a rather unique educational program that they call *Museum on Wheels* (MOW). MOW is a multicultural art educational program that brings a mobile museum of international folk art to schools in the city and surrounding areas. Integral to the school curriculum, MOW staff members work closely with classroom teachers to provide bilingual services for kindergarten through eighth grades (Van Der Stad 2005). When the long vehicle arrives at the school, you can be sure that the children sense that a special event is going to happen.

Culinary Special Events

Special events featuring food and drink are growing in number. Interestingly, culinary events have become a niche in tourism referred to as *culinary tourism*. The International Culinary Tourism Association defines *culinary tourism* as developing unique and memorable food and drink experiences and then marketing them to visitors (International Culinary Arts Association 2006). Culinary tourism can be seen as a subset of cultural tourism because cuisine is often an expression of a local culture.

Many culinary events include arts and cultural experiences. Some of these culinary special events are offered to promote new products; others market existing products. Some of these events are used to highlight locales, such as a winery. Others create awareness of local cuisine or popular chefs. And still other culinary special events, such as the Gilroy Garlic Festival (2006), are closely related to cultural tourism and are used to promote entire regions.

Often, culinary arts are embedded in other types of arts and cultural events. For example, the Cherry Creek Arts Festival has long featured culinary artists along with other artisans (Cherry Creek Arts Festival 2006). Culinary special events are of interest to us because art is typically a

major feature of most culinary events. In fact, some special events are dedicated to culinary arts, giving new meaning to the parental admonishment to stop playing with your food. The Cherry Creek Arts Festival and the Gilroy Garlic Festival both include food demonstrations. Juried fine arts and crafts, music, and other live performances are also part of both festivals.

Clearly, there are many special events in which it is impossible to separate experiences associated with arts and culture from experiences related to food and drink. In fact, the two types of experience are used to complement each other:

• The Scottsdale League for the Arts is a nonprofit volunteer organization in Arizona. The league hosts the Scottsdale Culinary Festival each year and raises money through this event to fund the arts and arts education (Scottsdale Culinary Festival 2006). This weeklong special event includes wine tasting and wine brunches; the James Beard Dinner that features influential chefs, culinary artisans who demonstrate their talents; the Great Arizona Picnic featuring outdoor performances; and several other activities.

• The Oklahoma Wine Harvest Festival is an annual special event commemorating the September wine harvest. Billed as more than just a wine festival, this event offers a fun-filled day in the country, live music, crafts, gifts, gourmet foods, guided tours, and a chance to visit with other folks interested in building the Oklahoma wine industry (Nuyaka Creek Winery 2007).

• The Art of Food and Wine in Palm Desert, California, promises cooking and tasting, concerts and cocktails, arts and outdoors, and golf and grilling (Moore 2006). This special culinary event costs $650 U.S. for one person to attend, and with additional events, attendees can expect the total cost to be $1,000 U.S. per person (Moore 2006). The 4-day program includes wine tasting, gourmet food, and music. At least two dozen vintners attend; there are culinary demonstrations, seminars on the taste and benefits of olive oil, and presentations on the fine points of champagne and sparkling wines. According to Lee Brian Schrager, the founder and director of the 2007 Food Network South Beach Wine and Food Festival in Florida, these kinds of food and wine celebrations help local economies and increase recognition of local products (Moore 2006).

Culinary special events include farmer's markets where participants can enjoy culinary goods, demonstrations, and entertainment.

Photo courtesy of Kim Still

Farmers' markets appear to be growing in popularity, and they offer another example of the merging of arts and culture through culinary special events. The National Farmers' Market Directory noted that the number of markets increased 111% between 1994 and 2004, and there are more than 3,700 farmers' markets operating in the United States alone (U.S. Department of Agriculture 2006). Farmers' markets are places where rural and city folks gather in ways that culturally define an area. The markets typically include demonstrations and entertainment. The farmers' market in Wolfville (Wolfville Farmers' Market 2006), Nova Scotia, for example, operates every Saturday. The market includes more than 50 venders and provides ongoing entertainment for a city whose population is just greater than 3,600. Though located in a small town in the rural Annapolis Valley of western Nova Scotia, the Wolfville farmers' market is similar to those found in larger cities across North America in terms of it being a gathering place for arts and cultural expression and experience.

Summary

This chapter discussed the myriad of special events associated with arts and cultural programming. Special events are a growing area of arts and cultural programming for many recreation and arts agencies. This chapter also examined the meaning of the term *special events* and presented many examples of these events. It described organizations not typically associated with special events along with those that are better known for their events. Special event areas relevant to arts and cultural programmers, such as cultural tourism, convention tourism, exhibits and openings, development and sponsorship events, public outdoor performances, educational events, and culinary events, were considered. Following are two case studies written by arts administrators to illustrate how they view special events in their organizations.

CASE STUDIES IN SPECIAL EVENTS

The following two case studies illustrate the importance of special events for arts and cultural organizations. The first discusses the many and varied events held by the Memphis chapter of the American Institute of Architects (AIA). In reviewing this case study, you will see links between cultural tourism and convention tourism and will see how professional societies, such as this Memphis group of architects, provide educational and recreational events designed to create awareness and generate income. In the second case study, you will learn about programs provided by the Seattle Art Museum (SAM). In addition to programming and maintaining several museum sites, SAM produces special events ranging from on-site festivals and conferences to many activities in the outdoor sculpture park that features a locale for performance and other events.

AIA Memphis

Heather B. Baugus, Executive Director

AIA Memphis is a professional association for the architectural community in western Tennessee. Its mission is to be an effective resource and advocate for its members and to inspire a better built environment. All activities of the organization, including management, membership services, and events, are produced out of a single office with one full-time director. The organization produces an average of 30 programs per year, including professional development meetings, public lectures, fund-raisers, and community outreach and educational events. Audiences include representatives from the architecture and design community, professional affiliates, arts and cultural organizations, government agencies, civic organizations, historic preservation agencies, and the general public. Design education programs for K-12 are held in a variety of academic settings and in collaboration with arts and cultural organizations such as museums, historic preservation groups, city and county arts programs, artists, professional associations, and cultural institutions. Program attendance varies from 20 to more than 1,000 and includes all ages, social classes, and economic backgrounds. Collaborations are a critical component of all design education programs and community outreach and

educational events. They encourage audience participation, expand the base of expertise, establish the credibility of new programs, and offset limited staff resources.

All AIA Memphis programs fall into one of three categories: meetings, fund-raising events, and community outreach and educational programs. The executive director plays a variety of roles depending on the objectives of the program. In every case, responsibilities include program development, promotion, implementation, and closure. Closure involves financial reconciliation, evaluation, and modification.

Meetings occur throughout the year to advance the organization or to offer professional development through educational lectures. With a target audience of association members, the primary role of the programmer is to assess the professional environment for time-sensitive topics, identify and secure expert presenters, manage all event logistics, promote the event to the target audience, secure sponsorships as needed, and evaluate success through surveys and financial analysis. The programmer, particularly in a single office, acts as manager, marketer, developer, accountant, and assistant. Given the limitations in time and budget, in many cases the programmer also takes on the role of graphic designer.

AIA Memphis produces two cornerstone events that provide substantial income while also offering opportunities for professional recognition, camaraderie, and recreation: the Celebration of Architecture Gala and the annual Golf Tournament. The gala provides association members and others in the design profession an opportunity to celebrate the outstanding achievements of their colleagues. This event has evolved from a 2-hour reception with 50 in attendance to a large-scale production that brings together more than 300 architects and designers for a multidimensional experience. Unlike meetings that involve planning in a series of short stages beginning 6 months in advance and that are limited in overall production, the gala requires substantial planning and involvement. Attendance, financial goals, and postevent satisfaction of attendees and sponsors measure success. Therefore, emphasis is placed on developing a strong event committee that clearly understands the motivations, needs, and expectations of two distinct audiences: attendees and sponsors. Satisfying these two audiences influences every aspect of event planning, including the schedule, presenters, musicians, food, and location. Even the smallest detail of the table centerpieces or point of entry becomes significant. Every opportunity to shape the participants' experience is considered. Technological advances and access to production experts have changed the look of the event, allowing for further theatrical displays and elaborate presentations. All of the elements come together to create an event that maximizes the experience for all of the senses. It is the responsibility of the programmer to see that a timeline is established 12 months in advance and that clear goals are developed by the committee. Success relies heavily on the programmer's ability to both manage the process and delegate the tasks.

All new and reoccurring programs are evaluated for success based on the program objectives established in advance. Every program must support the mission of the organization. There is, however, a distinction between programs that are intended to raise funds and programs that are purely educational. This is not to suggest that they are always mutually exclusive. Professional associations are beginning to take a more active role in their community by adding programs that are educational for audiences outside of their membership. AIA Memphis currently invests 50% of its resources in producing programs that respond to community needs and in offering opportunities for further education on a variety of topics. The goal of these programs is to encourage advocacy for more sustainable communities. This goal is achieved by offering members of the community opportunities for learning about the built environment; events encouraging further exploration of their city as it relates to architecture, art, and public spaces; and direct assistance with community design challenges.

Partnerships play a vital role in assessing the needs of the community and in establishing programs that reach intended audiences. AIA Memphis established two expanded programs to deliver education and outreach programs to the community as well as to children aged 6 to 18. Architecture Month was established in 2004 to celebrate architecture in a historical, a professional, an educational, and a design-centered context. Because of the interest in celebrating the past as well as the future of Memphis, a partnership was established with Memphis Heritage Inc., a local nonprofit whose mission is to educate and coordinate individuals and groups to save, improve, reuse, and

maintain architecturally and historically significant buildings, open spaces, streets, neighborhoods, parks, and cultural artifacts in Shelby County, Tennessee. Each year this partnership hosts 6 weeks of public lectures, architecture tours, youth initiatives, and community activities. Invited speakers offer national and international perspectives on design as a means to strengthen and positively affect communities and individuals. Every lecture is matched with an appropriate location that emphasizes the topic. To date these lectures have all been held in arts or cultural venues because these venues traditionally are the greatest innovations of their time architecturally and are destinations that attract larger audiences. In addition to providing spaces that resonate with the lectures, using these venues allows AIA Memphis to offer financial support to and build relationships with organizations that become partners in delivering youth programs on art and design.

With support for arts education in public schools dwindling, there has become a greater reliance on community-based organizations to provide access to the arts. Over the years, AIA chapters have taken a leading role in providing access to design education. Architects for Education, a program developed under AIA Memphis, works with arts and cultural organizations in collaboration with architecture professionals to provide programs for K-12. Design competitions held in the classrooms coordinate with a current exhibition at various museums within the city. This program provides students and teachers with additional curriculum options to explore design through instruction by local professionals and then to further that learning through site visits at local museums. AIA Memphis has also helped develop architecture and design lesson plans to be incorporated into the educational programs produced by the various museums. What evolves from these collaborations and the many others occurring throughout the year is an open dialogue in which ideas are shared and programs are developed by individual groups who know that they have a network of support. These collaborations enable the organizations to take on projects that may extend beyond their resources but have lasting effects on the community and meet needs.

Connecting With New Museum Audiences Through Special Events
Cara Egan, Manager of Communications, Seattle Art Museum

The Seattle Art Museum (SAM) is one museum in three locations: the downtown Seattle Art Museum (postmodern design by Robert Venturi and a new expansion scheduled to open in spring 2007), the Seattle Asian Art Museum in Volunteer Park (1930s art deco building set in an Olmstead park), and the Olympic Sculpture Park on the city's waterfront (9 acres, or 0.04 square meters, of green space and sculpture). Each facility has its own character and provides a unique atmosphere for holding a special event. One goal of SAM is to be a third place for the community—an active civic space where people can connect with art. Our special event program enforces this goal and allows us to bring in new audiences who come to the museum for a purpose other than an exhibition.

For many of the guests attending the special events, the event is their very first introduction to SAM. Our research indicates that holding special events at the museum is an effective way to bring new audiences to the museum and connect with them on a casual level so that they become future visitors and sometimes even members and donors.

The museum provides a unique environment that is spiritual and meaningful. This characteristic makes SAM a popular destination for holding milestone events such as weddings, memorial services, engagement parties, and special anniversaries or birthdays. These events are often booked months and even years in advance. Weddings are especially popular at the Seattle Asian Art Museum because of its Great Gatsby likeness and feel. Wedding guests who have never been to the museum discover the outstanding Asian art collection and the unique architecture and want to return with their family and friends.

Other nontraditional events held at SAM range from corporate retreats, company parties, annual meetings, film festivals, recitals, product launches, and wine tastings to fashion shows, press conferences, and chess competitions. Every event has a different audience, and most of these audience members are visiting SAM for the first time or are seeing the museum in a new light—one that is more comfortable and inviting.

SAM's special events are an important source of revenue for the museum. One full-time staff person manages and books all of the special events. He helps arrange catering, security, audiovisual equipment, and any other needs of the event planner.

The cost of the event depends on the type of the event, number of people, catering preferences, and amount of space utilized. SAM offers a deep discount to other nonprofit organizations that want to hold their event at SAM. The museum is also a resource for other arts organizations that may not have a facility of their own.

When its brand new facility, the Olympic Sculpture Park, came online in early 2007, SAM began holding new types of events. Many garden clubs, beach naturalists, Audubon societies, and the like started booking events at the park's pavilion, an indoor-outdoor space of 8,000 square feet (750 square meters). The sculpture park has captured the attention of a whole new audience for the museum, and it appeals to a wide range of people. It is a unique setting with incredible views of the Olympic Mountains, Puget Sound, and Seattle skyline. The park is free and open to the public, but the museum is able to close the pavilion to hold special events. The park also includes an amphitheater that is perfect for holding concerts, performances, and outdoor movies.

Recently SAM also doubled the size of its downtown museum, a project that included the addition of an event space large enough to accommodate a sit-down dinner for 600 guests. Meeting and convention planners often look for spaces that are unique to a city in which to hold dinners or host keynote speakers. The expansion of the museum, scheduled to open in May 2007, enables SAM to finally compete with other large special event venues and to appeal to the increasing number of conventions and meetings held in Seattle.

Community Arts

Lori L. Hager, PhD
University of Oregon

Recreation, leisure, and the arts have long been aligned in the United States. With the emergence of settlement houses, YMCAs, YWCAs, Boys and Girls Clubs, and the playground movement at the turn of the 20th century, the arts have played a central role in engaging and enriching people's nonwork and nonschool hours. The arts in community settings foster community development and civic engagement and serve as a bridge between communities and neighborhoods.

This chapter examines community arts as they intersect with leisure and recreation. First, it defines what the community arts encompass and presents characteristics that help distinguish community arts from other arts activities; second, it examines historical moments in the development of the field; third, it presents principles and practices that guide the field; fourth, it examines challenges that community arts practitioners face, along with the ways in which these challenges are met through leadership and research in best practices; and fifth, it includes two case studies that illustrate types of programs and shared values common to community arts.

Definitions

The terms *community cultural development, community-based art, arts-based civic dialogue,* and *community youth arts* are often used interchangeably to refer to arts practices that have shared values, goals, and approaches to teaching, learning, creating, and producing the arts that come together under the rubric community arts. While there are no hard and fast distinctions between the terms, each has a different focus, while they all share certain core principles.

Community arts may be distinguished from more traditional arts in that they are firmly rooted in the community they serve and in which they are identified. Community arts break down barriers between artist and audience and include everyone, no matter the skill level, in creating and presenting the arts. Community arts are a collaboration between artists and community members that addresses—through the arts—issues central to the local community, with a goal of improving local conditions.

The term *community arts* came into widespread usage in the United States in the 1960s and 1970s. It refers to a shared set of values, principles, and practices in teaching, creating, and producing in the arts world and is used as a way to distinguish its practice from that of the more traditional and formal mainstream arts.

At the core of community arts is the concept of community. In the early 20th century, neighborhoods were considered the heart of communities and were the point of daily departure and return. Contemporary community and neighborhood centers continue to represent this idea of place-based communities where local people convene in recreational and leisure activities, including the arts.

Community arts take place in arts centers, museums, schools, youth organizations, community centers, and other informal settings where people gather for social, recreational, political, educational, or civic purposes. Community arts, as distinguished from the more formal, or institutional, arts such as ballets, operas, and symphonies, are about fostering local dialogue, generating social capital, and stimulating positive community change. Community arts bring people together in common understanding for working toward common goals and civic democracy.

Two examples of community arts projects include the recent *The War Project* at the Sojourn Theatre and the American Festival Project. In *The War Project: 9 Acts of Determination* (2006), artistic director Michael Rohd and his company sponsored weeklong community workshops in which community members shared their stories about war. These stories were then crafted into a presentation that included both community members and professional actors.

The American Festival Project involves a group of internationally renowned arts organizations from all over the United States that travel to one city and spend more than 2 years working with local community organizations to develop story circles around local issues. The goals of this project are to foster community connections, create excellent art, and generate social discourse.

Community Cultural Development

The term *community cultural development* (CCD) came into common usage in the 1990s. It describes community arts practices that are contextualized in larger socioeconomic and political purposes. A

Rockefeller Foundation report titled *Creative Community: The Art of Cultural Development* (Adams and Goldbard 2005) helped to define the CCD field and its history, principles, and programs as "a range of initiatives undertaken by artists in collaboration with other community members to express identity, concerns, and aspirations through the arts and communications media, while building cultural capacity and contributing to social change" (Adams and Goldbard 2005, 107).

CCD is a useful term because it remains rooted in the local but still encompasses the whole range of cultural activities employed in the development process. The term is now more widely employed as cities contract with cultural planners to include the arts in urban revitalization and development efforts, and due to the recent emergence of community arts and CCD college degree programs. CCD engages community members in participatory art making that is often focused on issues and concerned with diversity, democracy, and social justice. It generally involves multiple art forms. It frequently engages collaborating practitioners in fields unrelated to the arts—people from government, social service, urban planning, and medicine—according to the needs of the community members and the nature of their aspirations. Finally, CCD practitioners recognize the transformative interdependence of quality process and quality product: They are inextricable (Burnham, Durland, and Ewell 2004).

Community-Based Art

The term *community-based art* refers to an intrinsically participatory collaborative process and to work that employs arts-based methods but emanates from settings other than the arts world. For instance, community-based art may include a play created around community issues or a mural depicting local history. Examples of community-based art projects include Suzanne Lacy's Mural Projects in Los Angeles, the Mural Arts Project of Philadelphia, and Jan Cohen-Cruz's work at New York University in community-based theater.

Community Youth Arts

The arts have always been at the core of recreation and leisure activities, especially for youths. Community youth arts (CYA) are non-school-based arts that typically reflect a partnership between arts organizations and any of the following: schools and school districts, community youth organizations, recreation and community centers, artists, universities, and state arts agencies. These activities may take place in juvenile justice centers, youth homeless shelters, community centers, public schools and universities, Boys and Girls Clubs, Girl Scout meetings, YMCAs—in short,

Partnering with a youth organization is a good way to involve teenagers in their community.
Photo courtesy of SouthEast Effective Development (SEED)

they may take place wherever youths gather. CYA programs have broadly defined goals, such as encouraging social development, mentoring youths, increasing community commitment, keeping schools open late, and fostering social bonds. Because CYA programs are largely voluntary—that is, young people are not required to attend—they focus on providing learning opportunities and fostering social development in fun and safe environments.

Arts-Based Civic Dialogue

Community arts assist in *civic dialogue*. The Animating Democracy Project of Americans for the Arts has coined the term *arts-based civic dialogue* to describe "community-based practice and civically engaged cultural work that engender[s] significant public discourse on issues of consequence such as civil rights, war, AIDS, globalization and more" (Korza 2002). For instance, the Flint Youth Theatre developed the play . . .*My Soul To Take* as a catalyst for grappling with an elementary school shooting. School discussion groups and community study circles were formed to address school violence. The Animating Democracy Initiative (ADI) project, an initiative of Americans for the Arts, "fosters arts and cultural activity that encourages and enhances civic engagement and dialogue. It is based on the premise that democracy is animated when an informed public is engaged in the issues affecting people's daily lives" (ADI, www.artsusa.org/animatingdemocracy/about/default.asp#gpals). Project materials are available at the ADI Web site, including extensive publications about the national projects, and includes a searchable database that illustrates the projects, discusses the documentation and evaluation, and illuminates best practices in the arts-based civic dialogue.

Community arts remain rooted in the unique characteristics of each community, and terms discussed in this section are not mutually exclusive. Other terms that share similar principles with community arts include *theater of the oppressed*, *theater for social change*, *community animation*, and *socially engaged arts,* among others.

Historical Moments in the Community Arts Field

Four significant historical moments influenced the development of the community arts field. The first surge in the community arts occurred at the turn of the 20th century with the progressive reformers and the emergence of the settlement houses, the little theatres, the Chautauquas, and the university extension programs in the arts. The second surge came in the 1930s in America and was catalyzed by the Works Progress Administration: "In literally thousands of out of the way places, art clubs, theatres, writing groups, choral societies, symphonies, and what have you, suddenly sprang into being—a wonderous florescence, with infinitely rich promise" (Kamarck 1975, 6). The third surge took place during the 1950s in response to increased bureaucratization and the emergence of an affluent middle class that helped to open up the educational system to the creative arts and added a burgeoning leisure class. The fourth surge, which occurred in 1975, highlighted "all the arts for all the people," broadening participation, and "pervasive social urgency for redefinition of experience" (Kamarck 1975, 8-9).

1900s—Settlement Houses as Community Centers

Early community arts efforts in the United States emerged with the progressive movement at the turn of the 20th century and were closely linked to the recreation and playground movements. In Chicago, Philadelphia, New York, and other major urban areas, civic-minded philanthropists led reforms in child labor, family health, education, welfare, and recreation. Progressives recognized the importance of building healthy minds and bodies and revolutionized the ways in which cities were constructed by incorporating public spaces into city planning. These spaces included playgrounds for children to play in and families and neighbors to gather in and community centers for helping the urban poor and recently arrived immigrants to acclimatize to American urban life. The settlement houses offered arts activities in music, drama, dancing, crafting, painting, and drawing. The arts

were viewed as a means to bring people together in the spirit of sharing each other's cultures and to transcend the language barriers. In the settlement ideal, the quality of the interaction between youths and adults was a measure of how well the settlements were doing. Consequently, the settlement houses were actively engaged with child welfare, health, housing, and child reform laws.

The positioning of the arts in settlements and other community groups such as YMCAs, Boy and Girl Scouts, and youth clubs helped to cement the arts' place in community organizations whose purpose was to fill young people's leisure hours with worthwhile pursuits. Tolerance for diversity and respect among people of different nationalities and ethnic and religious backgrounds were especially important.

The settlements offered classes and clubs for adults and youths. They also offered health care services. Due to the progressive idea that the arts help educate and develop the whole child, the arts were included in the settlements early on. The arts were neighborhood based and practiced in everyday life as "aspects of the rituals of association through church and home and as part of the background of the great crises of birth, death, and marriage. They were found in the local restaurants, cabarets, tea rooms, ice-cream parlors, and other gathering sites" (Kennedy 1920, 449). These early settlement efforts provided the foundation for community arts, and especially community youth arts, in community and recreation centers and informal organizations all over the country.

Community arts, particularly theater and pageants, were considered particularly useful in Americanization efforts. Early community arts can be viewed as precursors to contemporary arts in that they brought people together, addressed differences, provided a civic sphere, and explored American life.

1930s—Works Progress Administration

Following the Great Depression, the U.S. federal government created jobs for artists through the Federal Art Project of the Works Progress Administration (WPA). WPA workers not only created the highways, bridges, and dams of the interstate highway system and built national park trails and lodging centers but also generated some of the most well-renowned artists of the day. The WPA arts projects were divided into programs such as the Federal Writer's Project, the Federal Music Project, the Federal Art Project, and the Federal Theatre Project. Through providing jobs for musicians, actors, playwrights, dancers, puppeteers, muralists, poets, and many others, the WPA created a network of interstate arts organizations that exist to this day. Traveling children's theaters, fairs, and musical theaters provided free performances and classes to youth and adults in urban and rural areas.

Rachel Davis DuBois was concerned with the role that the arts play in improving people. DuBois viewed drama as a means of challenging Americanization efforts. In her 1943 book, *Get Together Americans: Friendly Approaches to Racial and Cultural Conflicts Through the Neighborhood-Home Festivals*, DuBois discussed cultural democracy as a way of critiquing the ideal of the melting pot. She said that for "half the melting pot to rejoice in being made better while the other half rejoiced in being better allowed for neither element to be its true self" (DuBois 1943, 5). In her view, cultural democracy could exist if differences were shared without annihilating one another. For example, DuBois created neighborhood festivals and pageants to bring together groups of people such as foreign-born adults in Americanization classes and people of different religious orientations, social levels, and ethnicities. She brought together settlement houses, YMCAs, refugee committees, English language classes, and representatives of various culture groups. DuBois' efforts foreshadowed contemporary community arts efforts that bring together communities of difference and echoed the settlement houses that sought to generate comfort, sympathy, and understanding among communities.

Other community arts practices of the early 20th century included Chautauquas, university extension programs, and junior leagues. By the 1940s, "hundreds of playgrounds all over the country were giving boys and girls the excitement and educational opportunities to be found in recreational dramatics" (McCaslin 1997, 137). Community and recreation centers continued to be important meeting places for youths.

1950s—The Wisconsin Idea

The Wisconsin Idea was a political notion that linked public education, public service, citizen participation, and community progress. Robert Gard, the founder of the Wisconsin Idea Theatre, is one of the pioneers of the community arts movement. He worked and wrote about his efforts to build community arts and theater throughout the 1950s. His Wisconsin Idea Theatre reached out from Madison and inspired literally tens of thousands of Wisconsinites to write plays, poetry, and books derived from their lives and from their sense of place as a way of building Wisconsin by developing personal creativity (Ewell 2000). Gard was also concerned with training future leaders of the community arts and envisioned university training programs that would prepare young people to address social problems and community issues through the arts.

1970s—The Surge in Community Arts

Community arts traces its historical trajectory with the major social movements in the United States, including the social revolution catalyzed by the Civil Rights movement. The establishment of the National Endowment for the Arts (NEA) in 1965 served to propel the nation's regional arts movement, and supported the founding of thousands of arts organizations. The NEA's Expansion Arts program supported the development of community arts centers and local arts programs that were neighborhood based. It was during the 1970s that the community art agencies expanded, and began to provide centralized services to communities helping to broaden and deepen the position of the arts in local communities.

The 1970s were a profound decade for community arts. Many community centers that presented arts also taught the arts. In smaller neighborhoods, community arts centers arose naturally out of activities already happening in city-run community centers, youth organizations, and recreation programs. During this time the relationship between the arts and civic programs was formally established through livable cities and other urban renewal initiatives. The arts became linked to labor issues through the Comprehensive Employment and Training Act (CETA), which helped to employ a cadre of artists and arts administrators and fueled arts organizations. The first complete study on the state of the arts and education was published in 1977. It was during the 1970s that the community arts agencies expanded and began providing centralized services to communities. These services broadened and deepened the position of the arts in local communities.

In *The Arts at the Community Level: A Report to the National Endowment for the Arts* (1977), James Backas defined three kinds of activities associated with community arts: participation and training of the non-artists, identified with a specific community, and the "outreach" programs of arts organizations. This typology continues to be useful today in helping to define community arts programming. With an emphasis on participation (not training of the artist), community arts are practiced as a part of community arts centers, and also in the education and outreach programs of many arts organizations. They may also be affiliated with any institution and arise naturally from local arts practices.

Community Arts Council Movement

With the emergence of the Community Arts Agencies (CAA) through the 1970s and 1980s, a wide range of services to communities and arts organizations became available, including grantmaking, arts education programming, fund-raising, facilities, and administrative services. Community arts networks include community arts agencies, colleges and universities, public and private schools, libraries, parks and recreation commissions, non-arts local government agencies, and performing and exhibiting centers, all having in common participation in a support system that developed, sustained, and delivered arts activities at the community level (Backas, 1977).

Principles and Practices

Contemporary community arts practices are firmly rooted in the historical development of community centers and community-based organizations, and carry on principles established over one

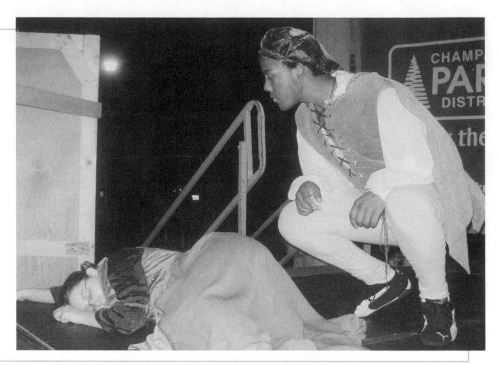

A local community arts council provides a support network for arts and cultural programming, such as performances of Shakespeare in the Park.

Photo courtesy of Ragen E. Sanner

hundred years ago to foster community connections, and promote social reform. The community arts field remains responsive to local conditions, and includes a wide variety of programs and activities that arise from local character, resources, and expertise. However, there are a set of guiding principles and practices which community-based programs generally share.

Contemporary Community Arts Practice

Community arts activities and programs can be found in neighborhoods and communities across the nation, and each reflects the multiplicity of voices, values, and diversity of each town and community. With the growth of leisure programming, the kinds of arts experiences available to people of all ages have proliferated. Intersecting the leisure and recreation fields, community arts stresses participatory arts experiences for everyone.

Issues confronting community arts include: who participates, who practices, what is the purpose of the arts practice. Community arts demand a place in neighborhood revitalization, cross-cultural communication, and improving academic performance. General principles and approaches that define the community arts field can be said to align themselves within four broad categories: *Place*, *Purpose*, *Principles*, and *Participants*. *Place* refers to geographically-based arts practices rooted in the local community; *Purpose* activates civic engagement, community building, social reform, and youth development. Community arts emphasize *Participation*, challenge assumptions that arts creation is only for professional artists, and stress that all community members are considered equal contributors. *Practices* are process-based, collaborative, and inclusive.

One does not have to look far to find examples of community arts in any neighborhood. The local mural that was a collaboration with a local artist, school children, and community members to celebrate an important moment in the community's history, digital storytelling projects, the many folk and traditional arts and crafts that are taught formally and informally, the art center downtown that sponsors the First Friday art walk, the country fairs and festivals that are unique to each community and draw visitors from all over the world, the tile art at the downtown bus shelter, the senior theatre troupe, and the photography exhibit at the local homeless shelter can all be considered community arts.

Community artists are working with prison populations to create poetry and theatre, they are working with people with disabilities in public art projects, with college students in zines—a

self-described "do it yourself democracy" in the form of homemade pamphlets and books that rebel against mainstream voices—they are working in senior dance projects, theatre projects with homeless populations, and with the displaced citizens of New Orleans in storytelling projects.

Community Youth Arts

Informal arts and out-of-school programs that take place in community centers, youth organizations, and recreation programs are receiving increasing national attention and federal and local support. Fueling the youth arts movement, in part, is the gap that exists between institutional time (such as time spent at school) and time spent at home with family in the evenings. Children spend 25% of their time in school. When schools close at 3 p.m. (or even at the lunch hour), and there is no possibility of active social engagement at home, where can youths go? Community youth organizations (CYOs) provide one answer to this question (McLaughlin 2000).

Young people are more likely to be involved in or victims of violent crimes between 2:00 p.m. and 6:00 p.m. Recent research emphasizes the lack of available youth services, adult involvement, and safe places to go after school as contributing to these statistics. Youths who participate in after-school programs are less likely to engage in high-risk behaviors such as drug use and are more likely to demonstrate greater academic achievement. An important factor determining whether inner-city youths go on to achieve employment is the amount of civic engagement in the neighborhood. Young people in neighborhoods with high levels of civic engagement, or social capital, are more likely to finish school, land a job, and avoid crime (Putnam 1993). Research presented in the recent report *Champions of Change: The Impact of Arts on Learning* (Fiske 1999) demonstrates that engagement in the arts nurtures the development of cognitive, social, and personal competencies and that the arts "can increase achievement, help decrease youth involvement in delinquent behavior and improve youths' attitudes" (Fiske 1999, 1). Many programs in housing developments and correctional facilities are a force in their communities.

Researchers have found that "creative youth-based nonschool organizations and enterprises that have sprung up in response to this 'institutional gap' engage young people in productive activities during nonschool hours" (Heath, Brice, Soep, and Roach 1998, 21). These organizations vary in structure, ranging from Boys and Girls Clubs and parks and recreation centers to an array of youth-initiated and grassroots endeavors. Programs may take place in existing community centers, such as settlement houses, Boys and Girls Clubs, city parks and recreation buildings, grange halls, and school campuses.

Challenges

During the summer, after school, and on the weekends, young people and their elders throng to city recreation facilities, local community centers, and arts organizations. Festivals, fairs, circuses, and parades are aspects of the exciting community arts field. Part of the rituals of association, the community arts are a growing national movement that encompasses virtual realities as well as public plazas.

Though the nonarts and arts fields intersect in multiple arenas, they do have significant differences that play into the success or failure of joint programming between arts and recreation, city services, or social services. Recreation staff members frequently view the arts as an add-on to sports and other recreational activities. Artists often find community and recreation centers challenging environments to work in because their expertise and needs are often undervalued. The time and space needs of the arts differ from those of sports and other recreational activities, and the goals and values of arts programs may be underrepresented or misunderstood.

The following list includes six factors that influence community arts programming in recreation and community settings. Paying attention to these six factors will help to increase the likelihood that the community arts program meets the expectations of everyone involved. Recent research in planning after-school programs that include the arts, in partnership development and collaboration,

will also assist the effective development of community-based arts projects with recreation programs. These factors include: expertise, time, space, organizational structures, goals, and values.

1. Expertise—Artists, arts administrators, and teaching artists are professionals who spend their lifetimes continuing their education in their respective crafts. Through their artistic skills and knowledge and their ability and experience in working with the target populations, arts professionals make a difference in the values and success of the programming. Arts classes offered by professional artists who are also professional teachers and educators affect the outcome of the arts events, and the success of the programs. The expertise of arts professionals needs to be recognized and utilized throughout the program planning, implementation, and evaluation.

2. Time—Time is critical to the success of any arts program. Often the time involved in planning, developing, and implementing arts programs is underestimated. Arts specialists and other community professionals who are working together must meet frequently and get acquainted with each other's knowledge and needs. For example, in a youth arts development project, all the participants, including artists, program staff, and youth leadership, should get to know the language and tools of the arts as well as the language and tools of the social service and community organizations involved. Time also affects the program participants: The time required for participation is frequently cited as a major difference between enrichment programs and arts programs. Arts classes require participation so that attendees build on the skills learned in the previous class sessions and so that participants can benefit from the teaching artist's expertise. Drop-in sessions common to recreation and enrichment programs can often work against the goals of an arts program. For instance, youths participating in a drama program at a Boys and Girls Club need to attend each class so that they can take part in the final productions that are planned as part of the community celebration.

3. Space—When arts and nonarts partnership programs are planned, it is critical to address the issue of space. When planning a music or drama program, space must be allocated for that program so that it does not interfere with the other activities of the organization and vice versa. Drama and music are loud activities—so be prepared! It is also important to establish expectations about the use of the space. When are students allowed in the allotted space? If there is a common area where participants convene before and after the program, who takes care of the common space? Also, where are arts supplies stored between classes?

4. Organizational structure—One of the biggest challenges that partnerships between arts and nonarts organizations face is negotiating their differences in organizational structures, leadership styles, and accounting systems. Blending the different organizational cultures takes leadership and careful attending to the steps necessary to achieving the desired outcomes. For instance, when arts programs are grant based, it is critical to decide who the fiscal agent is and how payment for personnel and supplies will be handled.

5. Goals—When arts and nonarts organizations join forces to create arts programming that dovetails with nonarts goals, the various groups involved in the programming will frequently define the purposes of the program in vastly different ways. Whereas the funding agency may believe that the purpose is to help kids stay in school, the kids may think that they are participating just to have fun. Meanwhile, the teaching artist may be planning to address social development or academic enhancement goals in very specific ways. The different program constituents may also have different ideas concerning the length of the program and issues of sustainability. Research has shown that creating a continuing relationship (lasting 2 years or longer) with a program participant influences the ability of an arts program to effect long-term change, and yet many artists and community organizations expect that their programs will stop at the end of a school term. Expectations regarding the length and the goals of the program need to be articulated from the outset.

6. Values—Articulating the values and missions of the participating arts and nonarts groups is essential to the success of the program. What are the various groups expecting from the program, and how will they know that they have achieved their objectives? How can the differing values of the participating organizations be respected and at the same time integrated to serve the larger goals of the program? As well, how the different partners articulate values for participation and outcomes affect the evaluation criteria of the program. How do the program partners define

successful implementation? Clarifying each partner's role and relationship to these six factors will make a significant impact on the attitudes and outcomes, as well as sustainability, of community-based arts projects.

Training Artists

The Community Arts Network lists 36 degree programs and 28 nondegree courses in community arts. Columbia College Chicago, California College of the Arts, and the University of Oregon's Arts Administration program all have research centers that operate in conjunction with their education programs in community arts. It is now possible to receive training to teach, manage, and research community arts programs through colleges and universities such as these.

Training community artists is especially critical. Universities are responding to the need to train people

Many arts education curricula include traditional arts experiences as well as nontraditional ideas and settings.

Photo courtesy of SouthEast Effective Development (SEED)

how to work with communities through the arts and how to deal with sensitive issues and populations that community arts often entail, but there is still a lack of comprehensive literature on training for artists to work in alternative settings. The handbook titled *Artists in the community: Training artists to work in alternative settings*, by community arts researchers and practitioners Grady Hillman and Kathleen Gaffney (1998) was one of the first to address this issue. This monograph also provided information about "the challenges, problems, and solutions of community arts programs" (6). Programs described in the handbook took place in schools, parks and recreation centers, religious centers, public housing, juvenile justice centers, and hospitals. For each of these organizations, problems and considerations for artists and arts administrators making first contact were discussed. Parks and recreation facilities were considered precious resources for the arts communities. Artists were counseled to prepare for last-minute space organization, changing class populations, and lack of storage for arts supplies.

The exponential growth of after-school programs across the United States has steadily increased the number of full-time positions needed to staff the programs, creating new roles and positions in a developing field. Research by the Afterschool Alliance has shown that the after-school field is growing faster than programs are able to train competent program managers who can bring together the values, missions, and goals of the arts and nonarts agencies. Since funding agencies are increasingly demanding demonstrable proof of the efficacy of the programs, more and more arts and nonarts partnerships are working with university faculty to design and conduct program evaluations in line with the outcomes articulated by all the program participants.

Trends in Community Arts Programming

The nonprofit arts sector will be undergoing profound change over the next decade. The founders of many of the U.S. arts organizations and community-based arts organizations will be retiring in

startling numbers over the next decade, which will have significant repercussions for the future of the field.

Like most of the nonprofit arts sector in the U.S., the community arts field will be undergoing significant transformation over the course of the next decade, which will change the ways that the arts leaders are educated and how the arts are practiced and funded.

Funding

Foundations such as the Nathan Cummings Foundation, the Dana Foundation, and the Wallace Foundation are putting considerable resources behind research and development in the community arts field. The recent emergence of several community arts centers housed at universities, the proliferation of community arts degrees, and several significant research studies reflect the commitment of foundations to the growth of the community arts field.

Communication

Communication structures and digital technologies allow community artists to share ideas and practices with colleagues across the globe, which will continue to shape the ways in which community-based arts are practiced. The Community Arts Network (www.communityarts.net) is the central communication hub for community arts practitioners, researchers, and educators in the United States.

Research

Many researchers have led the way in documenting contemporary practice and setting agendas for research in historical and contemporary criticism and theory in community arts. Among these are Don Adams and Arlene Goldbard (2005), Linda Frye Burnham and Steven Durland (1998), Jan Cohen-Cruz (2005), William Cleveland (1992, 2005), Grady Hillman and Kathleen Gaffney (1996), Bill Bulick (2003), and Doug Blandy and Kristin Congdon (1987).

Higher education researchers are working with community-based artists and practitioners to set priorities for educating future community arts leaders and establishing important research agendas. Foundations are supporting these efforts through establishing initiatives that result in pilot project implementation and evaluation demonstrating best practices, and providing important research compendiums to the field. Increased attention will be paid to the use of digital technologies in community-based arts practices, documentation, and evaluation.

Community-Based Arts

Careers in community-based arts include teaching youth and adults in the arts, managing and leading community-based arts programs at community and recreation centers, implementing partnerships between community-based organizations, education institutions, and arts organizations, evaluating and documenting best practices, and planning large festivals and events.

The community arts field is maturing, gathering a body of historical literature, demonstrating best practices which are based on sound theories, and making available advanced degrees in record numbers for those interested in pursuing a career in the community arts.

Summary

This chapter introduced community arts and the ways in which community arts intersect with leisure and recreation programming. Sharing common goals, communities, programming, and spaces, community arts and recreation often work on parallel yet divergent tracks. Differences in expertise, training, and expectations challenge efforts to offer both enrichment opportunities and substantive and sustainable arts experiences. Research suggests that there are significant gains for participants in arts and leisure programming, and it is in the interest of both fields to find ways to

work together, to include the arts in every recreational opportunity, and to acknowledge the time and expertise of the artists and arts administrators in each and every arts event. Cross-disciplinary training, education, and communication are key ingredients for building successful arts and leisure programming.

CASE STUDIES

Swamp Gravy

William Cleveland

This first case study illustrates a community-born arts event that began as a small idea and grew into an annual event that remains integral to its community while attracting thousands of visitors every year. *Swamp Gravy* is a community-born and community-bred event that includes everyone, regardless of talent or age.

This case study is excerpted, with permission, from *Making Exact Change: How U.S. Arts-Based Projects Have Made a Significant and Sustained Impact on Their Communities* (Cleveland 2005), a collaborative research project between Art in the Public Interest (API) and the Center for the Study of Art and Community. The purpose of this collaboration was to collect stories of community arts projects that have created a sustained positive effect on their communities. The result is a collection of 10 case studies of the community arts field that was published by API. The Community Arts Network, a program of API, "supports the belief that the arts are an integral part of a healthy culture, and that community-based arts provide significant value both to communities and artists" (http://communityarts.net/canabout.php). Author William Cleveland is a writer, a musician, and the director of the Center for the Study of Art and Community. He is also the editor of *Art in Other Places: Artists at Work in America's Community and Social Institutions* (1992). Linda Burnham and Steve Durland are cofounders of API and the Community Arts Network. They also coauthored *The Citizen Artist: 20 Years of Art in the Public Arena* (1998).

In the early 1990s, town leaders in Colquitt, Georgia, felt that the community needed something to reenergize its pride and economy. Joy Jinks of the Colquitt-Miller Arts Council felt that a historical pageant could provide an infusion of cultural energy, involve the county folks, and attract visitors from elsewhere. In 1991, Jinks met Richard Owen Geer, then completing a doctorate in performance studies at Northwestern University. Jinks related her idea and Geer got excited. Over many hours of discussion, they decided to work together to develop a play around the history of Colquitt. They called it *Swamp Gravy*.

Swamp Gravy is a musical play that celebrates rural southwestern Georgia folklife. Original songs and choreography are combined with traditional music and dance in a grand-scale stage production with a cast and crew of 100. Professionally written (by Tennessee playwright Jo Carson), directed, and designed, the play draws on folklore, tall tales, and family stories culled from oral histories gathered by a team trained by Carson. It is performed in Cotton Hall, a 60-year-old warehouse in Colquitt. It has also played in Washington, District of Columbia, at the Kennedy Center, and throughout the South.

Now in its 13th year, *Swamp Gravy* is what its artistic creator, Richard Owen Geer, calls "an experiment in a form of community performance—oral-history-based, large-scale, professionally produced amateur theater" that celebrates the lives and stories of the residents of Colquitt and Miller County.

The title, *Swamp Gravy*, refers to a local recipe for a stew, a kind of improvised soup made of whatever is at hand. The play sports the full-length stories of a handful of people and the sayings, phrases, and diction of literally hundreds of people. It blends folk remedies, ghost stories, jokes, well-known scandals, and deeply held secrets. It contains births, deaths, dressing up, dressing down, mother love, family violence, and a secret wedding in the woods. It's got folk tunes, sing-alongs, and blues songs.

The show runs four weekends each spring and fall and is rewritten each year. Although the theme of the play changes—in 2004 it was Brothers and Sisters and in fall 2005 it was Love and Marriage—the basic design of weaving stories into a theatrical tapestry remains the same.

The mission of the *Swamp Gravy* project is to involve as many people as possible in a theatrical experience that empowers individuals and bonds the community while strengthening the economy.

The following are the values of the *Swamp Gravy* project:

• *Community involvement*—*Swamp Gravy* began in 1991 when the Colquitt-Miller Arts Council voted to sponsor the project. Since that time, more than 1,000 citizens (16% of the county population) have been involved in the project as storytellers, story gatherers, actors, singers, seamstresses, painters, carpenters, ticket sellers, greeters, concession salespersons, souvenir salespersons, exhibitors, promoters, Swamp Gravy Institute consultants, and more.

• *Individual empowerment*—*Swamp Gravy* actors testify to developing self-confidence in their lives. Youth cast members carry their stage presence into the realm of classroom reporting. Two cast members have created a neighborhood after-school tutoring program for children who are at risk. Another has applied her creativity and initiative to help establish a Museum of Southern Culture and an outreach program training schoolteachers and students in storytelling techniques. Twenty-five cast members have been trained as Swamp Gravy Institute consultants and have shared their experience of arts-based community revitalization.

• *Community bonding*—According to "Swamp Gravy Artifacts," *Swamp Gravy* has united Miller County across the boundaries of age, race, class, and gender. The ages of the cast members range from 8 months to 87 years, and as many as 50% of the cast members are under the age of 18. Biracial participation has characterized the cast since the beginning of the project, and an increasingly diverse audience mix has been observed. Of the stories collected, 25% are from the Black community, and as much as 14% of the cast has been African American. All socioeconomic boundaries have been crossed, and one-third of the actors are male. Because many of the cast members encounter one another daily, the *Swamp Gravy* esprit de corps carries over into all facets of life and work in the community. *Swamp Gravy* is a way in which the arts create common ground on which diverse people can work and play together.

• *Stronger economy*—From 1994 to 2003, *Swamp Gravy* sold approximately 72,000 tickets. About 75% of the guests have been from out of town, which means that new dollars are coming into the community. Estimating that each guest spends about $53 U.S. ($18 in tickets, $15 for meals, $10 for gasoline, and $10 in souvenirs), more than $4,000,000 U.S. was generated in the small community during the 10 years from 1994 to 2003—an average of $400,000 U.S. per year.

"Swamp Gravy"
A case study from
"Making exact change: How U.S. arts-based programs have
made a significant
and sustained impact on their communities"
By William Cleveland; edited by Linda Frye Burnham
Saxapahaw, N.C.: Art in the Public Interest, November
2005, 140 pp.
Also available online at the Community Arts Network
<http://www.communityarts.net>.

Arts and Corrections—Communities in Schools

Grady Hillman

In this second case study, Grady Hillman describes the Communities in Schools (CIS) project in Mississippi, an arts-in-corrections project. The CIS project illustrates the kinds of research-based and sustained community arts programs that can be developed through comprehensive collaborative partnerships among artists, arts organizations, public agencies, universities, juvenile justice programs, and corporations for the benefit of youths and communities.

Hillman is an expert in helping communities to develop partnerships between arts and corrections. He has worked extensively as a resident artist, a program administrator, and an arts consultant for local, state, federal, and foreign agencies in the development of arts programs for community settings. Over the past two decades, he has worked with hundreds of schools, arts organizations, housing authorities, adult and juvenile justice institutions, religious organizations, and municipal governments. Hillman has published extensively in the area of community arts and humanities

programs and two monographs for Americans for the Arts, including *Artists in the Community: Training Artists to Work in Alternative Settings* (1996).

Located on Highway 82 in the Mississippi Delta, a predominantly rural area with a high rate of poverty, CIS has become a statewide provider of arts programs for youths who are at risk. Knowledgeable of data demonstrating that arts instruction enhances academic achievement, CIS reframed its mission toward educational enhancement, recreation, and workforce training through community-based arts programs. CIS emphasizes the placement of local arts professionals in after-school, extracurricular, and curricular settings. Its two primary offerings, ceramics and creative writing, derive from the cultural resources of Mississippi; all CIS offerings attempt to link participants to the cultural heritage of the state. CIS now owns and is renovating a building that is 19,000 square feet (1,800 square meters). It will be used as a training and arts center for area residents. At present, it hosts a community ceramics cooperative and provides summer media and ceramics camps for area youths. It also includes a street-side gallery of youth artwork.

In October of 2002, CIS received a 3-year Cultural Partnership Grant from the U.S. Department of Education Office of Innovation and Enhancement program to develop arts and humanities programs for middle school and high school youths who are academically at risk. The CIS Cultural Partnership project provides exemplary after-school curricula in the following areas: visual arts (ceramics and printmaking), performing arts (creative writing and poetry performance, drama, and video production), and heritage studies (local blues history, Native American history, and civil rights history).

CIS partnered with the Delta Center for Culture and Learning at Delta State University to create a Mississippi Delta culture curriculum for after-school youth programs. This curriculum surveys the same subjects that the Greenwood Department of Education program surveys and uses the same interactive, field-investigation teaching style. Called *The Delta Heritage Lighthouse Partnership*, the project has been operating for 3 years with funding from a Corporation for National and Community Service Grant and administered by the University of Southern Mississippi.

CIS currently provides core arts programming to court-involved youths in 10 counties spanning the state. CIS has operated yearlong after-school and summer visual arts and ceramics workshops at the Greenwood Adolescent Offender Program (AOP) since the spring of 2002. CIS provides 458 Mississippi court-involved youths with skill-based, artist-taught residency opportunities. The final component of CIS's core arts program occurs at Mississippi's two youth correctional facilities, at alternative schools, and at AOP and training schools.

CIS and the Mississippi Arts Commission (MAC) devised the strategy for program implementation from best practices in a federal partnership between the National Endowment for the Arts (NEA) and the Office of Juvenile Justice and Delinquency Prevention (OJJDP) titled *Arts Programs for Juvenile Offenders in Detention and Corrections*, (http://ojjdp.ncjrs.org/grants/grantprograms/discr14.html). Best practices included a rigorous, skills-based curriculum taught by practicing artists. The program conformed to the juvenile justice cycle so that court-involved youths would have access to arts programming at every stop in the system: prevention (after-school arts programs to engage youths along with programs at alternative schools where youths are remanded by schools for disciplinary reasons), intervention (arts programs in adolescent offender programs, detention centers, and training schools), and aftercare (arts programs in alternative schools where youths are remanded by the courts after incarceration or as a sentencing requirement).

CIS has facilitated the development of cultural plans, ensuring that residents have access to their cultural and artistic heritage. Each cultural plan generates community support for youth arts programs and includes proposals for developing community arts centers, youth heritage tours, and increased arts education both in school and after school.

Cultural Programming

Doug Blandy, PhD
University of Oregon

Culture is the way that individuals and groups come together to generate creative and symbolic forms such as "custom, belief, technical skill, language, literature, art, architecture, music, dance, drama, ritual, pageantry, handicraft" (American Folklife Center 2006). Integral to culture is material culture. Schlereth (1985, 5) understands material culture as that "segment of humankind's biosocial environment that has been purposely shaped by people according to culturally dictated plans." Thus material culture involves the objects, forms, and expressions associated with culture. In his definition of material culture, Deetz (1977, 24) "includes all artifacts, from the simplest, such as a common pin, to the most complex, such as an interplanetary space vehicle." As Bolin and Blandy (2003, 249-250) emphasize, "All human-mediated sights, sounds, smells, tastes, objects, forms, and expressions are material culture. When there is purposeful human intervention, based on cultural activity, there is material culture."

Cultural programming includes the formal and informal ways in which organizations and institutions address, cultivate, present, preserve, and celebrate the creative and symbolic forms associated with culture. These organizations and institutions may include community arts centers, museums, schools, places of worship, recreation centers, municipalities, social service organizations, festivals, local arts agencies, and hobby associations, among many others.

The individuals responsible for managing cultural programming "should carefully and mindfully consider the ways in which they facilitate, document, preserve, celebrate, curate, and educate" about culture (Blandy and Congdon 2003, 178). The development of policies, procedures, and implementation strategies that encourage mindfulness needs to be considered at all levels and in all settings in which cultural programming takes place. In chapter 3 of this book, Carpenter provided an overview of what constitutes arts and cultural programming as well as introduced theoretical models that inform programming. Her discussion considered development, content, planning, implementation strategies, policies, and assessment issues as well as the context in which programs occur.

This chapter delves into the issues, perspectives, methods, and ethical behaviors that should guide cultural programming across a variety of institutions and organizations. The United States and Canada are demographically and culturally diverse in multiple aspects, including race, ethnicity, political persuasion, sexual orientation, age, socioeconomic status, and religion. Cultural programming that takes place in democratic societies should encourage the multiple cultural perspectives that a healthy and functioning democracy requires. To this end I will specifically discuss the concept of cultural democracy and how it can inform cultural programming. Associated with this discussion is a synthesis of our conceptions of multiculturalism and an exploration of how these conceptions influence programming. I will also discuss characteristics of culturally competent personnel. Finally, I will turn to public sector folklore for a model that cultural programmers can look to for strategies, methods, and ethical behaviors. This chapter ends with two case studies that support the discussion of cultural programming: a study of the University of Oregon Disability Studies Film Festival and a study focusing on the El Camino Real International Heritage Center in Socorro, New Mexico.

Cultural Democracy

The idea that cultural rights are a human right has been circulating within the United States for at least a century and is sometimes referred to as *cultural democracy*. Cultural democracy is also a concern in Canada. It has come to be defined by a loose set of principles, rights, and freedoms. A nation that is culturally democratic is one where there is no official culture. Adults and children are guaranteed the right to their own history, to free and equitable access to culture, to tradition, to education, to public speech, and to the construction of culture. There is recognition of cross-cultural shared values, attitudes, and beliefs.

Cultural democracy has been traced to democratic ideals held by the Iroquois, to the writings of Thomas Paine, to the concept of justice found in some American religious traditions (Adams and Goldbard 1990), to the American antislavery movement, and to the women's movements of the 19th and 20th centuries (Stimpson 1990). The first use of the term *cultural democracy* was by J. Drachsler in his 1920 book *Democracy and Assimilation: The Blending of Immigrant Heritages in*

America (Adams and Goldbard 1990). However, contemporary conceptions of cultural democracy can be linked most directly to the early 20th-century writings of Horace Kallen on the importance of cultural pluralism within multicultural societies.

Kallen analyzed the unprecedented immigration of 30 to 40 million women, men, and children from eastern and southern Europe to the United States. He concluded that this immigration resulted in a transformation of American society that was perceived negatively by older immigrant populations. Terrorist activity directed toward newly arriving immigrants was not unusual, and school systems adopted policies that reinforced assimilation through Anglocentric curricula (Suzuki 1979). Kallen responded to what he perceived as the attempted destruction of newly arriving cultural groups by arguing that American democracy is inconsistent with the idea of a melting pot. He proposed that the United States should not be a nation of ethnic conformity but a commonwealth of national cultures (Ramirez III and Castenada 1974).

Within the United States, cultural democracy received its greatest governmental support during the Great Depression through the Federal Art Project (FAP). FAP included multiple divisions that were based either on media or around specific projects. FAP also included an Art Teaching Division. Teachers worked in a variety of settings, including hospitals, mental health facilities, settlement houses, and community arts centers. During this time, 100 art centers were established in 22 states. A typical art center included an exhibition space and classrooms.

It was within the community arts centers that cultural democracy was most fully realized as a principle for guiding public access to the arts. Community arts centers were a vehicle for bringing citizens' attention to the indigenous art of the United States in contrast to the works of contemporary or historical European artists. Community arts centers also developed programs that encouraged connections between art and the general public. This was part of an attempt to realize an authentic popular and mass culture in contrast to the culture encouraged by the entertainment industries (Harris 1995). FAP administrators believed that a culturally democratic orientation was congruent with an American democracy, in which people should have the right to contemporary cultural expression as well as to their cultural past (Harris 1995). Such an orientation, they argued, was appropriate for a country like the United States, who has a citizenry claiming cultural roots from all parts of the world.

During the 1950s and 1960s a few individuals working within community development sustained culturally democratic perspectives. For example, during the 1950s Baker Brownell, a Northwestern University scholar, began publishing on the role of art in community. He believed that the arts, economic development, and community planning are closely connected (Brownell 1950). Associated with community theater and political activism in Wisconsin, Robert Gard wrote extensively during the 1950s and 1960s on the important relationship that exists between art and place in rural communities. In his writings he proposed that artists must connect with other civic associations to ensure community health and vitality (Gard 1955).

Cultural democracy continues to be foundational to community cultural development and thus is fundamental to cultural programming. In *Creative Community: The Art of Cultural Development*, Adams and Goldbard (2001) write the following:

> Cultural democracy is predicated on the idea that diverse cultures should be treated as essentially equal in multicultural societies. Within this framework, cultural development becomes a process of assisting communities and individuals to learn, express and communicate in multiple directions, not merely from the top—the elite institutions of the dominant culture—down. (55)

Thus cultural democracy is vital to cultural programming. The following sections provide strategies for achieving a culturally democratic vision within cultural programming.

Orientations to Cultural Programming

Stern and Cicala (1991) observed that the fluidity of culture is in part associated with the ways in which members of groups "absorb, invigorate, modify, and transmit folk expressions in a multicultural,

This flamenco dancer, performing at an event held by a local library, is part of a cultural program that focuses on a single group but is marketed toward a diverse audience.

Photo courtesy of Hult Center for the Performing Arts/Eugene

pluralistic society" (xi). Cultural programming facilitates this process, if appropriate, in a public arena. Sleeter and Grant (1987) identified five ways that this process occurs in multicultural educational contexts. These five ways can be considered in relation to how cultural programming occurs within organizations and institutions:

1. One type of cultural program is designed for a particular cultural group independent of the larger pluralistic society. Examples include an ethnically oriented festival marketed to a particular ethnic community or a hobby show designed only for a particular category of hobbyist. The content of this programming is specialized and depends on insider perspectives and information for success.

2. A second type of programming focuses on a single cultural group but is marketed to a broad audience that includes members both inside and outside the group. Examples include festivals associated with a particular country or region marketed to people who have no connection to the country or region. The case study of the University of Oregon Disability Studies Film Festival that appears at the conclusion of this chapter is also an example of this type of program.

3. A third type of programming is multicultural and concentrates on the relationships existing between cultural groups and group members. An example is a folk festival that is designed around a theme such as *family* or *ritual* and provides examples of how various cultural groups attend to that theme.

4. A fourth type of programming is multievent oriented and is associated with an organizational or institutional mission to promote the idea that North Americans live in a diverse, culturally pluralistic society in which all cultural groups are equal. An example is parks and recreation programming that over time focuses on the many cultural groups living in the region. The case study associated with the El Camino Real International Heritage Center that appears at the end of this chapter exemplifies this type of programming.

5. A fifth type of programming is designed to correct or critique the disparities and biases inherent in the larger society. Such programming is social action and advocacy toward this end. Consider Fred Wilson's 1992 exhibit Mining the Museum and the associated programming that was held at the Baltimore Historical Society (Berger 2001). Wilson's installation focused on the history of slavery in the United States through the juxtaposition of objects in the museum's collection. Another example is Project Row Houses (2006) in Houston, Texas, a project that includes educational programming designed to reclaim inner-city neighborhoods.

Cultural Programming and Cultural Competence

Carpenter and Howe (1985) defined *programming* as the process of planning and delivering leisure experiences to an individual or a group. In chapter 1, Carpenter, using a phrase coined by Alvin Toffler, described people who plan cultural programs as *experience makers*. Designing experiences within a cultural programming context requires cultural competence. In turn, cultural competence requires that organizations have a defined set of values and principles, and demonstrate behaviors, attitudes, policies, and structures that enable them to work effectively cross-culturally. . . . Cultural

competence is a developmental process that evolves over an extended period. Both individuals and organizations are at various levels of awareness, knowledge, and skills along the cultural competence continuum. (National Center for Cultural Competence 2006)

Cross and colleagues (1989) further described cultural competence as an ongoing pursuit of self-reflection, knowledge acquisition, and skill development practiced at individual and systems levels in order to effectively engage a culturally diverse population. Using the work of Cross and colleagues, the National Center for Cultural Competence (NCCC; 2006) proposed a conceptual framework for achieving cultural competence. Within this framework, cultural programmers who are culturally competent

- value diversity,
- conduct self-assessment,
- manage the dynamics of difference,
- acquire and institutionalize cultural knowledge, and
- adapt to the diversity and cultural contexts of the individuals and communities served.

Programmers who are culturally competent design programs that are accessible to all, responsive to individual needs, responsive to participant interests, and planned in cooperation with interest groups representing cultural constituencies. These groups are associated with all of the organizations and venues mentioned earlier in this chapter or elsewhere in this book. Organizations and venues should infuse such competence into overall policies and practices. Readers are referred to NCCC (2006) at Georgetown University for tools to assist with assessing organizational and individual cultural competence. These tools address cultural competence in relation to physical environment, materials, resources, communication styles, and values and attitudes. They also provide suggestions for using the assessment results.

Committing to the principles of universal design will also assist in creating cultural programs that are accessible to culturally diverse audiences. As I have written elsewhere (Blandy 1999) and as Modrick emphasized in chapter 4, the goal of universal design is to minimize people's need to adapt. Universal design recognizes that there is no normal or average person. Individuals participating in universally designed programs can expect facilities and experiences to be flexible. The participant's right to choose based on personal preferences and abilities is emphasized. Regardless of previous experience, knowledge, or ability to communicate, participants can expect to be able to join in the program in some way. The user's sensory abilities and the multiple ways in which information about a facility or program can be perceived are held in high regard.

A Folkloric Orientation to Cultural Programming

Cultural programming is informed by a variety of academic disciplines and professional fields, including anthropology, history, art, education, folklore, leisure studies, recreation, tourism, international studies, and business. Of these, I have found folklore, particularly public sector folklore, to be the most directly useful. This is partly because public sector folklorists study and document the ways that people do and make things. This doing and making is sometimes referred to as *folklife*. Mary Hufford (2006) exemplifies what is meant by folklife and explains the reasons why folkloric perspectives are important to cultural programming. She writes,

> What is folklife? Like Edgar Allan Poe's purloined letter, folklife is often hidden in full view, lodged in the various ways we have of discovering and expressing who we are and how we fit into the world. . . . Folklife is community life and values, artfully expressed in myriad forms and interactions. Universal, diverse, and enduring, it enriches the nation and makes us a commonwealth of cultures. (American Folklife Center 2006)

Folklife is found in the names people use, the holidays people celebrate, the ways leisure time is spent, the ways homes are decorated, the music people participate with, the slang that is spoken,

Folklife can be manifested through dance.

Photo courtesy of Hult Center for the Performing Arts/Eugene

and the myriad other ways in which people express their values, attitudes, and beliefs in daily life.

In order to understand and appreciate folklife, folklorists go into communities to observe and talk to people about what they do and make. In doing so the folklorists gain insight into the rituals, celebrations, music, dance, crafts, stories, jokes, and plethora of other things that contribute to the manifestation of culture. Then, often in partnership with community scholars, the folklorists plan workshops, publications, conferences, symposia, concerts, tours, festivals, and exhibits for the general public. Community scholars are people associated with and recognized by various cultural groups that have particular insights into the communities and cultures to which they belong.

Collaborative Ethnography

One method for working with members of communities and cultures is referred to by Luke Eric Lassiter (2004) as *collaborative ethnography*. Lassiter promotes this method as one way to try and achieve a correct interpretation, representation, or description of a cultural group. Misrepresentation, according to Lassiter, often results in anger, frustration, and disappointment.

Lassiter's method includes the following:

- Participating in the lives of others (learning a new language or how to behave appropriately within a particular setting)
- Observing behavior (both that of the ethnographer and that of the community)
- Taking field notes (jotting down first impressions, drawing maps, or writing extensive descriptions of cultural scenes)
- Conducting interviews (both informal and formal)

Conducting Fieldwork

Peter Bartis' (2006) guidelines for fieldwork are useful in combination with Lassiter's guidelines for developing cultural programs. Bartis' guide, *Folklife and Fieldwork: A Layman's Introduction to Field Techniques*, is a classic and informs the work of both experienced and inexperienced field researchers. Bartis divides a project into three parts: background research and preparation, fieldwork, and organizing the material for archival preparation (or interpretation in a public event). His fieldwork

guide is particularly useful in introducing a variety of fieldwork techniques such as note taking, audio recording, and video recording.

Cultural Brokers

Robert Kurin (1997), the director of the Center for Folklife and Cultural Heritage at the Smithsonian Institution, describes his role of working between a cultural group and the public as that of a broker. In Kurin's view, a cultural broker works on behalf of the people being represented and interpreted in a cultural program. He contrasts this view with the exploitive "flea marketier" who is "anyone in or out of culture putting stuff up for people to encounter" (19). For Kurin, fieldwork is best accomplished by cultivating an "informal learning relationship with the represented" and by taking "the issue of how to represent a culture as problematic" (23). Relationships with those in the field are horizontal and weblike rather than hierarchical and vertical (23).

In developing a cultural program, the broker must do the following:

- Negotiate with all interested parties the way in which a cultural group and its members are represented and interpreted.
- Negotiate the perspectives of those who hold formal knowledge with those who have experiential knowledge.
- Broker the worlds of entertainment, scholarship, and politics as they come to bear on cultural programming.
- Broker the tension between cultural homogeneity and heterogeneity.

Conceptualizing, Designing, and Implementing Cultural Programs

As Kurin (1997, 21-22) observes,

> Culture brokers usually perform a series of sequential, progressive, goal-oriented tasks, though they may have to reiterate some of the steps as situations change during the course of a particular project. Culture brokers empirically and interpretatively study the culture to be represented, arrive at models of understanding, develop a particular form of representation from a repertoire of genres, and bring audiences and culture bearers together so that cultural meanings can be translated and even negotiated.

There are multiple models available for conceptualizing, designing, and implementing cultural programs. Of particular relevance are those that are community based. In addition, good models systematize the process for easy replicability. Following are two models that cultural programmers have used successfully and that are easily replicated in other settings.

Blandy and Congdon's Model

In 1986 and 1987, Kristin G. Congdon and I curated an exhibit for the Bowling Green State University School of Art Gallery. The exhibit was called *Boats, Bait and Fishing Paraphernalia: A Local Folk Aesthetic.* Our curatorial method exemplifies what Kurin (1997) described in his description of the work of cultural brokers. A folklorist as well as local, well-known fishers helped us plan the exhibit. This exhibit was on view during February 1987 and included a wooden fishing boat, fishing flies, fishing tackle, clothing worn by fishers, photographs of the northwest Ohio fishing landscape, and miscellaneous other objects (Blandy and Congdon 1988). A significant finding arising from this exhibit was the development of a method for partnering with community members to develop cultural programming (Blandy and Congdon 1993). This model is based on pedagogical guidelines from Freire (1970, 1981). The guidelines focus on building nonhierarchical and cooperative relationships among people, methods for critical inquiry, forging a common language, and a dynamic conception of culture. Our model facilitates nonhierarchical

relationships among the people participating in the program development. In the case of *Boats, Bait and Fishing Paraphernalia*, these people included object makers, object holders, exhibition facilitators, exhibition designers, and the public. For other cultural programs, participants in planning will include anyone associated with facilitating the cultural program as well as representatives of the cultural groups being interpreted.

The model consists of five overlapping and dynamic phases of activity:

1. Orientation—The primary facilitators pose questions regarding the context for the program and appropriate research strategies for investigating the problems. They also ask who, what, where, when, and why questions:

   ○ How can a specific cultural practice be represented in the program?

   ○ Who from the culture can assist us in planning the program?

   ○ When is it appropriate or not appropriate to share a cultural practice with the public?

   ○ What strategies will be used to interpret this culture?

2. Identification of partners—Problems and questions are posed regarding key partners in planning and implementing the program. These problems and questions may address the development of shared language, the clarification of program purposes, and the roles of various partners.

3. Planning—Problems and questions are posed regarding the process of deciding what to include in the program.

4. Implementation—Problems and questions are posed regarding the identification of key people participating in the program implementation. Questions also address the logistics of making the program available to the public.

5. Evaluation—Problems and questions are posed regarding appropriate qualitative and quantitative evaluation strategies for all aspects of program planning and implementation.

After this model was used at Bowling Green State University, it was adapted for an anthropological exhibit at the University of Oregon Museum of Natural History in 1989 (Gabai 1990), an exhibit on tattooing at the Maude Kerns Art Center in Eugene in 1990 (Brooks 1991), the New Mexico Van of Enchantment community programs beginning in 1996 (de Chadenedes 1996), the

Careful deliberation, including use of the model created by Blandy and Congdon, over an exhibition can create a more meaningful experience for visitors.
Photo courtesy of Jenny German

Zines and DIY Democracy exhibit at the University of Oregon Knight Library in 2005, and the online exhibit Zines: Witness this Moment in 2005 (Blandy and Voelker-Morris 2005).

Rhode Island Black Heritage Society Model

Similar to the cultural programming model that Kristin G. Congdon and I developed is the model titled Keepers of the Tradition: A Five Step Approach for Collecting African American Documents and Artifacts implemented at the Rhode Island Black Heritage Society and the Afro-American Historical and Cultural Museum in Philadelphia (Gaither 1992).

The steps of this model are

1. identifying an informal historian (keeper) of the family or group whose material is of interest,

2. enlisting the keeper's help in interpreting the objects, photographs, or documents for others associated with the materials,

3. introducing a professional historian to assist in establishing the larger context and the importance of the materials,

4. giving the materials back to the community through the design and implementation of an exhibit, and

5. developing and implementing a plan for education and publication by keepers and professionals.

Ethics and Cultural Programming

Cultural programming that has integrity requires methods that emphasize fair and equitable relationships among planners, consultants, and participants. Thus the planning and implementing of cultural programs requires programmers who behave ethically. In this chapter I advocate for a collaborative relationship with the members of the culture being represented or interpreted in a program. I agree with Lassiter (2004) that in representing and interpreting others, our first responsibility is to those who are being represented and interpreted. These individuals should be intimately involved as consultants in all aspects of the program. Kurin (1997, 24-25) sums up the ethics of cultural programming as follows:

• Public cultural representations that purport to be educational or scholarly should, to the extent appropriate, possible, and necessary, have the consent and collaboration of those represented as expressed by the people involved or their legitimate and recognized authorities.

• Public cultural representations should be based on sound knowledge and research as practiced by the scholarly community. They should be accurate and fair.

• Producers of cultural representations should be explicitly forthright about the agencies involved in sponsoring, supporting, and implementing the cultural programs. They should be willing to answer questions about their authority and qualifications and about the scope of their involvement.

• Producers must honor the legal and moral rights of ownership and stewardship of tangible cultural property and intangible cultural expression. They must compensate individuals, groups, and communities through royalties, fees, honoraria, and other forms of recognition of services or materials rendered.

• Producers should intellectually engage those represented, offering the best of their knowledge while recognizing the value of the knowledge of their subjects.

• Compromising a cultural group through unethical behavior can cause irreparable harm to an organization. Following ethical guidelines such as those described here will help establish the credibility of the organization sponsoring the programming and the credibility of the facilitators of the program. Such credibility contributes to an organization's ability to offer programs in the future by generating trust among current and future partners.

Summary

My purpose in this chapter was to present cultural programming as a practice that reinforces culture as a human right. Cultural programmers have the capacity, through their work with cultural groups and members of the community, to contribute to the environments necessary to a healthy democracy. I have detailed the perspectives and methods that can guide cultural programming in a variety of institutions and organizations.

CASE STUDIES

University of Oregon Disability Studies Film Festival: Reinforcing Accurate Portrayals and Subverting Stereotypes

Heidi von Ravensberg
  Outreach Liaison, Educational and Community Supports
  Co-Coordinator, Disability Studies Initiative, University of Oregon

Deborah Olson
  Assistant Professor, Research Associate in Special Education
  Co-Coordinator, Disability Studies Initiative, University of Oregon

The Disability Studies Advisory Committee (DSAC) at the University of Oregon in cooperation with the Downtown Initiative for the Visual Arts (DIVA), a nonprofit arts organization based in Eugene, Oregon, has held two film festivals devoted to the experience of disability. The purpose of the festivals was to increase awareness of disability, reinforce accurate portrayals, and to subvert stereotypes. The organizing framework is that disability is a recognized culture (Brown 1997). This perspective refutes general social misconceptions that disability is a condition requiring medical care and redefines people with disabilities as empowered and having the right to basic citizenship.

Open to campus and community members, films were screened over three nights. The event paid particular attention to access to programming and venues. One of the nights was held in the community at the arts organization.

DSAC members and a few other interested individuals make up the festival's work group and staff. The planning committee suggests and consults on festival themes, dates, venues, film titles, presenters, sponsors, distribution of promotional materials, access accommodations, and resources. A screening committee reviews the suggested films and recommends a program. A work group implements recommendations as well as arranges for needed media, promotional, and access materials, access services, and training. A student assistant works at the direction of the committee to provide support services. When the festival concludes, the DSAC reviews and evaluates all aspects of the event and makes recommendations for improving next year's festival.

Because the DSAC's budget is extremely limited, obtaining financial and in-kind support from university departments, campus organizations, and interested individuals is crucial to success.

Two issues emerged as being the key to the success and credibility of the festival:

1. Programming a disability film festival with an emphasis on the perspectives and issues important to disability culture
2. Creating a process and an event inclusive of persons with disabilities

Programming was a challenge each year. In year one, films were solicited through film festival Internet sites. We organized the submitted films into a distinct theme for each night of the festival. For the second year, we chose films that were suggested by DSAC members and again organized them around themes such as identity and right to life. In both years it seemed important to capitalize on themes that were present in current media, such as right to life. When time permitted in the first festival we were able to present panels consisting of community activists who led the audience in a discussion of important issues regarding disability. Both years we struggled with the dilemma of presenting films that perpetuated popular stereotypes (e.g.,

Million Dollar Baby directed by Clint Eastwood) versus films that portrayed a full and complete life of an individual (e.g., *Independent Little Cuss* directed by Jeff Patterson or *Touch the Sound* directed by Thomas Riedelsheimer).

Because film is primarily an experience of the eye and ear, it was especially important to accommodate persons with visual and hearing impairments. Video describers were provided for people who are blind, while American Sign Language (ASL) interpreters and closed-loop sound systems were provided for people who are deaf or hearing impaired. Braille programs were available, and the festival program was printed in large font for the entire audience. Attending to the details of these technologies required much time and effort, but besides allowing for inclusion, including these technologies created a consciousness-raising experience for all participants.

Recommendations

Based on the University of Oregon Disability Studies Film Festival, the following is recommended.

- Be aware that the field of disability studies has recognized leaders, particular views on what it means to be disabled, and ideas on how that intersects with social perspectives.

- Know and involve your audience. Select films and discussants with a clear purpose. Don't be afraid to screen films that perpetuate stereotypes. Programmed with care, they can generate lively and informative discussions that empower audiences.

- Involve persons with disabilities in the programming. Otherwise, the festival is like a group of men putting on a women's film festival. It lacks credibility.

- Expect that persons with disabilities will attend and plan to provide access.

- To create an event that reaches out to community and campus members, pay special attention to collaborations with relevant groups, whether they be film studies programs on campus or community advocacy organizations.

Film festival programmers are encouraged to carefully consider their film selection and to maximize the inclusiveness of persons with disabilities in all aspects of the festival. Films that refute stereotypes as well as those that perpetuate them can contribute to lively discussion. Principles of universal design can help programs to utilize technology to promote full inclusion.

El Camino Real International Heritage Center, Socorro, New Mexico

Marcia de Chadenèdes

The El Camino Real International Heritage Center is an interpretive center for the National Historic Trail El Camino Real de Tierra Adentro, which opened on November 2005 to a crowd of 3,000. The center was created through a partnership between the New Mexico State Monuments and the Bureau of Land Management. The center is remotely located in the Chihuahuan Desert, 35 miles (56 kilometers) south of Socorro and 40 miles (65 kilometers) north of Truth or Consequences, 5 miles (8 kilometers) off of Interstate 25.

The landscape design for the center took place over the 2 years preceding the center's opening. The installation was designed to promote awareness, create public ownership, and establish a community for the new cultural resource. Limited resources were enhanced by partnering with agencies interested in opportunities for educational outreach.

The overall design and related activities were closely tied to the concepts of professor Jim Kennedy of Utah State University: that humans are not born knowing or caring about human ecosystems and that our relationships with resources are learned and shaped by the culture and events of our childhood. Interactions with the intended audience address key social values of educational opportunities afforded in leisure and formal activities and the creation of family memories related to sustaining a resource.

Overall and individually the design and related activities address the exhibit themes: the formation and life forms of the Rio Grande basin and Chihuahuan Desert environment, the exchange with the indigenous people living along the trail route, the Hispanic settlement along the trail, the role of the historic military forts of New Mexico, and the contemporary cultural practices.

The Valencia County Xeriscape Club of Belen (90 miles, or 145 kilometers, north) was recruited to act as consultants for the landscape architect, located in Denver, for general landscaping and the creation of a Chihuahuan Desert Plants Garden. The New Mexico Museum of Indian Arts and Culture (170 miles, or 275 kilometers, north) donated an ethnobotanical garden design and list of plants with curative, ceremonial, dye, and dietary purposes. Elementary and middle school classes in Truth or Consequences helped create these gardens during the school year. The students researched and wrote about the plants, offering their efforts for the center's interpretive use, created the beds, and planted.

A similar project was facilitated for a Socorro elementary school. A *curandera* garden was designed with the donated expertise of the Albuquerque Biopark (110 miles, or 175 kilometers, north). This traditional garden of Hispanic healing plants was installed following a school field trip to the botanical park. Both of the school garden projects specifically addressed the New Mexico Department of Education standards and benchmarks in English, science, and history.

The majority of the project came to fruition on National Public Lands Day 2004 with the help of a work party of 130 children and adults. The beds for the two ethnobotanical gardens were established. Belen Girl Scouts installed the desert plants garden. Socorro Girl Scouts sowed a nearby field with a seed blend that replicated the natural fields that existed before overgrazing occurred. Socorro Boy Scouts mapped half of a 10-kilometer cross-country recreational trail planned to reach Fort Craig.

After a morning of frenzied labor, the volunteers gathered for a late lunch, a *metanza* (traditional Hispanic barbeque) served by the Sierra County 4-Hers, and were thanked by state legislators and local mayors. While serenaded by a mariachi band, they tried on Spanish colonial clothing and gear, were entertained by a presentation from the Food Museum, rode in wagons and buggies, petted the horses of Back Country Horsemen, and visited a mobile exhibit offered by the Bosque del Apache National Wildlife Refuge (18 miles, or 30 kilometers, north).

Museums

Janice Williams Rutherford, PhD
University of Oregon

The casual visitor, a person who visits museums only occasionally, might ask why museums would need to offer programs. The perception of the museum as an exclusive collection of rare objects held sway among much of the American public until recently. But during the past 30 years, museums have set about changing their image and their course. Museums do, indeed, plan activities that utilize their collections and their expertise to engage, entertain, and educate. Programming for these purposes means that museum professionals have begun to offer a wide array of leisure opportunities.

In 1991, the American Association of Museums (AAM), the largest museum professional association in the United States, charged museums with the mission of incorporating "an educational purpose in every museum activity" (Hirzy 1998, 3). The general assembly of the International Council of Museums (ICOM) amended its 1995 statutes to identify museums as "permanent institution[s] in the service of society . . . for purposes of study, education and enjoyment" (Hudson 1998, 85). Thus, during the past two decades, leaders in the profession have codified the changing role of their institutions. Museums of all stripes—art, history, science, natural history—have gone from institutions whose primary purpose was to house and preserve objects to institutions whose obligation is to make these objects available to the public for learning and enjoyment.

Defining education and outreach as primary objectives in museum management has resulted in a plethora of professional literature that explores museum education (see, for example, Donnelly 2002; Moffat and Woollard 1999; Roberts 1997) and the implications of embedding education in "every museum activity" (Hirzy 1998, 3). The imperative to enhance educational programs in museums throughout the United States is partly a response to the shrinking funding for the arts in the public schools (Floyd 2006). But museum programming is much more than curriculum; it provides an opportunity to socialize, a path to personal growth, and a form of entertainment. An informal longitudinal review of museum literature conducted by a museum consultant who specializes in audience development found that the reasons most people visit museums in their leisure time include social interaction, active participation in worthwhile activities, new experiences, and learning opportunities (Hood 2004).

Beyond its function as an educational and social hub, the museum can serve as a public forum. As consultant Alice Parman (2006) points out, museums are "potential gathering places for their communities." They do not "set entry requirements, ask visitors to follow a curriculum, or grade them on their efforts. Once visitors have paid the admission fee, they're free to learn in their own way" (Parman 2006). Museum professionals take advantage of these institutional qualities by programming for diverse learning styles in creative and exciting ways. Well-conceived museum activities do not dictate results: "Visitors, rather than the museum, determine the outcomes" (Parman 2006).

Museum Programming Enhances Leisure Experiences

Because new museums are established all the time and because many are short lived, no one has been able to determine exactly how many museums there are in the United States at any given time. According to the AAM, the most recent attempt estimated that there are 17,500 (American

Museum programming can incorporate technology to provide educational programs.

Taft Richardson's Folkvine Event
Photo courtesy of the Folkvine Team

Association of Museums 2007). Canada boasts more than 2,600 museums (ArtCyclopedia, 2007; Canadian Heritage 2007), and ICOM lists 24,000 members in 150 countries, likely only a fraction of the actual count worldwide (International Council of Museums 2007). In addition to museums of art, history, science, and natural history, museum directories and associations include zoos, arboretums, and aquariums. An infinite variety of specialty museums are included in the total. There is, it seems, a museum to serve virtually anyone's interests. That fact alone suggests the possibilities for piquing the curiosity of people who have leisure time to explore what museums have to offer.

Museum Theater and Living History

One of the current topics of professional discourse about history museums is their ability to present the complexities and debates inherent in the interpretation of the past. Historians point out that history is not the past but rather "the act of selecting, analyzing, and writing about the past" (Davidson and Lytle 1992). History museums typically use artifacts to portray earlier times, and since an artifact can convey to viewers only that which their own experiences enable them to understand about it, curators of history have traditionally relied upon written labels to tell the whole story. Writing succinct labels that hold a visitor's attention while relating the nuances, implications, and controversies in what can only be an imperfect and evolving interpretation of the past is a difficult task. Docents who tell stories to visitors enhance the museum experience, but those who do not encourage audience participation seem like lecturers. As Gail Dines points out in the film *Beyond Killing Us Softly* (Lazarus and Wunderlich 2000), today's college students are from the first image-based generation of learners, and they are often more receptive to visual stimulation than to text or lecture. Innovative museum programming that involves role-playing, costumed interpreters, and scripted theater can enhance historical interpretation for such learners. It can also develop more complicated interpretations than artifacts and text alone can convey.

History museums offer a wide range of role-playing programs, from docent-led script reading to conversation with costumed interpreters who pretend to be characters from the past (often called *living history)* to full-blown scripted theatrical performances. The interpretive tour of Campbell

House, a historic house museum in Spokane, Washington, is an example of docent-led script reading. Visitors are given leaflets that feature dialogues with historical characters who were friends, associates, or employees of the Campbell family. At appointed stops on the tour, the docent reads a dialogue with the visitor whose character frequented that part of the house. One leaflet, for example, features one of Mr. Campbell's gambling cronies, and the visitor who holds that leaflet has an exchange with the docent in the den where the men played cards. The script provides entertaining but accurate information about mine owners' attempts to stave off union activity in the early 20th century. Another visitor might read the part of young Helen Campbell's friend and discuss the social activities of the wealthy young set during the Gilded Age in Spokane (Rutherford and Shay 2004). This interactive interpretive tour accomplishes two goals: It makes the tour highly entertaining, and it allows the docent to impart historical details that might be difficult to get across through lecture alone. It also acknowledges the growing awareness that museum visitors have different learning styles.

The High Desert Museum in Bend, Oregon, is a museum of natural and cultural history that houses a variety of exhibits, including historical dioramas, art galleries, and wildlife habitats. Installations include a Plains Indian encampment, a pioneer homestead, and a working sawmill (Craig 2006, 9-10). The museum launched a theater program in the summer of 2006 that includes a living-history interpretation of Spirit of the West, an exhibit that consists of life-size dioramas depicting the history of the region. The dioramas originally had no interpretation and thus seemed to present a "linear progression of history" that omitted important aspects of white settlement of the western United States, such as "narratives about wars, [Indian] reservation life, [and] treaties" (Craig 2006, 14). Now, costumed living-history interpreters who portray figures such as wagon-train immigrants, temperance advocates, miners, and brothel madams give visitors a more complete picture (see figure 13.1) (Craig 2006, 54). As volunteers become available, interpreters from ethnic groups other than European Americans will represent Native Americans, Latinos, and Asians, all of whom played an important part in the history of the region. These historical characters enrich the learning experience, the entertainment value, and the social interaction of the museum visit.

History museums are not the only venues appropriate for performance. Museums of all types offer the opportunity to combine a number of art forms, among them theater and dance. In 2000, for a citywide festival called *Art and Soul*, the Dallas Museum of Art staged a performance by the

Figure 13.1 Mike Ford portrays a Wells Fargo messenger in one of the Spirit of the West dioramas at the High Desert Museum in Bend, Oregon.
Photo courtesy of Ann Craig and the High Desert Museum

Dallas Black Dance Theatre during a symposium that included lectures, discussions, and exhibitions. The festival "brought the diverse peoples of Dallas together . . . to explore the common yearning for a relationship with the divine" (Sachatello-Sawyer et al. 2002, 56).

The association of the Science Museum of Virginia with the Carpenter Science Theatre Company in Richmond, Virginia, has given birth to an ambitious professional museum theater program. Cofounded in 1996 by a musical director and a museum professional and funded by a grant from the Carpenter Foundation, the program first produced *Playing with Fire: After Frankenstein* by Barbara Field (Gard n.d., 2-3), a full-length piece that explored the moral questions surrounding human attempts to create life. Having established Onstage, a successful theater venue, the company and museum went on to develop short Character Cameos, or biographies of science figures, and a children's theater called *KidStage*.

The Carpenter Science Theatre has also produced classics about scientific discoveries and debates such as *Inherit the Wind*, the story of the Scopes trial that highlighted the 1920s controversy about teaching evolution. In the museum's version, the audience is invited to participate as the jury (Gard n.d., 3). As the artistic director of the Carpenter Science Theatre Company writes, museum theater is "a means of interpreting the content of museum exhibits" in "a compelling event." It "stimulates thought and learning by creating a passionate response in its audience" (Gard n.d., 1-2). Here, indeed, is programming that meets the goal of museum professionals to engage their audiences in powerful learning experiences.

Workshops

Workshops are perhaps the most interactive leisure programs that museums can offer. The Woolaroc Museum and Wildlife Preserve in northeastern Oklahoma is a good example of an institution that uses its heritage, collections, and site to present workshops of interest to both adult and young learners. The site was

> established in 1925 as the ranch retreat of oilman Frank Phillips. The ranch is a 3,700 acre [15-square-kilometer] wildlife preserve, home to many species of native and exotic wildlife, such as buffalo, elk and longhorn cattle. Woolaroc is also a museum with an outstanding collection of western art and artifacts, Native American material, [and] one of the finest collections of Colt firearms in the world. (The Woolaroc Institute 2003, 1)

Workshops that were scheduled for the summer and fall of 2006 included The Cowboy and His Gear, an "outdoor, hands-on experience"; The Woolaroc Landscape Story, a horticulturist's comparison of the landscape then and now; The Language of Branding, a workshop that allows participants to design their own brands; and Woolaroc Photography With Jerry Poppenhouse, a class taught by an Oklahoma State University photography professor (The Woolaroc Institute 2006). Developing workshops that will not only attract visitors, enhance their learning experience, and provide social interaction but also enlist them as regular attendees requires attention to several factors, according to the authors of *Adult Museum Programs*. Among the points to consider are the institution's mission, the instructor's understanding of the purpose of the workshop and of pedagogy, the number of participants and their preferences, and the facility (Sachatello-Sawyer et al. 2002, 22-23).

The workshops at Woolaroc clearly meet these requirements. The private, nonprofit foundation cites the following mission: "Woolaroc is committed to preserving the history and heritage of the people and peoples of Oklahoma and the values of early America" (The Woolaroc Institute 2003, 11). Programmers have enlisted the services of expert instructors; they have planned workshops on topics that pertain to the institution's history, site, and collections; and they have considered the preferences of the target audience by choosing activities that will draw visitors who are interested in Oklahoma ranching.

Workshops can be an engaging way to attract leisure-time learners of all ages. For example, the Art Complex Museum in Duxbury, Massachusetts, a regional art center organized around the collection of the Carl A. Weyerhaeuser family, offers teen workshops each summer. During the

summer of 2006, the museum conducted workshops on drawing, painting, clay, printmaking, and mosaics (The Art Complex 2006, 2). Leisure-time learners of all ages have proven that workshops related to the mission and collection of a museum are an excellent strategy for attracting visitors.

Demonstrations, Lectures, and Seminars

Museums with space that can accommodate larger audiences have the opportunity to enhance their educational mission through demonstrations and lectures. All museums must conserve their collections, and most use their collections for research purposes on a regular basis. Whether related to conservation or scholarship, both of these activities can double as outreach strategies. Audiences respond enthusiastically to the chance for a peek behind the scenes. Take, for example, the University of Pennsylvania's Museum of Archaeology and Anthropology, the large holdings of which include Egyptian mummies and remnants of excavated buildings. The following report summarizes a 2005 gala that drew a large crowd:

> Two demonstration stations, located in the galleries, welcomed guests all evening.
> In the Upper Egyptian Gallery, CT Scanning of Mummies, was hosted by Dr. Janet
> Monge. Here, a virtual archive of major skeletal collections was presented . . . . In
> the Chinese Rotunda, 3D Archaeological Structures from Subsurface Surveying were
> presented by Dr. Kostas Danilidis, and Dr. Alexei Vranich. Work investigating and
> developing methods for the recovery of underground structures was featured. (http://
> events.internet2.edu/2005/fall-mm/gala.html)

Art museums also use demonstrations as entertaining educational programming. The Asian Art Museum in San Francisco hosts AsiaAlive, a combination demonstration and hands-on program, in its Chong-Moon Lee Center for Asian Art and Culture (Asian Art Museum 2006). The museum uses this leisure activity as enrichment programming in conjunction with particular exhibitions. For example, in February 2006, the artist Shozo Sato demonstrated the type of Japanese painting, formatting, and materials seen in the exhibition, Traditions Unbound: Groundbreaking Painters of Eighteenth-Century Kyoto (Asian Art Museum 2006). Other demonstrations have included Tanjore relief painting, traditional Persian painting, Sashiko embroidery, tea-bowl pot throwing, and woodcut printing (Asian Art Museum 2006).

Lecture series associated with the mission and current exhibitions of a museum are time-honored programs that Sachatello-Sawyer and colleagues refer to as "bread-and-butter programs" (2002, 21). They are among the most common offerings in all types of museums. Field research conducted between 1996 and 2002 revealed that lectures were second only to docent training among the top three types of programs offered in art, history, and science museums (Sachatello-Sawyer et al. 2002, 22).

At the Henry Morrison Flagler Museum in Palm Beach, Florida, programmers tailor the annual lecture series to reflect the goals of the Gilded Age house museum. Flagler was among the magnates in the late 19th century who profited from investments in oil, railroads, and, notably in his case, hotels. His 55-room, 60,000-square-foot (5,574-square-meter) winter retreat, Whitehall, advertised his worldly success (Henry Morrison Flagler Museum 2007). Converted to a museum in 1959, the home attracts 100,000 visitors a year (Henry Morrison Flagler Museum 2007). The Gilded Age continues to fascinate museumgoers, and the mission of the Flagler Museum acknowledges that fascination. It states that part of the purpose of the organization is to preserve, research, and interpret

> Whitehall, its collections, and materials related to the life of Henry Morrison
> Flagler . . . [and to] preserve this important American historical site and provide a
> unique educational experience for visitors from around the world. Through the
> Flagler Museum, more than 100,000 visitors a year discover Florida's rich history
> and the indomitable spirit of America's Gilded Age. (Henry Morrison Flagler
> Museum 2007)

Accordingly, the 21-year-old annual lecture series provides "a detailed look at America's Gilded Age and its influence on history and culture" (Henry Morrison Flagler Museum 2007). The 2006

Andy Revkin, environmental reporter for the *New York Times*, introduces his fellow presenters during POLAR-PALOOZA's kick-off event.

Photo courtesy of ClimateChangeEducation. org

series included lectures on historical figures of the time, including Andrew Carnegie, Buffalo Bill, Thomas Edison, and Jack the Ripper (Henry Morrison Flagler Museum 2007).

As pedagogy assumes a larger role in museum missions, the character of the museum lecture is changing. In the introduction to *Creating Connections: Museums and the Public Understanding of Current Research*, Farmelo (2004) notes that both scientists and laypeople have become more and more interested in making sure that current research is presented in open forums (Chittenden, Farmelo, and Lewenstein 2004). Thus, the traditional lecture format has been called into question:

> There is an urgent need to move from a "monologue" model of communication, with scientists lecturing the public on what it should know, to a "dialogue" model, in which scientists meet the public in forums that are even handed, giving nonspecialists much more time to air their concerns and share them with the "experts." (Chittenden, Farmelo, and Lewenstein 2004, 10)

Programmers in science museums are in the position to host such discussions.

Docent Training

Docents have long been a staple of museum programming. Museums of all types use docents, or guides, to instruct visitors about the significance of their collections. In art museums, training programs for docents have typically attracted people who wish to learn more about art history, for art history has long been standard fare in these educational programs. And, as the researchers who developed *Adult Museum Programs* found, docent training was the most popular program in 95% of the art museums surveyed (Sachatello-Sawyer et al. 2002, 22). This activity serves another purpose, too. As Capitano (2004, 19) points out, "Volunteering typically fulfills a need. . . . Most people who volunteer want to better their community."

Recent developments associated with the new emphasis on different learning styles and frameworks of understanding have generated new ways of thinking about docent training. Some museums have even jettisoned the term *docent* in favor of labels perceived as less scholarly and elitist. For instance, the Jordan Schnitzer Museum of Art on the University of Oregon campus in Eugene, Oregon, launched an interpretive guide program when it reopened after a major expansion in 2004.

The original docent program had been established in 1969, long before there were any professional educators on staff. As education became a central part of the museum's mission, longtime docents resisted attempts to expand their training programs (Capitano 2004, 35). Eventually, a new Gallery Guide (later renamed *Exhibition Interpreter)* program emerged, and museum staff solicited volunteers. A carefully crafted application process helped staff to select 45 of the 61 respondents for interviewing. During interviews, volunteers expressed common motivations for becoming interpreters: They wanted to learn more about art, they wanted to give back to their community, and they wanted to interact with other people (Capitano 2004, 39). Thus, for some, museum docent or interpreter training programs provide an important leisure activity.

Family Activities

Museum programming can offer a plethora of leisure activities that attract families. Although this chapter cannot cover the broad and much-studied subject of children's education in museums, a specialized field that is explored in several works on museum education, it is certainly appropriate to mention family programming here.

Encouraging children to become comfortable in museums is one way to ensure their patronage as adults. A 1992 NEA study showed that art education correlates far more closely with later museum attendance than any other predictor does (Kolb 2000, 53). Two examples of successful programs that provide the opportunity for young children to make art after examining works in the museum collection are Toddler Thursdays at the High Museum of Art in Atlanta and the Discovery Gallery at the Jordan Schnitzer Museum of Art. Toddler Thursdays target preschool children, encouraging parents to "bring your child to look at works of art and create a masterpiece to take home. Drop by any time and stay as long as you like" (High Museum of Art Atlanta n.d., 2). At the Schnitzer, an exhibit of works by pop artist Roy Lichtenstein inspired the creation of a Lichtenstein activity center in the Discovery Gallery. Children could sit on a couch that resembled those in Lichtenstein's interior series, watch a video about Lichtenstein and pop art, and make their own creations with dots, waves, and zigzags on coloring-book outlines that resembled some of the works on exhibit.

Festivals and special events are treated comprehensively in chapters 9 and 10, but it should be noted here that museums are natural venues for events that enrich the museum experience. The SugarFest case study at the end of this chapter illustrates this opportunity. Many examples

Children can get a hands-on experience in frontier farm life at an outdoor exhibit.

Photo courtesy of Ragen E. Sanner

of such family events are sponsored by the Smithsonian Institution in Washington, District of Columbia. During the 2006 Art Night on the Mall, there were a number of activities that could be enjoyed by families. The National Museum of African Art presented Ghanaian songs and stories, the Hirshhorn Museum hosted an event called *Jazz on the Plaza*, and the Arthur M. Sackler Gallery and the Freer Gallery of Art held Lao dance classes for children aged 6 to 14 (Smithsonian Institution n.d.). Programming of this kind encourages families to visit museums during their vacations.

Community Discussions

The expanded educational and outreach role of museums in the past several decades has raised awareness of their capacity to provide a forum for exploring topics important to their communities. Incorporating public debates and discussions into programming requires careful planning; museum educators must always consider the appropriateness of current topics to their mission. But if a museum is to fulfill the AAM's (1992) call to "become more inclusive places that welcome diverse audiences" (3) and to realize its "potential for public service" (4), then it must widen its role in the community. One example of such far-reaching vision is the Community Conversations program at the Pratt Museum in Kachemak Bay, Alaska. The Pratt is "the only natural history museum in the 25,600-square-mile [2,378-square-kilometer] area of the Kenai Peninsula. It serves a regional population of more than 40,000 and hosts around 30,000 visitors each year" (Pratt Museum n.d., 1). Its role as the only museum in a large geographic area lends urgency to its inception of a community forum. Community conversations revolve around current topics of concern, such as immigration, global warming, and public vandalism. Its Web site explains that the museum is

> dedicated to the process of education, exploring the natural environment and human experience relative to the Kachemak Bay region of Alaska and its place in the world. The Museum seeks to inspire self-reflection and dialogue in its community and visitors through exhibitions, programs, and collections in the arts, sciences and humanities. (Pratt Museum, Education n.d., 1)

The Community Conversations program clearly supports this mission, and it also meets the requirements of attractive programming. It is educational, it provides social interaction, and it offers an opportunity for participating in socially valuable discourse that betters the community.

Museum Programming Challenges

Effective museum programming is not without its challenges. Museums must first serve their mission. As the foregoing example of the Pratt Museum suggests, serving the mission might sometimes involve a museum in public discourse on issues about which there is not public consensus. Even as we focus on activities that appeal to the leisure-seeking audience, we must acknowledge that some material appropriate to the educational mission of a museum will generate contention. Often by the very nature of the material explored, museum exhibitions can raise questions about ideological, cultural, and social values.

In addition, museums are challenged to find new ways to attract ever more diverse audiences. In order to fulfill the educational mission that has become central to museum programming, museum planners must reach out to audiences that have not traditionally felt included, as the Smithsonian's National Museum of American History has done with its Center for Latino Initiations.

Handling Controversy

As mentioned, because museums have become increasingly involved in their communities, and because exhibitions often explore topics that spark debate, museum planners sometimes confront controversy. At times, topics about which there is disagreement among stakeholders

(board members, donors, political leaders, and the public, for example) carry political implications. Sometimes an exhibit will generate discussion that stems from different values about patriotism, religion, war, or the environment.

A striking example of a museum controversy that ended in the Smithsonian Institution scrapping a major historical exhibit is the saga of the *Enola Gay*, the American B-29 bomber that dropped the first of the two atomic bombs that levelled Hiroshima and Nagasaki in August, 1945. The Air and Space Museum planned an exhibition featuring the restored aircraft as part of the 1995 commemoration of the 50th anniversary of the end of World War II. But when the proposed interpretive exploration of the bombing was made public, historians, veterans' groups, peace organizations, and politicians became embroiled in a dispute about the way the material was to be presented. One person lost his job, and the Smithsonian Institution found itself in the position of having to rethink the exhibit (Zolberg 1996, 72-76).

The 1999 exhibition at the Brooklyn Art Museum, Sensation: Young British Artists From the Saatchi Collection, brought forth a much-publicized skirmish in the so-called *culture wars*, the conflict between traditional and progressive values, when then-mayor Rudy Giuliani announced that he found some of the works disgusting (Sohn 2004, 37). Several of the pieces explored sensitive religious subjects using biological material such as elephant dung. The controversy centered partially on city funding of the show, but a lawsuit based on the mayor's decision to cut off the subsidy resulted in the court handing down a decision that upheld free speech in the case of art exhibits (Sohn 2004, 38-39).

Any museum must carefully consider the implications of potentially controversial programs. But if faithfully serving the mission of the museum is paramount, programmers need to weigh the loss to public service that might result from avoiding such events. In the case of the Sensation exhibit, its commercial success, whether in spite of or because of the controversy, generated valuable public debate about museums and social responsibility, cultural ethics, and free speech (Sohn 2004, 39). As for the cancellation of the *Enola Gay* exhibit, it might be argued that the Smithsonian Institution missed an opportunity for public discourse about the use of atomic weapons and war in general. As Luke argues, "Museums . . . possess a power to shape collective values and social understanding" (2002, xiii). Even in developing programs intended to attract leisure-time visitors, museums must remain true to their mission.

Fostering Inclusion and Respecting Cultural Identity

In 1992, the AAM set forth 10 principles for achieving both excellence and equity. These principles are laced with admonitions to "reflect the diversity of our society," to "assure that the interpretive process manifests a variety in cultural and intellectual perspectives," to "achieve diversity among trustees, staff, and volunteers," and to "carry out [the museums'] responsibility to their diverse public" (American Association of Museums 1992, 7). Reflecting diversity is a complex and comprehensive undertaking. Willson has noted that "as the American public becomes increasingly more diverse, art museums must utilize multicultural education theory and modify practices that do not effectively address diversity" (2005, 60).

The same prescription can serve all museums. In 1996, the Smithsonian's National Museum of American History acquired the Teodoro Vidal collection of Puerto Rican art. The museum had been working to incorporate the Latino experience into its programs; earlier in the decade, an internal audit had produced a report titled *Willful Neglect*, which urged more funding, staff, and exhibitions that interpreted Latino life. The resulting initiative encouraged a change in institutional thinking, and the Smithsonian Center for Latino Initiatives was created (Velasquez 2001, 115). The acquisition of the large Vidal collection cemented the determination to increase the Latino presence throughout the museum, and a collections manager was hired and a series of exhibits developed (Velasquez 2001, 117).

Planning programs to accompany the unveiling of these artworks forced staff to consider questions surrounding multicultural programming: how to maintain a specific, long-term cultural presence; how to attract a nontraditional audience; and how to change entrenched institutional policies and agendas. (Velasquez 2001, 118-119). The Smithsonian Institution has developed a variety of

programs from the initiatives that emerged during the 1990s. In September 2006, the celebration of Hispanic Heritage Month featured films, dance, a letters-from-home workshop, lectures, and a discussion of current Latino affairs in the United States (Smithsonian Institution n.d.).

Summary

Museums offer a wide variety of opportunities that invite the public to spend its leisure hours in constructive, educational, and entertaining activities. People are attracted to such programs because they provide social interaction and the chance to learn or to contribute to society. The foregoing discussion has offered some thoughts on what is possible in museum program planning, but I have purposely omitted a discussion of a critical component of good program planning: evaluation. Chapters in the first part of this volume treat theory and assessment. Presumably, readers will turn to these for assistance in developing program plans that incorporate sound evaluative measures. As for ideas about conceiving successful museum programs, the following case studies are excellent examples. Each illustrates various ways a museum can use its collections and promote its mission to host memorable experiences.

CASE STUDIES

The West Baton Rouge Museum's SugarFest: An Educational Event Designed as a Festival

Caroline Kennedy

The West Baton Rouge Museum is a rural, parish (county) historical museum supported in large part by a millage (property tax) levied on parish citizens. Although the museum is located just a few miles from the state capital, it lies on the opposite bank of the Mississippi River, which has kept the area fairly isolated from the city of Baton Rouge and the suburban sprawl associated with it. Sugar plantations cover the parish, and many buildings from before the Civil War remain, functioning similarly as they did 150 years ago. A sugar mill located in the center of the parish still produces raw sugar from local sugar cane.

In 1995, the museum developed SugarFest as a means to communicate its mission (to interpret the unique cultural heritage of West Baton Rouge) to local citizens and to attract visitors from outside the parish. The focus of the annual festival is sugar plantation life in the parish, both from a historical perspective and as it exists today. The goals are to publicize the museum to a broader audience, to instill pride among local citizens in their rural traditions, and to provide a unique educational opportunity within a festival format.

The museum staff includes four full-time and five part-time employees, complemented by volunteers who work as needed. The net cost of SugarFest, which is about $5,000 U.S., is offset by money brought in through food and drink sales. Food, drink, and music at the festival are carefully selected to highlight life on a sugar plantation, which in turn complements the exhibits and historic buildings on the grounds. To solicit more volunteers and to encourage more community involvement, local civic, church, and school groups help sell food and drinks for a portion of the profits. This gives the festival a built-in audience from the beginning and brings in stakeholders who want to ensure its success.

Folkways associated with plantation life are demonstrated by local people who still practice these traditions. They are invited to participate and are paid for their time. Paying craftspeople was a rarity in the area at the time—most festivals charged a booth fee to offset the costs of an event, with little thought given to the kinds of crafts presented. The West Baton Rouge Museum selects craftspeople who can demonstrate their craft and discuss it with visitors. The emphasis is on interaction with the public versus hawking wares. This fulfills the mission of the museum and provides an additional educational component to the event. It also helps instill pride and gives the selected craftspeople a financial incentive, encouraging them to continue in their endeavors.

A local Sugar Queen is asked to come as an honored guest to give each visitor a raw sugar sample and to explain how her title was bestowed on her through a ceremony that has been running for generations. SugarFest also features a sweets contest for local cooks, a traditional cake walk, and a recognition ceremony for visitors who have given the museum oral histories that encourages more citizens to recognize their own sugar stories as significant. Families are encouraged to share these stories with each other, and guides are stationed throughout to interpret local history. No admission fee is charged, which encourages families and community groups to attend together. A plantation big house and cabins that once housed slaves are available for viewing without charge. Living-history interpreters are on hand in each setting, recounting the lives of actual citizens of the parish, both from the past and the present. Controversial topics such as slavery and modern-day segregation are met head-on in discussions and activities moderated by trained multicultural interpreters. Collection replicas (e.g., farming implements, shackles, butter churns, and so on) are used in various activities so that visitors can see the items in action and understand how they reveal historical traditions.

Since 1995, SugarFest has grown into an annual community gathering that has attracted out-of-towners. It has been named a Top 20 Event by the Southeast Tourism Society and has been copied by other historical museums in the area. The millage that supports the museum has been renewed for another 10 years, and annual visitation includes many of the people who were first exposed to the museum through SugarFest.

The Mapmaker's Eye: David Thompson on the Columbia Plateau

Northwest Museum of Arts and Culture (MAC), Spokane, Washington
Marsha Rooney

David Thompson, a Canadian explorer and fur trader, spent the years from 1807 to 1812 establishing trade relationships with Inland Northwest tribes and charting the perplexing 1,200-mile (1,931-kilometer) course of the Columbia River and its eastern tributaries. His experiences provide an ideal lens for viewing the larger subjects of Western exploration and first contact between European and American Indian cultures.

Because of the Lewis and Clark Bicentennial, 2004-2006, interest was high as the Northwest Museum of Arts and Culture (MAC) in Spokane, Washington, began to plan the exhibit, The Mapmaker's Eye. MAC's American Indian Cultural Council supported the exhibition, and local author Jack Nisbet provided interdisciplinary expertise and educational vision. Above all, Thompson's explorations provided compelling material for regional partnerships that would last far beyond the installation dates of the exhibition. The Mapmaker's Eye spawned programs for all ages and spurred regional interest in future related projects.

Spokane is the primary cultural center for 1.9 million people living within a 200-mile (322-kilometer) radius that includes areas of Oregon, Idaho, Montana, British Columbia, and Alberta. The museum annually serves 10,000 students and teachers, more than 50% of whom are from underserved populations, including rural areas, Title I schools, American Indian reservations, and minority groups. The Mapmaker's Eye particularly appealed to those with strong connections to the land, and it provided a multidisciplinary experience linking geography, science, art, economics, and cultural history. This content easily filtered into interactive programming for MAC target audiences (adults, educators, families, and students) and reflected the museum's mission to engage visitors in lifelong learning about visual arts, regional history, and American Indian and other cultures.

During 4 years of project planning, museum curators and consultants met regularly with the American Indian Cultural Council, a diverse community program committee, and the U.S. David Thompson Bicentennial Committee. From its many curatorial, financial, and educational partnerships, a rich array of public arts and cultural programming evolved from the exhibit, all of which maintained the museum emphasis on key artifacts: the journals, field sketches, and equipment of Thompson's era of exploration. Cultural material enhanced the tribal perspective, and the Smithsonian Affiliate status of the museum facilitated a Smithsonian Institution loan of navigation instruments.

The Mapmaker's Eye provided excellent opportunities to improve museum–educator relationships, expand semiannual teacher nights and workshops, host a teacher institute to create and market exhibit curricula, host a regional musical performance, and participate in Teaching American History

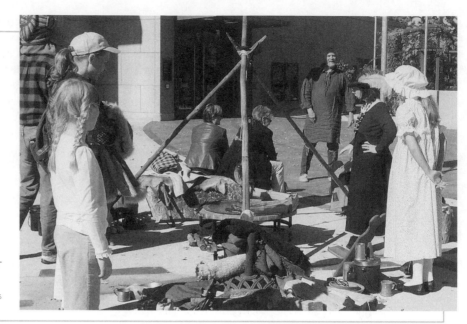

The Mapmaker's Eye encampment.

Photo courtesy of Northwest Museum of Arts & Culture

collaborations emphasizing the importance of regional objects, archives, and historic sites. The exhibition also drew two major events. The national Surveyor's Historical Society (SHS) located its annual Surveyors Rendezvous west of the Mississippi for the first time. The group attended The Mapmaker's Eye as well as a living-history reenactment at nearby Riverside State Park, the site of Thompson's trade post. The museum also hosted a 2-day regional forum for Canadian and U.S. museums and government agencies, during which it shared Lewis and Clark Bicentennial lessons and encouraged support for the Thompson Bicentennial and future interpretation efforts of regional fur trade. The exhibition underwriter, the Nature Conservancy, shared its fur-trade program as one example.

From simple exhibit text panels to Nisbet's readable companion book, the project provided written material for adult learners at various levels, including a newspaper feature on the curator of the Ontario archives hand-delivering Thompson's original journals for installation. A five-session speaker series, partially funded by Humanities Washington, tested demand for leisurely weekend afternoon presentations and linked Canadian and American scholars and American Indian elders with interested audiences, which averaged 65 attendees per session. A gallery take-home brochure emphasized additional options for all visitors, including reading lists, Web sites, videos, and related community programs. The museum's annual gala fund-raiser delighted a traditional, upscale dinner audience with living-history participation in staged fur-trade activities and comments by Nisbet, who also led docent field trips and a popular 4-day cultural tour to Canada.

A creative program idea involved geocaching, a Web-based activity suited in content and methodology to The Mapmaker's Eye. Using global positioning systems, participants located a geocache, or stash of treasure, on the MAC grounds and recorded comments on a blog at the museum Web site. The museum also incorporated fur-trade themes into regular family programs, including discovery backpacks for gallery use, Family MACFest Saturdays, and interactive stations within the exhibit.

The Mapmaker's Eye involved history aficionados and American Indians in its planning, and early conversations revealed the contrast between non-Native and Native sense of time and place. American Indian perspectives on first contact remain less than enthusiastic. As Nisbet's oral histories revealed, much was lost when extensive numbers of native populations fell prey to European American disease. On a positive note, Kalispel elders shared pride in reviving canoe-building traditions as they discussed their elegant reproduction canoe on exhibit. Exhibit audiences were surprised to learn that the fur trade attracted not only European Americans but also native people from the eastern woodlands and Hawaii to the region.

My two recommendations to arts and cultural programmers are (1) to look for the most creative ways to connect project content, methodologies, and subject disciplines and (2) to create the widest range of partnerships possible throughout all aspects of planning and implementation, from selecting objects and securing underwriting to developing and publicizing the programs. The Mapmaker's Eye not only met the museum's interdisciplinary mission but also produced a wealth of programs for all audiences and left a regional legacy of interest in fur-trade interpretation.

Performing Arts Programming

Steven Morrison, MFA
University of Cincinnati

Photo courtesy of Kagen E. Sanner

A householder opens her mailbox to find a glossy brochure from the local community theater. The brochure highlights next year's main-stage subscription series. Although she does not consider herself an arts aficionado, she certainly enjoys going out for dinner and a show on a fairly regular basis. She glances over the brochure that boldly announces the theme for the season, *Bringing You Broadway!* Fondly remembering the trip she took to New York City a few years back, she becomes more intrigued and begins to flip through the pages of the brochure. The titles and the playwrights are familiar and are ones she has enjoyed in the past. Through the concept of title recognition, the brochure accomplishes an initial objective by piquing her interest, and she reads on. She even begins to consider buying a season subscription for herself and her husband.

That evening she is reading the local newspaper and notices that the nearby regional theater has just announced the titles of its next season. Similarly to the community theater, the regional theater is hyping a five-show season ticket. She recognizes only one of the productions and the playwrights for one or two more. She does not necessarily think any less of the regional theater—it has a reputation of offering premier talent and high artistic quality—but she does ponder the differences in the choice of programming. She naturally wonders how titles are chosen, and why the two theaters take such different paths in their offerings. For that matter, she wonders what the considerations are when her local dance company chooses its programs, when the symphony puts together its series of concerts, and when the opera makes its title selections.

The purpose of this chapter is to offer arts managers and managing artists an understanding of the programming process and how that process affects nonprofit performing arts institutions. Challenges, distractions, useful systems, important considerations, and best practices from the profession will be examined. The ultimate goal of this chapter is to assist managers in devising their own systems for making sound programming decisions.

Challenges and Trends

The greatest dilemma that leaders of nonprofit performing arts organizations face is how to juggle their artistic mission along with fiscal solvency. These two concepts are often at odds, and leaders regularly practice skillful discretion and deliberate compromise in order to ensure a balance of both. Arts organizations have scarce financial and human resources that leaders must allocate wisely in order to best serve their mission in a financially sound manner. Most performing arts groups rely on ticket income as a primary source of revenue, which requires careful attention to programming choices.

The single event versus the season experience is especially relevant to fiscally conscious arts administrators in the context of audience attendance and revenue trends. The 2005 publication of *Theatre Facts* by the Theatre Communications Group (TCG) included a survey and analysis of conditions at regional theaters across the country. For the first time, the analysis revealed that average single-ticket income was greater than average subscription income. Arts organizations are seeing a decline in customers' interest in season tickets (subscriptions), and managers now have to pay more attention and allocate greater resources to the single-ticket customer.

Researchers ponder the causes for this trend. Perhaps it is caused by decreasing loyalty among audiences, or perhaps attendees' busier and less-predictable schedules promote a reluctance to make long-range time commitments. Regardless of the reasons, more arts organizations are challenged to market the value of each event as a single-ticket offering, to strive to sell the season as a whole, and to offer subscription packages that offer customers something in between, which are commonly called *flex tickets*. The same TCG survey revealed that flexible-subscription income

constitutes an increasingly significant proportion of total subscription sales. In 2001, flexible subscriptions accounted for only 5% of subscription income, whereas in 2005 that figure nearly doubled to 9%. To a programmer, this means that there is less assurance that all of the programs added to a season will actually be experienced by all of the customers. Audiences are demanding the right to pick and choose.

Good programmers are also mindful that society is finding greater value in leisure activities that fall outside the realm of the performing arts. Audiences are supporting countless competing activities that involve television, the Internet, podcasts, multiplex cinemas, and many other activities that are of a time-shifting nature, an attribute that is not inherent in a live performance. Time shifting enables users to do what they want, when they want. Further frustrating the programmer is the fickle nature of audiences. Some programs and titles inevitably sell better than others do, but it is often difficult to predict which ones those will be. This makes programming especially challenging when the organization needs to make reliable budget forecasts of single-ticket revenue. All of these concerns reiterate the importance of good programming decisions that result from a comprehensive process.

Seeking a Structured Programming Process

Performing arts administrators appreciate systematic processes. It is comforting to know that tried-and-true practices can help lead to desired outcomes. Managers enjoy such structure in their everyday work. They lead marketing departments that apply useful data to create value that is sufficient to overcome the customer's perceived costs. They work with development officers to identify suspects, nurture those suspects into prospects, and cultivate those prospects into patrons and donors. They devise financial management practices that provide the necessary resources for the organization and enable them to make decisions that stem from solid information systems.

Can managers enjoy that same level of comfort when they make programming decisions? Can they apply a similar system to the process? Do managers even know what their role is in the programming process? These are just a few of the questions that make the programming process more complex than other areas of management. One thing is for certain: Programming decisions, whether they concern core offerings or innovative programs, define nonprofit arts organizations. Programming is the means to a desired end, and it is the product of the organization's mission, as well as the organization's reason for existence. Programming decisions demand thoughtful consideration. A systematic process is elusive, but a checklist of careful considerations relevant to any nonprofit performing arts institution can be devised.

Nonprofit Influence on Programming

Programming decisions would have a much simpler and more logical focus if performing arts institutions operated in the private sector. In that sector, administrators seek the greatest degree of profitability and therefore make market-driven programming decisions that lead to the greatest possible paid attendance. Programming energies are targeted solely on the financial bottom line. If nonprofit managers worked in the for-profit sector, they would research attendance trends and select productions that offer title recognition, or at least the attributes of the most popular productions. Under these market-driven conditions, new dramas, avant-garde plays, experimental operas, and innovative musical compositions would rarely find their way onto the stage. From a purely business viewpoint, it simply does not make good business sense to allocate scarce resources to such unpopular programming. The risk is too great, or the return on investment is too small.

In reality, the vast majority of performing arts organizations in the United States operate as nonprofit corporations, and a primary reason for that status is the concept of market failure, a recognition that the organization could not survive in the private sector. Market failure leads to a gap in earned income. The nonprofit status of an arts institution, and therefore the manager's decision-making process, acknowledges that the programming does not financially sustain the

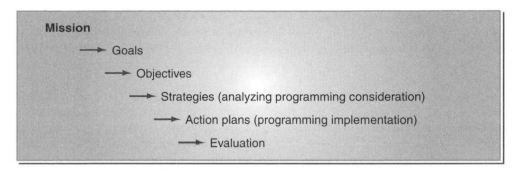

Figure 14.1 The planning process should have a logical flow, but the mission must form its foundation.

organization. Nonprofit administrators have to generate contributed income to fill that gap and balance the operating budget.

In the nonprofit sector, administrators realize that their products may not be commercially viable. Programming decisions are not market driven; rather, they are mission driven (Wolf 1999). This implies that their greater reason for existence is to deliver some sort of social service. Without the clarity of the profit motive, programming decisions and the definition of success become complex, but that does not mean that decisions are made without a focus on specific results. Good programming is influenced by both the mission of the organization and fiscal responsibility. Programming must logically flow from the mission, reflect the values inherent in that mission, have a definable and justifiable purpose, and offer evaluative criteria for measuring success.

Programming as a Function of Strategic Planning

As administrators struggle to apply some sort of formal process to the complex dynamics of programming, they should consider the concept of strategic planning as a framework. Since the primary outcome of strategic planning is to produce fundamental decisions, the planning process itself can form a logical progression for programming. In figure 14.1, the process is likened to a staircase. The mission is paramount and leads to each of the next steps (or planning concepts), with the function of each concept stemming from the preceding concept.

The mission, or the reason why the arts organization exists, will always provide the ultimate rationale for programming. Formulating the mission is the responsibility of the board of directors. A well-formulated mission motivates all of the stakeholders. In a culturally rich population with numerous arts organizations, the mission will also define the unique niche of an organization. The mission communicates to company members, the audience, and the arts community who the organization is and what it does. It should be internalized by stakeholders and easily communicated to potential audiences.

The mission leads to goals that are founded in the mission. Once goals are established, quantifiable and measurable criteria are needed in order for the organization to both measure its success and offer a tangible objective for everyone involved. Artists, in conjunction with tactical considerations offered by arts managers, must next consider the most effective and efficient work tasks, or strategies, to accomplish those objectives. Consider the objectives as ends and the strategies as means to the ends. The programming that an arts organization delivers to its constituents, the nonprofit equivalent of a product line, formulates its action plans. These offerings, hereafter referred to as *programming*, are the most powerful institutional resources for achieving goals, meeting objectives, and fulfilling the mission.

Programming can take different forms. Core programming is the main-stage or primary series of concerts, plays, or other performing arts offerings. Core programming draws on the majority of the production and marketing resources, both monetary and human. Although often drawing on fewer organizational resources, the second stage of a theater or the auxiliary seasonal offerings of an orchestra should be considered part of the core programming.

A second category of programming may be classified as *initiatives*, which are productions or services that supplement core programming. They serve specific goals that stem from the mission of

Nontraditional collaborations often form the basis for innovative programming. The collaboration between the Cincinnati Opera and the Allen Temple A.M.E. Church not only was fun and challenging for both organizations but also accomplished a variety of programming goals.

Photo courtesy of Cincinnati Opera

the organization and may be nonrecurring events. For example, a local dance company that primarily presents national touring companies as its core programming may supplement its season with initiatives such as juried competitions or contests to foster the development of young choreographers.

A third type of offering is often labeled as *innovative programming*, which is defined individually by the organization. Innovative programming is often the research and development aspect of an arts organization, and it can be the most exciting form of programming. Although it is difficult, if not impossible, to describe the impetus of innovation, such programs often start as an initiative to better serve the mission, reach out to a different audience, creatively raise funds, enhance public relations, or accomplish specific marketing objectives. Innovative programming may be core or initiative. For example, in order to reach a new audience, an opera company may join forces with a local church for a special concert that fuses jazz, gospel, and classical works performed by opera stars. This is what choir director Robert Gazaway had to say about the program:

> The collaboration between Cincinnati Opera and the Allen Temple A.M.E. Church is an exciting venture for several reasons. First, there is a spiritual element in every piece of music no matter what the style or who is performing. Also, this is an opportunity for the choir to share varied musical genres with a larger audience than those who attend Sunday service. Thirdly, the program selection for the concert is so diverse that we can literally say there is something for everyone. Finally, this innovative collaboration is a means to expand the audience for the Opera by moving the performance out into the community. (Bellin 2006)

Later in the chapter we will examine how each arts organization may have its own definition of innovative programming.

What to Program

All good programming decisions start with a solid mission statement, which will lead an organization to make appropriate programming decisions with clarity and specificity. The mission statement reflects an organization's community and its primary stakeholders. It also offers a sense of direction for the planning process, enables the establishment of quantifiable evaluative criteria, and is even inspirational. This is the mission statement of the Amas Musical Theatre:

Amas Musical Theatre is a non-profit, multi-ethnic theatrical organization located on MacDougal Street in Greenwich Village. Founded in 1968 by Ms. Rosetta LeNoire, the Amas mission is grounded in non-traditional, multi-ethnic production, education and casting. Amas Musical Theatre is devoted to the creation, development and professional production of new American musicals, the celebration of diversity and minority perspectives, the emergence of new artistic talent, and the training and encouragement of inner-city young people. (Amas Musical Theatre 2007)

This mission statement forms a solid foundation for making sound programming decisions, including the titles the theater might select and the services it offers. The mission highlights the proficiencies and core values of the organization, and it logically leads to a series of goals, objectives, potential strategies, and ultimately programs that will serve its mission and form the identity of Amas. Many of its goals are actually suggested in the latter part of the mission statement.

Now note a sampling of the programs offered by Amas. This sampling illustrates the theater's carefully chosen variety of core and innovative offerings that stem from the mission.

- **Theatre Programs at Amas**—Amas provides an artistic home for writers, composers, and lyricists to create and develop new work, from first drafts to full-scale production.

- **Amas Six O'Clock Musical Theatre Lab**—This lab is a development series for writers, lyricists, and composers to mount staged readings of their new musicals. New shows are presented for three consecutive evenings in hour-long concert versions. Recent productions include *Lone Star Love, or the Merry Wives of Windsor, Texas*; *Stormy Weather: The Story of Lena Horne*; *From My Hometown*; *Zanna, Don't!*; *Langston Hughes' Little Ham*; *Four Guys Named Jose and Una Mujer Named Maria*; and an adaptation of *Sheba*, a new pop-rock-gospel musical that examines what happens when cultures and politics collide.

- **Amas Workshop Program**—The workshop program gives composers and lyricists the opportunity to create a more polished and complete version of their new work. Developing a musical is a long and arduous process that requires much rewriting and adaptation. Workshop productions entail 2 weeks of rehearsal culminating in a series of performances using minimal costumes, lighting, and sets.

- **Amas Mainstage Program**—Select musicals are given a full Off-Off-Broadway run of 4 weeks. The shows are fully produced, including sets, costumes, lights, and live music. Critics are invited to attend.

Amas, like most performing arts organizations, chooses genres and titles that are consistent with its mission. The organization is further challenged to accomplish the right mix of offerings. These sorts of decisions require programming strategies that consider the effect the organization wants to have on its constituents as well as the allocation of scarce human and financial resources. At the beginning of this chapter, we saw a householder who received a brochure featuring the core programming of a local performing arts group. She not only considered the individual titles but also assessed her own degree of interest and the value of a season ticket. Programmers struggle with the understanding that the whole equals more than the sum of its parts. Individual titles and programs are examined for their virtues and consistency with the mission, but they must also be examined for how well they relate to each other in forming a total-season experience.

Edward Stern, producing artistic director at the Cincinnati Playhouse in the Park, is in charge of programming at the institution. He compares the precarious and thoughtful nature of programming an entire season to that of designing a roller-coaster ride. He strives to create a preconceived, intentional, and well-planned experience for the rider, or the audience. He wants a particular series of loops, ascents, and declines that results in a specific total experience for loyal subscribers. During the planning process, he carefully selects titles both on their individual merits and as part of a season in order to offer the variety he seeks. Should something happen during season planning to cause the elimination of one program, it would not be unusual for him to entirely reprogram titles in surrounding slots in order to recapture his planned aesthetic design—the total experience (Stern 2006).

The clarity of Amas' mission of public service is a best practice in the way it specifies certain types of programming. That clarity is important when an organization wants to deliver such a sophisticated range of services (multiethnic product creation, development of new work, and production of selected works) to such a targeted range of constituents (inner-city young people). Best practices also establish quantifiable criteria to evaluate the success of the programming efforts. Those criteria should be spelled out in the programming objectives. Evaluation is an essential part of the planning process, though it is often neglected because it is time consuming. This last step in the process assesses effectiveness and efficiency, and it also provides invaluable considerations for future programming. Evaluation allows for learning from mistakes and building on successes, and so it logically comes back to the planning progression and asks, "Did we meet our objectives?"

Best practices dictate that managers remain mindful of those objectives and how they were derived from the broader goals, which ultimately flow from the mission. Quantifiable criteria are of greater value when they are measured against an outcome-based objective. According to the grant guidelines of the NEA, outcomes are the benefits that accrue to the participants of programming; they represent the effect that the project has on participants. Typically, an outcome is a change in the participant's behavior, skills, knowledge, attitude, status, or life condition that occurs as a result of the project. For example, an outcome might be that students demonstrate an interest in theater. Employing outcome-based objectives means measuring some sort of preprogramming assessment against a postprogramming assessment.

Outcomes are measured by identifying characteristics or conditions that tell whether change has occurred; these objective measures are called *indicators*. To be useful, indicators must be countable or observable evidence of change. An example of an indicator is the number and percentage of students who attend at least two live theater performances during the life of a project. A good evaluator will create outcome-based objectives with indicators of change rather than simplistic outputs, which offer less informative data, such as an attendance number or subjective comments from participants about the likeability of a program.

At Amas, the evaluation process involves a preliminary step. Amas begins to measure success first in qualitative terms by asking the following questions about the programming:

- In the Amas development process, were the artists' goals achieved? Were they able to see what was necessary to take their project to the requisite next level?
- Were Amas audiences engaged and challenged? Were we able to provide both cultural mirrors and bridges to others?
- Do our choices for early development via readings bear out our faith and investment?
- Have our education programs enabled young people to make better choices in their lives?
- Do we maintain the financial soundness to continue the growth of our work?

Those qualitative questions are documented by Jan Hacha, managing director, who comments,

> Evaluation is key, but those criteria are soft and qualitative. Though we consider them an important first step, we really have to pair those criteria with specific, measurable objectives that offer us a more quantitative basis for evaluation. Then the challenge is to develop program-by-program metrics that offer real-world measurements, such as dollars raised per event, children reached at an after-school program, and the like. (Hacha 2006)

Amas does not consider criteria such as attendance or tuition-related revenue as a specific function of the evaluation. Rather, all revenue sources, earned and contributed, are assigned monetary goals as objectives that are consistent with the last question in the list. Also note that the criterion of audience or viewer satisfaction is specific in the context of being *engaged* and *challenged*, as opposed to something as vague as *enjoyment*. The concept of audience satisfaction is just one of several evaluative criteria. As the mission states, the organization exists not necessarily to satisfy the general public, but for defined audiences and participants. This introduces another primary consideration in programming—who are the programs for?

Cast of Amas Musical Theatre's 2001-2002 production of *Little Ham.*

Photo courtesy of Donna Trinkoff, Producing Artistic Director

For Whom to Program

Arts managers and the board alike must identify and define their constituency—for whom the organization exists. There is a strong connection between what you program and who you program for, and both should be evident in the mission. Unlike Amas, other performing arts organizations are less specific in their missions. They often have more generic goals such as, "To produce quality work," "To entertain," or "To educate." Arts administrators sometimes refer to such mission statements as *McMissions.* The term suggests that, like any McDonald's franchise, the enterprise lacks a sense of individualism, a defined market segment, or a characteristic niche. However, smaller arts organizations with a more limited range of services often sustain and even thrive with such a generic mission. Those organizations find a broad mission statement to be liberating and less restrictive when making programming decisions. Such organizations seek to be as inclusive and accessible as possible in order to serve the greatest number of constituents.

A generalized mission statement may be appropriate, even helpful, when the arts organization is without competition in the marketplace or when it is serving a smaller community that lacks sufficient population to support a variety of interests. For example, a community may be sufficient in size to support a live theater but not large enough to support a theater that only produces new or avant-garde works. A theater that exists in this type of area may enjoy the programming freedoms of an unrestrictive mission statement—a primary goal of entertaining the community is sufficient.

Inherent to community theater is the local, volunteer nature of the performers and technicians who produce the work. The performers and technicians are key stakeholders, and it is wise to reflect their needs in the mission and programming of the organization. However, an arts organization that serves a larger population or that coexists with similar organizations, such as Amas, would find a generic mission to be unwise. With the latter type of institution, the programming process can become riddled with frustration if it lacks a clear direction. Everyone involved with the programming must be on the same page in terms of interpreting and internalizing the mission. Additionally, everyone must understand for whom the organization exists, or key stakeholders may become frustrated and divided, especially those involved in making programming decisions.

Until now, this chapter has concentrated on inclusive programming considerations. Programmers must also consider exclusionary factors, usually stemming from the readiness to produce certain programs. For example, the music director of a small orchestra may find that a Mahler concert meets all the mission-rooted programming criteria from the standpoint of audience demand. If the orchestra considers its musicians as primary stakeholders, they too may desire the challenge.

The programmer must then consider all of the key stakeholders and their interests as well as the organization's capacity to present the work. Here is where exclusionary factors may influence the decision: Mahler's works are lavishly orchestrated for large numbers of musicians. They not only require either a large core orchestra or numerous extras but also an advanced degree of musicianship. Either criterion can put Mahler's work outside the reach of most community orchestras and many smaller to midsize professional orchestras. The programmer must carefully examine how a Mahler concert serves the mission of the orchestra against the ability to perform the work consistent with the orchestra's standards for artistic quality.

When making this type of decision, it is useful to systematically and objectively analyze the effect the program has on the goals of the organization against the capacity to perform the work within its defined artistic standards. This analysis may not be conclusive in isolation, but it will lead to constructive discussions such as the following:

- Should this program be considered a high or low priority?

- Are we artistically prepared to produce the program?

- If the program has great effects on the mission, what resources might be needed in order to build the necessary capacity to do the program? (This process is also associated with the management tool known as a *needs assessment.*)

- Should we table this program for another time or eliminate the idea altogether?

Where to Program

The venue can and will influence the programming. Often a performance space is not a tried-and-true venue with which the arts organization is familiar. The ideal location is safe, clean, and easily accessible. Be sure that the space is licensed for public events and that the local fire marshal has issued an occupancy certificate sufficient to accommodate the maximum audience. Confirm that the space is accessible for people with disabilities according to the guidelines in federal regulations. In the United States, these include section 504 of the Rehabilitation Act and the Americans with Disabilities Act.

Additionally, seemingly obvious considerations need to be formally assessed. Are the size and the style of the stage appropriate? Is a raked (sloped) stage a concern? Orchestral events often call for risers (platforms) that may be affected by such concerns. Some theatrical productions may call for the traditional proscenium stage (the picture-frame style), whereas others are best performed on a thrust or arena style. Dance events often call for a yielding stage floor, which may be accomplished with portable materials such as Marley dance flooring. Assess the size of the stage with regard to the productions needs, as well as the size and layout of the house (audience areas). Be sure to consider both the stage and the house with regard to sight lines. Avoid uncomfortable or obstructed audience views. Some found-space venues, or spaces not specifically intended for the performing arts, do not afford such amenities as raked seating areas or ideal sight lines. A sometimes overlooked preproduction consideration is an assessment of doorways and thresholds. Production personnel often have large pieces of scenery, props, or instrumentation that require larger entryways.

Venue accessibility can be more complex than concerns about space or the ability of audience members to locate the venue, safely and affordably park their car, and easily find their seat. Programming accessibility should also account for perceived obstacles or incentives. A venue that is perceived as inviting by some constituents may be perceived differently by others. Programming choices alone are not sufficient to overcome such perceptions.

One such obstacle was experienced by the Alabama Shakespeare Festival (ASF) in Montgomery, Alabama. In the 1990s, this regional theater presented more than 14 productions a year in their beautiful facility. The programming choices were generally consistent with those of other major regional theaters, and, of course, the works of Shakespeare were highlighted. The building is a majestic example of neo-Palladian architecture, featuring two state-of-the-art performance venues. It is located in a cultural park that is shared by an art museum, a majestic lake inhabited by swans, groomed botanical gardens, and a variety of nature-inspired public areas.

In the 1990s, the board and staff embarked on an institution-wide initiative to diversify their audience. Audience members were predominantly Caucasian, whereas the organization was located

The Carolyn Blount Theatre, home of the ASF in Montgomery, Alabama.

Photo courtesy of Alabama Shakespeare Festival

in a demographically biracial community, roughly half Caucasian and half African American. In the past 25 years, many performing arts organizations have launched sincere efforts to bring diversity to their audiences. Although such diversity efforts suggest some obvious title-selection strategies, the venue must also be considered.

When the ASF offered a play by African American playwright August Wilson, the *what* (play selection) was found to be appropriate, but the *where* became a barrier to attendance. Formal evaluation of the production found that the organization failed to attain its attendance objectives. Informal focus groups revealed that some members of the African American community perceived the facility as uninviting or intimidating. Their community was not visibly involved in building the $21.5 million U.S. facility and they did not feel any stake in that venture; if anything, they felt excluded from the venture. Many associated the building, its location, and its opulence with the wealthy elite who built and founded ASF.

In a concerted effort to address this perception, programming strategies were brainstormed and implemented by biracial staff, board members, and volunteer committees. The crux of the strategies to overcome the *where* stigma was to open the theater for community events that served and were sponsored by the African American community. Management created and booked numerous non-performing-arts events for the sought demographic in order for that target group to develop a sense of comfort and belonging about the building. Such events included the hosting of an African American scholarship banquet and even the development of a theater-sponsored award ceremony for special achievements by noted African American residents of Alabama. Over time and combined with several other diversity initiatives, including greater African American involvement and visibility on the staff, the targeted community began to feel more at home in the facility. When African American theatrical works were programmed in future seasons, the ASF was much more successful in attaining the attendance objectives.

To revisit the programming construct discussed at the beginning of this chapter, note how the evaluation process revealed a missed program objective. Further evaluation deemed the mission, programming goals, and attendance objectives to be sound, and new strategies were implemented to achieve those goals and objectives (see figure 14.2).

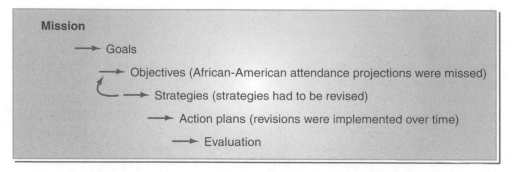

Mission

⟶ Goals

⟶ Objectives (African-American attendance projections were missed)

⟶ Strategies (strategies had to be revised)

⟶ Action plans (revisions were implemented over time)

⟶ Evaluation

Figure 14.2 The planning process is dynamic and cyclical. The evaluation step informed the ASF that it needed to make changes to its planning.

Is there room for innovation within the programming consideration of *where?* Jay D. Meetze, artistic director of the Opera Company of Brooklyn (OCB), offers an innovative approach to this aspect of programming. The company's mission is to make opera affordable and accessible to people who do not usually have the opportunity to attend performances in conventional venues. The company keeps production costs down by eliminating virtually all visual elements of production (costumes, scenery, and spectacle), and it even reduces, if not eliminates, venue costs. Instead, those scarce resources are allocated to the core values of the art form and the artists. Works are often presented in an intimate venue where the audience has a better opportunity to connect with the art, which is also a core value for the OCB.

Meetze admits to cutting the operas down to a 2-hour running time, but he defends the programming as traditional. As the primary programmer for the company, he respects titles that audiences will recognize, and he understands that such titles result in greater interest from the public. Although the titles are traditional, the venues most certainly are not. The organization often produces works at unpublicized anonymous venues, including private residences in and around Brooklyn. The logistics for such an innovative approach are unique: Audience members interested in attending must call the OCB box office for advance reservations. Once audience members pay for a ticket (usually around $15 U.S.), they are instructed to call back a few days before the event. When they call back, they are given the address of the performance. Title recognition, word of mouth, and world-class performers are among the OCB's most powerful allies as it works to fulfill its public service mission (Meetze and Osa 2006).

When the Program Occurs

Timing is everything. The success or failure of programming is often a function of when the event takes place. The most obvious consideration is venue availability. Arts organizations that do not own their own home are often at the mercy of the venue and its calendar policies. For example, an orchestra that shares a hall with other local arts groups may compete with those organizations on scheduling. Some programs

Kenneth Overton as Papageno in the OCB 2003 production of *The Magic Flute* at New York City College of Technology's Voorhees Theater in downtown Brooklyn.

© Vinepod, Inc. www.vinepod.com. Photo by Timothy Maggio.

have some flexibility with regard to their schedule, but many do not and can be affected by artists' availability, competing events, complementary events (outside events that might increase attendance at a program), or seasonal concerns. Scheduling conflicts are particularly common during the holiday season, when the ballet is offering its *Nutcracker*, the theater its *A Christmas Carol*, and the orchestra its annual holiday concert. Administrators are wise to establish the best possible relationships with their venue (or venues) and the other arts groups. Many local arts councils will serve as a coordinator for calendar concerns. Other considerations that present timing challenges include adverse weather for outdoor programs, lead time required to market and promote a program, availability of press coverage, and timing restrictions imposed by a sponsor's fiscal year.

How to Plan Programming

In Lewis Carroll's *Alice's Adventures in Wonderland*, the Cheshire Cat offers this piece of wisdom: "If you don't know where you are going, any road will take you there" (Carroll 1865). Every organization must devise its own road map for program planning. Figure 14.3 offers a simplified

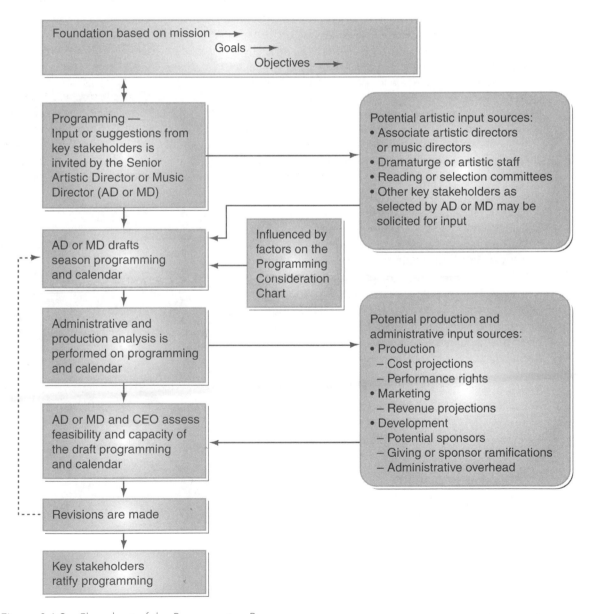

Figure 14.3 Flowchart of the Programming Process.

flowchart that summarizes the programming decision-making process. It is a sequential construct that identifies key considerations. The flowchart of activity leads to input for programming considerations, either for the executive director or the artistic director. These two directors are separately or ideally jointly involved in the programming process. Each arts organization will have its own unique considerations to add to the process. In a more established and experienced organization, the flowchart can cycle numerous times during a planning process that takes many months of research. Eventually, an informed and thoughtful programming plan will evolve.

The Programming Process sidebar elaborates the input sections of the flowchart on the right side of figure 14.3. The illustration offers specific considerations for making programming decisions. It is organized by revenue and expenses. Since a budget is a plan that is expressed monetarily, managers can also use this list of considerations in budget planning; most of the considerations can easily be expressed as a line item on a budget. Larger staff-driven arts institutions with sophisticated organizational charts will systemize the process to include input from various departments, such as general management, production, marketing, development, and so on. In that instance, each department should submit a succinct narrative and budget to the executive director and artistic director, as appropriate. The narratives and budgets form the basis for discussion among key stakeholders as to the feasibility, costs, and benefits of the programming. Smaller organizations may use the chart to develop a comprehensive process that heeds all the necessary input.

Analysis of the proposed programming should be considered against each criterion on the chart. One of the more significant criteria falls to the marketing director, who must forecast revenue for each proposed program. That projection should be conservative. Ticket revenue forecasts should be a function of the average ticket price multiplied by projected attendance. Projected attendance should consider such factors as the time slot (calendar) and documented attendance of past programs that were similar in nature or in the degree of title recognition. Once all criteria are analyzed, further discussion regarding capacity and effect should occur among leadership, aiming for a consensus decision about whether or not to proceed. The chart may also be used as a to-do list in order to bring programming to fruition.

Programming Process

Artistic or Mission Considerations:

- Extent to which the program services the organization's agreed-upon mission and goals, both as a single event and as part of a season.
- Extent to which the program services or benefits a defined constituency or certain key stakeholders, such as the core audience, a target audience, or target artists (i.e., playwrights, composers, the orchestra, the resident acting company, and the like).
- Availability and capacity of artists/talent or other artistic and production resources.
- Anticipated reception by the public (potential for controversy, strategy for managing or preventing controversy).

Capacity and Cost Considerations:

Facility or Venue

- Size, occupancy, and equipment appropriate to program and audience
- Availability of venue (calendar issues)
- Rental or usage fees
- Architecture or staging style
- Acoustics
- Sightlines
- Accessibility
- Safety and security inside and out

- Audience occupancy
- Insurance (property, event)
- Union requirements of the venue (on personnel)
- Licenses and permits (occupancy, liquor, building, business, and so on)
- Signage
- Parking
- Front-of-House staff

Production Elements

- Securing performance rights
- Artist salaries
- Scenic design and materials
- Lighting design and materials
- Costume design and materials
- Props design and materials
- Sound design and materials
- Sound reinforcement
- Makeup design and materials
- Composer needs
- Music Director, Choreographer, or other contract services
- Costume or scenery shop usage and personnel
- Shop crews
- Load-in and load-out costs and issues
- Transportation or vehicle needs
- Storage needs
- Running crews and stage hands
- Union benefits (housing, pension, health, and the like)

Administrative Elements

- Managerial staff overhead
- Managerial supplies
- Office space
- Box office
- Telephone and Internet
- Utilities
- Insurance (liability, business interruption)
- Taxes and users fees (varies as a function of local laws)
- Janitorial
- Bank charges
- Accounting and payroll
- Information systems (hardware and software)

Marketing and Public Relations Elements

- Printing
- Photography and media
- Mailing costs

- Supplies
- Advertising
- Web site
- Public relations expenses
- Telemarketing expenses
- Groups, buses, and tourism
- Special projects
- Cross promotion possibilities
- Special promotions possibilities
- Concessions
- Publications and printing
- Postage

Revenue Potential and Considerations

Earned Revenue

- Ticket income forecasts (based on past similar events)
- Tour (or runout) potential
- Education outreach (master classes, related educational programs, and the like)
- Concessions (refreshment or gift shop sales)
- Advertising (program ads or signage)

Contributed Revenue

- Federal, state, county, or municipal government grants
- Foundation grants
- Corporate sponsors
- Impact on membership, annual giving, or other fund-raising campaign

Henderson and Bialeschki (2002)

Obstacles to Good Programming Decisions

The partnership and working chemistry between the artistic CEO and the managerial CEO must be healthy, productive, and functional. Without such a relationship, the programming process can become dysfunctional. Artistic excellence, however an organization defines it, will always be paramount in programming decision making, and that is why it makes sense to have an artist at the helm of the process. The qualified artist's specialized knowledge and experience in programming is the key to successful programming. Although some artistic and music directors have a keen business sense, others must feel comfortable asking for managerial input. Good programming is the product of a communicative and mutually respectful relationship between the artistic and the managerial leadership.

Beware of shiny objects that may inhibit or distract the programming process. These objects take many forms, and one is the temptation to make a programming decision based on potential for funding. Foundations, corporate sponsors, or even generous individual donors all have their own agendas; think of those agendas as their missions. Only if their mission is consistent with your organization's mission and capacity is there good reason to program the mutually beneficial event. Be mindful that contributed revenue potential is just one of many criteria, and do not allow funding opportunities to cloud your objectivity regarding the other programming considerations discussed in this chapter. Similar distractions may include a program that is of special interest to a small number of key stakeholders. An example would be producing *Hamlet* primarily because a certain director seeks the challenge or to reward a certain member of the acting company with the

coveted role. Strive to be objective with all of the considerations, justify and articulate programming rationale, keep communication flowing among all input sources and key leadership, and be mindful of all programming considerations.

Summary

A nonprofit performing arts organization exists in a mission-driven environment and is charged with providing a public service. Programming decisions define an organization to that public and form the basis for serving its mission. Key ingredients in good programming decisions include not only a clearly defined mission but also artistic and managerial leadership who work well together, remain visionary, and understand their changing constituency. Since distributing profit to shareholders is not an objective, perhaps the most compelling characteristic of a nonprofit performing arts institution is the ability to experiment. Great works can culminate from that experimentation. Although leaders understand an underlying mandate of fiscal responsibility, they still strive to take risks and perhaps even fail as they create new art, produce works that may be unpopular yet address important artistic goals, and vary the means by which their audiences view traditional art. Good programmers must be able to manage those risks and make compromises as necessary in order to serve their artistic mission while also ensuring fiscal solvency.

CASE STUDIES

Pensacola Opera: Presenting Innovation in a Traditional Art

Marcus Glasgow, MA and MBA candidate

In the world of opera, innovative programming would seem to be difficult, if not impossible. Opera audiences tend to prefer proven titles by well-known (and often long-gone) composers. Furthermore, many opera directors feel these productions are best received when staged in a traditional manner.

The Pensacola Opera is no exception. As of 2007, the organization was in its 24th season, with a modest budget of approximately $240,000 U.S., a figure that doubled since 2004. In 2004, Opera America recognized Pensacola Opera as the fastest growing opera company in the United States. Artistic director Kyle Marrero has a detailed 5-year production plan to take it through its 30th season. It is only recently that others have become involved in the planning for a given season.

Marrero's talent is not limited to the artistic direction of the company; he also possesses a business savvy for the financial bottom line. He considers that ultimately the executive committee and board of directors must approve the coming season. His 5-year programming slate takes into consideration the cost of production, name recognition of repertoire, artistic value to patrons, availability of cast, availability of sets and costumes, forecast of ticket sales, and salability of the season subscription.

"In early fall of the preceding season I develop the detailed production budget, presenting the opera's five-year plan. I almost always offer alternative repertoire as a comparative choice for the executive committee," Marrero has said. In this way he allays fiscal concerns while also keeping the organization on track artistically. With the predictability required by this sort of programming process, it would seem that there is little room for innovation. However, this is not the case.

First, Marrero considers collaborations with other performing arts organizations as a means of attracting audiences: "Fortunately, opera as an art form necessitates collaboration since it encompasses the entirety of visual art. Collaboration with other arts organizations, such as the Pensacola Children's Chorus, Northwest Florida Ballet, and the Pensacola Symphony, always aids in audience development." However, the greatest innovation occurs in the Pensacola Opera's educational initiatives. "We have a responsibility to educate our audiences," Marrero claims. Traditional audiences are served by the main-stage product line, but innovations in education are invigorating younger audiences, from schoolchildren to young professionals. "In this way we can sustain growth while staying on the cutting edge," Marrero explains.

That cutting edge includes a new commission. According to Marrero, "It's called *The Window's Lantern* and it's based on local folklore that is very familiar to our community, so the story is very accessible. The opera is in English and only two hours long, the length of a movie." Works like this serve a twofold educational purpose: to offer programming that is relevant to the community and thereby better connects the Pensacola Opera with its community, and to appeal to new audiences, especially a younger audience.

The lesson learned from the Pensacola Opera is clear: Even the most traditional of art forms has room for innovation. Innovation can augment the traditional; it does not have to replace the traditional with an entirely new product. Would the organization be as popular if it ceased to produce *La Traviata* or *Le Nozze di Figaro [The Marriage of Figaro]*? Marrero does not think so. The operatic main stage will always involve the classics, but industrious programmers will continue to find ways to augment those with fresh ideas such as *The Window's Lantern* in order to better connect with their communities and find new audiences.

San Antonio Symphony Orchestra: An Orchestra Tweaks Its Award-Winning Programming

Some may consider the San Antonio Symphony Orchestra (SASO) the epitome of programming genius, having received many honors for its innovative programming under the baton of maestro Christopher Wilkins. In 1994, the American Symphony Orchestra League (ASOL) recognized the orchestra as "a model of inclusiveness and community-relevant programming for American orchestras" (Texas Cultural Trust). That same year SASO was named the winner of the first American Society of Composers, Artists, and Publishers (ASCAP) Morton Gould Award for Creative Programming. By the end of the millennium, the orchestra managed to earn five more awards from the ASCAP, including the Award for Programming of Contemporary Music. Throughout the 1990s, SASO used an operating budget of $2.7 million U.S. to create innovative presentations of traditional and contemporary repertoire.

But much has happened to the orchestra since then. The 1999-2000 season was Wilkins' last as music director, though he continued to serve as music advisor and was named music director emeritus during the 2001-2002 season. The orchestra declared bankruptcy in 2003, setting the stage for a talented and committed new music director to take the podium the following season. In the fall of 2004 Larry Rachleff began his tenure as music director, with a slightly different programming vision and the intent to overcome the orchestra's fiscal difficulties.

In their book *Standing Room Only: Strategies for Marketing the Performing Arts*, Philip Kotler and Joanne Scheff (1997) suggest that an effective strategy is to program according to the culture of the community. The authors single out Wilkins as having "an impressive long-term plan for involving the city's Hispanic population" (1997). This approach is exactly what earned the orchestra recognition for community-relevant and creative programming from organizations in New York City; but how did it fare with audiences in San Antonio?

Julianne Fish, the orchestra's vice president for operations, explains her view:

> I don't think the connection is as strong as people assume. The feedback that I've gotten is that sometimes it's slightly offensive to people to think that, because they're Mexican or of Latin decent, that the only type of music they will enjoy will be Latin based. There's obviously a large Hispanic population. We also have Mexican nationals that come from Mexico for the weekend or for whom San Antonio is their second home.

> I think what we're finding more often than not—with the Mexican nationals in particular—[is] that they are interested in the traditional programming: the Tchaikovsky, the Beethoven, the Mozart. Everybody always said, "Well, you're in San Antonio. You're right next to Mexico. You have to do Latin-based programming," . . . but that is not always the answer.

Traditional programming, or what Fish refers to as *traditional staples of the orchestral literature*, is exactly what Rachleff gives them. These staples, in addition to his dedication to living American

composers, are what define Rachleff's programming style. However, given the organization's mission to provide innovative and diverse programming, where is the potential for innovation?

Fish suggests that innovation pertains to how an organization excites its audience about what it does, rather than changing its programming altogether:

> Innovation doesn't mean you change what you're presenting; it's how you make it relate to people. Consider two different audiences: the young up-and-comings and the standard, long-time supporters of the symphony. The music means two different things to those two groups, but it is the same music.

Making that music relate to the different audiences is where innovation comes in. Fish has been known to offer concerts to younger audiences that offer orchestral classics with added visual spectacle, such as dance or movement artists.

What is next for SASO? Fish suggests part of the process that is often left out. "There is another element: Ask for feedback. We really want to follow up and invite input from the audience. Let them know that that's an important part of our process." In this way the organization can assess its innovations while informing the audience of its intent to remain true to its mission. An organization's innovations are only as good as what it learns from its efforts.

What are the lessons learned? A best practice in New York City is not necessarily a best practice elsewhere. The savvy arts administrator understands the need to connect with the community, but strategies to achieve that goal are a function of each community and arts organization. While SASO was garnering accolades from respected sources and academics for its programming, it was accumulating debt. Current management does not regard programming alone as the primary factor that led to bankruptcy, but the organization did learn the importance of listening to its constituents and tweaking the programming back toward traditional orchestra fare.

Imagining the Future of Arts and Cultural Programming

Gaylene Carpenter, EdD
University of Oregon

Doug Blandy, PhD
University of Oregon

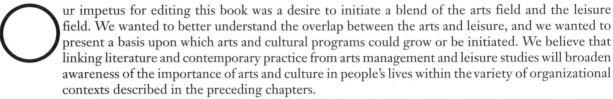

O ur impetus for editing this book was a desire to initiate a blend of the arts field and the leisure field. We wanted to better understand the overlap between the arts and leisure, and we wanted to present a basis upon which arts and cultural programs could grow or be initiated. We believe that linking literature and contemporary practice from arts management and leisure studies will broaden awareness of the importance of arts and culture in people's lives within the variety of organizational contexts described in the preceding chapters.

We now come to a point in this book when it is both prudent and essential to consider ways in which the planning and delivery of arts and cultural leisure experiences will be influenced by future trends and realities. What follows are précis that relate to the future of arts and cultural programming. Topics include changing demographics, technological innovation, economics, building community, enhancing research, and anticipating program interests.

Changing Demographics

Throughout this book, contributors have addressed the importance of access and cultural competence in providing arts and cultural programming. The necessity for keeping such concerns in mind is only going to increase as a result of the demographic shifts that are coming and are already evident in both the United States and Canada. Demographic shifts will occur in residence, ethnicity, and age. Demographic change will result in fresh opportunities for programming for new, diverse, and larger audiences in urban, suburban, and rural areas. A synopsis of what is occurring and what can be expected follows.

Hobbs and Stoops (2002) note that the population is growing faster in the western United States than it is in all other regions of the country. Changes in age are occurring as well. Overall, "as the United States entered the 21st century, most of the population lived in the South or the West, in metropolitan areas, was female, at least 35 years old, White (but much less so [than in previous years]), owned a home, and lived alone or in a household with one or two other people." (Hobbs and Stoops 2002, 3). More specifically, more than 50% of the U.S. population in 2000 was older than 35.3 years. Consider that in 1900 more than half of the U.S. population was 22.9 years or older. Hobbs and Stoops also indicated that the year 2011 will mark the beginning of growth in the number of U.S. residents who are 65 years and older.

A 2006 demographic study by Johnson considered trends in rural areas and small towns within the United States. Technology and ease of transportation are allowing people greater flexibility around work hours and place of residency. As a result, migration from rural areas has slowed, particularly in areas that are near cities. Johnson notes that growth in immigrant groups is not confined to urban regions. Particularly important for arts and cultural programming is the finding that people in their 50s and 60s are moving to rural areas for access to recreational opportunities.

Joseph Chamie, Chief Demographer of the United Nations, predicts that by 2050 the U.S. population will reach 420 million compared with the current 300 million. He believes that the evidence suggests that by 2050 21% of U.S. citizens will be 65 years old or older. Chamie also predicts that the number of people reaching age 100 or older will increase. He also confirms that the United States will continue to move away from an ethnic composition that is primarily European (Kawasaki 2006).

Foot, Loreto, and McCormack (2006) predict similar shifts for Canada. Low fertility rates coupled with increasing life expectancy is causing the average age of Canada's citizenry to increase as well. It is anticipated that Canada's overall population will grow only through immigration. Immigrants will primarily come from Asia, Central and South America, and the Caribbean.

These changing demographics mean that practices currently taken for granted in providing arts and cultural programs will need to be refined. The participant base for which current best practices developed will, of course, continue. However, new or refined best practices will be needed in order to serve new or growing constituent groups. It is anticipated that both preservice and in-service preparation of arts and cultural programmers will continue to evolve and that lifelong learning for arts and cultural programmers should be emphasized.

Technological Innovation

Technological innovation and the rate at which innovation takes place will have a profound effect on arts and cultural programming in the 21st century. One futurist argues that the innovation in this century will be the equivalent of what occurred in the preceding 20,000 years (Kurzweil and Meyer 2006). Kurzweil (2006) articulates some of what we can expect to experience within the next 30 years. What he imagines is based on current trends and has profound ramifications on how people will be able to choose to use their leisure time. The implications for art and culture are significant.

Consider, for example, that virtual environments are already taken for granted by those who play games or are part of social networking. Within the decade, virtual environments will be multisensory and include enclaves of real and simulated people. The difference between the real and the simulated will be difficult to perceive. The importance of time and space to personal relationships will continue to diminish. Computer technology will be present and invisible. Clothing, buildings, and our bodies, among other things, will be computer enhanced. People will be injected with nanobots that enhance intelligence and sensory experience. These same nanobots will help us navigate real and virtual environments. Experience beaming will be a pastime for those interested in experiencing another person's life. Experience beaming permits individuals to send digital representatives of their experiences and emotions to the Internet for consumption by others.

Trends and innovation supporting this future are already evident in social networking sites such as Second Life. Second Life is a virtual world that as of September 2006 was inhabited by 747,263 avatars (online digital representations of participants). This number is growing at an estimated rate of 20% per month (Special Report: Virtual Online Worlds 2006). People participate in Second Life for entertainment. Residents "fly over islands, meander through castles and gawk at dragons" (Special Report: Virtual Online Worlds 2006, 77). However, residents also "form support groups for cancer survivors. They rehearse responses to earthquakes and terrorist attacks. They build Buddhist retreats and meditate" (79). The creators of Second Life envision it to be an "engine of creativity" (79). As such, it is a destination for people who are focusing their leisure time on experimentation and artistic and cultural innovation in the company of others.

Programmers who are forward thinking will need to anticipate designing programs for such environments. Some programs will replicate activities that are successful in the nonvirtual environment. However, other activities will be based on those unique characteristics associated with virtual environments in which people can fly, shift shape, and assume other superhuman powers. The rapidly evolving nature of virtual environments reinforces that preservice and in-service preparation of programmers must evolve and that lifelong learning must be cultivated.

Economics

The American Assembly (2006) describes three arts and cultural sectors: nonprofit, for-profit, and informal or unincorporated. In many ways the American Assembly defined these three sectors according to their economic basis. Kreidler (2006), in one of the most significant assessments of the nonprofit arts and cultural economic environment, relates a history of the public funding of the arts to the close of the 20th century. Three distinct stages are described. The last stage is the one that we are currently leaving as we move toward a currently undefined state of being.

In his essay, Kreidler (2006) acknowledges, as some of the contributors to this volume do, that funding from both public and private sources is uncertain. In Kreidler's view this is not a temporary economic anomaly but more likely a long-term condition that will change the ways that arts and cultural activities are funded and delivered. Kreidler also predicts an even bigger problem. This problem is a loss of a labor force willing to work without benefits and at a reduced wage.

Emerging out of this environment is a trend in which arts and both nonprofit and for-profit organizations are providing cultural programming. This trend is evidenced in the way that cities are cultivating this relationship in an effort to attract a young and hip citizenry (Dewan 2006). Recognizing that young people are choosing locations over jobs, cities such as Portland, Oregon,

are promoting public policies such as zoning regulations and low-interest municipal loans that promote arts and cultural venues. One result, as described in the James Irvine Foundation report on the arts in California, is that the nonprofit arts sector is becoming less viable in an environment in which the distinction between commercial and nonprofit programming is disappearing (James Irvine Foundation and AEA Consulting 2006). Thus the arts and cultural managers, as well as artists, currently graduating from universities are looking very seriously at the for-profit sector, and the better wages it provides, as the best venue in which to pursue their professional goals. The report suggests that it is in the best interest of the for-profit and nonprofit sectors to work together toward mutually satisfying ends. A strong case is made that one sector is not viable without the other. As such, programmers with interests in promoting arts and cultural experiences, whether they are from public or private organizations, need to find ways to engage in dialogue with one another.

Building Community

At the start of the new millennium, the notion of social capital caught the nationwide interest of a range of professionals, including those in arts and leisure. Stimulated by Putnam's (2000) best-selling book, *Bowling Alone: The Collapse of American Community*, the idea of social capital refers to social networks and the norms of reciprocity and trustworthiness that arise from them (Putnam and Feldstein 2003; Infed 2005). Professionals in arts and leisure create venues that are conducive to building social interaction that contributes social benefits to individuals and their communities.

Working together on art projects can help build a sense of community.

Photo courtesy of SouthEast Effective Development (SEED)

In addition, collaborative relationships are becoming more prevalent in both the arts and culture and the leisure and recreation professions. These partnerships have been developing in part because granting organizations encourage joint efforts, because public and nonprofit organizations frequently find it necessary to share efforts due to limited funds, and because stakeholders value working with others to accomplish lofty goals that one organization cannot achieve on its own.

Collaborative efforts not only benefit our organizations but also contribute to building community. Collaborative programs generate trust and social connections among those individuals working together and frequently enable the development of programs that otherwise would not take place because of limited human and nonhuman resources. Forming partnerships, cooperative ventures, and collaborative agreements has long been practiced by recreation and leisure professionals in the public sector (Hensley et al. 2006). Arts organizations, for example, have expertise in the arts and access to various artists. Public leisure organizations have indoor and outdoor spaces and missions that stress that they should provide public access to recreation.

When it becomes evident that a community-based need exists, arts and leisure professionals who may already be programming together are well positioned to be proactive in coming together to seek solutions in newer ways. Professionals in parks and recreation who work in California were recently challenged by America's Promise: The Alliance for Youth regarding the findings of a study about America's youths:

A new study . . . finds that when youth are provided with at least four out of five fundamental resources, their chances for success dramatically increase and damaging racial and economic gaps are significantly reduced. The data also show that more than two-thirds of youth are not currently receiving enough of these resources. The in-depth study, *Every Child, Every Promise: Turning Failure Into Action*, measures the presence and impact of Five Promises that affect the development of youth: caring adults; safe places; a healthy start; effective education; and opportunities to help others. The Alliance has issued a call to action outlining recommendations for policymakers and other sectors that impact the lives of children and youth. (California Park and Recreation Society 2006)

It is plausible to infer that if parks and recreation professionals initiate communication with selected arts organizations in their local communities, they may be able to address what America's Promise: The Alliance for Youth found to be a contemporary failure. In the future, professionals working *together* to develop programs in arts and culture should want to be at the forefront in addressing local and social concerns such as the one presented here.

Luckily, there are ample examples of nonprofit arts organizations and public recreation organizations working together to provide arts and cultural leisure experiences. Citing Americans for the Arts data, one of us recently noted that 91% of local arts agencies are already collaborating with at least one public or community agency, and 78% are working with three or more (Carpenter 2006). There is every indication that these collaborations will continue to be pursued. Such programs foster positive working relationships among professionals, as evidenced by increases in the number of articles reporting on collaborations that appear in professional magazines and journals. We have also seen modest increases in the number of educational sessions related to arts and cultural programming being held at national and regional conferences. Professionals planning a recent National Recreation and Park Association congress included sessions on cultural arts and heritage (National Recreation and Park Association 2006). As a result, arts and cultural programming was a featured area for professional development of parks and recreation professionals.

Building community through arts and cultural programming requires arts managers and recreation professionals to purposefully work together in new ways. Arts providers have been content to make art and put it on a stage or gallery wall and believe that other community partners would deliver an audience (McDaniel and Thorn 1997). Recreation professionals all too often concentrate their programs on active sports and outdoor pursuits while minimizing opportunities for arts participation. Collaborative programming efforts intitiated by arts managers and recreation professionals, along with other community-based professionals who have a commitment to providing arts and cultural opportunities, contribute to positive community development.

Enhancing Research

What we *do* and *do not* know about the meaning of leisure as it is experienced by those participating in arts and cultural pursuits should be addressed by researchers and professionals. It is essential to shed much-needed light upon meanings associated with arts and cultural participation. Research is systematic investigation within a field of knowledge that is undertaken to establish facts and principles in order to contribute to that body of knowledge (Henderson and Bialeschki 2002). Research is concerned with theories and focuses on explaining deviations toward or away from theoretical principles. For our purposes, arts and cultural leisure experiences provide a context in which we can examine individual and group behaviors.

Much of what we know about arts and cultural behaviors is in the form of patterns of participation rather than meanings associated with arts and cultural behavior. Both points of knowledge are necessary when making programmatic decisions and planning comprehensive arts and cultural leisure experiences. Programmers must know patterns of participation when seeking funding sources and promoting comprehensive programs. Through program documentation and evaluation, astute programmers already collect and promulgate this information to various stakeholders. But what of the experience itself? Kelly (1996) reminds us that it is both the behavior and the meanings attached

to the behavior that we call *leisure*. Both the more transparent participation patterns and the more illusive entity that is signified by the behavior (i.e., the social psychological component of leisure) need to be part of our collective research agenda. The effect of activity involvement on psychological and social development has not yet received significant research attention (Kleiber 1999). What motivates people to participate in arts and cultural experiences instead of the wide variety of other leisure options? How do people make their choices in how they spend their discretionary time and money on arts and cultural experiences? The more that arts and cultural programmers know about how people make their decisions, the more they are able to implement program strategies that address people's interests.

Clearly, more research is needed, and seeking this kind of knowledge about arts and cultural leisure experiences is a goal for the future. However, challenges do exist. McCarthy and Jinnett (2001) note that current research on arts participation has its limitations: first, it oversimplifies the process individuals go through in deciding to engage in arts participation, and, second, it focuses more on demographics than on user motivations and attitudes. The arts participation model discussed in chapter 1 of this book attempts to address both needs, and thus it can give insight into what arts and cultural providers might address to encourage participation. Others have pointed out that arts-related research does not benefit from contracts between industry and universities, targeted research by private foundations, or industry research institutes located inside universities (Chartrand 2000). Research in the arts, like leisure, frequently has not been financially supported by government, business, or industry to the extent that research within other disciplines has been supported. As a result, our empirical knowledge derived from scientific research is less than what it could be to help us program arts and cultural leisure experiences. However, these current limitations should not stifle our motivation to engage in future research in arts and leisure.

Though our understanding of leisure has evolved from many disciplinary perspectives, the understanding coming from an arts and cultural perspective is minimal to date. More research toward understanding the motivation and conditions that lead to arts and cultural participation will improve programming by adding essential information to needs assessment. In addition, it will help articulate the value associated with the arts and cultural leisure experience in ways that will allow us to specifically design programs addressing those qualities that add to the worth of the experience.

People with keen research interests in arts and cultural programming can take heart, given the growth in leisure research. The theoretical and empirical examination of leisure and its place in the lives of individuals and social groups has gained momentum (Burton and Jackson 1999). Leisure has been the subject of much research over the past 30 years. Leisure, like art, tends to be obscure and difficult to understand in part because it is so individually experienced. This reality requires researchers to examine leisure within one of several theoretical constructs. The arts experience, like the leisure experience, can be systematically examined either from a theoretical basis or as a type of leisure pursuit or expression. If arts and cultural settings and experiences were examined more frequently, our understanding of them would be enhanced accordingly. Then our abilities

Beyond programming the events that provide arts and leisure experiences to the community, it is important to research the enjoyment of the participants so that future programs can better deliver these experiences.

Photo courtesy of Ragen E. Sanner

to create and deliver arts and cultural leisure experiences would be advantaged, as we would be able to use documented research findings when planning and implementing such programs.

Closely aligned with the trend toward research is the trend toward advocating and promoting the benefits of leisure. In their review of leisure as a profession, Parr, Havitz, and Kaczynski (2006) acknowledge that in the late 1980s, researchers and managers began to recognize the need to better document and communicate the benefits of parks, recreation, and leisure services and amenities. Called the *benefits approach to leisure*, these efforts, led by the Parks and Recreation Federation of Ontario, first took hold in Canada and then spread quickly to the United States.

The positive effects of leisure participation have been frequently researched in the past 25 years. Driver and Bruns (1999) recently compiled a list of positive outcomes; these include personal benefits (psychological, personal development and growth, personal appreciation and satisfaction, and psychophysiological), social and cultural benefits, economic benefits, and environmental benefits. These benefits are supported by several empirical research findings associated with leisure participation. In general, these benefits *should* include arts and cultural experiences along with recreation activities such as sport, outdoor recreation, and physical activity that often dominate leisure research. Reviewing the literature for evidence of benefits derived from arts and cultural participation has been minimal (Carpenter 2005), and research designed to identify the specific benefits of arts and cultural leisure experiences needs to be increased. Such research has the potential to further validate these positive outcomes and may also document currently unknown benefits derived from participating in arts and cultural leisure experiences.

Mannell and Kleiber (1997) caution us that as we arrange experiences for people, we need to remain cognizant of the possibility of undermining the perceived freedom and intrinsic motivation that are the foundations of leisure. Most people find leisure and make of it what they will based on their personal and social resources (Mannell and Kleiber 1997, 353). Mannell and Kleiber would probably also remind us how important it is to study how people's personalities and social situations encountered during everyday life shape their perceptions and responses to arts and cultural leisure experiences. Such study would put us in a better position to meet people's needs and interests in arts and cultural leisure experiences.

Anticipating Program Interests

Most of us reading this book would agree that programming arts and cultural leisure experiences for individuals and groups is a worthy calling. We can find ample reasons to support our thinking and ample evidence to assure us that arts and cultural expression is on the rise. As professionals and aspiring professionals interested in programming arts and cultural leisure experiences, we know the importance of developing new strategies that will help us do better at addressing people's interests. The intent toward our last topic about the future of arts and cultural programming is to briefly examine the factors that influence what, when, and how we program.

At this sociohistorical point in time, astute programmers must remain cognizant of relevant contemporary trends. We must remain aware of trends that potentially affect our programs or that suggest we need to develop new skills or gain additional knowledge in order to better deliver our experiences. What follows are several factors that we believe have ramifications for planning and developing programs. Some of the factors can be viewed as opportunities, others as challenges. As a group, they may seem somewhat trendy. The worthiness of many to be considered as factors in programming could be vigorously debated. Some were identified from popular literature sources; others were found in literature generated by futurists. If they seem too trendy, remember that both people's interests and organizational initiatives are frequently influenced by popular culture thinkers and writers in contemporary society. Thus programmers will want to closely examine each factor in order to determine its relevance to their programming situation and responsibility.

• More and more organizations are developing programs that educate consumers about arts and culture. Organizational initiative is a primary reason why this development is occurring. Results from program evaluations often suggest that participants enjoy an experience more when they have knowledge about the artists or the performers. The fact that the public schools have had

Keep in mind the popular trends regarding what people find exciting within the arts and cultural realm. These trends can be used to attract new participants to programs.

Photo courtesy of Conrad Weiler

to eliminate arts education due to budget limitations is another reason why more arts organizations are providing arts education. When such educational programs are designed, they frequently contain what we would consider to be a recreational component; that is, the educational experience is directed toward *learning as fun.*

• There is evidence of marketing efforts to promote experiences related to specific and unique cultural amenities found in certain place-related destinations. Generally referred to as *cultural tourism*, these opportunities offer visitors chances to experience the arts and cultural fabrics of local areas. They also enable communication between visitors and members of the cultural core of the experience (Carpenter 2004). Programmers will play a greater role in producing cultural tourism opportunities in the future.

• People of all ages have more and more arts and cultural programs from which to choose. Nonprofit arts organizations have greatly increased awareness of their programs for the general population and for selected groups such as older adults (i.e., Elderhostel programs) and youths (i.e., after-school and weekend programs). While this growth is a positive thing, it also suggests that programmers will be competing with one another for the attention of various publics.

• Businesses in the private sector have increased the number of arts and cultural programs available to the public (EventLister.com 2007). While various stores for hobbyists have long been in business (i.e., fabric, craft, bead, pottery, and scrapbooking stores), now these stores are offering programs designed to help customers learn more about their hobby and share their products with one another. These kinds of opportunities contribute to the competitive mix in arts and cultural leisure programming.

• Every 7.5 minutes, someone else turns 50 years old. The baby boomers have influenced and will continue to influence contemporary society. Most people of this generation were afforded the opportunity to learn about the arts in the public schools. Since leisure research tells us that people often return to pursuits they engaged in as children, arts and cultural programmers may well find themselves planning and implementing more leisure experiences specifically designed for baby boomers. This population is better off financially than their parents were, and we can anticipate that once retired, they will have plenty of free time for participating in arts and cultural leisure experiences.

- In *Megatrends 2010*, Patricia Aburdene (2005) presents seven future trends, two of which seem particularly relevant to programming arts and cultural leisure experiences. These are the power of spirituality and values-driven consumers.

  o Emerging information suggests that more and more people are seeking experiences associated with reinforcing or discovering their spirituality (Aburdene 2005). Arts and cultural experiences as spiritual expression or as conduits for realizing spirituality are programmable. The present growth in cultural tourism has had major effects on organizations offering arts and cultural programs. We can assume that as people *seek* spiritual experiences in the future, they will surround themselves by cultural and historical sites of importance. It has been suggested that Buddha helped set spiritual tourism in motion 2,500 years ago when he encouraged followers to visit sites important to his life (Garfinkel 2006). The growing trend toward spiritual vacations (Alexander 2006) appears to be one that arts and cultural programmers should explore.

  o The notion of values-driven thinking is intricately connected to what we do in arts and cultural programming. McDaniel and Thorn (1997), in their final report on adult arts participation and learning consciousness, found it essential that arts providers instill, reconnect, or intensify within adults a value and a need for the arts. The authors explored ways to do this and suggested that the arts providers who are more effective are the ones who include values-based thinking as relevant in everyone's life and the life of the community. We can anticipate that values-driven consumers will also be concerned about sustainable and responsible green practices in the delivery of programs and services.

- *Adultescence* is a term that is being used to describe a new life stage (trendSCAN 2006) that individuals aged 18 to 25 (and sometimes older) experience. This sizable group of young people, who are referred to as *disconnected* and *transitioning to successful adulthood*, could benefit from arts and cultural opportunities.

- Where people live and how they access arts and cultural leisure experiences will continue to vary. The notion that one size fits all has never been more inappropriate to use as a basis for making program decisions. We see more and more people who want to live in urban homes in the city core, often because of their proximity to arts and cultural scenes. We also see lifestyle centers in suburbia, ideal versions of urban streetscapes with cafes, performance spaces, offices, housing, and parks (Reno 2006). We see increased opportunities to program virtual arts and cultural experiences as a way for audiences to *be* there without *being* there. Creative programming using technology is going well beyond where it was just a year ago. Take for example, the virtual family dinner, in which families can interact while dining together around a screen as large as a television or as small as a picture frame (Baldwin 2006). This virtual programming option is not like the experiences of the millions who watch millions in New York City's Times Square on New Year's Eve. Those are media-driven, one-way, noninteractive arts and cultural experiences.

- Time scarcity will likely become a factor in programming decisions of the future. There are two sides of a coin that programmers must remain cognizant of when considering new or modified programs. One side of the coin shows that time is a finite number of clock hours. The other side of the coin reflects an ever-widening range of choices that individuals in a free society have for spending their free time.

  o There continues to be rich debate of whether time scarcity is a myth or a reality in a contemporary society in which the predominant paradigm stresses a linear, time-bound life pattern. Today, workers in the United States are working more than the medieval peasants did and more than the citizens of any other industrial country work. On average, we work 9 full weeks (360 hours) longer per year than our peers in Western Europe work. Americans, for example, currently average a little more than 2 weeks of vacation per year, while Europeans average 5 to 6 weeks of vacation each year. One-half of all Americans said they would trade a day of pay for a day off each week (DeGraaf 1994). Though it was thought that advances in technology, automation, and cybernation would give us more leisure time and less working time (Fabun 1967; Murphy 1981), the anticipated leisure age has not arrived (Kelly 1996). Instead, contemporary society seems to have contracted a social condition

referred to as *affluenza*. Affluenza, described as a painful, contagious, socially transmitted condition of overload, debt, anxiety, and waste resulting from the dogged pursuit of more, carries with it symptoms of time scarcity and time urgency (DeGraaf, Wann, and Naylor 2002). It seems that productivity gains have come in the form of more money and more stuff rather than more time (DeGraaf 2003). This phenomenon creates a continuing sense of complexity for many.

○ The other side of the time coin is that of choice. Schwartz (2004) argues that the paradox of choice creates feelings of *more is less* for many people. When there are more things to do than individuals feel they have the time for, immobility and inaction may negatively affect their interest in our programs. Too much of a good thing has proven to be detrimental to our psychological and emotional well-being (Schwartz 2004). Quite simply, if potential program participants feel pressures associated with time and choice, they will find responding to even our best arts and cultural programs overwhelming. This reality both explains and challenges our programming successes and failures.

Summary

The field of future studies promotes the analysis of contemporary trends in order to anticipate future developments within disciplines as well as within culture and society. In keeping with the futurist agenda of noting trends, in this chapter we have described trends that are likely to shape and inform arts and cultural as well as leisure programming within the coming decades. Our intent is not to offer prescriptions for but suggestions of the social and cultural forces that arts and cultural programmers will be working with and within. Science fiction writer Octavia Butler (2000) believes that speculating about the future is an act of hope. It is in this spirit that we conclude this volume. We are confident, based on the collective wisdom of those who have contributed to this book, that the fields associated with arts and cultural programming will respond to these trends, and others, with vigor and imagination.

references and resources

Aburdene, P. 2005. *Megatrends 2010: The rise of conscious capitalism*. Charlottesville, VA: Hampton Roads Publishing Company.

Academy of Leisure Sciences. 2006. White paper #7: The benefits of leisure. www.academyofleisuresciences.org/alswp7.html.

Accessible Arts, Inc. 2006. www.accessiblearts.org.

Adams, R.M. 1992. Secretary Adams comments: Smithsonian horizons. *Smithsonian* 23(2): 12.

Adams, D., and A. Goldbard. 2005. *Creative community: The art of cultural development*. New York: Rockefeller Foundation.

Adams, D., and A. Goldbard. 2001. *Creative community: The art of cultural development*. New York: Rockefeller Foundation.

Adams, D., and A. Goldbard. 1990. *Crossroads: Reflections on the politics of culture*. Talmage, CA: DNA Press.

Akron, Ohio. 2007. www.citytowninfo.com/places/ohio/akron.

Allen, J. (2000). *Event planning*. Toronto: John Wiley & Sons Canada, LTD.

Alexander, N. 2006. A spiritual retreat is not a vacation. It's a journey within. *The Sunday Oregonian*, December 24.

Alliance for the Arts. 2006. *Olympism & culture*. www.olympic.org/uk/games/past/innovations_uk.asp?OLGT=1&OLGY=1912.

Amas Musical Theatre. 2007. www.amasmusical.org.

American Assembly. 2006. The arts and the public purpose. Available: www.americanassembly.org/programs.dir/prog_display_ind_pg.php?this_filename_prefix=arts_purpose&this_ind_prog_pg_filename=report.

American Association of Museums. *About Museums*. Retrieved October 14, 2007 from www.aam-us.org/about-museums/abc.cfm#how_many.

American Association of Museums. 1992. *Excellence and equity: Education and the public dimension of museums*. Washington, DC: American Association of Museums.

American Express Performing Arts Fund. 2006. http://home3.americanexpress.com/corp/giving_back.asp.

American Folklife Center. 2006. Introduction: What is folklife? www.loc.gov/folklife/fieldwork/introduction.html.

American Life Inc. 2007. Economic trends. www.amlife.us/economic_trends.html.

Americans for the Arts. 2007. Arts and economic prosperity. New York. www.artsusa.org/information_resources/research_information/services/economic_impact/default.asp.

Andrew W. Mellon Foundation. 2006. www.mellon.org.

Arlington Arts. 2003. Arlington County services. www.arlingtonarts.org/ cultural_affairs/default.htm.

Arlington, Virginia. 2006. www.co.arlington.va.us.

Arnold, N.D. 1978. Pop art: The human footprint infinity. *Leisure Today*, 24-25.

The Art Complex. *Workshops*. Retrieved July 11, 2006 from www.artcomplex.org/workshops.html.

ArtCyclopedia. 2007. *Museums in Canada*. Retrieved October 14, 2007 from www.artcyclopedia.com/museums/art-museums-in-canada.html.

Arts, Education, and Americans Panel. 1977. *Coming to our senses: The significance of the arts for American education*. New York: McGraw-Hill.

Asian Art Museum. 2006. *Programs*. Retrieved July 11, 2006 from www.asianart.org/asiaalive.htm.

Asian Art Museum. *Highlights and resources from past AsiaAlive and public programs*. Retrieved July 11, 2006 from www.asianart.org/pastasiaalive.htm.

Austin, Texas. 2006. www.austin.about.com.

Avgikos, J. 1995. Group material timeline: Activism as a work of art. In *But is it art: The spirit of activism*, ed. N. Felshin, 85-116. Seattle: Bay Press.

Backas, J. 1977. *The arts at the community level: A report to the National Endowment for the Arts*. Unpublished manuscript. Available from the National Endowment for the Arts, Nancy Hanks Library.

Baldwin, C.K., L.L. Caldwell, and P.A. Witt. 2005. Deliberate programming with logic models: From theory to outcomes. In *Recreation and youth development*, ed. P.A. Witt and L.L. Caldwell, 219-239. State College, PA: Venture.

Baldwin, D. 2006. Virtual family dinner whets the appetite. *The Sunday Oregonian*, December 24.Balfe, J.H., and M. Peters. 2000. Public involvement in the arts. In *The public life of the arts in America*, ed. J.M. Cherbo and M.J. Wyszomirski, 81-107. New Brunswick, NJ: Rutgers University Press.

Barboza, S. 1993. A mural program to turn graffiti offenders around. *Smithsonian* 24(4): 62-70.

Bartis, P. 2006. Folklife and fieldwork: A layman's introduction to field techniques. www.loc.gov/folklife/fieldwork/.

Bateson, M.C. 1990. *Composing a life*. New York: Plume.

Bellin, J., with the Cincinnati Opera. June 2, 2006. Cincinnati Opera and Allen Temple A.M.E. Church Present Opera goes to Church [Press release].

Bender, S. 1989. *Plain and simple: A woman's journey to the Amish*. San Francisco: Harper.

Bennett, C.F. 1982. *Reflective appraisal of program (RAP): An approach to studying clientele-perceived results of Cooperative Extension programs*. Ithaca, NY: Cornell University.

Berger, M. 2001. *Fred Wilson: Objects and installations, 1979-2000*. Baltimore: Center for Art and Visual Culture, University of Maryland.

Best, F., and B. Stern. 1976. *Lifetime distribution of education, work and leisure: Research, speculations and policy implications of changing life patterns*. Washington, DC: Institute for Educational Leadership, George Washington University, 26-50.

Better Business Bureau Wise Giving Alliance. 2003. BBB Wise Giving Alliance standards for charity accountability. www.give.org/standards/newcbbbstds.asp.

Blandy, D. 2000. Introduction. Community arts councils: Historical perspective. *CultureWork: A Periodic Broadside for Arts and Culture Workers*. 5(1): 5 paragraphs. http://aad.uoregon.edu/culturework/culturework12.html#com.

Blandy, D. 1999. Universal design in art education: Principles, resources, and pedagogical implications. In *Built environment education in art education*, ed. J.K. Guilfoil and A.R. Sandler, 220-227. Reston, VA: National Art Education Association.

Blandy, D. 1991. Conceptions of disability: Toward a sociopolitical orientation to disability for art education. *Studies in Art Education* 32(3): 131-144.

Blandy, D., and K.G. Congdon. 2003. Administering the culture of everyday life: Imagining the future of arts sector administration. In *The arts in a new millennium*, ed. D. Pankratz and V. Morris, 177-188. New York: Praeger.

Blandy, D., and K.G. Congdon. 1993. A theoretical structure for educational partnerships and curatorial practices. *Visual Arts Research* 19(2): 61-67.

Blandy, D., and K.G. Congdon. 1988. Community based aesthetics as an exhibition catalyst and a foundation for community involvement in art education. *Studies in Art Education* 29(4): 243-249.

Blandy, D., and K.G. Congdon. 1987. *Art in a democracy*. New York: Teachers Press.

Blandy, D., and R. Voelker-Morris. 2005. Zines and do-it-yourself democracy: Witness this moment. *CultureWork*. [Online]. http://aad.uoregon.edu/culturework/zines/index.html.

Blumenthal, R. 1996. Arts are backed as aid for troubled youth. *New York Times*. April 26.

Bolin, P., and D. Blandy. 2003. Beyond visual culture: Seven statements of support for material culture studies in art education. *Studies in Art Education* 44(3): 246-263.

Brooks, K. 1992. *Exhibiting tattoos*. Unpublished master's project, University of Oregon, Eugene, OR.

Brooks, K. 1991. Living art: Tattoo show. Master's project, University of Oregon, Eugene, OR.

Brown, S.J. 1997. "Oh, don't you envy us our privileged lives?" A review of the disability culture movement. *Rehabilitation in Practice: Disability and Rehabilitation* 19(8): 339-349. www.dimenet.com/disculture/archive. php?made=A&id=7;&sort=A.

Brownell, B. 1950. *The human community: Its philosophy and practice for a time of crisis.* New York: Harper.

Bulick, B. 2003. Cultural development in creative communities. *Americans for the Arts Monograph.* www.artsusa.org.

Bumbershoot History. 2007. www.bumbershoot.org/history.htm.

Bumbershoot Info. 2007. www.bumbershoot.org/info.htm.

Burnham, L. 2000. Reaching for the Valley of the Sun: The American Festival Project's untold stories. *Tulane Drama Review* 44(3): 75-112.

Burnham, L., S. Durland, and M. Ewell. 2004. The CAN Report: The state of the field of community cultural development: Something new emerges. www.communityarts.net/readingroom/archive/canreport/rpt2-charge.php#_ftn1.

Burnham, L., and S. Durland. 1998. *The citizen artist: 20 years of art in the public arena.* Gardiner, NY: Critical Press.

Burton, T.L., and E.L. Jackson. 1999. Reviewing leisure studies: An organizing framework. In *Leisure studies: Prospects for the twenty-first century,* ed. E.L. Jackson and T.L. Burton, xvii-xxiv. State College, PA: Venture.

Butler, O.E. 2000. A few rules for predicting the future. Available: http://exittheapple.com/applesauce/2007/04/a-few-rules-for-predicting-the-future/.

Cady, M.H. 2005. Supporting a vibrant arts sector in California: An interview with Arts Program Director March Hinand Cady. *IQ: Irvine Quarterly* 5(2, Fall 2005).

Caldwell, G.N. 2000. The emergence of museums as a brand. *International Journal of Arts Management* 2(3): 28-34.

Calhoon, M. 2006. Food, fun and philanthropy. *The Weekly,* July 6.

California Park and Recreation Society. 2006. What's new. www.cprs.org.

Camhi, L. 2002. Peering under the skin of monsters. *New York Times.* March 17.

Canadian Heritage. *Summative Evaluation of the Museums Assistance Program and Canadian Museums Association Program.* Retrieved October 14, 2007 from www.pch.gc.ca/progs/em-cr/eval/2005/2005_05/3_e.cfm.

Capitano, J. Exhibition interpreters: Creating a new volunteer program at the University of Oregon museum of art (Master's project, University of Oregon, 2004).

Carmichael, E., and C. Sayer. 1991. *The skeleton at the feast: The Day of the Dead in Mexico.* Austin, TX: University of Texas Press.

Carpenter, G. 2006. Arts and culture. In *Introduction to recreation and leisure,* ed. Human Kinetics, 333-352. Champaign, IL: Human Kinetics.

Carpenter, G. 2005. Research update: Awaken your agency with art. *Parks & Recreation* 40(4): 26-32.

Carpenter, G. 2004a. Assessing arts and cultural programming in Oregon's recreation organizations. *Culture-Work.* [Online]. 8(4): 15 paragraphs. http://aad.uoregon.edu/culturework/culturework.html.

Carpenter, G. 2004b. Collaborating to address cultural tourists' interests for experience. *e-Review of Tourism Research (eRTR).* [Online]. 2(1). http://ertr.tamu.edu/appliedresearch.cfm?articleid=52.

Carpenter, G. 1999. Economic and leisure factors impacting participation in the arts by middle aged adults. *CultureWork.* [Online]. 3(3): 19 paragraphs. http://aad.uoregon.edu/culturework/culturework10.html.

Carpenter, G.M., and C.Z. Howe. 1985. *Programming leisure experiences: A cyclical approach.* Englewood Cliffs, NJ: Prentice Hall.

Carroll, L. 1865. *Alice's Adventures in Wonderland.* London: Macmillan and Co.

Center for Universal Design. 1997. *The principles of universal design. Version 2.0.* Raleigh, NC: North Carolina State University.

Center of Creative Arts. 2006. www.cocastl.org.

Charity Navigator. 2007. Find a charity you can trust. www.charitynavigator.org.

Chartrand, H.H. 2000. Toward an American arts industry. In *The public life of the arts in America,* ed. J.M. Cherbo and M.J. Wyszomirski, 22-49. New Brunswick, NJ: Rutgers University Press.

Chautauqua Institution. 2007. www.ciweb.org.

Cherbo, J.M., and M.J. Wyszomirski, eds. 2000. *The public life of the arts in America.* New Brunswick, NJ: Rutgers University Press.

Cherry Creek Arts Festival. 2006. www.cherryarts.org.

Chittenden, D., Farmelo, G., & Lewenstein, B. V. (Eds.). 2004. *Creating connections: Museums and the public understanding of current research.* Walnut Creek, CA: AltaMira Press.

CHLY 101.7 FM. 2007. www.chly.ca.

Chong, D. 2002. *Arts management.* London: Routledge.

Chronicle of Higher Education. 1997. Sculptures welcome Long Island U. Freshmen. Short subjects. October 17.

Chubb, M., and H. Chubb. 1981. *One-third of our time?* New York: Wiley.

Clawson, M. 1963. *Land and water for recreation—opportunities, problems, policies.* Resources for the Future Policy Background Series. Chicago: Rand McNally.

Clawson, M., and J. Knetsch. 1966. *Economics of outdoor recreation.* Baltimore: Johns Hopkins University Press.

Cleveland, W. 2005. *Making exact change: How U.S. arts-based projects have made a significant and sustained impact on their communities.* Art in the Public Interest. www.communityarts.net/readingroom/archive/mec/index.php.

Cleveland, W. 1992. *Art in other places: Artists at work in America's community and social institutions.* Portsmouth, NH: Greenwood.

Cohen, C. 1999. A patchwork of our lives: Oral history quilts in intercultural education. *CARTS Newsletter* 3(1): 3-4.

Cohen, R., T. Filicko, and M.J. Wyszomirski. 2002. *National and local profiles of cultural support: The national survey.* Washington, DC: Americans for the Arts / Columbus, OH: Arts Policy and Administration Program, Ohio State University.

Cohen-Cruz, J. 2005. *Local acts: Community-based performance in the United States.* New Brunswick, NJ: Rutgers University Press.

Colbert, F. 2001. *Marketing the arts.* 2nd ed. Montreal, PQ: HEC Montreal.

Colbert, F., C. Beauregard, and L. Vallée. 1998. The importance of ticket prices for theatre patrons. *International Journal of Arts Management* 1(1): 8-16.

Colbert, F., et al. 2007. *Marketing Culture and the Arts.* 3rd ed. Montreal: Chair in Arts Management, HEC.

Congdon, K.G. 2006. Folkvine.org: Arts-based research on the web. *Studies in Art Education, 48* (6): 36-51.

Congdon, K.G. 2004. *Community art in action.* Worchester, MA: Davis.

Craig, A. S. 2006. Creating historical consciousness: A case study exploring museum theater (Master's project, University of Oregon, 2006).

Craine, K., ed. 2005. A position paper on cultural & heritage tourism in the United States. http://cultural-heritagetourism.org/documents/WhitePaper_001.pdf.

Crompton, J.L. 1979. Recreation programs have life cycles, too. *Parks and Recreation* October: 52-57.

Cross, T.L., B.J. Bazron, K.W. Dennis, and M.R. Isaacs. 1989. *Towards a culturally competent system of care: Vol. I.* Washington, DC: National Technical Assistance Center for Children's Mental Health, Georgetown University Child Development Center.

Crouch, G.I., and K. Weber. 2002. Marketing of convention tourism. In *Convention tourism: International research and industry perspectives,* ed. K. Weber and K. Chon, 57-78. New York: Haworth Press.

Csikszentmihalyi, M. 1993. *The evolving self: A psychology for the third millennium.* New York: Harper Collins.

Csikszentmihalyi, M. 1975. *Beyond boredom and anxiety.* San Francisco: Jossey-Bass.

Danford, H., and M. Shirley. 1964. *Creative leadership in recreation.* Boston: Allyn & Bacon.

Davidson, J. W. & Lytle, M. H. 1992. *After the fact: The art of historical detection.* New York: McGraw-Hill.

Davidson, T. 2006. *Meetings* market report. *Meetings* 20(1): 1, 11-13.

de Chadenedes, M. 1996. Personal communication.

Deetz, J. 1977. *In small things forgotten.* Garden City, NY: Anchor Books.

DeGraaf, J. 2003. *Take back your time: Fighting overwork and time poverty in America.* San Francisco: Berrett-Koehler Publishers.

DeGraaf, J., producer. 1994. *Running out of time in America.* [Television broadcast]. Seattle: Public Broadcasting Service.

DeGraaf, J., D. Wann, and T.H. Naylor. 2002. *Affluenza: The all consuming epidemic*. San Francisco: Berrett-Koehler Publishers.

Delamere, T.A. 2001. Development of a scale to measure resident attitudes toward the social impacts of community festivals: Verification of the scale. *Festival Management and Event Tourism* 7(1): 25-38.

Delamere, T.A., L.M. Wankel, and T.D. Hinch. 2001. Measuring resident attitudes toward the social impact of community festivals: Pretesting and purification of the scale. *Festival Management and Event Tourism* 7(1): 11-24.

Delamere, T., and R. Rollins. 1999. Measuring attitudes toward community festivals: Social impact priorities in Parksville. *Recreation and Parks BC* Spring 1999: 33-35.

Delamere, T.A., and T.D. Hinch. 1994. Community festivals: Celebration or sell-out? *Recreation Canada* 52(1): 26-29.

Dewan, S. (2006). Cities compete in hipness battle to attract young. *The New York Times*. Retrieved September 24, 2007 from www.nytimes.com/2006/11/25/us/25young.html?_r=1&oref=slogin.

Donnelly, J. F. (Ed.). 2002. *Interpreting historic house museums*. Walnut Creek, CA: Altamira Press.

Doss, E. 1995. *Spirit poles and flying pigs: Public art and cultural democracy in American communities*. Washington, DC: Smithsonian Institution Press.

Dreeszen, C. 2003. Program evaluation: Measuring results. In *Fundamentals of arts management*, 4th ed., ed. C. Dreeszen and P. Korza, 251-291. Amherst, MA: Arts Extension Service.

Driver, B.L., and D.H. Bruns. 1999. Concepts and uses of the benefits approach to leisure. In *Leisure studies: Prospects for the twenty-first century*, ed. E.L. Jackson and T.L Burton, 349-369. State College, PA: Venture.

Driver, B.L., P.J. Brown, and G.L. Peterson, eds. 1991. *Benefits of leisure*. State College, PA: Venture.

Dubois, R. 1943. Get together Americans: Friendly approaches to racial and cultural conflicts through the neighborhood home-festivals. New York: Harper.

Edginton, C.R., D.M. Compton, and C.J. Hanson. 1980. *Recreation and leisure programming: A guide for the professional*. Philadelphia: Saunders.

Edginton, C.R., S.D. Hudson, R.B. Dieser, and S.R. Edginton. 2004. *Leisure programming: A service-centered and benefits approach*. 4th ed. Boston: McGraw-Hill.

EventLister.com. 2007. www.eventlister.com.

Ewell, M. 2000. Community arts councils: Historical perspectives, part one. *CultureWork: A Periodic Broadside for Arts and Culture Workers*. [Online]. 4(1): 35 paragraphs. http://aad.uoregon.edu/ culturework/culture-work12.html.

Fabun, D. 1967. *The dynamics of change*. Englewood Cliffs, NJ: Prentice Hall.

Fall 2005 internet 2 member meeting: Gala museum reception and program. *Internet 2*, September 21, 2005. Retrieved July 11, 2006 from http://events.internet2.edu/2005/fall-mm/gala.html.

Fargo, North Dakota. 2007. www.city-data.com/city/Fargo-North-Dakota.html.

Farnum, M., and R. Schaffer. 1998. *The YouthARTS handbook: Arts programs for youth at risk*. Washington, DC: Americans for the Arts.

Farrell, P., and H.M. Lundegren. 1991. *The process of recreation programming: Theory and technique*. 3rd ed. State College, PA: Venture.

Fish, J. 2007. Interview by Marcus Glasgow. San Antonio Symphony Orchestra, San Antonio.

Fiske, E., ed. 1999. *Champions of change: The impact of arts on learning*. Washington, DC: The Arts Education Partnership and the President's Committee on the Arts and Humanities.

Florida, R. 2002. *The rise of the creative class*. New York: Basic Books.

Floyd, Mark. 2006, January 5. Oregon book award winner decries increasing lack of art education in schools. *OSU New & Communication Services*. Retrieved June 9, 2006, from http://oregonstate.edu/dept/ncs/news-arch/2006/Jan06/caveman.htm.

Foot, D.K., R.A. Loreto, and T.W. McCormack. 2006. *Demographic trends in Canada, 1996-2006: Implications for the public and private sectors*. Ottawa, ON: Industry Canada.

Foster, E. 2003. Art matters. *Camping Magazine* 76(6): 22-28.

Foundation Center. 2006. Gain knowledge. http://foundationcenter.org/gainknowledge.

Freire, P. 1970. *Pedagogy of the oppressed*. New York: Seabury.

Freire, P. 1981. *Education for critical consciousness*. New York: Continuum.

Funk, B.A. 1987. The arts. In *Recreation and leisure: An introductory handbook*, ed. A. Graefe and S. Parker, 101-104. State College, PA: Venture.

Gabai, C.J.N. 1990. Ethiopia's braided traditions: Integrating multicultural elements into a natural history museum exhibit. Master's project, University of Oregon, Eugene, OR.

Gaither, E.B. 1992. "Hey! That's mine": Thoughts on pluralism and American museums. In *Museums and communities: The politics of public culture*, ed. I. Karp, C.M. Kreamer, and S.D. Lavine, 56-64. Washington, DC: Smithsonian.

Garcia, B., and A. Miah. 2006. The Olympics is not a sporting event. Available: http://newmediastudies. com/art/olympic.htm.

Gard, L. Introduction to Carpenter Science Theater Company. Retrieved July 11, 2006 from http://larrygard. freeyellow.com/page32.html.

Gard, R. 1975. The arts in the small community. *Arts in Society* 12: 82-91.

Gard, R.E. 1955. *Grassroots theater: A search for regional arts in America.* Madison, WI: University of Wisconsin.

Garfinkel, P. 2006. Spiritual tourism infuses vacations with purpose. *The Bend Bulletin*, December 25.

Getz, D. 2005. *Event management and event tourism.* 2nd ed. New York: Cognizant Communication Corporation.

Getz, D. 1997. *Event management and event tourism.* Elmsford, NY: Cognizant Communication Corporation.

Gibans, N. 1982. *The community arts council movement: History, opinion, issues.* New York: Praeger Publishers.

Gilroy Garlic Festival. 2006. www.gilroygarlicfestival.com.

Godbey, G.C., L.L. Caldwell, M. Floyd, and L.L. Payne. 2005. Contributions of leisure studies and recreation and park management research to the active living agenda. *American Journal of Preventative Medicine* 28(2S2): 150-158.

Goldblatt, J. 2002. *Special events: Twenty-first century global event management.* 3rd ed. New York: Wiley.

Gray, D., and H. Ibrahim. 1985. Recreation Experience—The Human Dimension. *Leisure Today/Journal of Physical Education, Recreation, and Dance* 55(10): 27-32.

Guidestar.org. 2007. www.guidestar.org.

Hacha, J. May-July 2006. Personal communication.

Hager, L. 2003. *Who owns the glass slipper: Transformation ideology in community drama with youth. Report no. CS 512 476.* Washington, DC: Office of Educational Research and Improvement. www.eric.ed.gov/ERIC-WebPortal/Home.portal.

Harris, J. 1995. *Federal art and national culture: The politics of identity in New Deal America.* New York: Cambridge University Press.

Hayt, E. 1998. Far from "the troubles," agitprop for both camps. *New York Times.* October 16.

Heath, S. Brice, E. Soep, and A. Roach. 1998. Living the arts through language-learning: A report on community-based youth organizations. *Americans for the Arts Monograph* 2(7).

Henderson, K.A., and M.D. Bialeschki. 2002. *Evaluating leisure services: Making enlightened decisions.* 2nd ed. State College, PA: Venture.

Henry Morrison Flagler Museum. 2007. Whitehall. Retrieved October 14, 2007 from http://flaglermuseum. us/html/whitehall.html.

Hensley, S., S. Markam-Starr, E. Montague, and J. Hodgkinson. 2006. Public recreation. In *Introduction to recreation and leisure*, ed. Human Kinetics, 110-142. Champaign, IL: Human Kinetics.

Heritage Festival Edmonton. 2007. www.heritage-festival.com.

Hess, E. 1989. Mapplethorpe goes to Washington. *Village Voice.* August 8.

Hickey, D. 1997. *Air guitar: Essays on art and democracy.* Los Angeles: Art Issues.

High Museum of Art. Family programs. Retrieved July 20, 2006 from www.high.org/experience/education/family.aspx.

Hillman, G., and K. Gaffney. 1996. *Artists in the community: Training artists to work in alternative settings.* Washington, DC: Americans for the Arts.

Hirzy, E. C. (Ed.). 1998. *Excellence and equity: Education and the public dimension of museums* (2nd ed.). Washington, DC: American Association of Museums.

Historica. 2007. *Canadian Encyclopedia*. [Online]. www.thecanadianencyclopedia.com.

Hobbs, F., and N. Stoops. 2002. Demographic trends in the 20th century. Washington, DC: U.S. Government Printing Office.

Hood, M. G. 2004. Staying away: Why people choose not to visit museums. In G. Anderson (Ed.), *Reinventing the museum: Historical and contemporary perspectives on the paradigm shift*, 150-157. Walnut Creek, CA: Altamira Press.

Howe, C.Z. 1993. The evaluation of leisure programs: Applying qualitative methods. *Leisure Today/Journal of Physical Education, Recreation, and Dance* 64(8): 43-46.

Howell, D.W., D. Wright, N. Reynolds, M. Bateman-Ellison, and R. Ellison. 2006. *Passport: An introduction to the tourism industry*. 4th Canadian ed. Toronto: Thomson Nelson.

Hoyle, L. H. 2002. *Event marketing*. New York: John Wiley & Sons.

Hudson, K. 1998. The museum refuses to stand still. In B. M Carbonell (Ed.), *Museum studies*, 85-91. Malden, MA: Blackwell.

Hufford, M. 2006. American folklife: A commonwealth of cultures. www.loc.gov/folklife/cwc.

Hultsman, W. 1998. The multi-day, competitive leisure event: Examining satisfaction over time. *Journal of Leisure Research* 30(4): 472-497.

Infed. 2005. *Social capital*. www.infed.org/biblio/social_capital.htm.

International Council of Museums (ICOM). 2007. Retrieved on October 14, 2007 from http://icom.museum/mission.html.

International Culinary Arts Association. 2006. www.iacp.com.

Iso-Ahola, S.E. 1980. *The social psychology of leisure and recreation*. Dubuque, IA: Brown.

Ivey, B., and S.J. Tepper. 2006. Cultural renaissance or cultural divide? *Chronicle of Higher Education*. May 19.

Jackson, E.L. 2005. Leisure constraints research: Overview of a developing theme in leisure studies. In *Constraints to leisure*, ed. E.L. Jackson, 4-19. State College, PA: Venture.

Jackson, E.L., and D. Scott. 1999. Constraints to leisure. In *Leisure studies: Prospects for the twenty-first century*, ed. E.L. Jackson and T.L Burton, 299-321. State College, PA: Venture.

James Irvine Foundation and AEA Consulting. 2006. *Critical issues facing the arts in California: A working paper from the James Irvine Foundation*. San Francisco: James Irvine Foundation.

Jazz Festivals. n.d. www.thecanadianencyclopedia.com/index.cfm?PgNm=TCE&Params=U1ARTU0001748.

John Michael Kohler Arts Center. 2006. www.jmkac.org.

Johnson, K. 2006. *Demographic trends in rural and small town America*. Durham, NH: Carsey Institute.

Jordan, D.J., D.G. DeGraaf, and K.H. DeGraaf. 2005. *Recreation programming for parks, recreation, and leisure services: A servant leadership approach*. 2nd ed. State College, PA: Venture.

Jordan Schnitzer Museum of Art. Events. Retrieved on July 20, 2006 from http://uoma.uoregon.edu/events/index.php.

Junk to Funk. 2007. www.junktofunk.org.

Kamark, E. 1975. *Arts in society: The surge of community arts* 12(1).

Katz, S. 2000. Busy bodies: Activity, aging, and the management of everyday life. *Journal of Aging Studies* 14(2): 135-152.

Kawasaki, G. 2006. June 05, 2006: Addendum to ten questions with Dr. Joseph Chamie. How to change the world: A practical blog for impractical people. http://blog.guykawasaki.com/2006/06/addendum_to_ten.html.

Kelly, J.R. 1996. *Leisure*. 3rd ed. Boston: Allyn & Bacon.

Kennedy, A. 1920. *The arts as function of local community life*. Biographical material. Unpublished manuscript. 1920-1931. Box 1, folder 1. Albert J. Kennedy Collection. The Social Welfare History Archives Center, University of Minnesota Libraries.

Kennedy, R. 2006. Lessons in new ways to see. *New York Times*. July 5.

Kimmel Center for the Performing Arts. 2006. www.kimmelcenter.org.

Kinzey, D.W. 2005/2006. The death of performing arts subscriptions—or not? *The Voice of Chorus America* Winter: 29-32.

Kleiber, D.A. 1999. *Leisure experience and human development: A dialectical interpretation.* New York: Basic Books.

Knowles, M.S. 1980. *The modern practice of adult education: From pedagogy to andragogy.* New York: Cambridge.

Knowles, M.S. 1970. *The modern practice of adult education: Andragogy versus pedagogy.* New York: Association Press.

Kolb, B. M. 2000. *Marketing cultural organisations: New strategies for attracting audiences to classical music, dance, museums, theatre and opera.* Cork, Ireland: Oak Tree Press.

Korza, P. 2003. Program development: Connecting art with audiences. In *Fundamentals of arts management,* 4th ed., ed. C. Dreeszen. Amherst, MA: Arts Extension Services, University of Massachusetts-Amherst: 117-149.

Korza, P. 2002. INROADS: The intersection of art and civic dialogue. www.communityarts.net/readingroom/archivefiles/2002/08/inroadsthe_inte.php.

Korza, P. 1994. Program development. In *Fundamentals of local arts management,* ed. C. Dreeszen and P. Korza, 67-107. Amherst, MA: Arts Extension Service.

Korza, P., B. Schaffer Bacon, and A. Assaf. 2005. *Civic dialogue, arts and culture: Findings from animating democracy.* Washington, D.C.: Americans for the Arts

Kotler, P., and J. Scheff. 1997. *Standing room only: Strategies for marketing the performing arts.* Boston: Harvard Business School Press.

Kraus, R. G. (1985). *Recreation today: Program planning and leadership.* Glenview, Illinois: Scott, Foresman, and Company.

Kreidler, J. 2006. Leverage lost: The non-profit arts in the post-Ford era. www.inmotionmagazine.com/lost3.html.

Kurin, R. 1997. *Reflections of a culture broker.* Washington, DC: Smithsonian.

Kurzweil, R. 2006. Accelerated living. *PC Magazine.* [Online]. www.pcmag.com/article2/0,1895,32901,00.asp.

Kurzweil, R., and C. Meyer. 2006. Understanding the accelerating rate of
change. KurzweilAI.net. www.kurzweilai.net/articles/art0563.html?printable=1.

Lane Arts Council. 2007. Welcome to Lane Arts Council. www.lanearts.org.

Lane Arts Council. 2005. Annual Report. www.lanearts.org/advocacy/LAC2005AR.pdf.

Lapierre, L. 1999. The Ravinia Festival under the direction of Zarin Mehta. *International Journal of Arts Management* 1(3): 70-84.

Lassiter, L.E. 2004. Collaborative ethnography. *AnthroNotes* 25(1): 1-9.

Lazarus, M. & Wunderlich, R. (Producers). 2000. *Beyond killing us softly: The impact of media images on women and girls* [Videorecording]. (Available from Cambridge Documentary Films, Cambridge, MA).

Leider, N. 2006. Millennium Park or millennium museum? *Chicago Tribune.* June 29.

Leonard, R., and A. Kilkelly. 2006. *Performing communities: Grassroots ensemble theaters deeply rooted in eight U.S. communities.* Oakland: New Village Press.

Lilly Endowment Inc. 2006. *Frequently asked questions.* www.lillyendowment.org/faq.html.

Lippard, L. 1997. *The lure of the local: Senses of place in a multicentered society.* New York: The New Press.

Los Angeles Philharmonic Association. 2006. www.laphil.com/home.cfm.

Luke, T. W. 2002. Museum politics: power plays at the exhibition. Minneapolis: University of Minnesota Press.

Mannell, R.C., and D.A. Kleiber. 1997. *A social psychology of leisure.* State College, PA: Venture.

Mannell, R.C., and D.J. Stynes. 1991. A retrospective: The benefits of leisure. In *Benefits of leisure,* ed. B.L. Driver, P.J. Brown, and G.L. Peterson, 462-473. State College, PA: Venture.

Marrero, K. 2007. Interview by Marcus Glasgow. Pensacola Opera, Pensacola.

Massachusetts Cultural Council. 2006. www.massculturalcouncil.org/.

McCarthy, K.F., and K. Jinnett. 2001. *A new framework for building participation in the arts.* Santa Monica, CA: RAND.

McCaslin, N. 1997. *Historical guide to children's theatre in America.* Studio City, CA: Players Press.

McDaniel, N., and G. Thorn. 1997. *Learning audiences.* New York: The John F. Kennedy Center for the Performing Arts and the Association of Performing Arts Presenters.

McEvilley, T. 1992. *Art and otherness: Crisis in cultural identity.* Kingston, NY: McPherson and Company.

McKercher, B., and H. du Cros. 2002. *Cultural tourism: The partnership between tourism and cultural heritage management.* New York: Haworth Press.

McLaughlin, M. 2000. Community counts. www.publiceducation.org/pdf/Publications/support_services/communitycounts.

Meetze, S., and S. Osa. April-June 2006. Personal communication.

Meyer, H.D., and C.K. Brightbill. 1956. *Community recreation: A guide to its organization.* Englewood Cliffs, NJ: Prentice Hall.

Michigan State University. 2006. Welcome to the MSU applicant page. www.jobs.msu.edu.

Moffat H., & Woollard, V. (Eds.). 1999. *Museum and gallery education: A manual of good practice.* London: The Stationery Office.

Moore, S., with The Press-Enterprise. July 21, 2006. Palm Desert: This festival promises fine wine, food and music, but it's pricey. [Press release.]

Morrison, A. 2002. *Hospitality and travel marketing.* 3rd ed. New York: Thomson Delmar Learning.

Moscardo, G. 2000. Cultural and heritage tourism: The great debate. In *Tourism in the twenty-first century,* ed. B. Falkner, G. Moscardo, and E. Laws, 3-17. New York: Continuum.

Murphy, J.F. 1981. *Concepts of leisure.* 2nd ed. Englewood Cliffs, NJ: Prentice Hall.

Murphy, J.F., J.G. Williams, E.W. Niepoth, and P.D. Brown. 1973. *Leisure service delivery system: A modern perspective.* Philadelphia: Lea & Febiger.

Nanaimo Blues Society. 2007. Nanaimo Blues Festival. www.nanaimobluesfestival.com.

National Assembly of State Arts Agencies. 2003. *Design for accessibility: A cultural administrator's handbook.* Washington, DC: Author.

National Center for Cultural Competence. 2006. www11.georgetown.edu/research/gucchd/nccc.

National Endowment for the Arts (NEA). 2004. *Outcome-based evaluation: A working model for arts projects.* www.nea.gov/grants/apply/out/faq.html#16.

National Overhead Cost Study. 2004a. Brief #3, Getting what we pay for: Low overhead limits nonprofit effectiveness. http://nccsdataweb.urban.org/kbfiles/311/brief%203.pdf.

National Overhead Cost Study. 2004b. Brief #4, The quality of financial reporting by nonprofits: Findings and implications. http://nccsdataweb.urban.org/kbfiles/520/brief%204.pdf.

National Overhead Cost Study. 2004c. Brief #5, The pros and cons of financial efficiency standards. http://nccsdataweb.urban.org/kbfiles/521/brief%205.pdf.

National Recreation and Park Association. 2006. NRPA Congress and exposition. www.nrpa.org/congress.

Neulinger, J. 1974. *The psychology of leisure.* Springfield, MA: Thomas.

Neulinger, J. 1981. *To leisure: An introduction.* Boston: Allyn & Bacon.

Noteboom, L. 2006. A champion for orchestras. *Symphony* July-August: 56-63.

Nuyaka Creek Winery. 2007. Taste Oklahoma wines. www.nuyakacreek.com.

Oaxaca's Tourist Guide. 2007. www.oaxaca-travel.com/guide/ cultural.php?section=cultural&lang=us.

Olympic Art Competition 1936 Berlin. 2006. http://olympic-museum.de/art/1936.htm.

Oregon Council for the Humanities. 2007. www.oregonhum.org.

Oregon Country Fair. 2006. www.oregoncountryfair.org.

Orlando Sentinel. 1996. Younger adults aren't flocking to the arts, NEA study finds. May 19.

Parks and Recreation. 2006. Chicago mayor talks parks. May.

Parman, A. 2006. The museum's community role. CultureWork, 10. Retrieved April 19, 2006 from http://aad.uoregon.edu/culturework/culturework33b.html.

Parr, M.G., M.E. Havitz, and A.T. Kaczynski. 2006. The nature of recreation and leisure as a profession. In *Introduction to recreation and leisure,* ed. Human Kinetics, 353-375. Champaign, IL: Human Kinetics.

Patton, M.Q. 1978. *Utilization-focused evaluation.* Beverly Hills, CA: Sage Publications.

Philadelphia and the Countryside. 2007. www.gophila.com.

Philadelphia Folk Festival. 2006. www.pfs.org/PFF.php.

Pine II, B.J., and J.H. Gilmore. 1999. *The experience economy: Work is theatre and every business a stage.* Boston: Harvard Business School Press.

Polivka, E.G. (Ed.) 1996. *Professional meeting management* (Third edition). Birmingham, AL: Professional Convention Management Association.

Posavac, E.J., and R.G. Carey. 1992. *Program evaluation: Methods and case studies.* Englewood Cliffs, NJ: Prentice Hall.

Pratt Museum, Art, Science, Culture of Kachemak Bay, Alaska. Retrieved July 24, 2006 from www.prattmuseum.org/index.html.

Prison Arts Foundation. 2006. www.prisonartsfoundation.com.

Project Row Houses. 2006. Welcome. www.projectrowhouses.org.

Putnam, R. 1993. The prosperous community: Social capital and public life. *American Prospect Online* 4(3). www.prospect.org/cs/articles?article=the_prosperous_community.

Putnam, R.D. 2000. *Bowling alone: The collapse of American community.* New York: Simon & Schuster.

Putnam, R.D., and L.M. Feldstein. 2003. *Better together: Restoring the American community.* New York: Simon & Schuster.

Raines, K., and S. Gee. 2006. Are there holes in your marketing? *Arts Professional* 114: 10.

Ramirez III, M., and A. Casteneda. 1974. *Cultural democracy, biocognitive development, and education.* New York: Academic Press.

Ravanas, P. 2006. Born to be wise: The Steppenwolf Theatre mixes freedom with management savvy. *International Journal of Arts Management* 8(3): 64-76.

Reno, J. 2006. Scenes from a new mall. *Newsweek,* December 4. www.newsweek.com/id/43924.

Riley, K., and M.A. Stanley. 2006. Art programs for older adults. *Parks and Recreation.* February. www.nrpa.org/content/default.aspx?documentId=3613.

Roberts, L. C. 1997. *From knowledge to narrative: Educators and the changing museum.* Washington, DC: The Smithsonian Institution.

Robinson, B.J. 1987. Vernacular spaces and folklife studies within Los Angeles' African American community. In *Home and yard: Black folk life expressions in Los Angeles,* 19-27. Los Angeles: Afro-American Museum.

Robinson, J.P., and G. Godbey. 1997. *Time for life: The surprising ways Americans use their free time.* University Park, PA: The Pennsylvania State University Press.

Rohd, M. 1998. *Theater for community, conflict, and dialogue: The hope is vital training manual.* Portsmouth, NH: Heinemann.

Rollins, R., and T. Delamere. 2007. Measuring the Social Impact of Festivals. *Annals of Tourism Research* 34(3): 805-808.

Rollins, T. 1990. Making art, making money: 13 artists comment. *Art in America* 7:136-137.

Rosoff. July 6, 2006. Personal communication.

Rossman, J.R., and B.E. Schlatter. 2003. *Recreation programming: Designing leisure experiences.* 4th ed. Champaign, IL: Sagamore.

Ruegg, D.L., and L.M. Venkatrathnam. 2003. *Bookkeeping basics: What every nonprofit bookkeeper needs to know.* St. Paul: Amherst H. Wilder Foundation.

Ruppel, W. 2002. *Not-for-profit accounting made easy.* New York: Wiley.

Russell, M. 2006. A consistent upward trend. *PCMA Convene,* pp. 32-45.

Russell, R.V. 2005. *Pastimes: The context of contemporary leisure.* Champaign, IL: Sagamore.

Rutherford, J. W. & Shay, S. E. 2004. Peopling the age of elegance: Reinterpreting Spokane's Campbell House—a collaboration. *The Public Historian, 26*(3), 27-48..

Sachatello-Sawyer, B. et al. 2002. *Adult museum programs: Designing meaningful experiences.* Nashville, TN: American Association of State and Local History.

Sarbey de Souto, M. 1993. *Group travel.* 2nd ed. Albany, NY: Delmar Publishers.

Schaumburg Park District. 2006. www.parkfun.com.

Schlereth, T.J., ed. 1985. *Material culture: A research guide.* Lawrence, KS: University Press of Kansas.

Schlereth, T.J. 1980. *Artifacts and the American past.* Nashville: American Association for State and Local History.

Schor, J.B. 2003. The (even more) overworked American. In *Take back your time: Fighting overwork and time poverty in America,* ed. J. DeGraaf, 6-11. San Francisco: Berrett-Loehler.

Schor, J.B. 1991. *The overworked American: The unexpected decline of leisure.* New York: Basic Books.

Schwartz, B. 2004. *The paradox of choice: Why more is less.* New York: Harper Collins Publishers.

Scott, C. 2000. Branding: Positioning museums in the 21st century. *International Journal of Arts Management* 2(3): 35-39.

Scottsdale Culinary Festival. 2006. www.scottsdaleculinaryfestival.org.

Seattle Art Museum. 2006. www.seattleartmuseum.org.

Seattle World Percussion Society. 2006. www.swps.org.

Seligmann, J., and A. Cohen. 1993. New grounds for child's play. *Newsweek.* November 1.

Shaw, G., and A.M. Williams. 2002. *Critical issues in tourism: A geographical perspective.* Malden, MA: Blackwell Publishers.

Sheehan, S., and H. Means. 2002. *The banana sculptor, the purple lady, and the all-night swimmer: Hobbies, collecting, and other passionate pursuits.* New York: Simon & Schuster.

Sheffield, E. 1984. Are you providing multiple-option programming? *Parks and Recreation* 19(5): 56-57.

Shim, J.K., and J.G. Siegel. 1997. *Financial management for nonprofits: The complete guide to maximizing resources and managing assets.* New York: McGraw-Hill.

Sleeter, C.E., and C.A. Grant. 1987. An analysis of multicultural education in the US. *Harvard Educational Review* 57(4): 421-444.

Smithsonian Institution. Events. Art Night on the Mall. Retrieved July 20, 2006 from www.si.edu/events/artnight.asp.

Smithsonian Institution Hispanic heritage month calendar of events. Retrieved July 26, 2006 from www.dclatino.com/sihhm/.

Sohn, H. 2004. Public funding for the arts and government policy on free expression: Mutual implications and influences (Master's project, University of Oregon, 2004).

Sonder, M. 2004. *Event entertainment and production.* Hoboken, NJ: Wiley.

Southwestern Association for Indian Arts. 2006. www.swaia.org.

Special Report: Virtual Online Worlds. 2006. Living a second life. *The Economist,* September 30.

Spiller, J. 2002. History of convention tourism. In *Convention tourism: International research and industry perspectives,* ed. K. Weber and K. Chon, 3-20. New York: Haworth Press.

Springen, K. 2006. Fashion corn clothes. *Newsweek.* April 17, 2006.

Statistics Canada. 2000. Canadian culture in perspective: A statistical overview. www.statcan.ca/bsolc/english/bsolc?catno=87-211-X&CHROPG=1.

Stebbins, R.A. 2005. The role of leisure in arts administration. Occasional Paper Series. http://aad.uoregon.edu/index.cfm?mode=research&page=occasional.

Stebbins, R.A. 1992. *Amateurs, professionals, and serious leisure.* Montreal, PQ: McGill-Queen's University Press.

Stebbins, R.A. 1982. Serious leisure: A conceptual statement. *Pacific Sociological Review* 25:251-272.

Stern, E. Current Issues Forum lecture, February 8, 2006.

Stern, S. 1991. Introduction. In *Creative ethnicity: Symbols and strategies of contemporary ethnic life,* ed. S. Stern and J.A. Cicala, xi-xx. Logan, UT: Utah State University Press.

Stern, S. and Cicala, J.A. (eds.) 1991. *Creative ethnicity: Symbols and strategies of contemporary ethnic life.* Logan, UT: Utah State University Press.

Stewart, W. 1992. Influence of the onsite experience on recreation preference judgments. *Journal of Leisure Research* 24(2): 185-198.

Stimpson, C. 1990. What's current about being politically correct: A vision of cultural democracy. Paper presented at the University of Oregon, Eugene, OR.

Suzuki, B.H. 1979. Multicultural education: What's it all about. *Integrateducation* 17(1-2): 43-50.

Tedrick, T., and K. Henderson. 1989. *Volunteers in leisure: A management perspective.* Reston, VA: American Alliance of Health, Physical Education, Recreation and Dance.

Texas Cultural Trust Web site. www.txculturaltrust.org/partners_b_03h.html.

Thorn, G. November 1999a. Arts and Administration Program Presentation, University of Oregon.

Thorn, G. November 1999b. Discussion with arts management master's degree students at the University of Oregon, Eugene, OR.

Tillman, A. 1973. *The program book for recreation professionals.* Palo Alto, CA: Mayfield.

Toffler, A. 1970. *Future shock.* New York: Random House, Inc.

Torino Olympics. 2007. www.zerodelta.net/speciali/xx-giochi-olimpici-invernali-torino-2006.

Toronto Fringe Festival. 2006. http://fringetoronto.com.

Tourism Mexico. 2007. www.visitmexico.com/wb/Visitmexico/Visi_Actividades.

trendSCAN. 2006. Adultescence: Extended life stage in 21st century. www.cprs.org/training-trendscan.htm.

trendSCAN. 2004. www.cprs.org/training-trendscan.htm.

U.S. Census Bureau. 2006. www.census.gov.

U.S. Department of Agriculture. 2006. Farmers market facts. www.ams.usda.gov/farmersmarkets/facts.htm.

U.S. Department of Justice Civil Rights Division. 1996. A guide to disability rights laws. www.ncchem.com/american.htm.

Van Der Stad, S.G. 2005. Program assignment fall 2005 AAD 522. Unpublished paper, University of Oregon.

van der Wagen, L. 2001. *Event management for tourism, cultural, business, and sporting events.* Melbourne: Hospitality Press.

Veal, A.J., and R. Lynch. 1996. *Australian leisure.* Frenchs Forest, NSW, Australia: Pearson Education.

Velasquez, L. S. 2001. The Teodoro Vidal collection: Creating space for Latinos at the National Museum of American History. *The Public Historian, 23*(4), 113-124.

Virshup, A. 1988. The great art explosion. *Artnews* 87(4): 102-109.

Voss, V.G., G.B. Voss, C. Shuff, and I.B. Rose. 2005. *Theatre facts 2005: A report on practices and performance in the American not-for-profit theatre based on the annual TCG Fiscal Survey.* New York: Theatre Communications Group.

Vradenburgh, E. 2005. The Portal Program: Arts programming, tourism, and authenticity in traditional arts. Unpublished paper, University of Oregon.

VSA Arts. 2006. *Program development files.* Washington, DC: Author.

VSA Arts. n.d. *Very special arts festival program guide.* Washington, DC: Author.

Walker, C. 2004. Participation in arts and culture. *Arts Reader.* [Online]. 15(1 Winter): 5 paragraphs. www.giarts.org/library_additional/ library_additional_show.htm?doc_id=296047.

Walle, A.H. 1998. *Cultural tourism: A strategic focus.* Boulder, CO: Westview Press.

The War Project: 9 Acts of Determination. 2006. Sojourn Theatre. Retrieved 7/07/07. www.sojourntheatre.org/2006_warprojecttickets.asp.

Watson, B. 2005. World's unlikeliest bestseller. *Smithsonian* 36(5): 76-81.

Whiteford, A.H. 1988. *Southwestern Indian baskets: Their history and their makers.* Seattle: University of Washington Press.

Whitt, L.A., and J.D. Slack. 1994. Communities, environments and cultural studies. *Cultural Studies* 8(1): 5-13.

Willson, J. L. G. 2005. Expanding multicultural discourse: Art museums and cultural diversity (Master's project, University of Oregon, 2005).

W.K. Kellogg Foundation. 2001. *Logic model development guide.* Battle Creek, MI: Author.

Wolf, T. 1999. *Managing a nonprofit organization in the twenty-first century.* New York: Simon & Schuster.

Wolfville Farmers' Market. 2006. www.wolfvillefarmersmarket.com.

Woolaroc Institute. 2003. The Woolaroc Institute general information. Retrieved July 10, 2006 from www.woolaroc.org/geninfo/overview.html.

World Rhythm Festival. 2007. www.swps.org.

Wyszomirski, M.J. 2002. Arts and culture. In *The state of nonprofit America*, ed. L.M. Salamon, 187-218. Washington, DC: Brookings Institution Press.

Ybarra-Frausto, T. 1991. Rasquachismo: A Chicano sensibility. In *Chicano art: Resistance and affirmation, 1965-1985*, ed. R.G. del Castillo, T. McKenna, and Y. Yarbro-Bejarano, 155-162. Los Angeles: Wright Art Gallery, University of California.

Yeoman, I., ed. 2003. *Festival and events management.* Amsterdam: Elsevier.

Yeoman, I., M. Robertson, J. Ali-Knight, S. Drummond, and U. McMahon-Beattie. 2004. *Festival and events management: An international arts and culture perspective.* Oxford: Elsevier.

Zibart, R. 1998. In Seattle, child prisoners find outlet for art. *Christian Science Monitor.* August 14.

Zolberg, V. L. 1996. Museums as contested sites of remembrance: The Enola Gay affair. In Macdonald, S. & Fyfe, G. (Eds.), *Theorizing museums: Representing identity and diversity in a changing world*, 69-82.

Zuzanek, J., and T. Beckers. 1999. Time pressure, time use, and leisure: What makes people feel rushed in Canada and the Netherlands? Paper presented at the Ninth Canadian Congress on Leisure Research, Wolfville, NS.

index

about the editors

Gaylene Carpenter, EdD, is emerita associate professor in the arts and administration program at the University of Oregon in Eugene, where she teaches graduate-level courses in arts program theory.

As an author, Carpenter has written several publications on program theory, including a program theory textbook, *Programming Leisure Experiences* (Prentice-Hall, 1985).

Carpenter is past president of the American Leisure Academy (ALA) and an ALA senior fellow. She also served as an elected board member for the Society of Park and Recreation Educators and the American Association for Leisure & Recreation. Carpenter is a member of the National Recreation and Park Association (NRPA), where she has maintained her certification since 1984. In addition, Carpenter holds membership in the Association of Arts Administration Educators, the Canadian Association for Leisure Research, the International Festivals & Events Association, the World Leisure Association, and both the Oregon and Pennsylvania Recreation and Park Associations.

Gaylene Carpenter

In 2004 Carpenter received an Ovation Award from the Oregon Festivals and Events Association. She has been awarded twice with the Teaching Innovation and Excellence Award from the Society of Park and Recreation Educators (1996 and 2001). Carpenter also received the Professional Award for Leadership in 1998 from the Northwest region of the NRPA.

In her leisure time, Carpenter enjoys spending time with her family and friends, gardening, and attending festivals and events. She resides in Eugene, Oregon.

Doug Blandy, PhD, is a professor in the arts and administration program and associate dean for academic affairs for the School of Architecture and Allied Arts at the University of Oregon in Eugene. He is also the director for the university's Institute for Community Arts Studies (ICAS).

Blandy has more than 30 years of experience in community arts and arts administration as a teacher, researcher, consultant, national and international presenter, and administrator. He is the author of numerous publications, including 6 books, 10 book chapters, and more than 100 articles, proceedings, reports, and book reviews. Blandy also is the founder and publisher of CultureWork, the Web-based advisory of the Center for Community Arts and Cultural Policy (CACP).

Blandy is currently the coeditor for *Studies in Art Education*. He also serves on the review board of *Journal of Gender Issues in Art Education*, *Journal of Social Theory in Art Education*, and *Journal of Cultural Research in Art Education*. He is a member of the National Art Education Association (NAEA) and the American Folklore Society.

Doug Blandy

In 2007 Blandy received the Faculty Excellence Award from the University of Oregon. His other notable awards include the NAEA Women's Caucus Mary Rouse Award (1997) and the NAEA Manuel Barkan Award (1991).

Blandy and his wife, Linda, live in Eugene, Oregon. He enjoys reading, listening to music, hiking, and traveling.

about the contributors

Chris N. Burgess

Chris Burgess is currently a visiting assistant professor in the Arts Management program at the College of Charleston in South Carolina and is completing work on his PhD in Cultural Policy from The Ohio State University, where he also received his MA in Arts Policy and Administration. He is a former Barnett Fellow at Ohio State and his recent work consists of publications and speaking engagements across various cultural policy topics including theory model extension, arts education, creative sector interrelationships, the intersection of art and law, and arts financial management. Additionally, in 2006 Burgess received a State Department U.S. Speaker and Specialist Grant to discuss cultural diplomacy at an international seminar in Belgrade, Serbia based on past collaborative work co-commissioned by Arts International and the Center for Arts and Culture. Burgess has also worked both on a professional and volunteer level with a variety of arts organizations across multiple disciplines primarily in marketing, development, and finance.

Francois Colbert, MBA, MSc

Francois Colbert

Francois Colbert is professor of marketing and holder of the Carmelle and Rémi Marcoux Chair in Arts Management at HEC Montréal. In addition to his duties as academic supervisor for the Diplôme d'études supérieures spécialisées en gestion d'organismes culturels (DESSGOC – Graduate Diploma in the Management of Cultural Organizations), he is editor of the *International Journal of Arts Management*, published by the Chair in Arts Management. In May 2002, he was awarded the Order of Canada for his many achievements and for his unique contributions in developing the field of arts management and he was made Fellow of the Royal Society of Canada in 2005; he also received the ACE Award 2006 from the Association of Cultural Executives.

Professor Colbert has been active in the field of arts and culture for over 30 years, particularly in the performing arts, museum, and film sectors. He has given numerous training and professional development seminars in arts management, with a focus on the field of marketing management in a cultural context. He is a past or present member of the board of directors of many cultural organizations and served as vice-chair of the Canada Council for the Arts for eight years, until 2003; he has been on the board of other large organizations such as Les Grands ballets canadiens and Radio-Québec. He is also the founding president and co-chair of the scientific committee of the International Conference on Arts and Cultural Management (AIMAC).

Kristin G. Congdon, PhD

Kristin G. Congdon has taught art in a variety of settings, including public schools, correctional settings, treatment facilities, museums, and universities. She is a professor of Film and Philosophy at the University of Central Florida and Director of the Cultural Heritage Alliance. She has published extensively on folk art, community arts, and feminism in an effort to celebrate artists who have had little visibility in the art world. Her most recent books include, *Artists from Latin American Cultures* and *20th Century United States Photographers* (co-authored with Kara Hallmark), *Just Above the Water: Florida Folk Art* (co-authored with Tina Bucuvalas), *Community Art in Action*, and *Uncle Monday and Other Florida Tales.* Dr. Congdon has been president of the Florida Folklore Society and a member of the Florida Folklife Council. She has also been a World Congress Member for the International Society for Education Through Art, and the president of the National Art Education Association's Women's Caucus.

Kristin G. Congdon

Tom Delamere, PhD

Tom Delamere is a professor of Recreation and Tourism Management at Malaspina University-College in Nanaimo, British Columbia, Canada. Tom has worked for over 25 years in the recreation field, including 10 years part- and full-time programming with the City of Mississauga Recreation and Parks Department, and over 15 years as an educator, researcher, and facilitator. His specific research focuses on understanding the social impacts of community-based festivals, and the need for a coordinated approach to the measurement and interpretation of resident attitudes toward these impacts.

Tom is active in the Nanaimo music community, as a baritone saxophonist with an assortment of groups including the Malaspina Stage Band, Malaspina Saxophone Quartet, and the Nanaimo Musicians' Association Big Band. Using the moniker "DJ Doc," he also volunteers as an on-air programmer with CHLY-FM, Radio Malaspina where he hosts two shows: "The Impending Loom" and "Vitamin J." In addition, Tom is currently a Board Member with the Canadian Association for Leisure Studies.

Photo courtesy of Scott Littlejohn

Tom Delamere

Lori L. Hager, PhD

Lori Hager, (PhD Theatre for Youth, Arizona State University), is an assistant professor in the University of Oregon's Arts and Administration Program, where she codirects the master's program in Community Arts and serves as associate director of Community Arts for the UO Center for Community Arts and Cultural Policy. Hager is responsible for the graduate level professional practice internship courses and oversees the undergraduate minor in Community Arts and the undergraduate practicum program. Dr. Hager founded and directs the ePortfolio project, which supports students in Arts and Administration and the School of Architecture and Allied Arts to develop and maintain ePortfolios as part of their research and professional preparation (http://ePortfolio.uoregon.edu). Dr. Hager also presents and conducts research in the area of community youth arts policies and practice, and is currently conducting research which examines professional development for teaching artists who work with youth in school and after-school settings.

Lori L. Hager

Karla A. Henderson, PhD

Karla A. Henderson is currently a professor in the Department of Parks, Recreation, and Tourism Management at North Carolina State University. She has given numerous presentations throughout North America, Europe, Asia, and Australia and publishes regularly in a variety of journals in the field. Among her authored or co-authored books are: *Both Gains and Gaps* (with Bialeschki, Shaw, and Freysinger), *Dimensions of Choice, Introduction to Recreation and Leisure Services*, and *Evaluation of Leisure Services* (with Bialeschki). She is currently coeditor of *Leisure Sciences*. Dr. Henderson has contributed to the profession in a number of ways by serving as president of SPRE, president of the AAHPERD Research Consortium, President of the Academy of Leisure Sciences, and on numerous state, national, and international boards and committees. When not working, Karla enjoys hiking in the Rocky Mountains, running and playing her trumpet in North Carolina, and reading and writing wherever she goes.

Karla A. Henderson

James E. Modrick, MA

James E. Modrick is an arts administrator who has built a professional career that combines practical organization management experience, knowledge of public policy processes, and a passion for learning. He has published and presented papers that explore and advance the role of the arts in education through policy and practice focusing on the topics of creativity, leadership, politics, and accessibility of the arts at national and international conferences. For the past six years, Mr. Modrick has been the vice president of Affiliate and Education Services for VSA arts, an international nonprofit organization committed to advancing the arts in the lives and learning of people with disabilities. He joined VSA arts in 1999 as the manager of Affiliate Services and quickly advanced his influence and visibility. He was promoted to vice president in 2001. Prior to this, Mr. Modrick was the director of membership for the National Art Education Association, the largest professional association supporting visual art educators in the United States. He also received an Arts Administration Fellowship in the Office of Policy Planning and Research with the National Endowment for the Arts in 1994. Mr. Modrick holds a Master of Arts in Arts Administration from Indiana University in Bloomington.

James E. Modrick

Steven Morrison, MFA

Steven Morrison is an assistant professor and the associate director of the Arts Administration Graduate Program at the University of Cincinnati. His career experience includes general manager (1998-2001) and assistant managing director (1992-97) at the Alabama Shakespeare Festival, an LORT B major regional theatre. He also served as the orchestra manager for the Alabama Symphony Orchestra and business manager and director of development at Theatre Albany. Other professional activities include technical consultant for Wolf Trap Center for the Performing Arts' stART smART Institute, board retreat facilitator and consultant on strategic planning for community theaters, and performing arts grants panelist for the Alabama and Ohio Arts Councils. He taught at the University of Alabama and Alabama Shakespeare Festival Master of Fine Arts program. He has also served on the board of the Association of Arts Administration Educators. Steven has a BFA in Theatre Arts from Valdosta State University and an MFA from the University of Alabama.

Steven Morrison

J. Robert Rossman, PhD

J. Robert Rossman is an author, speaker, and consultant on designing and staging engaging recreation programs and events. His work in public recreation includes programming community art and sport events. For thirty years he held university appointments, serving most recently as Dean of the College of Applied Science and Technology at Illinois State University where he holds the titles of Dean and Professor Emeritus.

He is the lead author of *Recreation Programming: Designing Leisure Experiences* that has been used since 1989 to teach recreation programming at over 100 universities in the United States, Canada, Australia, New Zealand, Thailand, and Taiwan. Dr. Rossman has served on the board of directors and as president of the Society of Park and Recreation Educators. He was invited to deliver lectures on programming as the 2006 Jay B. Nash Scholar Lecturer and the 2007 George Butler Lecturer. He is recognized throughout the world as an expert on programming theory and techniques. He recently delivered keynote addresses on programming at the annual conferences of the New Zealand Recreation Association and the New Zealand Association of Event Professionals. He believes that arts and cultural programs should be designed and staged to deliver engaging experiences for participants.

J. Robert Rossman

Janice Williams Rutherford, PhD

Janice Rutherford is the Museum Studies Coordinator on the faculty of the Arts & Administration Program at the University of Oregon. She received her PhD in history from Louisiana State University and taught U.S. history and public history at Washington State University from 1997 until 2002. She has also taught at Eastern Washington University, Southeastern Louisiana University, Clayton State College and State University, and Georgia State University. As a practicing public historian from 1977 until 1990, Rutherford served as historic preservation officer of Spokane and Spokane County, Washington; executive director of the Heritage Trust of Clark County, Washington; director of the Louisiana Association of Museums; and program director of the Southeastern Museums Conference. She currently serves on Oregon's State Advisory Committee on Historic Preservation. Publications include: *Selling Mrs. Consumer: Christine Frederick and the Rise of Household Efficiency* (University of Georgia Press, 2003); "Peopling the Age of Elegance: Reinterpreting Spokane's Campbell House—A Collaboration," co-authored with Steven E. Shay, The Public Historian 26, no. 3 (2004); "An Interdisciplinary Collaborative Experiment in Art Education: Architects Meet Arts Administrators," Art Education, 58, no. 4 (2005); and "Historic Corbin Park: Preservation Success Story or Study in Challenges?" The Public Historian 27, no. 4 (2005).

Janice Williams Rutherford